"Merle leads Kerasote to ponder, make mistakes, love and learn. The unapologetic imperfection of Kerasote's choices proves that relationships with dogs are as complicated as human ones, a reflection of our own essential humanity." —*BookPage*

"A joyous, sad, gripping, and deeply moving testament to the fulfilling relationship that can grow between human and dog."
—Juliet Clutton-Brock, author of
A Natural History of Domesticated Mammals

"This exquisitely written book is sure to be controversial, but it raises important questions that every thoughtful dog owner should consider." —Patricia B. McConnell, Ph.D., author of *For the Love of a Dog: Understanding Emotion in You and Your Best Friend*

"*Merle's Door* is a love story for grown-ups—an intense reciprocal relationship between a dog and his man, and how we and our dogs genuinely share feelings and emotions."
—Dr. Bruce Fogle, D.V.M., author of *The Dog's Mind*

"To be entertained and educated at the same time is rare in dog books, which makes this one definitely worth reading."
—Stanley Coren, author of *How Dogs Think* and *The Intelligence of Dogs*

"We see the world of dogs through Merle, and we also come to know Merle personally, just as we know our own dogs. It is beautifully written, a real page turner, often funny, always fascinating, and very moving. It's a book you will never forget."
—Elizabeth Marshall Thomas, author of *The Hidden Life of Dogs*

D0011319

PRAISE FOR

Merle's Door

Merle's Door

Also by
TED KERASOTE

TED KERASOTE

Merle's Door

Lessons from a Freethinking Dog

A HARVEST BOOK
HARCOURT, INC.
Orlando   Austin   New York   San Diego   London

Requests for permission to make copies of any part of the
work should be submitted online at www.harcourt.com/contact
or mailed to the following address: Permissions Department,
Houghton Mifflin Harcourt Publishing Company,
6277 Sea Harbor Drive, Orlando, Florida 32887-6777.

www.HarcourtBooks.com

Epigraph from *Dogs Never Lie About Love* by Jeffrey Moussaieff Masson
reprinted courtesy of Crown Publishers. Excerpt from "Wild Geese"
is from *Dream Work* by Mary Oliver. Copyright 1986 by Mary Oliver
and reprinted courtesy of Grove/Atlantic, Inc.

This book is printed on FSC (Forest
Stewardship Council)–certified stock.

The Library of Congress has cataloged the hardcover edition as follows:
Kerasote, Ted.
Merle's door: lessons from a freethinking dog/Ted Kerasote.—1st ed.
p.   cm.
Includes bibliographical references and index.
1. Dogs—Wyoming—Anecdotes.   2. Dogs—Behavior—Wyoming—
Anecdotes.   3. Human-animal relationships—Anecdotes.   4. Dog
owners—Wyoming—Anecdotes.   5. Kerasote, Ted.   I. Title.
SF426.2.K47   2007
636.7092'9—dc22   2006038041
ISBN 978-0-15-101270-1
ISBN 978-0-15-603450-0 (pbk.)

Text set in Bodoni Book
Designed by Linda Lockowitz

Printed in the United States of America

First Harvest edition 2008
K J I H G F E D C B A

For Donald and Gladys Kent

CONTENTS

Just as being in jail or in exile will produce a loneliness of spirit in a human being, so, it seems, will captivity produce the same in a wild animal. Perhaps even dogs, the most domesticated of all domestic species, long for their original lupinelike freedom.

—JEFFREY MOUSSAIEFF MASSON
Dogs Never Lie About Love

Merle's Door

PROLOGUE

This is the story of one dog, my dog, Merle. It's also the story of every dog who must live in an increasingly urbanized world, and how these dogs might lead happier lives if we changed some of our behavior rather than always trying to change theirs.

Merle had the good fortune to live in a rural place—northwestern Wyoming—where the boundary between civilization and the wild is still very porous. He enjoyed an enormous amount of open space and personal freedom, coming and going as he wished through his own dog door. Yet what he taught me about living with a dog can be applied anywhere. His lessons weren't so much about giving dogs physical doors to the outside world, although that's important, but about providing ones that open onto the mental and emotional terrain that will develop a dog's potential. His lessons weren't about training, but about partnership. They were never about method; they were about attitude. And at the heart of this attitude is a person's willingness to loosen a dog's leash—in all aspects of its life—and, whenever practical, to take off its leash completely, allowing the dog to learn on its own, following its nose and running free.

CHAPTER 1

From the Wild

He came out of the night, appearing suddenly in my headlights, a big, golden dog, panting, his front paws tapping
the ground in an anxious little dance. Behind him, tall
cottonwoods in their April bloom. Behind the grove, the San Juan
River, moving quickly, dark and swollen with spring melt.

It was nearly midnight, and we were looking for a place to
throw down our sleeping bags before starting our river trip in the
morning. Next to me in the cab of the pickup sat Benj Sinclair, at
his feet a midden of road-food wrappers smeared with the scent of
corn dogs, onion rings, and burritos. Round-cheeked, Buddha-
bellied, thirty-nine years old, Benj had spent his early years in
the Peace Corps, in West Africa, and had developed a stomach
that could digest anything. Behind him in the jump seat was Kim
Reynolds, an Outward Bound instructor from Colorado known for
her grace in a kayak and her long braid of brunette hair, which held
the faint odor of a healthy, thirty-two-year-old woman who had
sweated in the desert and hadn't used deodorant. Like Benj and
me, she had eaten a dinner of pizza in Moab, Utah, a hundred miles
up the road where we'd met her. Like us, she gave off the scents of
garlic, onions, tomato sauce, basil, oregano, and anchovies.

In the car that pulled up next to us were Pam Weiss and Bennett Austin. They had driven from Jackson Hole, Wyoming, to

Moab in their own car, helped us rig the raft and shop for supplies, joined us for pizza, and, like us, wore neither perfume nor cologne. Pam was thirty-six, an Olympic ski racer, and Bennett, twenty-five, was trying to keep up with her. They had recently fallen in love and exuded a mixture of endorphins and pheromones.

People almost never describe other people in these terms— noting first their smells—for we're primarily visual creatures and rely on our eyes for information. By contrast, the only really important sense-key for the big, golden dog, doing his little dance in the headlights, was our olfactory signatures, wafting to him as we opened the doors.

It was for this reason—smell—that I think he trotted directly to my door, leaned his head forward cautiously, and sniffed at my bare thigh. What mix of aromas went up his long snout at that very first moment of our meeting? What atavistic memories, what possibilities were triggered in his canine worldview as he untangled the mysteries of my sweat?

The big dog—now appearing reddish in the interior light of the truck and without a collar—took another reflective breath and studied me with excited consideration. Might it have been what I ate, and the subtle residue it left in my pores, that made him so interested in me? It was the only thing I could see (note my human use of "see" even while describing an olfactory phenomenon) that differentiated me from my friends. Like them, I skied, biked, and climbed, and was single. I had just turned forty-one, a compact man with chestnut hair and bright brown eyes. But when I ate meat, it was that of wild animals, not domestic ones—mostly elk and antelope along with the occasional grouse, duck, goose, and trout mixed in.

Was it their metabolized essence that intrigued him—some whiff of what our Paleolithic ancestors had shared? Smell is our oldest sense. It was the olfactory tissue at the top of our primeval nerve cords that evolved into our cerebral hemispheres, where thought is lodged. Perhaps the dog—a being who lived by his nose—knew a lot more about our connection than I could possibly imagine.

His deep brown eyes looked at me with luminous appreciation and said, "You need a dog, and I'm it."

Unsettled by his uncanny read of me—I had been looking for a dog for over a year—I gave him a cordial pat and replied, "Good dog."

His tail beat steadily, and he didn't move, his eyes still saying, "You need a dog."

As we got out of the cars and began to unpack our gear, I lost track of him. There was his head, now a tail, there a rufous flank moving among bare legs and sandals.

I threw my pad and bag down on the sand under a cottonwood, slipped into its silky warmth, turned over, and found him digging a nest by my side. Industriously, he scooped out the sand with his front paws, casting it between his hind legs before turning, turning, turning, and settling to face me. In the starlight, I could see one brow go up, the other down.

Of course, "brows" isn't really the correct term, since dogs sweat only through their paws and have no need of brows to keep perspiration out of their eyes, as we do. Yet, certain breeds of dogs have darker hair over their eyes, what might be called "brow markings," and he had them.

The Hidatsa, a Native American tribe of the northern Great Plains, believe that these sorts of dogs, whom they call "Four-Eyes," are especially gentle and have magical powers. Stanley Coren, the astute canine psychologist from the University of British Columbia, has also noted that these "four-eyed" dogs obtained their reputation for psychic powers "because their expressions were easier to read than those of other dogs. The contrasting-colored spots make the movements of the muscles over the eye much more visible."

In the starlight, the dog lying next to me raised one brow while lowering the other, implying curiosity mixed with concern over whether I'd let him stay.

"Night," I said, giving him a pat. Then I closed my eyes.

When I opened them in the morning, he was still curled in his nest, looking directly at me.

"Hey," I said.

Up went one brow, down went the other.

"I am yours," his eyes said.

I let out a breath, unprepared for how his sweet, faintly hound-dog face—going from happiness to concern—left a cut under my heart. I had been looking at litters of Samoyeds, balls of white fur with bright black mischievous eyes. The perfect breed for a winter person like myself, I thought. But I couldn't quite make myself bring one home. I had also seriously considered Labrador Retrievers, taken by their exuberant personalities and knowing that such a robust, energetic dog could easily share my life in the outdoors as well as be the bird dog I believed I wanted. But no Lab pup had given me that undeniable heart tug that said, "We are a team."

The right brow of the dog lying by me went down as he held my eye. His left brow went up, implying, "You delayed with good reason."

"Maybe," I said, feeling my desire for a pedigree dog giving way. "Maybe," I said once more to the dog whose eyes coasted across mine, returned, and lingered. He did have the looks of a reddish yellow Lab, I thought, at least from certain angles.

At the sound of my voice, he levered his head under my arm and brought his nose close to mine. Surprisingly, he didn't try to lick me in that effusive gesture that many dogs use with someone they perceive as dominant to them, whether it be a person or another dog—a relic, some believe, of young wolves soliciting food from their parents and other adult wolves. The adults, not having hands to carry provisions, bring back meat in their stomachs. The

pups lick their mouths, and the adults regurgitate the partly di-
gested meat. Pups who eventually become alphas abandon subordinate licking. Lower-ranking wolves continue to display the
behavior to higher-ranking wolves, as do a great many domestic
dogs to people. This dog's self-possession gave me pause. Was he
not licking me because he considered us peers? Or did my body
language—both of us being at the same level—allow him to feel
somewhat of an equal? He circumspectly smelled my breath, and
I, in turn, smelled his. His smelled sweet.

Whatever he smelled on mine, he liked it. "I am yours," his
eyes said again.

Disconcerted by his certainty about me, I got up and moved
off. I didn't want to abandon my plans for finding a pup who was
only six to eight weeks old and whom I could shape to my liking.
The dog read my energy and didn't follow me. Instead, he went to
the others, greeting them with a wagging tail and wide laughs of
his toothy mouth. "Good morning, good morning, did you sleep
well?" he seemed to be saying.

But as I organized my gear, I couldn't keep my eyes from him.
Despite his ribs showing, he appeared fit and strong, and looked
like he had been living outside for quite a while, his hair matted
with sprigs of grass and twigs. He was maybe fifty-five pounds, not
filled out yet, his fox-colored fur hanging in loose folds, waiting for
the adult dog that would be. He had a ridge of darker fur along his
spine, short golden plumes on the backs of his legs, and a tuxedo-
like bib of raised fur on his chest—just an outline of it—scattered with white flecks. His ears were soft and flannel-like, and
hung slightly below the point of his jaw. His nose was lustrous
black, he had equally shiny lips, and his teeth gleamed. His tail
was large and powerful.

Every time I looked at him, he seemed to manifest his four-
eyed ancestry, shape-shifting before me: now the Lab I wanted;
there a Rhodesian Ridgeback, glinting under some faraway Kala-
hari sun; an instant later he became a long-snouted coydog, born

of the redrock desert and brought to life out of these canyons and cacti. When he looked directly at me—one brow up, the other down, his cheeks creased in concern—he certainly appeared to have some hound in him. Obviously, he had belonged to someone, for his testicles were gone and the scar of neutering had completely healed and the hair had grown back.

As I cooked breakfast at one of the picnic tables, he rejoined me, sitting patiently a few feet away while displaying the best of manners as he watched the elk sausage go from my hands to the frying pan. He gave not a single whine, though a tiny tremor went through his body.

When the slices were done, I said, "Would you like some?"

A shiver ran through him once again. His eyes shone; but he didn't move. I broke off a piece and offered it to him. His nose wriggled in delight; he took it delicately from my fingertips and swallowed. His tail broomed the sand, back and forth in appreciation.

"That dog," said the Bureau of Land Management ranger who had come up to us and was checking our river permit as we ate, "has been hanging around here for a couple of days. I think he's abandoned, which is strange because he's beautiful and really friendly."

We all agreed he was.

"Where did he come from?" I asked her.

"He just appeared," she replied.

The dog watched this conversation carefully, looking from the ranger's face to mine.

I picked up a stick, wanting to see how well he could retrieve. The instant I drew back my arm, he cringed pathetically, retreated a few paces, and eyed me warily.

"He can be skittish," the ranger said. "I think someone's beat him."

I flung the stick away from him, toward the moving river. He gave it a cool appraisal, then looked at me, just as cool. "I don't fetch," the look said. "That's for dogs."

"He doesn't fetch," the ranger said.

"So I notice."

She checked our fire pan and our portable toilet—both required by the BLM for boaters floating the San Juan River—while the dog hung around nearby, hopeful but trying to look unobtrusive.

"I'd take that dog if I could," the ranger said, noting my eyes lingering on him. "But we're not allowed to have dogs."

"Maybe we should take him down the river," I heard myself say.

"I would," she said.

When I discussed it with the others, they agreed that we could use a mascot, a river dog, for our trip. Taking a dog on a wilderness excursion is hardly a new idea. In fact, it's a North American tradition. Alexander Mackenzie had a pickup mutt who accompanied him on his landmark first journey across the continent to the Pacific in 1793, via southern Canada. The dog was unnamed in Mackenzie's diary but often mentioned for surviving swims in rapids and killing bison calves. Meriwether Lewis also had a dog on his and William Clark's journey up the Missouri and down the Columbia from 1803 to 1806. The acclaimed Newfoundland Seaman protected camp from grizzlies and caught countless squirrels for the pot, as well as pulling down deer, pronghorn antelope, and geese. Although the expedition ate dozens of other dogs when game became scarce (they were bought from Indians), there was never a question of grilling Seaman. An honored member of the expedition to the end, he may have kept the depression-prone Lewis sane on the arduous journey. Three years after returning to civilization, unable to reintegrate into society, and with no mention of what happened to his dog, Lewis committed suicide. John James Audubon had a Newfie as well, a tireless hiker named Plato, who accompanied him across the countryside and retrieved many of the birds the artist shot for his paintings. Audubon called him "a well-trained and most sagacious animal."

With such august precedents, it would have seemed a shame not to take this handsome, well-behaved dog with us. What harm could come of it? No one raised the issue of what we'd do with him when we pulled out at Clay Hills above Lake Powell in six days. We'd cross that bridge when we came to it. In the meantime, this wasn't the nineteenth century. There'd be no living off the land; we needed to get him some dog food. Benj and I drove into the nearby town of Bluff, Utah, returning with a bag of Purina Dog Chow and a box of Milk Bones.

The only one who wasn't aware that the dog was going with us was, of course, the dog himself. After loading the raft with dry bags and coolers of food, I patted the gunwale and said to him, "Jump in. You're a river dog now." I had been designated to row the raft for the first day while the others paddled kayaks.

Dubiously, he eyed the raft. "No way," his eyes said, "that looks dangerous."

I tried to pet him, but he danced away, making a "ha-ha-ha" noise, half playful, half scared, as he pumped his front paws up and down in that energetic little dance he'd done the previous night as he appeared in our headlights.

"You'll like it," I said. "Shady canyons, great campsites, petroglyphs, swimming every day, Milk Bones, Purina Dog Chow, and"—my voice cajoled—"elk sausage."

I opened my waterproof lunch stuff sack, cut off a piece of the elk summer sausage, and held it out to him. He came closer, leaned his head forward, and snatched it. "Come on, jump in."

He shivered, knowing full well he was being gulled, but letting me pet him nonetheless, torn between wanting to come and his fear of the raft. Carefully, I put my arms around him, under his chest, and lifted. Whining in protest, he struggled. I managed to deposit him in the raft as Benj tried to push us off.

The dog leapt out of the boat, but instead of fleeing danced up and down the shore, panting frantically, "Ha-ha-ha, ha-ha-ha," which I translated as "I really want to go, but I don't know where we're going, and I don't like the raft, and I'm scared."

I talked to him in a low, soothing tone and got him calmed down enough so I could pet him again. Resting his head on my knee, he gave a huge sigh, like someone who's emotionally wrung out. For a moment, I could sense his many dashed hopes and his fear of people and their gear—not an unreasonable one given how he had cowered when I raised the stick to play fetch.

The others were in their kayaks, ready to go. Carefully, I got my arms around him again, but when I lifted him he struggled mightily, calling out in desperate whining yelps. I put him in the boat, and Benj shoved us off as I held the dog until the current took us. Then I let go of him and started to row. We were only yards from shore. With a leap and a few strokes he could easily return to land. Stay or leave—the choice was his. The dog jumped to the raft's gunwale, put his paws on it, and stared upstream without showing any fear of the moving water. Rather, he watched the retreating shore as if watching his natal continent disappear below the horizon.

His ambivalence filled my mind with questions. Had he been abandoned, or gotten himself lost? In either case, was he waiting faithfully for his human to return? Was his friendliness toward me his way of asking for my help in finding that person? Had I misread his eyes, seeming to say, "You are the one I've been waiting for"? Was his longing gaze back to shore simply his attachment to a known place—a familiar landscape where he might have been mistreated but which was still home? How many abused souls—dogs and humans alike—have remained in an unloving place because staying was far less terrifying than leaving?

"Easy, easy," I murmured as he began to tremble.

I stroked his head and shoulders. Turning, he looked at me with an expression I shall never forget. It mingled loss, fear of the unknown, and hope.

Of course, some will say that I was being anthropomorphic. Others might point out that I was projecting. But what I was doing—reading his body language—is the stock-in-trade of psychologists as they study their clients. All of us use the same technique as we try to understand the feelings of those around us—friends, family members, and colleagues. There'd be no human intercourse, or it would be enormously impoverished, without our attempting to use our own emotions as templates—as starting points—to map the feelings of others.

But something else was going on between the dog and me. An increasing amount of research on a variety of species—parrots, chimpanzees, prairie dogs, dolphins, wolves, and domestic dogs themselves—has demonstrated that they have the physical and cognitive ability to transmit a rich array of information to others, both within and without their species, sometimes even using grammatical constructions similar to those employed in human languages. Individuals of some of these species can also identify themselves with vocal signatures—in human terms, a name.

These studies have corroborated what I've felt about dogs for a long time—that they're speakers of a foreign language and, if we pay attention to their vocalizations, ocular and facial expressions, and ever-changing postures, we can translate what they're saying. Sometimes we get the translation spot-on ("I'm hungry"), sometimes we make a reasonable guess ("I'm sad"), and occasionally we have to use a figure of speech to bridge the divide between their culture and our own ("I love you so much, my heart could burst").

Dog owners who hold "conversations" with their dogs will know exactly what I mean. Those who don't—as well as those who find the whole notion of conversing with a dog absurd—may want to consider that humans have shared a longer and more intimate partnership with dogs than with any other domestic animal, starting before civilization existed. In these early times—before speech and writing achieved the ascendancy they enjoy today—

dogs had a greater opportunity to make themselves understood by humans who were still comfortable communicating outside the boundaries of the spoken and written word.

Charles Darwin, as keen an observer of domestic dogs as he was of Galápagos finches, commented on the relative equality that once existed between dogs and humans, and still exists, if you look for it: "[T]he difference in mind between man and the higher animals, great as it is, certainly is one of degree and not of kind." Darwin went so far as to say that "there is no fundamental difference between man and the higher mammals in their mental faculties," adding that nonhuman animals experience happiness, wonder, shame, pride, curiosity, jealousy, suspicion, gratitude, and magnanimity. "They practice deceit and are revengeful," he asserted, and have "moral qualities," the more important elements of which are "love and the distinct emotion of sympathy." These were breathtaking notions when he set them down in 1871 and remain eye-opening today, even to many who believe that animals can think.

The dog now took his eyes from mine, looked back to the shore, and let out a resigned sigh—I was to learn that he was a great sigher. Stepping down into the raft, he gave our gear a brief inspection and finally let his gaze settle upon the cooler sitting in the bow of the raft, surrounded by dry bags. Padding over to it, he jumped on it and lay down with his back to me. Another sigh escaped him. Within a few moments, however, I could see him watching the bluffs and groves of cottonwoods with growing interest, his head snapping this way and that as he noted the countryside moving while he apparently did not.

"Pretty cool, eh?"

He moved his ears backward, acknowledging my voice without turning his head.

As we entered the first canyon, and its walls blocked out the sky, he took a glance upstream and gave a start—the campground had disappeared. He jerked into a sitting position and stared around apprehensively. Without warning, he pointed his snout to the sky and let out a mournful howl, beginning in a bass register and climbing to a plaintive alto crescendo. From the canyon walls came back his echo: "Aaawooo, Aaawooo, Aaawooo."

Stunned, he cocked his head at the unseen dog who had answered him. Where was the dog hiding? He looked up and down the river and at the high shadowed cliffs. He seemed never to have heard an echo before. A moment later, he howled again, and again he was surprised to hear his voice rebounding from the cliffs. He looked around uneasily before giving another howl—this time as a test rather than to bemoan his situation. When the echo returned, a look of dawning realization crossed his face. It was remarkable to see the comprehension light his eyes. His lips turned up in a smile, and he howled again, long and drawn out, but without any sadness. Immediately, he cocked his head to listen to his echo. As the canyon walls sent back his voice, he began to lash his tail back and forth with great enthusiasm. He turned around and gave me a look of surprised delight—the very same expression people wear when they hear themselves for the first time.

I leaned forward and put a hand on his chest.

"You are quite the singer," I told him.

Throwing back his head, he laughed a toothy grin.

From that moment on, he never looked back. He sat on the cooler like a sphinx, his head turning to watch the cliffs and side canyons go by. He hiked up to several Anasazi cliff dwellings with us and stood attentively as we examined petroglyphs. On the way back to the river, he'd meander off, disappearing for long minutes, only to reappear as we approached the boats, dashing toward us through the cactus without a glance at the obstacle course he was threading. He seemed about as home in the desert as a dog could be.

At camp that evening, he supervised our shuttling the gear from raft to higher ground and watched as we began to unpack our dry bags. Then, satisfied we weren't going to leave, he vanished.

I caught glimpses of him, exploring a large perimeter around our campsite, poking with his paw at some object of interest, sniffing at bushes, and raising his leg to mark them. When I began to pour his dinner into one of our cooking pots, he soon appeared, having heard the tinkle of kibble on steel. Inhaling his dinner in a few voracious gulps, he looked up at me and wagged his tail. Cocking his head, he raised an eyebrow and clearly added, "Nice appetizer. Now where's the meal?"

I poured him some more, and after he gobbled it he gave me the same look: "Is that all?" Likewise after the next bowl.

"Enough," I told him, crossing my hands and moving them apart the way an umpire makes the signal for "Safe."

His face fell.

"We've got five more days," I explained. "You can't have it all tonight." Stowing his food, I said, "Come on, help me with the latrine."

He followed as I took the large ammo box inland and placed it on a rock bench with a scenic overlook of the river. After lining it with a stout plastic bag, I gave it its inaugural use as the dog sat a half dozen feet off, wagging his tail in appreciation as the aromas wafted toward him. Each day's bag had to be sealed and carried downriver to be disposed of properly at the end of the trip, and we had brought along a can of Comet to sprinkle on the contents so as to reduce the production of odors and methane. This I now did, leaving the can of Comet and the roll of toilet paper by the side of the ammo box. As I walked back to camp, the big golden dog followed me, his nose aloft, his nostrils dilating.

At dinnertime we sat in a circle around the stoves and pots, and the dog lay on his belly between Benj and me, looking alertly at each of us when we spoke. We were discussing what to call him besides "hey you."

Bennett proposed "Merlin," since the dog seemed to have some magic about him. Benj, who was opening a bottle of wine, wanted something connected to our trip, like, for instance, "Merlot." He poured us each a cup and offered some to the dog for a sniff. The dog pulled back his head in alarm and looked at the cup with disdain.

"Not a drinker," Benj commented.

"What about 'Hintza'?" I suggested. "He was the Rhodesian Ridgeback in Laurens van der Post's novel *A Story Like the Wind*. He looks like Hintza."

There were several attempts to call the dog Hintza, all of which elicited a pained expression on his face, as if the vibratory second syllable, "tza," might be causing him auditory distress. "So much for literary heroes," I said.

Someone threw out the name of the river, "San Juan." This brought about universal nays.

The sky turned dusky, the stars came out, the river made its soothing whoosh along the bank below us. We got into our sleeping bags. I watched the still nameless dog pad down to the river, take a drink, then disappear. I don't know how much later it was that I felt his back settle against mine. He was warm and solid, and he gave a great, contented sigh.

He wasn't there in the morning, but appeared shortly after I woke. Bounding toward me, he twirled around in excitement, pumping his front paws up and down and panting happily.

I roughed up his neck fur, and he closed his eyes in pleasure, going relaxed and easy under my hands.

We had breakfast and broke camp. Benj, who had been the last to use the latrine, carried it down to the beach. The dog was at his heels.

"I know what we can name him," Benj called out, twisting his face into an expression of disgust, "'Monsieur le Merde.' He ate the shit out of the ammo box."

"Ick," said Kim.

"No," I exclaimed in disbelief, watching the dog to see if he was foaming at the mouth or displaying some other sign of having been poisoned by the Comet. He looked absolutely tip-top, wagging his tail cheerfully.

"Are you sure, Benj?" I asked. "Did you actually see him eat it?"

"No, but it's empty, and who else would have done it? I saw him coming back from the latrine when I walked to it."

"He could have been someplace else." I knelt in the sand and said "come here" to the dog.

He came right up to me, and I leaned close and smelled his mouth. "Yuck!" I exploded, falling backward, as the stench overwhelmed me. "You are a vile dog."

He wagged his tail happily.

"You must be really hungry," I added.

"The question," said Pam, "is who's gonna row with him?"

We decided to draw straws, and Benj lost. "At least," he said, staring at the short straw, "someone on this trip has worse eating habits than me."

We paddled downriver, the morning breeze cool, the sun sprinkling the wavelets with glister. As the canyon widened, opening upon a grassy shoreline, the dog sat up smartly on the cooler. A dozen cows grazed along the left bank, raising their heads to watch us pass. They were Navajo cattle, the entire left bank of the San Juan River being the northern boundary of the Navajo Nation, which covers a sizeable portion of Utah, Arizona, and New Mexico.

The dog gave them a sharp, excited look, and leapt off the cooler. Flying through the air with his front and back legs extended, he hit the water in a mushroom of spray. He surfaced and began to paddle rapidly to the shore. Scrambling up the rocky bank, he shook himself once, and, as the cows watched in disbelief, he sprinted directly at them. They wheeled and galloped downriver.

Nose and tail extended, he chased after them, his wet coat flashing reddish-gold in the sunlight. Through willow and cactus he sprinted, closing the distance with remarkable speed and cutting out the smallest calf with an expert flanking movement. Coming abreast of the calf's hindquarter, he forced it away from the herd and toward the cliffs. It was clear he intended to corner it against the rocks and kill it.

Stunned, we watched in silence. Besides, what could we do? Yell, "Hey, dog, stop!"?

Yet something about his behavior told me that he hadn't totally lost himself to that hardwired state into which dogs disappear when they lock onto fleeing prey. Focused solely on the animal fleeing before them, they can run for miles, losing track of where they or their humans might be.

This dog wasn't doing that. As he coursed alongside the terrified calf, he kept glancing toward the raft and the kayaks, heading downriver to a bend that would take us out of sight. And I could see that he was calculating two mutually exclusive outcomes: the juicy calf and the approaching cliffs where he'd corner it, or the fast-retreating boats and the family he had found.

I saw him glance again at the bend of the river where we'd vanish—and right there I realized that dogs could think abstractly. The calf was as real as real could be, a potential meal right now. The boat people, their Purina Dog Chow, and the affection they shared with him were no more than memories of the past and ideas about the future, or however these English words translate in the mind of a dog.

Instant gratification . . . future benefits. The choices seemed clear. And mind you, we weren't calling or waving to him. Without a word, we floated silently down the river.

He chose the future. He broke off his chase in midstride, cut right, streaking past the group of startled cows who had gathered in a protective huddle. Reaching the bank, he raced along its rocky apron, trying to gain as much ground on us as he could before having to swim. Faced by willow, he leapt—again legs stretched fore and aft, ears flapping like wings—before belly crashing into the water. Paddling with determination, he set a course downriver that would intercept our float.

After a long haul—mouth open, breathing hard, eyes riveted upon us—he reached Kim's boat, swam up to her gunwale, and tried to claw his way aboard. She grabbed the loose fur on his back and hauled him onto her spray skirt. He looked suddenly very thin and bedraggled, especially when he turned to gaze wistfully after the cows. He heaved a great sigh of disappointment when the cliffs cut them off from view, then turned to me, floating fifty feet off. Springing from Kim's boat, he swam to mine. I helped him aboard, and he stared into my face with what appeared to be distress.

"You look like you've done that before," I said.

His eyes coasted away from mine.

Sensing his guilt, I tried to praise him. "You're quite the swimmer."

For the first time, he leaned forward and licked my mouth— just once before jumping out of my arms and into the water. The dunking had at least cleared his breath. He swam to the raft, allowing Benj to haul him in. Standing on the cooler, he shook himself vigorously, then reclined in his sphinx position to let the sun dry his fur.

Paddling up to the raft, I heard Benj talking to the dog and calling him "Monsieur le Merde." The dog stared straight ahead, paying no attention to him. Bennett pulled up on the opposite side of the raft. "Merlin, you're a cow killer," he sang out.

The dog flicked his eyes nervously to Bennett, then away.

I had an inspiration. This dog, though a little rough around the edges, was a survivor. He was also proud and dignified in his own quiet way. He reminded me of some cowboys I knew.

"I think we should call him 'Merle,'" I said. "That's a good, down-to-earth name."

At my voice, the dog sent me a glance, gauging my intentions. He held my eyes only a second before staring straight ahead. He seemed to know that chasing cattle wasn't going to win him friends. More than likely, he had either paid the price for it or had had a narrow escape. Dogs who chase cattle on Navajo lands are routinely shot. Maybe he had been creased by a bullet or perhaps someone had given him a second chance, letting him off with a sound beating. That could have been why he had flinched when I raised the stick. The dog now appeared to be waiting stoically for our reprimand, and perhaps that's why he had tried to appease me by licking my mouth.

"Merle," I said in a soft low voice. "Merle." He gave me another quick look, one brow up, the other down.

"Will that name work for you?"

The dog looked away, downriver, trying to ignore me. Then he began to tremble, not from his cold swim, but in fear.

In central and southern Italy during the 1980s, about 800,000 free-ranging dogs lived around villages, among cattle, sheep, pigs, chickens, deer, boar, hare, other domestic dogs, and wild wolves. To estimate the impact these free-ranging dogs were having on livestock and wildlife, and particularly on the small, endangered wolf population, a team of biologists captured, radio-collared, and then observed one group of dogs in the Velino-Sirente Mountains of Abruzzo. The group consisted of nine adults—four males and five females—to whom forty pups were eventually born, only two surviving into adulthood, a testimony to the many dangers the free-ranging dogs faced as they eked out a livelihood. They were killed by people—primarily herders—as well as by foxes, wolves, and predatory birds.

Contrary to popular belief, the biologists discovered that the dogs didn't prey on wildlife or livestock. Instead, they scavenged at garbage dumps, as did most of the wolves. Since large groups of dogs prevented the smaller packs of wolves from feeding, the wolves sometimes went hungry. The researchers also noted that a small percentage of the dogs hunted deer and other wildlife, their prey varying by locale. In the Galápagos Islands, for instance, free-ranging dogs had been seen to prey on marine iguanas. On occasion, the Italian researchers added, such dogs were known to take down livestock, especially calves.

Among these dogs there were some individuals the researchers described as "stray" and others as "feral." The two are quite distinct. "Stray dogs," the scientists wrote, "maintain social bonds with humans, and when they do not have an obvious owner, they still look for one. Feral dogs live successfully without any contact with humans and their social bonds, if any, are with other dogs." Merle—for the name quickly stuck—was clearly a stray, and his previous experience with people had apparently left him both friendly and wary.

Stepping ashore that evening, he kept a low profile, still trying to gauge our reaction to his cow-chasing incident from a distance. Even when I filled his bowl with kibble, he studied me with caution. I slapped my hip and called, "Come on, chow's on." I rattled the bowl, put it down, clapped my hands, and extended them to his dinner.

His mistrust evaporated in an instant. Bounding forward, he devoured his food. When he was done, he let me rub his flanks. I put my face between his shoulder blades and blew a noisy breath into his fur. This made him wriggle in delight. Then I opened my lunch bag and cut him a piece of elk summer sausage. He plumped his bottom in the sand, whisking his tail back and forth as I handed him the tidbit. He took it from my fingers with care.

I knew that I was probably sending him a mixed message, since elk and cattle are both red meat. But if he and I stayed together, I reckoned we could sort this out in time.

During the next few days, he rode on the cooler and swam among the kayaks. He slept between us and sat around the stove, as polite and amiable a dog as one could wish for. The river became wilder, losing itself in deep canyons, and no more cattle appeared to tempt him. We also kept the latrine covered. Merle would follow us to it and sit a ways off, his expression turning wistful when the user of the latrine rose and closed its lid.

Once, after we climbed to an overlook high above the river, Benj, who is an avid herpetologist, caught a desert spiny lizard. I had seen Merle chase several jackrabbits—unsuccessfully—but when Benj offered him the ten-inch-long lizard, its tongue flicking in and out, to gauge his reaction, Merle backed up several paces, his eyes filled with worry. "That is a dangerous animal," they seemed to say, which was somewhat true—although desert spiny lizards eat mainly insects, and sometimes other lizards, they have powerful jaws that can inflict a nasty bite. Benj brought the lizard closer to him, but Merle would have nothing of it. He snorted several times, continuing to back up.

"Maybe he got bit by one," Benj said, "or just doesn't like reptiles."

A couple of days later, I saw Merle behave in a way that lent some credence to both of Benj's guesses. As Merle and I walked along a bench above the river our path joined that of a sidewinder rattlesnake, its trail curving through the sand. Merle took in a noseful of the spoor, lifted his head sharply, and studied the terrain ahead with concern.

"Snake," I said, trying to teach him the English word.

He glanced back at me, only the very tip of his tail moving, acknowledging what I had said. Then he took several steps to the side of the sidewinder's trail and walked parallel to it, keeping his eyes peeled.

On our way back to camp, we passed some coyote scat—two turds, each about four inches long and an inch in diameter. Merle's reaction to them was entirely different. He gave the coyote poop a sniff, then poked at the turds with his right paw, his nails taking them apart. He gave them another deep smell, like a wine connoisseur who has swirled his glass and is appreciating the wine's bouquet. His gaze became excited.

"*Coyoté*," I said, giving the word its Spanish pronunciation.

He wagged his tail hard, cocked his leg, and squirted the coyote turds before enthusiastically scraping his hind legs over them. Puffing himself up, he trotted down the trail with his head swiveling dramatically from side to side, his entire body language announcing, "I will beat the living shit out of you if I find you."

His familiarity with the creatures of the desert impressed me; his burnished golden coat attracted me; his eyes wooed me. Yet for all the time we spent together, and despite sleeping by my side, Merle wasn't overt in his affections. He didn't put his head on anyone's lap; he didn't lick; he didn't offer his paw. Though still a pup, he was reserved and dignified. Life had taught him that trust needed to be earned.

On our last morning, as we came in sight of the muddy beach at Clay Hills and our waiting cars, which a shuttle company had driven down for us, I began to wonder whether this stray dog, with his mixture of fear and equanimity, would stick around or head off into the desert. I had once met a stray dog in Nepal whom I had thought was attached to me, but he had fooled me completely.

Like Merle, he simply appeared, walking into our camp in the remote Hunku Valley that lies beneath the great divide on which Mt. Everest looms. A young, black-and-brown Tibetan Mastiff, what Tibetans call a *Do Khyi*, he also had good manners and a highly evolved sense of how to feather his nest. He tagged along, eating our food and sleeping pressed to my sleeping bag, as my two companions and I trekked up the valley.

At the head of the valley, as we entered an icefall, the dog (whom we had named simply "the Khyi") went off to the left. Shortly he returned, sending us beseeching looks as he ran off again, trying to get us to follow him. We ignored him, keeping to our path, which we could see from the map was the direct route to the pass we had to climb. Many torturous hours later, we emerged from the icefall, only to find the Khyi, sitting there, waiting for us, an "I told you so" look on his face. Clearly, he had been this way before and knew a shortcut.

The next day we had to climb the Amphu Labtsa, a pass at the head of the valley that is the only way to exit the Hunku without retracing your steps. It's nineteen thousand feet above sea level, and to approach it you have to ascend increasingly steep snow-fields, which the Khyi, still at our heels, navigated handily. However, when the last snowfield turned into a gully full of ice bulges, the Khyi was stopped short. We had fixed ropes for our four porters, and I brought up the rear, "jumaring" on the rope (using a mechanical device with teeth to assist in the ascent) and pushing the Khyi ahead of me, boosting him over the ice bulges.

At last, we came to a bulge too long and steep for the Khyi to surmount even with a push from me. He sat, unable to go up or down. Had he attempted to do either, he surely would have slipped and tumbled to his death. Like Merle, he was a four-eyed dog, with two tan patches on his black forehead, directly above his very brown eyes. He was unable to move them independently, as Merle could, yet, when furrowed, they gave him an expression of sobriety and command. Now, they seemed to say, "You know what we have to do."

I took off my pack and opened it wide. Since the ropes and ice-climbing gear were being employed on the mountain, I now had extra room. Lifting the Khyi by his armpits, I slipped him into the pack tail-first. He didn't protest in the least, and I continued up the ropes. He wasn't quite as big as Merle, maybe forty-five pounds. Still, given the other gear I was carrying, it meant I was toting about sixty-five pounds. Occasionally, the load pulled me off my stance, my crampons scraping across the ice as I swung on the rope.

The Khyi didn't stir. When I looked around, he met my eye and gave me a steady look, unfazed by the steep angle. Not once did he lick me.

At the top, we cramponed along the ridge crest, searching for an exit and discovering that we were at an impasse. The only negotiable descent was via a ledge whose far edge connected to a steep snowfield that in turn led to the glacier and valley far below. However, the ledge was about a hundred feet below us and we couldn't climb down to it, a fact that was brought home to us by one of the porters who, shifting his backpack nervously, dropped his sleeping bag. We watched it grow smaller and smaller as it tumbled several thousand feet through space until it hit the glacier.

The only way down, we could see, was to follow the sleeping bag's fall—a free rappel, with nothing beneath our feet but the dizzying drop. Since my friends had led up, I offered to lead down. When I swung off into space, aiming for the tiny ledge, the Khyi, immobile till then, gave a small whine. Braking myself on the rope, I turned and saw him peering down into the abyss, his eyes enormously wide. He glanced at me and whined again. He did not like the exposure.

When I reached the two-foot-wide ledge, I let him out of the pack, for he had begun to struggle. He ran several feet to the right, where the ledge ended, and a dozen feet to the left, where it merged into the steep snowfield on which it was obvious he'd get no purchase with his claws. He sat down, looking as if the wind had been knocked out of him, and stared to the distant valley. When the others arrived, he came over to me, sat by my pack, and let me put him in it. This was a dog without illusions.

We did two more rappels before the steep angle of the snowfield lessened. I took the Khyi from my pack, and without so much as a backward glance he ran off into the approaching night, his dark form vanishing on the glacier below.

Out of water, almost out of food, we camped in a sandy swale, glad to be down and looking forward to the morning, when we could cross the glacier and moraine in safety. When the sun rose, we found a trickle of ice melt, and as we sat drinking our tea who should come trotting up but the Khyi. He greeted each person briefly with his plume of waving tail, then came and sat before me. Looking me in the eyes, he raised his paw. I clasped him on the shoulder, and he put his paw on my arm in a comradely gesture. He stared into my eyes for a long moment, then whirled and disappeared among the ice.

I never saw him again, though a good friend of mine met him the next climbing season when the Khyi approached his camp only a few miles from where he had departed from us. He was convivial and well mannered, and attached himself to my friend's party, accompanying them to Island Peak's 20,300-foot-high summit.

Now, as we floated toward Clay Hills, I watched Merle sitting on the cooler and wondered whether he'd walk off into the desert to await the next group of river runners—like the Khyi, a canine adventurer and opportunist, a professional stray, a dog who liked scenic trips, his luminous eyes having said to how many others, "I am yours . . . for some elk sausage and a free ride."

We de-rigged the raft and loaded it in Benj's truck. We lashed down the kayaks, and Merle watched our every move with attention and without the least inclination to take off. We gathered in a circle, and he looked at us quizzically.

"What should we do with him?" I asked.

Pam had a little Husky named Kira and couldn't take on another dog. Bennett wasn't sure of his future. Benj lived and worked at the Teton Science School, where dogs weren't allowed, and Kim said a dog didn't fit into her lifestyle. I wondered whether a dog really fit into mine, and what I might do with him when I traveled on assignments. When I voiced this concern, Pam and Benj volunteered to dogsit.

Merle stared at me from under his crinkled brows. The thought of leaving him on this riverbank suddenly struck me as one of the great blunders I might make in my life.

"You want to become a Wyoming dog?" I asked him, thinking of how his back had felt against mine in the night and the expression on his face when he had realized that the howls echoing from the canyon walls were his own.

He gave his tail a slow, uncertain swish, having read the somewhat uneasy tenor of our discussion.

Our decision was delayed momentarily as Pam and Bennett, needing to be off, began a round of hugs with us. After they had driven off, Kim climbed into the truck, as did Benj. I held the door open for Merle. "Let's go. You're a Wyoming dog now—if you want."

A warm, sloppy grin spread across his face: "Me? You mean me?"

"Yep, I mean you," I said gently. "Come on, let's go home."

He bounded in, and settled himself behind the front seats on the floor.

An hour later, I turned around and said, "Hey, you guys, how you doing back there?"

Kim gave a thumbs-up, and Merle, who had fallen asleep, opened one eye and gave me a contented thump of his tail.

CHAPTER 2

The First Dog

We left Kim in Moab, where she picked up her truck and drove east to Colorado. We headed north, stopping on the pass between Vernal, Utah, and Flaming Gorge Reservoir in the time-honored tradition of all male travelers for a roadside pee.

Merle took a few sniffs along the shoulder and, more particular about where he should relieve himself than Benj or me, moved off a few paces and urinated for an incredibly long time. When done, he looked up at the snowbanks—still piled alongside the road from the winter's plowing—and an expression of happiness suffused his face. Without a glance at us, he bounded to the top of the nearest one and stood at its summit, a good fifteen feet above our heads, wagging his tail slowly at Benj and me until he was certain that we were looking at him. Then, much as he had launched himself off the raft in pursuit of the cattle—front and rear legs extended—he leapt into the air and landed with a belly flop on the snowbank's sloping face, which was firm, smooth, and slippery in the spring sunshine. Like an otter, front legs before him, rear legs trailing, he slid downward, steering himself by pushing and pulling with his front paws so as to make gliding turns. At the lip of the bank, he went airborne again, landing lightly on all four paws and giving us a huge grin. Shaking off the moisture from his fur, he wagged his tail so hard that it slapped his flanks.

"Are you a ski dog as well?" I asked him.

By way of an answer, he galloped to the top of the snowbank, once again made sure we were watching him, then repeated his performance. This time, however, when he got to the edge of the snowbank, he braked himself with his front paws, slid sideways, rolled over, and rubbed his back in ecstasy on the snow, all four paws waving in the air. Then he threw himself to his feet, shook again, and looked at us with an expression that said, "That was the best!"

"There's a lot more of that in Wyoming," I told him, holding open the door of the truck for him.

Looking refreshed and restored, he jumped in and sprawled across the backseat.

"Better?" I asked him.

Thump, thump, thump went his tail.

Turning forward, I stared at the road ahead, cutting north through pines and mountains, and I wondered, as I often had, about how much pleasure dogs and humans give each other and when their destinies first intertwined. Many popular and scholarly writers have repeated a version of Merle's and my first meeting: A wolf walks out of the night into a campfire-lit scene, sniffs at some humans who smell of aurochs or mammoth, and snatches a scrap of meat tossed its way. The reality of the first interaction between wild dogs and humans was probably more complicated than this.

For starters, it isn't necessarily true that it was a wolf who threw in its lot with humans. It might have been a coyote or a jackal. Charles Darwin, whose work frequently returns to the subject of dogs and their domestication, noted that numerous domestic breeds around the world resemble specific wild canid species. He therefore believed that domestic dogs had a variety of wild ancestors. A century later, Konrad Lorenz, one of the founders of modern ethology and famous for having demonstrated that young geese could be imprinted upon a human, agreed. In his classic work *Man Meets Dog,* he maintained that certain breeds, such as German Shepherds, whom he called "Lupus" dogs, were the descendants of wolves, whereas such breeds as Poodles and Cocker Spaniels had golden jackals for progenitors. "The submissiveness of the childish jackal dog," Lorenz wrote, "is matched in the Lupus dog by a proud man-to-man loyalty that includes little submission and less obedience."

This notion—that dogs had their origins in several wild canid species whose traits re-expressed themselves in modern breeds—was steadily eroded, however, by a growing body of fossil evidence. When excavated, early dog bones looked a lot like wolf bones from the same region. The evidence, though, was literally fragmentary—part of a jaw from one site, a skull discovered in another, a foot in a third. The entire skeleton of a puppy, dating from twelve thousand years ago, was unearthed in northern Israel in the mid-1970s, and its excavators were hard-pressed to say whether it was that of a young wolf or a young dog. Then, in the 1990s, Robert K. Wayne, a molecular biologist at UCLA, and his team of researchers applied mitochondrial DNA analysis to the centuries-old question.

All plant and animal cells contain mitochondria. These tiny bodies are found outside the cell nucleus, in the cytoplasm, and mix calories and oxygen to produce energy. We then use that energy to read this page, to throw a ball, and, if you're a dog, to fetch it.

What's important to know about mitochondrial DNA, or mtDNA for short, is that it's a powerful search engine. Unlike the DNA in our chromosomes, which we inherit from both our parents, mtDNA is received only from our mothers. By tracing the occurrence of mutations back through time—in the DNA of living people as well as in that harvested from skeletal remains—geneticists have been able to determine how long ago two matrilineal clans diverged, in other words, when someone's maternal ancestors shared common mutations in their mtDNA and when they didn't. By calibrating these divergences with fossil remains of known ages (calculated by the radioactive decay of the isotope carbon-14), scientists have then been able to create what are called "molecular clocks." This sort of analysis has led geneticists to conclude that everyone alive today is related to one woman—dubbed "mitochondrial Eve"—who lived in Africa about 150,000 to 175,000 years ago.

Robert K. Wayne applied these techniques to dogs. He looked at 162 wolves from 27 locations around the world and compared the sequences of their mtDNA to that of 140 domestic dogs, representing 67 breeds. For good measure, he also sequenced five coyotes and twelve jackals. The results were stunning: Merle, the Khyi, the dog lying on your bed as you read this, in fact, every domestic dog alive today, during the last century, and going back for thousands upon thousands of years, from the smallest Pekingese to the largest Great Dane, is descended from wolves.

That's not to say that some coyote or jackal genes, here and there over the ages, haven't found their way into domestic dogs, since these wild canids can interbreed with wolves. Yet, as Wayne has stated, "Dogs are gray wolves, despite their diversity in size and proportion." What's more, Wayne's research showed that dogs could have been domesticated as long as 135,000 years ago.

At the time Wayne published his research, 1997, the oldest fossils of domesticated dogs had been dated at between twelve thousand and fourteen thousand years old. His findings therefore made everyone sit up and take notice. In fact, many scientists expressed skepticism about his date, saying that the randomness of mutations creates large variances in the reliability of molecular clocks. These variances could make Wayne's 135,000-year figure off by as many as tens of thousands of years. Even with that much wiggle room, however, his date for the domestication of dogs still fell roughly within the window of time during which the ancient people to whom we're all related left Africa and reached lands where wolves lived. There were no wolves in Africa at this time.

Because no written records exist from this period, nor even any oral histories, we will probably never know whether a wolf really walked into a circle of people sitting around a campfire, stared into the eyes of someone whose sweat smelled of reconstituted gazelle, and said, "I'm your dog." There are enough clues, however, to suggest that the domestication of wolves occurred in two different ways. The first hypothesis argues that we tamed wolves quite early on in our history while we were still hunter-gatherers; the second that wolves tamed themselves rather late in our history, as we settled in villages about twelve thousand years ago and were in the process of becoming farmers.

Both theories rely on the phenomenon known as "flight distance," a term that describes how close wildlife will let a person (or another potentially threatening animal) approach before fleeing. Even within the same species, flight distance varies among individuals. Some animals are nervous of humans and keep their distance. Some are indecisive—unsure whether to approach or flee. And some are bold, coming close to satisfy their curiosity and maybe to seek a handout. Anyone who visits a city park can see flight distance in action. Those geese and squirrels who have been fed, and haven't been harmed, will lead their offspring close to people. Those who have never learned the behavior, or who have narrowly escaped being snagged by a homeless person for dinner, will not. In any given batch of offspring, however, there are always going to be some individuals who are congenitally more or less cautious than their siblings. These factors are part of the broader discussion about which factor has the most effect on an individual—nature or nurture, what we inherit or what we learn.

When it comes to the ancestors of domestic dogs, both factors had to be operating. There were some wolves who were congenitally more curious, a bit more willing to take a risk and see what was up with those unusual bipedal creatures. Some of those wolves were immediately speared or arrowed, or got the fright of their lives in return for their curiosity; others managed to snatch a scrap of meat or a bone from a carcass. Eventually, these wolves learned to associate loosely with a band of humans, tracking their kills and scavenging them. In the meantime, the human hunters tracked the kills wolves made and, likewise, scavenged them.

At the heart of this relationship was energy conservation, a principle still operating today. If you can buy exactly the same groceries at a nearby store as at one five miles away, you'll shop at the closer location. If wolves could pick over a deer killed by humans, and supply themselves with extra calories, they would. If humans could scavenge a deer killed by a wolf pack rather than kill one themselves, they would, too. Such alliances were matters of convenience. Admiration, and love, came later.

Among this pool of wolves with short flight distances, some were especially willing to get close to humans. This wasn't an expression of friendliness, but of stress. Such a wolf could have been a female who had lost her mate to an accident and was thus unable to provide enough food for her pups. Left alone in the den while their mom hunted and scavenged, these pups would also have been the very sort of wolves who were first stolen by humans. After all, what could be more fun, if you were a young person growing up without a Game Boy, than to bring home a roly-poly wolf pup to play with?

Most of these pups were going to be too shy or already too mature—too imprinted on other wolves—ever to become domesticated. But some were going to be young enough and have just the right mixture of genes that would predispose them to live comfortably among people.

An example of how these events may have taken place was documented by Adolph Murie in his 1944 study *The Wolves of Mount McKinley.* Murie was a U.S. Fish and Wildlife Service biologist sent to Alaska on what today seems an almost unbelievable mission: to determine whether the American government should allow wolves to continue to exist in Mount McKinley (now Denali) National Park or exterminate them.

From 1939 to 1941, Murie watched a wolf family on the park's East Fork River—seven adults and five pups—and their interaction with Dall sheep, caribou, moose, grizzly bears, and other wildlife. On May 15, 1940, Murie took a pup from the pack's den so as to familiarize himself, as he put it, "with wolf character." The pup was a dark furry female, so young that her eyes were still closed. Unable to walk, she could only crawl about on her stomach. She was bottle-fed until June 25, when Murie gave her a ground squirrel, which she shook repeatedly, then ate. Murie kept the pup chained as she grew but allowed her to run loose every day. She permitted strangers to pet her, played with other dogs, and would come when Murie whistled. Murie named her Wags because of her avid tail wagging. Once, the alpha female visited her pup, and tried to lead her away. Wags followed to the end of her chain, where she whined and jumped, trying to follow her mother. "If the pup had been loose," Murie wrote, "it surely would have gone with the band."

In the photographs accompanying Murie's monograph, Wags appears to be a great big happy dog—one that could easily be mistaken for a Malamute. In one photo, Wags is smiling expectantly at a small girl who is holding a stick that she's about to throw. Murie noted that he knew of two other wolves who also had been removed from their dens at an early age, and who had similar, friendly dispositions.

It's not hard to see, then, how a wolf like Wags, taken from her den by humans some hundred thousand years ago, and bred with other friendly wolves, could have been the first proto-dog to give a gleeful wag of her tail when she saw a human—a long, furry wolf tail that would eventually evolve into a Golden Retriever's tail, a Beagle's, a Collie's, or Merle's.

When we arrived in Kelly, Merle bounded out of the truck and gave a quick look around. My silver trailer, which I used as an office, was permanently parked under a grove of cottonwood trees. Behind it, fields of sage rolled toward the snowcapped Tetons. Snuffling his nose over the porch's steps, he wagged his tail in slow appreciation: "I know who lives here: Ted." He cocked a leg and anointed the adjacent grass.

We unloaded my kayak; Benj and I exchanged a hug, and he headed home in his truck, four miles up the road. Merle jumped into my Datsun hatchback and we bumped along the dirt lane from the trailer until reaching the potholed blacktop of the one paved road that ran through Kelly. In 1950, the village was subsumed by the expansion of Grand Teton National Park and until the present day it has remained remarkably undeveloped—a half-mile square of private land between the park, the National Elk Refuge, and the Gros Ventre Wilderness. To our left was the main feature of the village, a twenty-acre field of wildflowers and sagebrush in which moose often bedded, around it a mix of old cabins, canvas-side yurts, 1960-ish tract houses, and several newer log homes. There was a covered wagon, left from the 1890s, ancient farm machinery collapsing into the sage, and several rusting cars. I could see horses in half a dozen corrals.

The ninety-odd people who lived in Kelly—ranchers, climbers, national park rangers, carpenters, nurses, auto mechanics, plumbers, retired folks, and the odd filmmaker and writer—all wanted to be here because the land was empty of development and full of weather and animals. The thirty or so dogs who lived in Kelly also enjoyed the place, I suspected, because virtually all of them lived unleashed, in houses without fences.

Merle and I crossed the Gros Ventre River and drove another

mile and a half to "Upper Kelly," the crest of a long ridge where eight trophy homes lay secluded in Douglas firs and aspens. The views were grand: all of Jackson Hole, the length of the Teton Range, and Yellowstone National Park to the north. A widow who liked my writing had rented me a cozy, well-appointed cabin, the only structure on her property.

I unpacked as Merle began to explore the field around the house. Not a minute later, he came bounding in, pumping his paws up and down and panting "ha-ha-ha."

"What is it?" I asked him.

He did a circle, lifting his head up and down the way an excited horse does.

"Show me," I said, walking toward the door.

He raced ahead of me, toward the willows south of the house, and stopped over a pancake of fresh bison poop.

He looked up at me, his tail whipping back and forth.

"Bison," I said.

He looked around. Male bison, the first to leave the National Elk Refuge in the spring, often bedded near the cabin while grazing on the new grass.

"He's around here someplace."

Deep tail wag.

I wondered how much bison poop smelled like cattle poop, and if Merle were already cutting out bison calves in his mind.

Returning to the cabin, I ate dinner, and it was almost dark when I got into bed, Merle curling up on the floor next to me. In what seemed like only a few seconds, but was in reality several hours later, I felt him put his snout under my arm and lift. I opened my eyes and stared into his. His tail was beating hard. Then I heard coyotes howling, not a hundred yards from the house.

"*Coyoté*," I said.

He gave an excited snort in agreement, "You're damn right they're *coyotés*," and ran to the front door, waiting for me to open it.

At fifty-five pounds, he was already ten pounds heavier than the biggest coyote, but a pack of them could probably kill him.

"Uh-uh," I said. "There's too many of them."

He circled frantically, ran to me, blowing breath though his lips, shivering all over, and whining.

"No. Lie down."

"Ha!" he exclaimed in frustration.

I pointed a finger at the floor. "Lie down."

He stamped his feet. I put my hand on the floor. "Lie down. You're not going out. Executive decision. Lie down."

He stared at me. I stared at him. I pointed at the floor again and said in a softer tone, "Lie down, please." I put a hand on his shoulders and gently pushed. "Please lie down."

His shoulders deflated and without disguising his displeasure he lay down, his head pointed toward the window. His ears pricked and an electric spasm went through his body every time the coyotes howled. But he didn't move.

"Thank you," I said, and saw his ears flick toward me.

About an hour later, I was awakened by the crinkling of paper and the trash can in the kitchen falling over. The coyotes were now silent. Getting up and going into the next room, I found Merle, his head in the trash can. He emerged with white freezer paper in his jaws. The elk steak that I'd cooked for dinner had been wrapped in it, and I had given him some of the meat. Coffee grounds darkened his muzzle and a piece of tomato was stuck to the end of his nose. Looking up at me, he wagged his tail with great contentment.

Taking the elk wrapper from him, I said, "No, no, no." He gave me a surprised look.

Repeating "No!" and punctuating it with a downward cut of my index finger, I returned the paper to the trash and put the plastic can on the counter, out of reach. He gazed up at it longingly.

"No dumpster diving," I said. "Come on, let's get some sleep."

I went to the bedroom door. He stayed put, looking from the trash to me and giving me a hopeful wag of his tail.

Shaking my head, I said, "Nope," then, "Come," as I beckoned to him with a come-along gesture. Taking one more look at the trash, he obeyed.

Anyone who has lived with a dog has more than likely experienced a version of this scene. After all, long before there were trash compactors, there were dogs. Researchers who believe wolves domesticated themselves, rather than humans having had a hand in the process, point out that trash was the motivating factor.

Raymond Coppinger is the best-known advocate of this theory. A biologist at Hampshire College and an accomplished sled-dog racer and trainer of sheep guard dogs, Coppinger notes that the archaeological evidence suggests dogs began to look more like dogs than wolves about twelve thousand years ago, when humans began to switch from hunting and gathering to herding and farming. Both activities gave rise to permanent settlements and refuse dumps.

"The wild wolf, *Canis lupus*," Coppinger writes in his book *Dogs: A New Understanding of Canine Origin, Behavior, and Evolution*, which he co-authored with his wife, Lorna, "began to separate into populations that could make a living at the dumps and those that couldn't." Those that could, he goes on to say, had shorter flight distances. Over time, these wolves began to evolve. They lost their long canines and large strong jaws, both necessary to kill big animals. Their head and teeth became smaller—just big enough to survive on the low-quality human leftovers. In addition, their brains became smaller, adequate to the job of scavenging trash in this new niche but not to organizing and coordinating hunts for elusive and formidable prey. Because these smaller dump wolves expended less energy to survive and reproduce, they were able to outcompete their brawny cousins.

Elaborating on his theory, Coppinger cites the work of the Russian geneticist Dmitry K. Belyaev who, starting in 1959, decided to replay the evolutionary history of the domestic dog by breeding silver foxes solely on the basis of their tameability. Within thirty-five generations, Belyaev and his colleagues observed some amazing results. The foxes lost pigment in their coats and developed a star-shaped pattern on their faces, similar to some breeds of domestic dogs. They lost their upright, pricked ears—one of the distinguishing characteristics of all wild adult canids—and retained the floppy ears of their puppyhood into maturity, just as many breeds of domestic dogs do. The level of corticosteroids in their plasma also dropped dramatically, a change in hormonal chemistry that left the animals calmer. Generation by generation, the foxes selected for tameability became less wary and ever more eager for human contact, whimpering to attract attention and sniffing and licking the researchers.

Coppinger concluded that the trends Belyaev had described in his forty-year-long experiment were precisely what happened in village dumps twelve thousand years ago, when wolves with shorter flight distances began to become transformed, by natural selection, into today's domestic dogs. He thought it extremely unlikely that early people would have embarked on such a long-term wolf-taming and breeding project.

They probably didn't—at least not intentionally. But by stealing wolf pups from dens and keeping the most friendly ones—pups such as Wags, Adolph Murie's McKinley wolf—they became engaged in the very sort of experiment that Belyaev conducted with silver foxes. Their initial selection may have been random, but given how fast changes took place in Belyaev's test, our ancient ancestors could have seen similar results in fairly short order. Let a friendly pup like Wags mate with an equally friendly wolf, and let their offspring mate with other friendly wolves, and within ten or so canid generations—one-half to one-third of a human lifetime back in those days—you'd have wolves on their way toward becoming dogs.

Until recently the archaeological evidence has supported both theories—that wolves domesticated themselves when we began to live in villages, and that we domesticated wolves when we were still nomadic hunter-gatherers—although the balance was slightly tipped in favor of domestication having taken place while we were hunters. A skull fragment with the proportions of a domestic dog was discovered in Yorkshire, England, and found to be ninety-five hundred years old, a date that precedes the arrival of agriculture to that part of the British Isles by thirty-five hundred years. A mandible of what is believed to be a domestic dog was also discovered in a grave in Oberkassel, Germany. The dog who owned that jaw lived fourteen thousand years ago, six thousand years before agriculture reached its home. Then, in 2002, new evidence emerged to support the theory that we domesticated wolves long ago. Two Russian researchers announced that they had carbon-14-dated a pair of adult canid skulls found in a camp of mammoth hunters in the Dneiper River Valley, west of Moscow. Both skulls had shortened snouts—the diagnostic feature of domestic dogs—and their age created a stir. They were seventeen thousand years old.

Additional proof for early domestication came during the same year when the geneticist Peter Savolainen and a team of Swedish researchers used mtDNA analysis to determine that the domestication of dogs took place between fifteen thousand and forty thousand years ago in several locations in East Asia. The genetic evidence also led Savolainen to conclude that "the first domestication of wolves would not have been an isolated event, but rather a common practice."

Savolainen's findings flew in the face of some of the most accepted notions about the origins of dogs, specifically that North American dogs were domesticated from North American wolves, European dogs from European wolves, and so on. However, when Robert K. Wayne and his colleagues analyzed the mtDNA of ancient domestic dogs from the New World—skeletal remains from archaeological sites in Mexico, Peru, and Bolivia, as well as the remains of Alaskan dogs that predate the first arrival of European explorers—their findings confirmed Savolainen's. The lineages of all these North and South American dogs could be traced back to Old World wolves. It was the domesticated descendants of these wolves who subsequently trekked over the Bering land bridge with humans, between thirty thousand and thirteen thousand years ago, and eventually became the dogs of the Western Hemisphere. Traveling in the opposite direction, these early dogs also accompanied humans to western Asia and Europe, where they founded some of today's breeds.

Dogs and people, it's now clear, have been partners for a long, long time.

When I opened my eyes in the morning, the first thing I saw was sunlight streaming through the windows; the second was Merle. His chin lay on the edge of the bed and he was staring directly at me. The instant he saw that I was awake, his tail, which had been wagging steadily at about 120 beats per minute, doubled in velocity.

"Good morning," I said. "Did you sleep well?"

He wagged his tail harder. When I went to pet him, he whirled and went to the front door. He had not forgotten the coyotes.

When I opened the door, he burst outside, cocked his leg for a quick pee, then sprinted into the sage where the coyotes had been singing. He coursed through the bushes, unraveling their story. I went back inside, and as I brushed my teeth he came into the bathroom.

"You are really wasting time," his impatient look said. "You can't believe what's out there."

I had some breakfast and gave him the last of the Purina, after which we walked down the hill to the trailer. Where the dirt road made a bend, following the buckrail fence along the boundary of the National Elk Refuge, Merle came to a stop and raised his right paw, his head extended in the classic pose of a Pointer. I doubted Merle had any Pointer genes, but most dogs will point—a behavior seen in wolves, who, when hunting together, will often extend their noses toward their prey, alerting other pack members to what they've spied.

Following Merle's nose, I saw a Uinta ground squirrel standing near its burrow, thirty feet ahead of us. Commonly called "chiselers," these squirrels are ten inches high and live by the thousands in and around Kelly, emerging from their underground dens each April.

Merle began a slow and deliberate stalk toward the ground squirrel, pausing after a few steps. I could see him turn the corner of his eye back to me. Seeing that I remained motionless, he took a few more gliding steps toward the chiseler, lifting his paws in a fluid motion that was hypnotic. The chiseler, its tiny paws raised to its mouth, its black eyes shining in the morning sun, didn't move.

There was no warning. Merle charged. The chiseler squealed and dashed. Merle emerged from a cloud of dust, the squirrel in his jaws. He shook it violently, pinned it to the ground, ripped it open, and swallowed it in half a dozen gnashing gulps.

I was stunned.

By the time I reached him he was slurping the blood off the dusty shoulder of the road. He gave me a satisfied wag of his tail and licked his lips with his long pink tongue.

"You've done that before," I said.

His tail beat harder.

Looking very proud of himself—glowing, in fact, with the sleek fullness of a well-fed diner—he trotted down the road, tail high, shoulders thrown back, head swiveling left and right as chiselers popped up and spied us.

If the squirrels were more than thirty feet away, Merle trotted by them with only a cursory glance. If they were less than thirty feet away, he went into point-and-stalk mode. Most of these chiselers whistled and disappeared down their burrows like miniature submarine commanders who have spotted a destroyer. One, however, let him get too close. Merle sprinted. The chiseler bolted, reversing course at the last second. Merle's jaws snapped on thin air. The chiseler squirted between his legs and dove into its hole.

Merle looked up at me with a self-effacing grin. "Hey—a dog can't get all of them."

"No," I answered, "he can't."

We continued down the hill and started along the alfalfa field that the Teton Valley Ranch cultivated for horse feed. There, directly in the road and blocking our path, stood a large male bison, more than likely the one who had left his calling card near the cabin. His fur was a deep chocolate brown; his head was massive.

Merle stopped. He did not point. He did not wag his tail.

"No," I told him.

The tip of his tail, still held high, wagged a tiny bit, acknowledging that he'd heard me.

Before I could get out another word, he charged the bison, who lowered his head and hooked Merle with his horn. Merle leapt aside—narrowly missing being disemboweled—planted his front paws, lowered his head, and woofed at the bison. If I hadn't been so worried for Merle, the scene would have been comical: a fifty-five-pound dog taking on a two-thousand-pound bison. The bison promptly hooked at him again, brushing Merle's left hip with his horn, and then, having become annoyed at this gadfly, charged.

Merle cast honor to the wind and galloped toward me, doing a 180 behind my legs and peering at the bison from around my knees. The bison, of course, had stopped after a few feet. If you weigh two thousand pounds, you're not going to waste energy chasing a dog who can't hurt you.

"So," I said, kneeling and putting an arm around Merle's shoulder. "That's a bison." I pointed at the animal, looking at us malevolently from about seventy-five feet away. "Bison," I repeated. "Bison you leave alone. Bison will kill you."

Merle didn't shiver with excitement, as he had when I told him he couldn't chase the coyotes, his electric shiver having implied "Just let me at them." Instead, he studied the bison with sober concentration. I stood. "Come on," I said, gesturing with my hand, "this is how you get around a bison."

Making a wide circle, I climbed the barbed-wire fence that surrounded one of the ranch's horse pastures, holding the bottom two strands apart for Merle. He jumped through the opening, but kept looking back at the bison as we skirted him. Eventually we recrossed the fence and stood on the dirt road, a hundred yards away from the huge animal. As we had walked around him, the bison had turned to face us, wheeling as steadily as the arms of a clock.

"That's how you get around a bison," I told Merle. "Let's go." I gave another motion with my hand and simultaneously walked away at an increased pace. Merle made one of his "ha-ha-ha" pants—indicating "I get it, don't mess with bison"—and fell in by my side.

That he did get it—that he was a quick study both of hand gestures and big, dangerous animals—became apparent over the ensuing days, weeks, and years. With little prompting he learned the signals for no, come, sit, lie down, go away, and be quiet. And as for bison, he never confronted another for as long as he lived.

The sort of unregimented training I was giving Merle is how dogs have learned to live with humans for thousands of years. Its loose methods are different from those employed in dog obedience school, where a dog is taught stylized behaviors by issuing commands that, when obeyed, are rewarded, often with food. However, the aim of both loose and strict dog training is the same: to create a well-socialized dog. Obedience school (whether done on one's own or in a formal group) uses top-down management to get results. The loose method doesn't use bottom-up management, leaving everything to the dog, but joint management. Its underlying assumption is that dogs are clever and quickly "get it" by simply watching and listening.

Once—when most of our learning took place outside of schools—this easy communication between dogs and people was taken at face value, a phenomenon to which the Victorian scientist Francis Galton paid homage when he wrote, "Every whine or bark of the dog, each of his fawning, savage, or timorous movements is the exact counterpart of what would have been the man's behaviour, had he felt similar emotions. As the man understands the thoughts of the dog, so the dog understands the thoughts of the man, by attending to his natural voice, his countenance, and his actions."

Galton goes on to say that this relationship is exclusive. A man, he declares, has to work to communicate his thoughts to an ox or a sheep, but he "irritates a dog by an ordinary laugh . . . frightens him by an angry look . . . calms him by a kindly bearing." Over most other life forms we have no power whatsoever. "Who for instance," he asks, "ever succeeded in frowning away a mosquito, or in pacifying an angry wasp by a smile."

Galton didn't investigate what underlying factors predispose dogs and humans to communicate so easily, other than saying dogs had an "inborn liking" for us. More than a century had to go by before Brian Hare, a biological anthropologist at Harvard University, sought the roots of this "inborn liking." He asked human volunteers to gaze at, point to, or tap on containers in which food had been hidden. (Odors were controlled, so smell wasn't a factor.) Wolves raised by humans, chimpanzees, and domestic dogs were all tested to see if they could then identify the container that contained the food. Ironically, the chimps, our closest genetic relatives, did the poorest; the wolves didn't do much better. Dogs, on the other hand, almost inevitably chose the correct container.

Hare then tried to answer the question that logically grew out of his experiment: Had each dog learned to read the social cues of people by living with them, or was the skill hardwired? He tested puppies from nine to twenty-six weeks of age, some of whom had been reared in human families, others in litters. They were all able to choose the correct container by observing the gestures given by humans: a nod, a stare, a tap. Hare concluded that sometime during their domestication, dogs had evolved the ability to read us extremely well.

The reverse is also true. Sometime during our history, we evolved the ability to read dogs with as much precision as they read us. In 1950, Konrad Lorenz suggested that the key factor underlying this ability was our almost universal love of dogs. This love, he claimed, has its roots in how we feel about our own infants, their juvenile features triggering what he called "innate releasing mechanisms." These releasing mechanisms then express themselves in nurturing behavior. The important juvenile features he noted are a relatively large head, large and low-lying eyes, pudgy cheeks, short and thick extremities, clumsy movements, and a generally pliant body. Lorenz might have been describing wolf puppies as well as human babies, and this was precisely his point: We often transfer our evolved responses to our own infants to substitute objects like dogs.

The anthropological evidence bears out Lorenz's theory. Virtually everywhere that explorers and anthropologists have encountered aboriginal people, they have found that they treat dogs, especially young dogs, with great affection. The Norwegian Carl Lumholtz, for instance, noted how the dingo was an important member of an Aborigine's family. "It sleeps in the huts and gets plenty to eat," he wrote, "not only of meat, but also of fruit. Its master never strikes, but merely threatens it. He caresses it like a child, eats the fleas off it, and then kisses it on the snout."

The diarist George Forster, who accompanied Captain James Cook to the Society Islands in the late 1700s, also observed a close bond between native people and their dogs when he wrote that Polynesian women nursed puppies at their own breasts with what he called "ridiculous affection." A memorable illustration of such affection can also be seen in the American painter George Catlin's

1844 pen-and-ink drawing *Sioux Moving Camp.* It shows men, women, and children mounted on horses. The horses pull travois, and the dogs run alongside them, dragging their own travois. Leading the entire band is a woman on foot, a child slung on her back and a puppy at her waist, perched in her shawl and looking out at the world with an eager and happy expression on its face.

Yet, as any parent who has watched a baby grow into a teenager knows, cuteness wanes with age. So, too, with wolf pups. As adults, they're no longer cuddly. They have long pointy snouts, big canines, and alert ears. By contrast, domestic dogs don't lose as much of their babyish cuteness when they grow into adults. Their ears stay floppy; their snouts remain relatively short; they still love to play; and, most important, they're willing to roll over on their backs and remain subordinate to those who raised them. The retention of such childlike characteristics into adulthood is called neoteny, and it's why so many people find dogs endearing—we are genetically predisposed to nurture the young. Such behavior, Lorenz observed, would have high survival value for any species.

The Dog Genome Project, an international effort based at the Fred Hutchinson Cancer Research Center in Seattle, Washington, may eventually discover whether some wolves have a similar predisposition to find us likable. The gene or complex of genes that underlies this trait may have helped to turn some wolves, thousands of years ago, into astute, human-reading dogs. The project may even be able to fix a date to that transformation, one stretching back to the time before our direct ancestors left Africa. After all, wolf and human remains—dated to 400,000 years before the present—have been found side by side in Kent, England. These wolves may be the very first "dogs," even though, as Robert K. Wayne has pointed out, they "may not have been morphologically distinct from their wild relatives." Dogs in wolfish clothing, they may already have begun an alliance with early primates—an alliance that became so valued that people chose their dogs to accompany them not only on their earthly journeys, but also on their final ones.

The most remarkable of these memorials was discovered in northern Israel, where, twelve thousand years ago, the Natufian culture began the transition from hunting and gathering to farming. Natufians lived in circular dwellings, and in one of these structures, under a limestone slab, the skeletons of an elderly person and a puppy were found. The person lay on its right side, its knees drawn up, its head bowed forward. The person's sex couldn't be determined because its pelvis had been damaged. Researchers later determined that the puppy was a transitional animal—a newly domesticated wolf.

We will never know whether the puppy and the human died at the same time and were buried together or whether the human died and the puppy was then sacrificed. What is known—and can be readily seen in a photograph of the grave—is that the fingers of the person and the paws of the puppy touch, the person's and the puppy's heads so placed that they are nodding toward each other in a final gesture of mutual regard and affection.

The grave wasn't unique. Two other dogs and a human skeleton were later uncovered in a nearby burial site, arranged similarly. The forehead of the human nods to the forehead of one of the dogs—no better symbol of our thoughts passing so easily between us.

On our arrival at the trailer, Merle did a thorough exploration of its interior as I listened to my phone messages. After he had sniffed every room, he stood in front of me, giving his tail a clipped little beat that I had come to understand meant that he wanted something. Then he made a lisping noise by slightly opening his mouth. I went to the kitchen and filled a bowl with water. I had been correct in my read of him. He slurped it up immediately.

"Hey," I said to him. "We'll go to town later, and I'll get you some bowls of your own and also your shots."

He wagged his tail enthusiastically.

"Let's see if you feel that way after we're done at the vet's," I told him. "In the meantime, would you like to go outside and do some exploring? I've got some work to do before we go."

I let him out and he stood on the porch a moment, surveying the fields and mountains before setting off.

A couple of hours later, as I was working at my desk, I heard him jump on the porch. Looking over my shoulder, I saw him standing patiently by the door.

"Want to come in?"

"Ha!" he panted.

I let him in and he immediately pumped his paws up and down in his excited little dance.

"What did you find?"

He whirled around, clearly enthused by what he had smelled and seen during his excursion.

I knelt and gave him a hug, and he sank into my hands, groaning in pleasure. Then he lifted his head, regarded me tenderly, and sat back on his haunches, putting his paws on my shoulders. We held each other's gaze.

Many modern dog trainers would view this moment as a red flag, claiming that a dog who puts its paws on your shoulders and looks you in the eye is trying to assert its dominance. This may be the case with some dogs, but not all of them. In fact, David Mech, one of the world's most eminent wolf biologists, has watched wolves behave in just this fashion and has called their "hugging"—the two wolves facing each other on their haunches or lying on their sides and placing their front legs around the opposite wolf's head and shoulders—"a deliberate display of friendliness and affection."

"Give me fifteen more minutes," I told Merle, "and we'll walk up the hill and get the car."

When I stood, he dropped to all fours and went to the screen door to look outside. Leaving him to his gazing, I went to my desk.

A couple of minutes later, I heard him lie down directly behind my chair. I turned. He was lying on his side, looking coyly at me from the corner of his eye.

"Everything okay?"

Thump, thump, thump—his tail hit the carpet hard, and I thought of how long humans have heard that contented sound. Whether 12,000, 50,000, or 400,000 years, it mattered little. All that mattered was the timeless refrain, echoing down through the ages, the human voice asking, the dog's tail responding:

How are you?

Better now.

I am glad.

So am I.

Eyes locked: together.

CHAPTER 3

The Synaptic Kiss

Unlike one of my childhood dogs—a Beagle-Terrier cross named Tippy, who began to whimper the instant she saw the vet's front door—Merle waltzed into the Jackson Hole Veterinary Clinic as if he had booked himself into a spa. He greeted the receptionist heartily but politely, allowed me to pick him up onto the stainless steel table without the least bit of fuss, and stood calmly for his vaccinations, swallowing his deworming pills as if they were candy. Inspecting his teeth, the vet, a square-jawed man in jeans and a western shirt, named Jack Konitz, declared Merle about ten or eleven months old and probably a yellow Lab with some Golden Retriever mixed in.

"Any hound?" I asked.

He stared at Merle's face. "Could be."

From the vet we went to Valley Feed and Pet, where I bought Merle a forty-pound bag of kibble and a red collar on which to put his rabies tag, his Teton County registration tag, and a tag inscribed with his name, our address, and phone number. I also bought him a rubber ball with a bell in it, a rubber bone that squeaked when pressed (sounding like the noise of a chiseler), and a rawhide chew.

"Oh, boy, do I have some treats for you," I told him as I got back into the car. He was in sphinx mode, occupying the entire

cargo space of the Datsun, its rear seat down, as he watched cus-
tomers enter and leave the store, the end of his nose twitching in
appreciation as a rancher pulled in with a pickup truck. Merle's
eyes gleamed. The man must have smelled of cattle.

Back in Kelly, we got out of the car, and without delay I began
his training as a bird dog. I threw the rubber ball across the small
field in front of the trailer. Merle watched the arc of the ball with
disinterest. I waited. He didn't move. Retrieving it myself, I shook
it under his nose so its little bell tinkled, and tossed it again. Unfazed, Merle watched its fall.

"Go get it," I said. "You've got Retriever blood on two sides."

He gave me a look that said: "I don't do balls."

I held the rubber bone in front of his nose. He sniffed it perfunctorily. I squeaked it. His ears pricked but he made no move
to grab it. So I pulled out the pièce de résistance—the rawhide
chew—and held it under his nose. Another superficial sniff.

"Mmm-mmm-mmm," I said in the tone of voice that adults use
when trying to feed reluctant children. So as not to wound me too
grievously, Merle tried to wag his tail, but his lack of enthusiasm
was clear.

"Oh, come on!" I exclaimed. "This is a rawhide chew. Dogs
go wild for them."

I pushed it between his lips. He parted his teeth and took it.
I let it go, and as it touched his tongue, he opened his jaws and
let the chew fall to the porch. He backed up from it—one step,
two, three—then gave me the tiniest wag of his tail, just its tip,
as if to say, "I apologize, I really do, but I don't do chews."

I sighed.

In her perceptive book *The Other End of the Leash,* dog behaviorist Dr. Patricia McConnell states that dogs who have been
raised in an environment without stimuli, like those poor dogs who
begin life in the bins of puppy mills, often develop "into adults
who won't play with any object, ever, not with balls, rawhide chew
bones, or Frisbees."

I wondered whether this had been the puppyhood Merle had experienced. Had he been raised in the Navajo equivalent of a puppy mill? Yet he seemed pretty well socialized—at least to people. McConnell goes on to say, "Perhaps there is a 'critical period' for object play, just as there is for socialization, in which dogs are hardwired to learn how to play and what to play with."

I collected the dog paraphernalia and toted the bag of kibble into the trailer, emptying a healthy portion into a new stainless steel bowl.

Merle waited, now wary of Ted bearing gifts.

"Have at it," I said, sitting on the floor nearby and waiting for another rejection.

He walked to the bowl, sniffed the surface of the kibble with care, and began to wag his tail approvingly. He finished his dinner in a dozen ravenous gulps, licking the bowl clean.

"Phew," I said as he came over to me and put the top of his head against my chest.

A few days later, Steve Heksel, a river guide who lived in a one-room cabin south of my trailer, brought home a black-and-white Border Collie pup named Jack. Only about ten weeks old, Jack began to romp with Merle, and, in the stylized behavior of puppies toward older dogs, fawned on him. Merle would let Jack crawl on his shoulders and chew his ears, closing his eyes in patient toleration, then spring up and run away from Jack, a move that sent the puppy into a high-pitched frenzy of barking: "I'm going to catch you! I'm going to catch you!"

About this time, a young Vizsla named Zula also arrived in Kelly, moving with her family into one of the yurts that dotted the twenty-acre sage meadow that lay north of our trailer. She had a smooth, amber coat, long ears, like those on a Maasai woman, tender hazel eyes, and a moist, wide, flesh-colored nose—the canine equivalent of *Cosmo* lips. Her waist was pulled in and there wasn't an ounce of fat on her.

Merle went gaga over her. She would make her way over the decrepit wooden bridge spanning the creek that separated our field from the main meadow, stepping daintily over the teetering boards, then race to our porch, where Merle would already be bounding down the steps. Round and round they would tear, cutting a circle about thirty yards in diameter, first Zula leading, then Merle, round and round, heeled over like cyclists at a velodrome, until I thought their hearts would burst.

Poor Jack would try to enter their blistering race only to be bowled over by the two of them. Recovering from his tumble, he'd sit in the circle they were scribing in the grass, his head swiveling to follow them, a plaintive but eager look on his face. Finally, Zula and Merle would pile up together, lying nose-to-nose, sides heaving, while Jack climbed over them, pulling their tails and ears, trying to get them to play.

It now occurred to me that Merle must have learned how to play with other dogs at some point in his young life. Actually, more than just play. Refreshed from the brief nap they had taken, he would sit up and look around with an air of anticipation. He'd test the wind, nostrils dilating, then take a deep breath, and throw his snout to the sky. Opening his mouth wide, he'd let out a howl, starting low and climbing through his considerable register. One howl completed, he'd wait for Zula and Jack to chime in before going on. The three of them would sit together, muzzles pointed at the cottonwoods and the mountains, having their morning songfest. At least three times a day, they would gather to chase each other, to nap, and to sing, each of them then returning to his or her respective yurt, trailer, or cabin. Merle would stand on the porch and watch Zula go over the bridge with a fond expression on his face, his tail doing a slow, appreciative wag: "Gosh, I like her."

His collar, with its trio of jangling tags, stayed on a hook by the door, for there seemed to be no need for him to wear it in Kelly. He was willing to walk near me as we went between the office and our cabin on the hill, lagging to investigate a smell, then galloping to catch up. When I would hear him coming, I'd crouch to face him, opening my arms, as he'd race headlong at me. At the last possible instant, he'd veer off, brushing my knee with his flank and laughing, "Ha-ha-ha!" In fact, if I noticed anything about our walks, it was that he didn't want to let me out of his sight.

As for my fears of his chasing wildlife, they were quickly allayed. When we'd see the bison, who continued to hang around the cabin, Merle would stand by my side, wagging his tail in a lazy arc, and look up at me with a humorous glint in his eye, implying, "Yep, I remember." When we'd walk by mule deer, he'd watch them—one ear pricked toward them, one ear angled back in my direction—as I'd repeat, "Deer, no, stay," my voice low and rumbling. And he'd look up at me with an expression that contained a hint of exasperation, the canine version of "I get it. I get it. I'm not supposed to chase wildlife."

For a few blissful days, therefore, I believed that I had found the model dog. All those training books that advised using a clicker to indicate to your dog the precise instant it has performed the desired behavior instead of saying, "good," or "yes," or "well done"; that counseled using the "alpha roll-over," during which the human acts as the alpha wolf and disciplines the dog by rolling it over on its back and growling in its face; that advocated a nothing-in-life-is-free approach to training, in other words that no food or treat should be given unless the dog earns it by sitting or lying down—these training books had it wrong. All you had to do was give your dog space, talk to him sensibly, show him what needed to be done—placing a hand on the floor for "lie down," gesturing here and there for him to "come" and "stay"—while generally letting him learn from the world around him, and he'd respond like the clever being he was.

Blinded by my rapid success—and not considering that I'd found a smart and compliant dog who hadn't been seriously tested—I took a bike ride along the foothills of the Gros Ventre Mountains. It was a hot afternoon and we went through the rolling sagebrush on an abandoned jeep road. Merle loped a few yards ahead of me, mouth open, tail streaming, ears flapping. We came over a small rise and saw twenty Black Angus cows. My perfect dog didn't hesitate. Going into hyperspeed, he rushed them.

"No!" I yelled.

It was like yelling at the space shuttle to come back. The cattle, thoroughly frightened, also went into overdrive as Merle dashed among them and cut out one of their calves. Downshifting, I raced after him.

We must have been quite the sight: the panicked cattle, the pursuing dog, and the man on the bike, shouting, "Merle, no! Merle, no!"

I continued to yell, to no effect. I was terrified. The rancher who owned these cows had a reputation for shooting dogs who chased them, and I could see the ranch house approaching in the distance. I could imagine the rancher, or his manager, lining up a scope-sighted .270 over the hood of his pickup.

That gave me the adrenaline burst I needed to accelerate up to Merle's tail and dart between him and the calf he was chasing. I kicked him in the ribs as I went by and yelled, "No chasing cows!"

Startled, Merle looked up with a "Huh?" expression. Talk about being hardwired! He hadn't even heard me. Furious, and frightened that I'd lose him, I went into hardwired mode as well. I jumped off the bike, rolled him over, held him by the ruff of his neck, and snarled in his face, "No!"

He cringed and whined, trying to escape my grasp. I let him go. He immediately jumped to his feet, surveyed the scene, saw the cows in the distance, and galloped after them. I couldn't believe it.

I leapt on my bike and chased him down, swerving in front of him and flying off to tackle him. This time I hit him soundly on the butt, ranting in his face, "No, no, no, you're gonna die!"

He cried out in fear and shock. His eyes were wild. His world had come undone. The one person he had trusted had betrayed him. And I felt shoddy and demeaned for having struck him.

Putting on his collar and leash, which I carried in my fanny pack, I said, "I'm sorry. I'm sorry. Let's go home."

I picked up my bike, got on, and set off. He trotted alongside me, breathing much harder than the pace warranted, for he was very upset. As was I. In fact, I was shaking.

On the drive back to Kelly, I watched him in the rearview mirror. He looked withdrawn and somber. Nor did his mood improve with dinner. He ate it and curled up in the living room.

I petted him before going to bed, but he wouldn't acknowledge me, staying curled up nose to tail.

Lying in bed, I wondered what to do. Clearly, I had been mistaken. For one set of behaviors, voice reinforcement could change his behavior. Since he was one of those highly social dogs who respond so well to praise, he listened to what I said. Watching me closely, he also imitated what I did. In short, he wanted to please me. But for other behaviors, those fixed-action ones such as chasing cattle, talking to him was like trying to speak to someone who is deaf.

This particular hardwired characteristic of the canine personality—chasing prey that runs—was compounded by the fact that Merle had probably received tremendous positive reinforcement for capturing calves in his early days on the San Juan River. Killing such an animal would have produced huge benefits for him—life itself. That sort of reinforcement was going to be hard to break, but I needed to break it, for I didn't want a dog who couldn't roam freely, especially in a rural place like Kelly.

As I mulled this over, I heard him stir and come into the bedroom. He put his chin on the bed, his nose just touching my arm. Taking his face between my hands, I kissed his forehead. "I am very sorry I hit you," I said. "I was so worried about you. I will never do that again." I could feel his head move as he wagged his tail.

"Come here," I said and patted the bed. He leapt up and I threw an arm around him. He put his head on my shoulder, wrapping a paw around my neck. Looking at me, he waited. Regarding him tenderly, I made a smooching noise with my mouth. He gave a relieved sigh and his body relaxed. Within minutes, he was asleep.

But apologies didn't solve the problem of his chasing cattle, and, to make my anxiety worse, two dogs were shot within the next month for chasing cattle near Kelly. This was before electric shock collars were readily available. In fact, though it's hard to imagine life without Google, that search engine didn't exist in 1991—you couldn't answer virtually any question with the click of a mouse. So I asked friends and vets what to do, and many of them recommended a choke collar.

The problem with a choke collar, however, was that Merle couldn't be on a leash. To duplicate the behavior that I wanted to terminate, he had to be running full-tilt. One person recommended throwing cold water on him while he chased cattle. That was how he had broken his dog of chasing cars—by throwing a bucket of ice-cold water on him from the passenger seat. But I didn't think cows would let me ride them. This person had the right concept, though. To counteract the huge positive reinforcement Merle had gotten for chasing cattle, he'd need to be given a large and unpleasant deterrent—one that I hoped he wouldn't associate with me.

Distracting him and then rewarding him with a treat and praise—the sort of training that gives something coveted as a way of pointing a dog away from disagreeable behavior—didn't seem to hold much promise. How do you distract a dog who is far away from you and deep in hardwired mode?

After sleeping on it for a few nights, I reluctantly bought a choke collar, slipped it over Merle's head, and set out on the same two-track where we'd found the cattle. As luck would have it, they were still nearby, and Merle, despite having been rolled over by his supposed alpha, took off after them as if he remembered nothing.

I had attached fifty yards of light climbing rope to his choke collar, and, as he sped away, I braked the bike while letting several coils of rope unravel from my hand.

"Merle, no!" I yelled and jerked the rope.

He came to an abrupt stop, shook his head like a fighter who's been punched hard, and looked around in perplexity. I pedaled forward as fast I could as he took off again, making straight for the fleeing cows.

"Merle, no!" I yelled, jerking the rope and wrenching him to a stop.

He shook his head. He caught sight of the cattle again. Off he went at a dead run. This was too painful to watch. Could he really be this hardwired?

Once more, I yelled, "Merle, no!" and snubbed the rope.

He tumbled into the sage, shook himself, stood up, and caught sight of the cattle. But this time he paused and slowly sat down. Staring at them, he trembled with unabated eagerness to resume his chase.

I pedaled up to him, crouched by his side, and said, very quietly, "No. You can't chase cattle."

He gave a small whine and his body shook—not in fear, but with pent-up longing.

"No," I repeated.

At the word, he turned and looked at me. Our heads were at the same level, and his eyes were bright and glowingly alive. They had cattle written all over them.

"No," I said. "You can't do this anymore. You'll be shot and killed. And I will miss you terribly."

He took a deep breath and glanced back at the cows, who had with excellent sense come to a stop a hundred yards off.

"No," I said. "Never again. No, no, no."

His posture visibly slumped, his shoulders sagged about half an inch, as if he were losing one of the greatest fortunes a dog could own.

"No," I repeated.

Stoically, he stared at the cattle.

"No," I said, and very slowly took off the choke collar.

I waited a moment. He sat, watching the cows.

"Okay, let's go."

I coiled the rope, got on the bike, and began to ride.

"Come on."

Reluctantly, he started after me as I deliberately rode parallel to the cattle. They jerked their heads up and began to gallop away. Merle was trotting by my side and I repeated, quietly, "No, no, no. No chasing."

He trembled violently, but he stayed alongside me. I stopped the bike, reached into my fanny pack, and gave him a biscuit. "Very good," I said. "Very, very good."

Taking it without enthusiasm, he held it in his mouth while staring at the departing cattle. What more could a dog say about his priorities?

"Good," I repeated. "Well done." And I patted him lavishly.

Still, he stared at the cattle.

"You can eat that now," I told him.

Turning to me, he sighed.

"I'm sorry," I replied. "Beef is out."

He looked back at the vanishing cattle, heaved another sigh, then began to chew his biscuit as if it were sawdust, leaving pieces of it on the ground.

"Okay," I said. "Your feelings about this have been noted. But it's nonnegotiable. Let's go."

I began to pedal, and he followed at a sullen trot. Within a few minutes, however, he picked up speed and galloped ahead of me as if he had put the incident behind him. He hadn't. When we got to the car, I tossed the choke collar into the back, and he made a point of sitting on the opposite side of the car from it, looking at it with great distaste, a feeling that he immediately extended to all collars. Even if we were heading off to do something that he enjoyed, like skiing, and I fastened his comfortable red collar around his neck, he became instantly poker-faced, as if he were a young boy being forced to wear a suit.

It was a small price to pay. He never chased cattle again, though he never lost his passion for them. Far into his old age, he would become terribly excited if we passed a herd of them. Trembling with eagerness, eyes fixed upon them, he'd watch their every move.

The events of our first weeks together—the bison, the deer, the cattle, Merle's unwillingness to fetch, and his quick grasp of both the words and the hand signals for No, Come, Sit, Lie Down, Go Away, and Be Quiet—made me reflect on how dogs learn. Some of the ways in which they take in, process, and then utilize information are identical to ours. Touch a stove, get burned, you don't touch stoves again. Work hard, get paid, you can buy the things you want. These examples of operant conditioning explain how most of us avoid harm and acquire the things we want. They don't explain why some dogs, like some people, are smarter than others, why many of us are in the middle ranks of intelligence, and why some of us have such difficulty simply getting by. Granted, we can fall back on the notion that some individuals are born smarter, or are more talented, than their peers. And there's some truth to this. Lots of people have written plays—there's only one William Shakespeare. Lots of theoretical physicists were working during the early 1900s—only one Albert Einstein emerged. Yet Shakespeare could never have come up with the startlingly elegant equation $E=mc^2$, and Einstein, for all his brilliance, would never have written, "He jests at scars that never felt a wound."

We see precisely the same kind of specialization in dogs. A Border Collie does a magnificent job of herding sheep, a Labrador Retriever of hauling ducks out of icy water. One can probably do

the other's job with training, but not as well as if it has been bred
to perform certain tasks—a dog who has it in its genes, so to
speak. A more accurate way of putting this would be to say that
the dog has inherited a set of physiological attributes. Oily hair,
for instance, would be one of these attributes. Repelling water, it
makes swimming comfortable and thus predisposes the dog to that
behavior.

The really interesting question, though, involves how a dog's
environment affects not its specialized behavior but its overall
intelligence. Will the dog who has more experiential input be
smarter? In an increasingly urbanized world, the question is particularly relevant because dogs who live in New York, Delhi, or
Sydney can't learn about deer, tigers, and kangaroos, all once in-
trinsic parts of their culture, the way children can learn, through
books and television, about theirs. In other words, it may be impossible for dogs to become knowledgeable, and eventually wise,
if they're not outside, being dogs.

There's a wealth of research that supports this contention. One
of the first people to set the stage for this research—in general
terms, determining how mammals learn—was Santiago Ramón y
Cajal, a Spaniard, who in 1906 shared the Nobel Prize in Physi-
ology or Medicine with an Italian, Camillo Golgi. Cajal demonstrated that the brain was composed of individual nerve cells and
also wrote about its workings in a lyrical way. Explaining how dendrites send out random conductors in the course of their formation, he wrote, "What mysterious forces precede the appearance
of the processes, promote their growth and ramification, stimulate
the corresponding migration of the cells and fibers in predeter-
mined directions, as if in obedience to a skillfully arranged archi-
tectural plan, and finally establish those protoplasmic kisses, the
intercellular articulations, which seem to constitute the final ecstasy of an epic love story?"

It was Cajal's "neuron doctrine" that laid the groundwork for
how we now view the nervous system, namely as individual neu-

rons, or nerve cells, communicating with each other at junctions, or switching stations, called synapses. Here is where a nerve impulse triggers the release of a chemical neurotransmitter, which then modifies the adjacent neuron. A single brain nerve cell has thousands of these synaptic connections on its cell body as well as on hairy appendages called dendrites. Think of the most densely branched tree you've ever seen, amplify its branches considerably, and that will give you an idea of how the dendrites of the brain reach out across their synaptic spaces to, in Cajal's terms, kiss each other.

In the 1960s, researchers at the University of California Berkeley began to focus their attention on whether experience could produce observable changes in these complex structures of the brain. Beginning with a group of genetically similar rats (to reduce the chance of genetic differences skewing the results), they divided the twenty-five-day-old, just-weaned rats into three groups. Group 1 was called "the Isolation Condition," the rats caged singly in a dark, quiet room, with ample food and water, but unable to touch or see another animal. Group 2 was named "the Social Condition." These rats lived three to a cage while being fully exposed to the conversation and activity of the lab technicians. Group 3 was labeled "Environmental Complexity and Training." Here, a dozen rats lived together in a big cage and got to play with toys and run through mazes, the arrangements and patterns of which were changed each day. In addition, these rats were frequently handled by people.

Within four to ten weeks, remarkable changes began to take place. The cerebral cortexes of the rats in the complex environment weighed on average 5 percent more than those of the other rats. Their average body weight was also 7 percent less than that of the sedentary rats because of their daily exercise. This phenomenon—a high brain-to-body-weight ratio—is also found in wolves who live in physically demanding, experientially rich environments. Pound-for-pound, they have about 20 percent bigger brains than domestic dogs.

Using another series of experiments, the Berkeley scientists then explored whether intelligence was a function of brain size. They found that the rats who had lived in an enriched environment were more adept at moving through problem-solving mazes than those in the less stimulating environments. It appeared that having a bigger brain might mean being a smarter rat, though the researchers hedged their findings, noting that some human geniuses with triple-digit IQs have had smaller brains than humans with only double-digit IQs.

In the 1970s, William T. Greenough, a psychologist at the University of Illinois, continued this line of investigation and demonstrated that it wasn't brain size alone that made for intelligence. The rats he reared in complex environments had more dendritic synapses per neuron than rats raised in isolated environments. The increased branching created a greater capacity for processing information.

A similar phenomenon is seen in the world of canids. Wolves are better than domestic dogs at solving problems such as opening doors or escaping from pens, and they can plan and execute coordinated attacks on prey much larger than themselves, which packs of dogs are unable to do. In short, those animals who live in more challenging terrain have more synaptic kisses going on in their brains.

Then, in the 1990s, Greenough began collaborating with another researcher, James Black, in a series of experiments that attempted to outline the attributes of stimulating environments. They compared rats who were confined to a cage with no exercise to rats who ran a treadmill each day. These two groups were, in turn, compared to acrobatic rats, individuals who were taught to wend their way through and over an elevated obstacle course. The brains of the couch-potato rats and the treadmill rats weighed the same, but the cerebral cortexes of the acrobatic rats were significantly heavier. Black and Greenough concluded that learning engaging tasks rather than merely exercising was critical.

These findings dovetailed with what the Berkeley researchers had come to understand through additional experiments designed to identify which stimuli had the most powerful effect on brain development. They, too, found that it wasn't exercise alone. Nor was it visual stimulation. Handling, petting, and love didn't produce large brains, either. Nor did pressing a lever for a food reward. The only thing that consistently improved rats' neural development was the freedom to roam a large, object-filled space.

These findings helped me to understand why Merle might not be interested in balls that jingled, in rubber bones that squeaked, or even in rawhide chews. He had grown up in one of the largest open spaces imaginable, one filled with all sorts of interesting creatures: some that would bite him, some that would kill him, some that—if he caught them—were delicious to eat and stopped his hunger pangs. He had been occupied in the most primal and engaging of tasks—staying alive. No wonder that toss-and-fetch wasn't quite his game.

Brain research has also given us a greater understanding as to why animals who live in zoos become depressed, even when they have balanced diets, sex, and authentic though miniaturized habitats. Compared to the real thing, captivity is dead boring.

This may also be why there are so many neurotic dogs in the world: the barkers, the furniture chewers, the biters; those who defecate in their homes when left alone, who run along their fences, threatening passersby, and who will swallow most any object no matter how distantly it resembles food. As Jon Katz notes in his thoughtful book *The New Work of Dogs,* "Dogs are rarely permitted to solve problems." They're not given "a chance to figure out what to do. They look to humans for direction." And we humans are all too willing to give them that direction.

Some dogs, thankfully, can break us of our patronizing habits— as Merle did for me. The first time this happened, I was trying to teach him to heel. I had put on his red collar and a leash—instant sobriety—and we were practicing walking around Kelly. Not only sobered by the collar and the leash, he was also confused by the command to heel. There were so many interesting smells to investigate. Why was I intent on bypassing them? And even if I wanted to maintain that metronomic pace, why should he? He could catch up to me whenever he wished. Why this sudden boot camp, when our life had been so free and easy? I could see his eyes ask these questions, and I could also sense his confusion, so I took off the leash. "You'll see," I said as he jumped up and down joyfully by my side. "Heeling might seem silly now, but when we're walking on a road with cars, it'll come in handy. Now heel." I offered him a biscuit by my thigh.

"Ha!" he exclaimed, "sure." Taking the biscuit, he fell in by my side.

For a while he heeled quite nicely. Then we came to the main road and set off for the post office. This meant going against the oncoming traffic had there been any. Immediately, he insisted on trotting in front of me and in the middle of the blacktop, instead of upon the shoulder to my left.

I did an end run around his right flank, forcing him toward the shoulder with the sharp command "Heel!"

"Ha-ha-ha," he panted, signifying, "You don't really mean that." Grabbing the biscuit I offered him, he immediately slipped behind me, back into the center of the lane. Back and forth we went, as if doing some kind of tango.

I wondered whether he didn't want to walk on the shoulder because the gravel hurt his paws. But this couldn't possibly be the case; he ran on the gravel road from the cabin to the river virtually every day without any sign of it bothering him. Then I decided that he was just being obstinate, a strong-willed dog who was going to make his choices and mine an ongoing contest.

The following day, the same thing happened. We had a reasonable practice session in the village, but as soon as we got to the main road, he broke heel even when I offered him biscuits as reinforcement. On the third day, as we walked toward the post office, I saw some sandhill cranes gliding across the sky, calling out in their high-pitched warbles. Taking my attention from Merle, I watched the cranes for a good fifteen seconds. When I looked down, he was back in the middle of the road. I was about to yell "Heel!" when I noticed how he was walking: He had his head cocked slightly to the right, his right ear tilted back, as he both listened and looked to his rear. At the same time, his left ear and left eye were trained on the road ahead. Just at that moment, his right ear came to attention, and he instantly drifted toward the shoulder of the road. A second later, I heard it—a car approaching from behind us. It went by, and Merle drifted back into the center of the lane, his head cocked so he could monitor traffic in both directions.

I had been so intent on getting him to heel that I hadn't paid attention to what he was doing. He had developed his own way of walking down the road safely. When I tried to make him heel on my left side, his frustrated "ha-ha-ha" wasn't an indication of his being disobedient; it was his way of saying, "You're blocking my view, and I can't hear as well."

I wondered if he had learned his road-walking method by watching cars go by as he made his rounds through the desert, occasionally using the tarmac to speed his travel. Perhaps he'd actually had a close call.

Suddenly, I saw him in the desert—growing up among snakes, coyotes, and cows—his dendrites becoming denser, reaching out for each other, their tips just kissing, the synapses firing, and the doggish equivalent of an "aha!" lighting his brain. Did it give him a sense of accomplishment? Given his reaction to the bison—"I get it!"—I thought probably so.

I knelt and called to him, roughing up his fur as he stood before me. "You are one smart dog," I said. "I am sorry."

He immediately looked serious. He didn't like my tone of voice when I apologized. So I stood up and motioned him down the road with my extended hand. "Lead on, Sir."

"Ha!" he snorted and gave his head a happy shake. Then he set off in front of me, prancing like a Lipizzaner stallion. I had seen the light.

He never heeled again, at least not on roads. And his method worked. He walked on the park road for his entire life without incident. In the backcountry, however, he evolved an entirely different strategy, one relying on his nose and my eyes. Watching him there, I learned that it was perhaps the dogs, not the humans, who had first realized what a team the two could be.

CHAPTER 4

In the Genes

Merle and I were walking on the ice of Yellowstone Lake, only a few yards from shore, when I heard a slow rumble. Under my feet, the ice began to move.

Merle's eyes widened with wonder and a little fear. Together, we whirled toward shore. Too late. The ice broke and we plunged into the freezing water. For a moment, we floated. Then the current took us. I heard a roaring and looked ahead. Iceberg after iceberg fell over the horizon. The lake had turned into a cataract.

Merle and I glanced at each other. His eyes were now calm, and his calmness filled me. Side by side, we began to swim.

Waking, I shook my head. Sunlight streamed through the windows.

Then I remembered the coyotes howling around the cabin, sometime around 3:00 A.M.

Merle had been beside himself with agitation—rushing to the window, going to the door, whining, waking me up by shoving his nose under my arm, his bright eyes saying, "I need to go out there! I want to go out there! I must go out there!"

This was nothing new. For the past few evenings the coyotes had been howling in the field below the cabin, sending Merle into an ever-increasing frenzy. This morning, unable to stand him any longer, I had jumped from bed and cried, "Okay! You want to go out there, go ahead."

I had thrown open the door, and he was gone in a flash, his long golden form streaking through the moonlight and disappearing into the sage. I listened. Silence. I listened some more, the moon hanging over the Tetons, the hum of the Gros Ventre River coming up through the forest. I called his name. I whistled. He didn't come.

I had left the door open and gone back to bed, regretting my decision. Yes, dogs long for freedom, I told myself, but sometimes they needed to be protected from their own instincts or their lives could be very short. Nor did familiarity with the wild always improve a dog's odds. The wolves of Yellowstone, for instance, live only 3.4 years on average. They die at the hooves of elk and moose; they drown fording rivers; they're caught in avalanches; and they're killed by other wolves.

When I awoke from my dream of swimming with Merle toward an icy cataract, he wasn't by my bed. I went to the door, called, and whistled. When he didn't appear, I ran into the sage field. No sign of coyotes or my dog. I threw on a pair of shorts and a T-shirt, got in the car, and drove down the hill, calling out the window and stopping periodically. Driving through Kelly, I looked left and right. Still no Merle. I turned onto the dirt road that led to the trailer, and there he was, pressed so hard against the trailer's front door that it looked as if he were trying to break in.

He heard the car, looked up, and saw me. As I parked, he ran to greet me, standing and hanging his paws inside the open window. "Arowh, rowh, rowh, arowh," he said in a kind of yowling parlando. "You can't believe what happened to me! Those coyotes. There was a whole pack of them—" On and on he went, throwing his head from side to side.

I got out of the car and looked him over, running my hands along his flanks, turning up his ears and paws, peering under his belly. He appeared unscratched. I gave him his favorite massage, kneading the thick fur around his neck and shoulders, and crooning to him that he was a brave dog. But he didn't relax. Instead, he pressed himself to my legs, trembling.

"Come on," I said. "Let's go in. You look like you're thirsty."

Tail between his legs, he glued himself to me as we went inside the trailer. He drank almost the entire bowl of water I put out for him. As I went to the bathroom and washed up, he followed me. As I answered the phone, he lay over my feet. As I switched on my computer and sat down to work, he huddled against the back of my chair. Turning around and looking down at him, I tried to imagine what had happened.

He had probably chased the coyotes down the hill toward the river, they sprinting ahead of him and leading him away from the security of the house. But someplace along the way, chaser and chasee must have reversed roles, the coyotes turning on him in numbers. He had fled to the safety of the trailer.

I lay down on the rug with him, nose to nose. "So tell me"— up went one brow, down went the other—"what happened with those *coyotés?*"

At the sound of their name, he blew out an anxious breath, his eyes becoming deeply worried.

I petted his head, and he sighed, a sigh that seemed to imply that things hadn't turned out quite the way he had expected.

Holding his head and stroking his shoulders, I tried to feel what he was feeling, imagining him as a pup on the Navajo Nation. Given his love of chasing cattle, he'd probably been shot at by a herder, or beaten soundly, and had fled into the desert. Starving, he'd caught rodents and finally taken down a calf. But while eating his first good meal in days, he'd been startled to see a coyote slink into view, size him up in an instant, and charge at him with fangs bared. Young Merle had backed off and watched from a distance as the coyote had eaten his prize.

And in Merle's mind, as in the mind of every creature who lives in the wild, had begun the exquisitely fine calibration of size.

Elk watch the arc that other elks' antlers make against the sky,
noting the angle subtended. Elephants study other elephants as
they demonstrate their strength by pushing over trees. Tigers measure how high another tiger has sprayed on a bush, and surely
Merle had noticed that the coyote was bigger than he.

But as he grew, Merle must have realized that he'd gotten
larger than every coyote he saw. So when they howled outside our
windows, he had decided to settle a score. However, he hadn't
reckoned on their numbers. I wondered if his sad, shaken state
was not merely a result of his having been roughed up. Perhaps
he was also ruminating on his error in judgment.

It became apparent, though, that he hadn't been completely
intimidated by his experience. The next time he saw a coyote, we
happened to be driving to town. The coyote was sitting alongside
the road, head cocked quizzically at the ground where a rodent
had hidden. Merle leapt to his feet, his eyes lit with a terrible rage.
Shaking with fury, he began to growl. I feared he might try to jump
through the windows, though they were rolled up. As we went by
the coyote, Merle whipped around and stared out the back window, continuing to tell the coyote, with sharp whines and growls,
what he'd do if he ever caught him.

"You be careful, Sir," I said. "There's strength in numbers."

He turned to me and snorted powerfully.

He wasn't just boasting. It took awhile, but he picked his moment and had his revenge.

The summer ripened, and so did Merle's education. As we drove
up to the cabin from town one balmy July evening, he jumped out
of the car, sniffed the air, and disappeared into the willows. A few
seconds later I heard a thrashing, followed by his howls. Bursting
from the trees, he rushed to me, screaming in pain. He was wearing a beard of porcupine quills.

He pawed at his cheeks miserably, crying out without stopping, which only made it worse since his tongue was also bristling

with the sharp needles. Getting pliers, I wrapped an arm around his shoulders and began to pull out the quills. He jumped out of my arms, crying in agony and foaming at the mouth. I couldn't put him, or me, through such an ordeal. Rushing into the house, I called Jack Konitz, who said he'd meet me at the vet clinic in forty-five minutes. Hustling Merle into the car, I drove the sixteen miles back to Jackson. There, Jack anesthetized him and took out the quills.

At home, I carried Merle, still unconscious, into the cabin and lay him on his new, green L. L. Bean dog bed. I was finishing dinner when I heard three hard thwacks. Lying on his side, he was looking at me and banging his tail on the floor. I knelt by his head and petted him.

"You look like you're feeling better," I said.

He put a paw on my hand and continued to thump his tail.

"You're not going to do that again, are you?" I asked him.

Jack Konitz had warned me, "I've got dogs that are so dumb they've done this six or seven times." Judging from the bill, chasing porcupines could become an expensive habit.

Not a week later, however, while on a bike ride, we came upon a porcupine. It was standing in the middle of the trail, regarding us with that resolute and somewhat put-upon air that porcupines have—knowing that they're almost invulnerable yet annoyed that they have to interrupt their business, turn their backs, and waddle away. Which is exactly what this one did.

I was about to call out, "Merle, no!" when I saw him glance at the porcupine and then at me.

"That's a porcupine," said his eyes. "You don't want to mess with them." And without waiting for me, he trotted down the trail, passing within five feet of the porcupine and giving it a respectful glance as he went by.

We had gotten through coyotes and porcupines, bison and cattle, and I figured that since these were the most common dangers facing a dog in Kelly, the worst was behind us. I didn't have a clue that Merle's greatest challenge might be his attachment to me.

We had driven into Jackson to run some errands, and I had parked one block from the town square with its famous elk-antler arches. It was a hot day, and I rolled down the windows, telling Merle I'd be back shortly. But I kept remembering things I needed to buy. I was gone for over an hour, and when I finally returned to the car I did a double-take. There was no dog in it. Astonished, I looked up and down the street, making sure I had the right car. Of course, I was in denial.

Frantic, I started canvassing the blocks around the car, calling out his name as tourists stared at me. No Merle. After an hour, I was ready to go to the police. Coming onto the busy thoroughfare of Broadway from a side street, I passed a jewelry store. Merle lunged from the door. He was tethered to a rope and greeted me wildly, twirling in the air, moaning in happiness, and panting, "We've found each other. We've found each other."

I knelt and hugged him. He put his chin on my shoulder and let out two great sighs, shuddering at the end of the second one.

A blond woman in jeans came around the counter and said, "I saw him trot by the store. He looked in, then went on, and I stepped out to look after him since he's such a pretty dog, but he didn't have a collar. He was looking into every single store all the way to the square. Looking for you, I guess. A little while later he came back, and I grabbed him, figuring he might get hit by a car."

I thanked her profusely and asked if I could borrow the rope. Merle had navigated Broadway safely once, but I wasn't going to take another chance. I led him to the car, and he bounded in as if getting into a lifeboat. Looking exhausted, he lay down and pounded his tail in relief. Then, as if suddenly remembering his ordeal, he began to express himself in his half-baying, half-talking way, wagging his head from side to side and crying out, "Yarowh, youroh, roowah." ("I was alone once in my life. I don't want that to happen again. Never. It's too horrible.")

Consoling him with many pets, I replied, "I don't want that to happen either." Thinking that this would be a good learning opportunity, I added, "And so that it doesn't happen, I want you to stay here. Right here. Stay." I pointed my finger at him and then at the floor of the car. "I'll be back. Promise. I will always, always come back. I will never leave you." Suddenly, I remembered my dream of swimming with him in the icy water, and how safe and calm he had made me feel despite our plight. "I will never leave you," I said again. "But you need to stay here." I roughed up his fur, and he watched me as I backed out of the car. "Stay. I'll be back."

Leaving the windows open, I returned the shopkeeper's rope, then positioned myself across Broadway, watching the car for the next hour. When I walked to it, Merle was lying on his side, sleeping peacefully.

The rivers ran clear and low, the long, green brome cured and yellowed, the nights turned sharp, frost whitening the sage in the early morning. When I opened the front door for Merle, the first thing he did was roll onto his back and wiggle his spine across the frozen grass, front paws hanging limply at their wrists, his head thrown back in an ecstatic grin. Leaping to his feet, he shook himself from nose to tail, took a deep breath of the September air, and looked at me with an expression that said, "Cold at last!" Which is hardly a surprising reaction from a creature who has to wear a fur coat through August.

The elk began to bugle, their thin, haunting calls hanging like veils in the forest. The freezing nights gave a hallucinatory brilliance to the gold aspen and amber cottonwoods. And the lowering sun bathed the trees and mountains in a lucent glow that made it impossible to stay indoors.

One afternoon during the first week in September, I took my shotgun from the shed and fastened Merle's red collar around his neck, adding two orange streamers of surveyor tape so that he'd be visible to other hunters. We drove up Ditch Creek to the boundary of Grand Teton National Park and the Bridger Teton National Forest. There, a trail wound up through a small valley of tall, old-growth aspen, their leaves filtering the sun like the stained glass of a cathedral.

Merle loped in front of me, his amber coat flashing among the dry leaves. Occasionally, he stopped to investigate interesting scents, prodding with his paw. A few moments later he rushed by me, brushing my calf with his flanks and making his "ha-ha-ha" pant: "Got you." He seemed to have put the loathsome collar out of his mind. He was no bird dog yet, but I suspected that once he had flushed a grouse or two, he'd get the drill.

I took a great breath of the sharp heady air. What could be better than this: walking through the September woods with my side-by-side shotgun, which had provided so many grouse dinners; wearing my old bird vest, its pocket holding the scent of feathers; and now accompanied by this wonderful dog.

We reached the head of the valley, made a pass through some alder, and came out on the crest of a ridge that faced the grand sweep of the Tetons. Merle grew still, raised his right paw, and pointed. Ahead, I could see two ruffed grouse, necks hunched over, as they began to scurry off. He charged; they flushed; I shot and downed one.

"Good dog!" I shouted, bursting with pride for him.

I looked around. He was nowhere to be seen.

"Merle?" I called.

I walked over and picked up the grouse, admiring its soft, gray-and-black feathers and sending my thanks its way.

"Merle!" I called, putting the bird in the pouch of my vest. "Here, Merle! Come."

Thinking that he might have chased the other bird, I followed the path of its flight. The crest of the ridge was open, covered with knee-high grass. I could see down its far side to the Gros Ventre River, two miles away; but I could see no golden dog.

I began to walk in bigger and bigger circles, as I might have done had I lost some small object in the woods. I knew this was ridiculous—a sixty-five-pound dog isn't a dropped flashlight. Slowly, I allowed the unwelcome thought to enter my mind: The shot had spooked him and he'd run away. Still, I persevered, walking this way and that, shouting his name. Finally, I retraced my steps to the car and drove the five miles to home.

There he was, sitting on the trailer's porch and looking forlorn. Unlike when he had been chased by coyotes, he didn't rush to greet me. Head hung, eyes shifting, he waited uneasily.

I knelt in front of him. He trembled. "You don't like guns, do you?" More trembling.

Oh well, I thought, not a bird dog.

Brightening my tone, I asked him, "How about some dinner?"

I fed him and his mood improved. Noticing that the light on my answering machine was blinking, I listened to the message, and Merle's speedy arrival was explained. A rancher who lived up the Gros Ventre River had found Merle sitting on the asphalt, howling mournfully. She had read his name tag and dropped him off on her way into Jackson.

"So," I said, "that's how you got here so fast." Sitting in front of him, I rubbed the inside of his ear flaps, circling the tips of my index fingers gently on the openings of his ear canals. He pushed his head into my chest and wagged his tail softly. He loved this particular massage.

His behavior on our grouse walk reinforced my belief that he had been shot at when he was younger. As is often the case with young dogs, that one incident could have been enough to make him permanently afraid of gunfire, though not necessarily of other loud noises. This I knew firsthand, since I had seen him napping in the cabin when a thunderclap had burst directly overhead, making me jump out of my skin. Merle had raised his head, and his benign look had said, "Hmm, quite the storm."

On the Fourth of July, however, as soon as the kids in Kelly had begun to set off fireworks, Merle had stood up and nervously looked out the screen door of the trailer. When the sound of another firecracker came from down the lane, he had winced, turned, and gone into the back room of the trailer, where he had curled up with his nose under his tail, trembling. Either children had thrown firecrackers at him in Utah or the sound of a firecracker reminded him of gunfire.

Some animal behaviorists suggest that, in the case of gunfire, some dogs can be cured of their fear through gradual exposure to what they call "an increasing range of potentially traumatic experiences from an early age." Merle might already be too old for such acclimatization, but I was willing to try.

On the day after he had been spooked by the blast of the shotgun, I took him to a secluded meadow. Getting out of the car, I slammed the door hard. He gave me a quizzical look, as if to say, "Why did you do that?" Clearly, most loud noise had no effect on him. Putting on his leash, so he wouldn't run away, I loaded a .22 target pistol. He watched me with apprehension. I was certain that he hadn't been able to place the pistol into the same category of objects as the shotgun simply from looking at it. Rather, he was listening to the metallic sound of its opening and closing, a sound similar to that of the shotgun being loaded.

He cocked his head. I fired the pistol in the air. He tried to flee. I held him. Panting terribly, he looked at me with distress.

"Easy," I said, "easy," stroking him affectionately and offering him a biscuit. He wouldn't take it.

I fired once again. Compared to the shotgun's report, the noise of the pistol was hardly noticeable—at least to me. But Merle began to yelp wildly.

Accustoming him to gunfire seemed utterly stupid. I unloaded the pistol, cased it, hugged him, and took him off the leash. He immediately jumped at my face in relief.

"No more bird dog training," I exclaimed, roughing up his fur. He bucked up and down with exuberance, turning round and round, and dancing his paws in a mad patter.

"You don't have to be a bird dog," I told him, crouching before him. "Honest. You are the best dog just the way you are." I scratched him from his shoulders to his hips, and he pushed his head so hard into my chest that he knocked me on the ground. I laughed as he stood over me, rubbing his forehead into my neck.

The next few weeks proved hard. I'd go to the shed and he'd follow me. After all, that's where I kept my mountain bike and backpacks, the gear he associated with fun. Out would come the shotgun, and his face would fall. He'd turn around, walk back to the porch, sit down, and, as I loaded the car, he'd look off into space as if counting the clouds.

When elk season opened in the last week of September, I figured I might be able to cajole him into coming along—not because I thought he could help me to hunt elk, but because I valued his company. Finding an elk usually took several mornings and afternoons, often a week or more of hunting, and during all this time no shooting was involved. In fact, unlike in grouse hunting, during which a hunter may shoot half a dozen times in the space of a few hours, an elk hunter tries to shoot only once each year, just enough to get one elk and fill the freezer.

Waiting until Merle was off on his rounds, I put the cased rifle in the car, then, later in the afternoon, called him. When he appeared after a few minutes, I snapped on his collar with its orange streamers. I had taken off the jangling tags—they made too much noise for elk hunting—and with indelible black marker had written his name, address, and phone number on the flat red webbing. He took a few steps toward the door, then stopped in his tracks. Twisting his head, he tried to look at the collar. He gave his head a shake, listened—no noise—and gave his tail a hearty wag, indicating: "Hmm, a quiet collar, nice."

Why hadn't I thought of this before? How many of us would want to walk around with a bunch of tags jangling around our necks? His reaction reaffirmed my determination to make him wear his collar only when necessary.

We drove to the same trailhead where we had started our grouse walk, and he jumped out of the car excitedly. But when I took the rifle from its case, he gave me a grievous expression. No sound was involved—the rifle had the same shape as the shotgun. I held it out to him and let him smell it. Without moving his feet, he stretched his neck forward, his nostrils dilating and his eyes filled with a mixture of caution and interest. One brow went up, the other down. After years of hunting elk with the rifle and carrying it after I had field dressed them, it smelled like elk—the same elk he smelled on me, in our house, and whose meat he had now eaten plenty of. Holding his tail low, he gave it a rapid, conflicted wag.

"Okay," I said softly. "We probably won't see any elk, and if we do, we can decide what we'll do then."

I motioned to him with my hand and I started off. He didn't move. "Come on," I said, kneeling, and patted my palms encouragingly against my chest. He came to me and put his head against me. Rubbing his flanks, I began to sing, "I know a dog and his name is Merle, I know a dog and his name is Merle" to the tune of "Blue," the song about the hound dog. I had sung it to him many times, changing the original words—"I had a dog and his name was Blue, betcha five dollars he's a goodun too"—to "I know a dog and his name is Merle, he's the best dog in the world."

At the sound of his name, Merle wagged his tail hard. At the words "He's the best dog in the world," my voice rising enthusiastically, he shivered with delight and sighed, pushing his head harder into my chest.

"Come on," I said, "we'll figure this out together." I stood up and clapped my hands. He yawned mightily—often a sign of anxiety—and off we went up the trail, the rifle hanging from its sling on my shoulder, which gave him some relief. It wasn't in the discharge position. Still, he was cautious. Instead of ranging ahead of me, he followed at my heels, making sure he could keep me in sight at every moment. I walked slowly, watching and listening.

We crested the ridge on which we had found the grouse, continued down into Turpin Creek, and climbed the next mountainside. As the sky grew dusky, we began to stroll up a basin, its upper reaches hidden from sight by a knoll that rose before us.

All of a sudden, Merle rushed around me, his head lifted, his mouth open, his nose chewing at the drift of evening air, a drift so slight I found it nonexistent until I took my lighter from my pocket and struck it. The flame bent toward us as the twilight's cooling thermals began to make their way down the valley.

Merle looked as if he were going to sneeze as he sucked on whatever scent was coming to him. He half closed his eyes, then opened them wide and began to pant excitedly, pumping his front legs up and down. He twirled once, his eyes glowing in the twilight.

"What do you smell?" I asked.

He shook his head in a circle and began to run forward.

"Merle," I called in a stage whisper. "Come."

He gave me an impatient look. I caught up to him, put my finger to my lips, hunched my shoulders and lowered my body, whispering, "Shhh. Quiet."

Imitating me, he sunk a little bit.

"Let's go, very quietly."

Side by side, we began to move forward. A few minutes later, my hand on his shoulders, we peeked over the top of the knoll.

Two hundred yards in front of us, across the next meadow and at the very edge of the pine forest, stood a large bull elk, thrashing his antlers against a tree. We had walked only a couple of hours, this was the opening day of elk season, and there stood a year's supply of meat. Since I ate no domestic meat, and hadn't done so for nearly two decades, getting an elk was no small matter.

I glanced at Merle. He was staring at the elk as if magnetized. I didn't know what to do. Should I watch the elk until he walked into the forest and come back tomorrow morning, alone? Or should I shoot and traumatize Merle again?

I leaned over and put my mouth on his ear. "Stay," I said. Our eyes were but a few inches apart. He looked at me defiantly: "Not on your life."

Returning my mouth to his ear, I repeated, "Stay." And I jabbed my index finger into the ground. "Stay."

"Ha," he panted. "Okay."

But he lied.

As I began to crawl forward, I turned around and saw him creeping after me on his belly. I put out my palm in the "stay" gesture he was supposed to have learned and glowered at him. "Stay," I mouthed.

Stretched out, he wagged his tail imploringly—"Oh, don't make me stay"—but this time he didn't move.

With oozing slowness, I swiveled on my hip and faced the elk. I exhaled slightly, held my breath, and felt the rifle become quiet in my hands. In that moment, I sent an apology toward him. Then I shot. He fell in a heap, and I turned around quickly, hoping to catch sight of Merle before he disappeared.

He was galloping away, but not in the direction I had expected. He was flying up the meadow toward the elk with a passion that made me spring to my feet. Racing after him, I saw him prancing around the elk and burying his nose in its mane. By the time I reached him, he had hold of the elk's neck and was shaking it up and down as if the great deer were a ground squirrel. He began to rip out mouthfuls of hair, trying to get at the meat underneath, all the while moaning and whining in a joyous frenzy.

"What a good dog you are!" I shouted.

He began to twirl in the air, jumping up toward my face and woofing—this from the dog who virtually never barked. Had he been a human, he'd have been saying, "Oh, my god. This is un-believable. An elk. We did it! We did it!"

I sat down and watched him bury his nose in the elk's mane, drinking in its enormous, wild, musky smell. I let him be and reached over to put my hand on the elk's head. Closing my eyes, I felt this place I'd loved so long—its grass, its water—made manifest in him. Thanking him for his gift of food, I sent his spirit on its way.

Seeing my stillness, Merle suddenly became very quiet. He sat by the elk's head and watched me with intense concentration, one brow going up, the other down, as he gauged my emotions.

"Elk," I said. "Elk. They're the best."

His tail broomed the duff.

"Okay," I told him. "Now the work begins."

For the next two hours, by headlamp, I skinned and quartered the elk, Merle going into what could only be described as rapture of the meat. He nibbled at the intestinal fat. He slurped the blood. He picked scraps of backstrap off the vertebrae. I fed him pieces of rib meat and neck meat and flank meat. Finally, his belly round and full, he fell asleep nearby, sprawled in the pine needles as he mut-tered excited little yips, his paws running and his eyes blinking.

The Milky Way arced above us as we hiked toward the road-head—he trotting in front of me now, instead of walking behind, his tail held high and waving gently back and forth. Watching him, I tried to piece together what I had just witnessed.

Here was a dog who had fled the blast of a shotgun, yet, three weeks later, had sat not six feet behind me while I had shot a high-powered rifle. The two acclimatization shots with the .22 had prob-ably done nothing to bring about this end. If anything, they had likely made him even more fearful of firearms. How had he made this turnaround?

The only thing I could think of was that somehow, in his cal-culus, he had come to the conclusion that getting an elk was worth the price of being close to a gun going off. And that he had been fully aware that I had been trying to get the elk standing in the distance seemed obvious. My body language as I stalked it was like his body language when he stalked ground squirrels. That I wasn't attributing false powers of reasoning to him became ever clearer over the next weeks, and in the following hunting seasons. Whenever I took the shotgun from the shed, he would give it a disgruntled look, walk back to the porch, sit down, and stare at me with an expression that said, "I just remembered—I have something else to do." Whenever I took out the rifle, he would be waiting at the car door with his tail beating happily. Sometimes I tried to fool him and would emerge from the shed with a cased firearm. At the roadhead, when I uncased it, and he saw the shotgun, he'd get back into the car. If he saw the rifle, he'd come to my side with his tail wagging.

Over the years, as we walked nearly every valley in the Gros Ventre Mountains on the eastern side of Jackson Hole, I began to see why early peoples so valued their dogs. Many times, when I couldn't detect any breeze, not even with my lighter, Merle would come to a stop and step out from behind me. (It had become apparent that he preferred that I walk first in the backcountry—at least on the outward-bound leg. On the way home, he would lead.) Raising his head to scent the air, he'd open his mouth, curl his upper lip, and half close his eyes. Nostrils dilating, he'd begin to wag his tail, indicating, "Elk."

What he was doing, particularly by opening his mouth and curling his upper lip, was facilitating the access of odors to his vomeronasal organ, which in dogs lies above the upper incisors. This type of behavior, called the Flehmen response, is seen in many ungulates, such as horses, wild sheep, and bison, as well as in members of the cat family. It helps them determine whether another individual is in estrus, or the physiological state of the animal, or how long ago it passed by. Some dogs exhibit the Flehmen response and some don't.

Merle would also take several rapid sniffs as he diagnosed a batch of drifting air. Interspersed between his normal breathing, these sniffs would pass the air he was inhaling over a bony structure called the subethmoidal shelf and then across the lining of the nasal membranes. When Merle exhaled, these odor-packed molecules stayed in place, giving him an extra few moments to appraise their contents.

Humans don't have a subethmoidal shelf. We do have two tiny pits on both sides of our septums, just inside the opening of the nose, but whether the nerves running from this vomeronasal-like organ to the brain are functional or vestigial has yet to be determined. The Human Genome Project has found that the gene believed to be essential for vomeronasal sensory neuron function in other mammals is nonfunctional in us, as well as in our cousins, the apes, and other Old-World primates. The olfactory bulbs, to which the vomeronasal nerves normally run in dogs, have also not been identified in humans. Nonetheless, some scientists believe that the location and structure of our vomeronasal-like organ suggests that it might be responsive to airborne chemicals.

With that in mind, I let Merle teach me how to smell. I began to throw my head back, open my mouth, and curl my upper lip, letting the wafts of air circulate through the intermingled passages of mouth and nose. Occasionally, I, too, would catch the evanescent drift of the big, musky deer.

Merle's hearing was also better than mine. Often, he would turn his head to the side, concentrate on some far-off sound, and look at me with his bright golden eyes that said, "Elk." Cupping my hand behind my ear, I would occasionally hear their faraway bugles sounding faintly from what seemed another universe. Acoustically, it *was* another universe. The average young human can hear sounds up to 20,000 hertz. Dogs can hear sounds up to about 45,000 hertz, and I was no longer a young human while Merle was a young dog.

In addition, Merle's brain could make an instantaneous calculation about the direction of the sound by relying not only on his movable ear flaps but also on the minute time lapse between the sound striking first his ear nearer to the sound, then the one farther away. The calculus itself was done in two time-sensitive bundles of neurons on each side of his brain stem called the superior olive, which can detect differences in stimulation of only one-millionth of a second. By cocking his head, Merle was providing his brain with ever-finer spatial information that was then triangulated into the sound's distance and position.

Humans use these very same anatomical structures to locate the direction of a sound, and, in fact, our hearing is superior to that of dogs in this regard. We have a spatial acuity of less than 1 degree, whereas dogs can localize sounds only in a 4- to 8-degree range. For this kind of auditory discrimination, the hearing of dogs is far better than that of horses and cattle, not as good as that of cats, and not nearly as good as that of elephants and dolphins, both of whom are slightly better than we are at determining precisely where a sound is coming from.

Why such different hearing abilities evolved in various mammals illustrates how our senses act synergistically, in this case the two senses being hearing and vision. Consider what we do when we hear an unexpected sound: We instantly orient our head and eyes to it. In fact, this reflex is faster and more accurate than the one that turns our head and eyes toward a brief flash of light. What is actually happening is that we're focusing the central area of our eyes—the portion of our retina which contains the maximum density of nerve cells and thus the highest visual acuity—directly at the sound. In humans, this area encompasses 1.5 degrees of the retina. In dogs, it's about 6 degrees. In ungulates, like horses and elk, it's 30 degrees.

Our hearing localization must therefore be this precise—1.5 degrees—so as to point our best vision directly at what might be ready to spring upon us. On the other hand, if you're a dog, with a 6-degree area of visual acuity, your hearing localization only has to be that good to enable you to spot a saber-tooth tiger rustling in the brush or a tasty elk sneaking away.

Taking his eyes from mine, Merle would stare into the distance—still listening to a sound I couldn't hear—and wag his tail for emphasis: "Yep, my friend, there are elk in them thar hills."

Interestingly enough, Merle chose not to point out the presence of mule deer to me. When we'd come upon them, the wind blowing from them to us, so that I was certain he had smelled them, I'd look down at him, my eyes asking, "Didn't you know they were there?" And he'd look back at me, his eyes saying, "Of course I knew they were there." I suspected he made no fuss over deer because we rarely ate them.

I saw him act similarly even when he'd encounter fresh deer spoor. He'd give a faint, dismissive snort: "Oh, just mule deer." If it was elk spoor, his interest would increase according to its degree of freshness. Old, dry pellets or tracks, he'd ignore. If the spoor was under a day old, he'd consider it reflectively. Fresh spoor, deposited within the hour, would electrify him. His tail would begin to lash; he'd look around; he'd gaze at me with gleaming eyes: "Yes, yes, elk ahead. Let's go."

As the years went by, and he observed more of the animals among whom we lived, his body language—as he smelled their tracks and droppings—would display how he felt about them. Of coyote spoor, he remained forever disdainful. He'd prod the turd with his front paw—always the right one—then give it a quick shot of pee, a scrape, a grin, a rapid "ha-ha-ha" pant, and move on. Wolf scat, he'd take apart with the same poking motion of his paw that he used with coyote sign, but after a sniff, his face would fill with deep consideration. No grin, no pant, no pee. He'd give me a sidelong glance from under his brows: "Yes, the big dog has stood here."

If he'd come across the ropy pies of grizzly bear, he'd take a deep, shuddering breath, finishing with a tremor at the bottom of the intake. A slow and steady look around the forest would follow—almost always we found grizzly scat in the forest—his eyes calm but very watchful. A small, respectful wag of the tail. "The great shambling one. Let's watch our step." With black bear, he'd give no more than several quick snorts, a little poke with his claws to reveal half-digested fruit, an off-handed grin. "The little bear. Maybe we'll see him. Not to worry. No trouble here."

The round prints of mountain lion would send him into a cascade of frustrated breaths. It was the only animal whose spoor Merle smelled without having seen the animal itself—not that he was unobservant. In nearly forty years of walking through lion country, I've seen only five of the secretive cats, one of them with Merle by my side; but the cougar had been so far away that I had had to use a spotting scope to make it out. When we came upon lion spoor, I loved to watch him breathe in the cat scent, for surely he recognized that brand of odor from the domestic cats of Kelly. Yet there must have been orders of magnitude difference between the two. His concentration over lion scat or prints reminded me of a scholar poring over a fragile manuscript, written in a language barely discernible to him, the ancient roots of the words familiar, the grammar almost parsable, but the meaning—a physical shape for the animal—just beyond his grasp. He'd go down the trail with his brow furrowed, his nose returning again and again to the track.

Pronghorn antelope excited him as much as elk, but in a different way. It was as if the antelope's speed gave Merle an extra burst of eagerness to be stalking, and, because pronghorn live in open country, he'd raise his head above the sage, looking far and wide. "Ah, there!" He'd fix his gaze upon them, cantering in the distance, and send me a quick look that said, "Have you spotted them, Ted?"

Moose was the one ungulate who had chased us with determination, the one animal who seemed truly dangerous and unpredictable to Merle, barreling out of the snow, teeth clacking, hair on its hump erect, ears back, eyes blazing. When he'd encounter their big oblong pellets, he'd take several cautiously respectful inhalations, as if recollecting our close calls.

Bison. A tremor ran along his fur, making it shimmer. A sigh escaped him. So much like cattle. A plaintive look at me. "If you would only let me chase them."

Some of the people to whom I mentioned Merle's distinct reactions to different spoor suggested that I might be projecting my feelings about these animals onto my dog. However, I frequently observed Merle encounter sign when ranging far ahead of me. Stopping, he'd put his nose to ground and I'd see his body language change while I was still too far away to identify the spoor. He'd turn toward me, and the way he held himself, the concern or merriment in his eyes, the angle of his tail, and the noises he would make would clearly indicate "Grizzly—heads up," or "The big dog has been watching us," or "Crazy moose around."

This sort of response from a dog who spent so much of his life in the wild shouldn't surprise us. Our own body language changes when we see a group of schoolchildren, a nun, or a band of mercenaries armed with AK-47s. All of us who are versed in human culture have the ability to make these sorts of discriminations instantly and to communicate our feelings to others. Dogs simply do this with their noses and communicate their findings in nonverbal ways. The olfactory process, however, is similar to the visual one. In fact, in some respects, it's far more precise.

Coming upon the middle of a track, for example, dogs can identify the direction in which the maker of the track has gone even when there are no visual clues. I often saw Merle do this when we'd come upon an elk track, so ill-defined on a rocky trail that it was impossible for me to ascertain which way the toes were pointing. Merle would zip up and down the tracks for a few feet and, inevitably, turn in the direction that the elk was traveling— something I could determine only when we came upon the elk's prints incised in softer ground.

Dogs are able to "read" tracks in this fashion by gauging the minute differences between each subsequent print's olfactory strength. The ability to smell with this level of acuity may seem incomprehensible to us, relying as we do on our eyes. But as the veterinarian Linda Aronson points out, being able "to discriminate between the age of two footsteps left 30 minutes earlier by a person walking at one stride per second, is an acuity of one part in 1,800.... [H]uman visual acuity is this good, it's just a matter of what your senses are programmed to compute."

To people who have been professionally trained to use their noses, these highly evolved canine olfactory skills aren't nearly as foreign as they appear to the rest of us. The French perfumer Jean-Claude Ellena, for instance, can tell from just one sniff of a jasmine essence the flower's country of origin and whether the machine that distilled it was made from stainless steel, aluminum, or steel. To Ellena, who has created scents for some of France's best-known perfume houses, a great perfume has a memorable *sillage*—a word that means "wake," "slipstream," or "vapor trail"—and is "the sense of a person being present in the room after she has left."

Merle, his nose lovingly caressing the invisible and airborne trails of elk, knew all about *sillage*.

And finally there were bighorn sheep. He'd inhale a quick, almost wistful breath over their diminutive pellets and then immediately glance at the cliffs around us, for we always found sheep scat in precipitous terrain. A dreamy look would cross his face, mixed with a bit of slyness. Sheep were the only large wild animal I had seen him chase, and he had perfected his method with amazing duplicity. The road on which we ski-skated ran under a series of cliffs where the sheep wintered, and the sheep would periodically cross the road on their way to the river for a drink. Scenting them on the wind, Merle would speed up, vanish from my sight, and chase them down the steep banks of the river, but only so far.

Rushing back to the road, he'd be waiting innocently for me. His tracks, though, told me what he had done.

"You are a very bad dog," I'd say. Of course, it would do no good to try to punish him after the fact. He'd laugh: "Me? I've just been standing here waiting for you."

On a couple of occasions, however, when the wind was blowing perpendicular to our line of travel, we crested the hill by the cliffs and found thirty bighorns crossing the road. Merle—forgetting the lesson of the choke collar and that I was right behind him on my skis—went from zero to sixty in an instant, heading directly for the flock.

At the top of my lungs, I shouted, "Merle, no!" He piled up in the snow, literally slamming on the brakes with his front paws, his head going down between his legs in a show of utter disappointment. Bringing himself erect, he emitted a huge sigh and looked back at me with chagrin.

"No!" I repeated.

"Ha-ha-ha," he replied, his eyes twinkling. "Don't worry." And he gave his tail a barely apologetic wag, meaning, "I wasn't serious. I was just testing them."

Why he would chase bighorn sheep and not other wildlife, I couldn't fathom. Around the house, when he wasn't aware I was watching him, he'd walk to within forty feet of mule deer and simply glance at them. Not so much as a flicker of interest in chasing them. Perhaps his abiding interest in bighorn sheep had been kindled when he was on his own in the desert. Like cattle, sheep might have helped him to survive. He might have caught a lamb on the cliffs of the San Juan River, and ever afterward bighorns were like a remembered ice-cream cone for an orphan—seeing or smelling one, even years later, evoking a memory of comfort during a dark time.

This, then, was the olfactory world in which Merle lived, and in which I did as well, for I often got down on my knees and tried to smell what he was smelling, to appreciate, even faintly, what he knew. It's a world that has, by and large, vanished from the consciousness of most dogs and most humans, a world in which he and I reveled, for we were living in a one-to-one relationship between those animals we smelled and those we ate and those who might eat us. It made walking outside an intimate, mindful adventure.

Occasionally, I would notice things Merle didn't, particularly animals standing still in the distance—a function of humans having more cone photoreceptors in their eyes than dogs. The cones let us see colors well, especially in bright light. Dogs, contrary to popular belief, can see colors, predominantly blues and yellows, but they can't differentiate between red, orange, and green objects. They probably see these colors as tints of yellow or blue. On the other hand, dogs have more rod photoreceptors than we do, and these allow them to see better in dim light.

On the darkest night, Merle would walk through the forest as if it were lit by spotlights, while I would stumble along behind him. Finally I'd light my headlamp, and he'd turn around, his eyes yellow and lit like two ghoulish orbs. This striking phenomenon, seen in many crepuscular and nocturnal animals, is caused by the tapetum lucidum, a layer of cells located behind the animal's photoreceptors. It reflects light back through the retina, in essence giving the retinal photoreceptors a second opportunity to react to each quantum of light and promoting better low-light vision.

Without uttering a sound, he'd give me and my headlamp an impatient look: "Do you really need that?"

But I had my moments as well. I would often have to hold his head, pointing his eyes at some elk only two hundred yards off.

"Elk," I'd say. He'd wag his tail tentatively. "Where?" Then they'd move, and he'd exclaim in several breathy gasps, "Of course, of course. Now I see them."

At other times, his ability to see motion was uncanny. Dogs not only have more motion-sensitive rod photoreceptors than humans, but also possess a 250-degree field of view, 70 degrees wider than ours. Many a time, I'd see him suddenly fix his gaze to tree line a thousand yards off. Scanning with great attention, I'd finally spy several tiny dots moving into the forest. Raising my binoculars, I'd see elk.

All in all, our individual strengths and weaknesses complemented each other. With contacts, I have 20/10 vision. Extensive behavioral tests reveal that most dogs have about 20/75 vision. My greater visual acuity was a result of my optic nerves having 1.2 million nerve fibers as compared to Merle's 167,000. On the other hand, he had 200 million scent receptors in his nasal folds compared to my five million. One might say, then, that my visual acuity for stationary objects was seven times better than his; but his nose, in all respects, was forty times better than mine.

He was also constantly monitoring what was going on around him, rather than being distracted, as I often was, by assumptions, projections, and hopes. Once, for example, Merle, my friend Bob Ciulla, and I were sitting on a bald ridge. Bob and I were panning our binoculars across the valley to tree line where we believed some elk would emerge.

Merle made the tiniest whine from behind me.

"Shh," I whispered, "be quiet."

A moment later, he whined again in an undertone, but more agitated.

"Shh," I said. "Look over there." And I pointed across the valley.

A few seconds later he nudged my shoulder with his snout and whined again. I turned and saw his eyes dancing with eagerness. Rotating his head, he pointed behind us with a leading motion of his nose.

I followed his gaze and there were three elk, walking in a line into the forest. They had crossed not a hundred yards behind us, and I could have easily shot one. Merle turned to me with a look that said, "I was trying to tell you."

There were many, many times he acted in this way, discreetly nudging me with his snout or alerting me with a tiny whine—the way a person would whisper—while I was intent upon searching in only one direction. I'd follow his gaze and see elk, or suddenly smell or hear them. And what always impressed me about his behavior, especially when he'd lope back through the forest to fetch me, was his absolute sense that we were a team—that it was only through me and the rifle that he'd fulfill one of his greatest desires: to eat an animal as big as an elk.

This suite of skills—his keen senses and his unflagging passion for hunting elk and antelope—led me to conclude that it was the newly domesticated wolves who were the initiators of the dog–human hunting partnership. They were the ones who scented and heard game first. They led the way toward it. They reaped the immediate benefits as the animals were field dressed. Subsequently, it was the humans who realized, just as I did, that these were pretty handy friends to have around.

On some mornings, when Merle and I had found nothing, though we'd been walking since dawn, we'd stop on a high vantage point and have a snack in the warm sun: a bit of elk jerky, dog biscuits, a cup of tea, a muffin. Merle would eat everything I had. Occasionally, if I ran out of food, I'd eat one of his dog biscuits—dry, but edible. He would then hang his paws over the edge of the precipice on which we'd stopped and gaze out across the valleys and mountains, sweeping his eyes over the country with what appeared to be both appreciation and an intent reconnaissance for game. I saw him do this virtually every time we were out, even when we had set up camp in the trees. He would lie on the edge of a grand prospect, paws hanging over the edge, gazing from valley to ridge crest to mountain peak. It seemed important to him to be able to watch over big distances.

After a while, our morning snack done, I'd lie with my head on my pack and pull my cap over my eyes. Before long I'd hear

Merle get up from his perch, come to my side, lie down next to me, and put his head on my chest. I'd put an arm around his shoulders, and we'd sleep that way for a half hour or so. Waking—his warm fur under my hand, his ribs rising and falling—I'd have the sense that time had disappeared. There was no such thing as the twentieth or twenty-first centuries—no cars, no rifles—only him and me in a place that seemed as familiar as our own skins.

This sense of utter familiarity with a place that was more of a home than the one I had grown up in often piqued my curiosity. It was a feeling that friends of mine—who hadn't grown up in the Rockies but had lived here a long time, as I had—sometimes spoke about: this sense of walking old ground. From where, I wondered, did this feeling come?

Then I heard of the Oxford University geneticist Bryan Sykes and his work tracing our ancestry through the use of mitochondrial DNA. Sykes became well known when he examined the Iceman, a 5,300-year-old corpse that had been found in 1991, well preserved, in the melting ice of an Italian glacier. In the course of his mtDNA analysis, Sykes discovered that the Iceman had the same mtDNA as one of the women who worked in his lab, Marie Moseley, whose mtDNA scan happened to be on file in the lab's records.

Overnight, Moseley became an international celebrity—the living relative of one of the most ancient humans ever found. She also developed, as Sykes reported, a warm connection to the Iceman. She began to think of him as a real person, a relative who, with his ancient ice ax, had lost his way and perished in the Alps.

This inspired the dreamer in Sykes. "It began to dawn on me," he wrote, "that if Marie could be genetically linked to someone long dead, thousands of years before any records were kept, then so could everyone else." With that in mind, he set out to map the mtDNA of modern people so as to give the fossil record a richer context. "The past," he wrote, "is within us all."

Within the next decade, Sykes applied mtDNA analysis to several long-standing controversies: the origins of Polynesians (he

confirmed that they came from Asia, not South America as was
once thought); the authenticity of one of the claimants to the Ro-
manov throne (the claimant, he found, was not related); whether
Neanderthals were our direct ancestors (they were not, the mtDNA
evidence showed); and whether Europeans were the descendants
of hunter-gatherers who had first reached Europe fifty thousand
years ago or farmers and pastoralists who had walked into Europe
relatively recently, from the Middle East, only ten thousand years
before the present.

This last question was of keen interest to me, because my ancestors were originally from Greece and had not been known to
have the slightest interest in wildlife except how to keep it from
eating their crops. Some of my ancestors had also been fishermen.
How had I become fascinated with great, alpine mountains, with
elk and grizzly bears, and with a dog whose idea of hearth and
home was to hang his paws over two thousand feet of empty space
and gaze into glacial distances? What unlikely pull had this place
exerted upon me?

At the time Sykes was doing his research, most genetic, archaeological, and linguistic evidence had corroborated the theory
that it was the farmers who had overwhelmed the hunter-gatherers
in Europe and thence passed their genes on to those of us who are
of European ancestry. Sykes, however, remained unswayed by his
scientific colleagues in other disciplines. He believed that his
evidence was correct—that mitochondrial DNA matches between
people today and those of the past, going back far beyond ten thousand years, was "the genetic echo of the hunter-gatherers."

An answer finally came from "Cheddar Man," a skeleton excavated in 1903 from the Cheddar Gorge near Bath, England. The
remains had been dated to nine thousand years before the present, at least three thousand years before farming had reached the
British Isles. Sykes extracted some DNA from one of Cheddar
Man's teeth and the sequence of his nucleotide bases—the four
key components of DNA, known as adenine, cytosine, guanine,

and thymine—were unequivocal. Their exact arrangement lay at the heart of the largest of the seven mtDNA clusters that Sykes had found in modern Europeans. "The Upper Paleolithic gene pool," Sykes wrote with undisguised glee, "had not been fatally diluted by the Middle Eastern farmers. There was more of the hunter in us than anyone had thought."

I wondered, though, where I had come from. Given my Greek ancestry, and the long history of agricultural and seafaring life in my family, wasn't it probable that I was related to Sykes's seventh and last cluster—those nouveaux arrivés farmers who had first settled between the Tigris and Euphrates rivers in the Fertile Crescent before moving to Europe relatively recently? But why, then, did I feel that "echo" coming from cold, northern mountains, that sense in my fingers, as I stroked Merle's fur, that he and I had lived this hunting life before?

I had nothing to lose but my illusions. I sent a DNA sample to Sykes's lab in Oxford, a saliva swab from the inside of my cheeks. Six weeks later, I found a thick envelope in my post office box. Not since I was a child at Christmas had I opened a package with more excitement.

And there it was: My great-great-great-great-going-back-20,000-years grandmother was a woman Sykes named Helena. She had lived at a time when the last ice age was at its peak. Her family fished and gathered shellfish during the winter along the south coast of France and migrated each spring up to the Massif Central to hunt big game.

Her DNA is my DNA, just as it is the DNA of about 45 percent of Europeans presently alive, for she had many descendents. She spent a considerable portion of her life at the foot of glaciers, relying on red deer for her sustenance. And what Europeans call red deer, North Americans call elk. It is the same circumpolar species, *Cervus elaphus,* and the relationship between the two—elk and humans—has gone on for more than fifty thousand years, according to M. R. Jarman, a scholar of Paleolithic and Neolithic

European deer economies. "Broadly speaking," he writes, "the same individual human populations and their descendants exploited continually the same individual red deer populations and their descendants. . . . This in itself implies that a mutually favorable relationship was achieved between the two species; it is not likely that so successful and so well-balanced a relationship could survive for such long periods if it were simply a case of a parasitic predator exploiting a prey population to the latter's detriment."

My fingers deep in Merle's reddish-gold fur, I thought of his 30,000-year-old wolfish ancestor, walking from someplace in Eurasia, as my long-gone great-grandparents walked by his side. I saw them resting on an escarpment, looking to the west, and seeing below them the great herds of red deer who fed them along the way.

I stretched and sat up. Merle also got up and did a doggy bow, bending his neck upward in muscular delight. It was an invitation I accepted. I went into the yoga pose called the downward-facing dog, modifying it so I rested on my forearms. Raising my face so I was nose to nose with him, I wagged my butt. He batted me playfully on the shoulder with his paw.

Then he came erect and lifted his snout sharply, opening his mouth, curling his lip, and sucking in the air. His tail began to beat strongly; he looked me in the eye: "I smell elk."

Picking up my pack, I said, "Lead on."

And tail high, he began to lope into the breeze. I followed at his heels, forgetting and remembering who we were as we slid back and forth through time.

CHAPTER 5

Building the Door

We became inseparable. Which isn't to say he dogged my heels. I'd go to work; he'd do his rounds through Kelly. When he'd return to the trailer, he'd stand by the screen door and make a lisping sound, clucking his tongue on the roof of his mouth, indicating, "Hello, could you please let me in?" Sometimes he would substitute a glottal stop, a sound akin to the pause between the two syllables in the interjection "uh-oh" or in the paused inflection native speakers give to the word "Hawai`i."

It astonished me that he didn't bark or whine or scratch as most domestic dogs would. When and where had he learned the merits of silence? Perhaps it had been during his days wandering the desert, stalking ground squirrels and cattle, and avoiding coyotes, rattlesnakes, and Navajo herders with guns. In this respect—moving quietly through the world—Merle wasn't that unusual.

Charles Darwin paid particular note to the atavism of domestic dogs who became feral and quickly stopped barking, opting, instead, for the silence of their wild cousins. Wolves, for example, though great howlers, will often give no more than a "woof" when they're startled or protecting their den or territory. Occasionally, they'll intersperse these woofs with a howl and sometimes even a growl, but compared to domestic dogs, wolves are practically mute.

Coyotes, too, lead relatively quiet lives. Despite their taxonomic name, *Canis latrans,* which means "the barking dog," they never resort to that mind-numbing "rau, rau, rau, rau, rau, rau, rau" that characterizes domestic dogs the world over. In fact, a coyote's bark is often a prelude to a howl song, in the pattern of "yip-yip-howl, yip-yip-howl." When coyotes do bark without howling, they vary their tones and keep it short. And jackals—the small, omnipresent wild dog of Africa and Asia—are even less vocal than coyotes.

Yet wild dogs are impressionable, as the ethologist Desmond Morris points out. Kept near domestic dogs, they can lose their silent ways and pick up the habit of barking. Why, then, didn't Merle learn to bark when he moved to Kelly from the San Juan River?

The answer to the mystery had to do with both his breed and his surroundings. The latter was easier to unravel—he simply had no tutors. Bucking a planet-wide trend, the dogs of Kelly rarely barked. This curious phenomenon was, I believe, the result of the village's lack of fences, a custom fostered by a couple in their seventies, Donald and Gladys Kent.

Descended from homesteaders, they had kept the central feature of the village—its twenty-acre field—unfenced. Many of Kelly's habitations, including the silver trailer that they rented me, surrounded this grass-and-sage prairie, which, over the years, had evolved into a commons—one that people, dogs, and wildlife used to get from one side of the village to the other. In addition, there were quite a few national park holdings scattered throughout Kelly, and these, too, were unfenced or, at best, partially enclosed by buckrail fences that dogs would go under and people over. Taking a cue from these traditions, the rest of us didn't erect fences on our land, and this casualness over where one's property ended and the commons began was transmitted to the dogs, always keen observers of their own humans' reactions to strangers and boundaries.

More often than not, as Merle and I walked down the road, we'd see a dog snoozing on the front step of its house. The dog would lift its head, but instead of running toward us and barking to defend its territory, it would amble across its lawn and sniff noses and butts with Merle, each taking in the scents of the other's anal gland secretions, indicating a dog's status, mood, and sexual condition. Then both would amicably wag their tails.

A lack of fences wasn't the only reason that the village's dogs were quiet. Kelly's homes lacked doorbells. You announced your presence by a soft knock, and, if there was no reply, by opening the door (all kept unlocked) and calling, "Anyone home?" The response from the resident dog wasn't a cacophony of high-pitched barks, warning its humans, "Possible burglar, all systems alert!" Rather, the resident dog wagged its tail and grinned, often giving a delighted whine of welcome.

Seeing as how rarely the dogs of Kelly barked, it seemed fitting that Merle wouldn't make a fuss when he wanted to come into the trailer or the house. The lisping cluck and the glottal stop worked perfectly well while the weather was warm, since my desk was only a dozen feet from the front screen door. But when it got cold, and the inner door was closed, he'd stand outside for an hour or more—unlike his dog friends, without a single scratch against the jamb or the tiniest yip of frustration—until I'd remember that I hadn't seen him in a while and go to the door.

I'd find him wearing a look of relief mixed with reproach. "At last! And what were you doing all this time?" He'd bound in, and I'd rough the fur on his flanks and bury my nose in his ruff. The scent of his golden hairs was mild and nutlike, something between a chestnut and an acorn, with almost none of the oily tinge that is the hallmark of Labrador and Golden Retrievers.

"What are you, anyway?" I'd ask him.

Up went one brow, down went the other, crinkling his forehead and giving him the appearance of a yellow Lab trying to imitate a Bloodhound's furrowed and attentive regard. If, indeed, Merle had some Bloodhound genes in him, his unwillingness to bark wouldn't have been that surprising. It's in the nature of Bloodhounds not to express themselves by barking, though they can be great bayers when hot on a trail.

Even if Merle had some hound in him, I would have thought that as October gave way to November, and the temperatures fell below zero, he might have been moved to utter more than a patient cluck while standing stoically by the door, waiting for me to let him in. But no, not once.

We might have gone on like this for years, as so many dog and human couples do, their days punctuated by the repeated beseechings of the dog to be let in or out, and the compliance, sometimes willing, sometimes grudging, of the human. However, an event intervened. On one bitterly cold day, the thermometer hanging at 20 below zero, I had to spend the entire day in town—first at the library, then having a crown put on a tooth, and finally going to a meeting. Thinking that Merle would be more comfortable in the trailer than in the car, I had left him in the office and didn't return until eight hours later—something dog owners do all the time. When I came home, I found two big turds near the front door and Merle lying by my desk, as far from his deposit as possible, his head between his paws and a look of abject mortification on his face.

"I am sorry," I said and went to him immediately. "Totally my fault."

He rolled on his side, put a paw on my arm, and closed his eyes in shame.

"Hey, hey, hey," I told him, rubbing my face in his neck. "Not to worry. And you left it right by the door. What more could you do?"

He clicked his teeth—"tatta-tatta-tatta"—implying, "Oh, thank you. I thought you'd be so angry."

"Look," I said. "Tomorrow we build you a doghouse."

The Ritz, as I nicknamed it, took a week to finish. It was set off the ground on a cinder-block foundation and had four inches of insulation in its floor, walls, and roof. Painted a deep burgundy, it was carpeted with plush, open-cell foam over which I laid a wool afghan. The final touch was a radiant heat lamp. When it was 20 below zero outside, it was 50 above inside the doghouse.

"*Voilà, Monsieur,*" I said with a flourish, upon its completion, "*ta maison est enfin prête. Et elle est magnifique, n'est-ce pas?*"

I had been working on Merle's French and Spanish, thinking that as long as I often expressed myself in several languages he might enjoy being multilingual as well.

Leaning forward cautiously, he sniffed the entrance of the doghouse with the same suspicion he'd displayed when smelling my rifle for the first time. His nostrils dilated, and he took several steps backward, giving me a look that made my heart sink: "No, thanks."

"Come on," I cajoled, "give it a try."

It was late afternoon; I was going into town; it was a few degrees above zero and light snow was falling.

"Look," I explained, "wouldn't you prefer to be in this wonderful, warm, dog *lodge* rather than sitting in the very cold car, the freezing car, while I have dinner and go to the movies?"

He gave me a deadpan look in return. Putting my hands on his shoulders, I began to guide him into the Ritz. He didn't so much as get his head through its door before he leapt away.

"Ha-ha-ha!" he cried. "Very nice, but that's enough."

Since the doghouse had cost about $400 worth of material and time, I wasn't about to give up.

"Watch me," I said, and crawled in. Turning around, I put my head on my folded palms. "Oh, my god! Is this ever comfortable and warm! You'll love it." I made room at the door and beckoned to him. "Come on in."

He trotted away. I poked my head out and saw him sitting by the front door, his expression clear. "Doghouses are for dogs. I want to be in our house."

"Be that way," I called to him.

I fetched my things and, to make my point, left him at the front door as I drove away. If a dog's jaw could drop, Merle's did.

Five hours later, the snow now falling heavily, I drove up the

lane and there he was, running from the front door to cavort in front
of my headlights. There wasn't a single golden hair on the afghan.

For the next week, I continued my tough-love approach, going
to town only to find him running to the car upon my return, his
back covered with snow, his doghouse spurned, a melted-out nest
at the front door where he had slept. Sometimes he wasn't home
when I arrived, and in a few hours—if it was daylight—I'd see
him come up the lane, tail held high, golden paws supple in their
tireless trot. I'd hold the door open for him, and he'd greet me lavishly, making a soft whining sound in his throat: "Good to see you.
You were gone a long time." Putting my nose to his head, I'd smell
perfume, occasionally cigarette smoke, other times fried food.
He'd been visiting neighbors.

"You've been two-timing me, haven't you?"

He'd laugh. "What's a dog to do if he gets left at home?"

I gave up on the hard line. If he was willing to sleep wolflike
in the snow at the front door at 20 below zero, could it be any worse
for him to sleep in a cold car for a few hours? Coming out of a
movie, I'd find my car windows thick with interior frost. Opening
the door, I'd see Merle curled nose under tail. He'd blink his eyes
under the globe light, stand up, do a languorous doggy bow, and
hold it as he simultaneously gave a sleepy wag of his tail. "Oh,
what a lovely nap! Are you back already?"

But even though Merle now accompanied me, there were days
on which I had to work in the library or go to some wildlife conference. He was car-bound for eight to ten hours, his confinement
relieved only by two or three short walks. By the end of the day,
he looked utterly bored. I'd take him for an hour of ski-skating,
but it seemed like a sop. I had been mentally engaged for the entire day. At best, he had gotten to watch traffic go by.

I would never think of treating friends this way, making them
prisoners of my schedule. Why should I treat Merle—who had become the best of friends—like an indentured servant, at my beck
and call in return for food and lodging simply because he didn't

have an opposable thumb with which to manipulate the knob on the front door?

Feeling guilty, I drove to Valley Feed and Pet to buy him one of the liver-flavored dog biscuits he liked. As I paid for it, my eye caught a line of what appeared to be small, plastic-covered windows on the wall adjacent to the checkout counter. They were dog doors, and they came in a variety of sizes. Intrigued, I examined them. They had white, aluminum frames and sturdy, flexible flaps made of clear plastic that swung in or out, allowing ingress and egress. Suddenly, I had a flash of inspiration. Here was the solution to Merle's and my dilemma.

To those who have installed such a door, my little eureka may seem feigned. It wasn't. At the time, I didn't know of a single other house in Kelly that had a dog door, nor, when I was growing up, did my dogs or any of my friends' dogs have their own door. I had no precedent for giving my dog command of his own life. Like millions of other dog owners, I was rooted in the assumption that it is the human who is in control and decides when the dog will come and go.

The consequences of changing this relationship would be profound, I knew, but in some ways I had already committed myself to the experiment. I had learned to trust Merle. He wasn't a nuisance to people or a threat to livestock and wildlife. He had also become savvy enough to avoid cars and dangerous animals. Nonetheless, when it came to his most fundamental needs—to relieve himself, and when to be inside or out—it was I who decided.

Considering our relationship from this light, I had to admit that my power over him soothed me on a subconscious level. Having him at my disposal transported me back to that normal but narcissistic state of childhood when we want our wishes to be everyone's wishes, our schedule to be everyone's schedule, our universe to be the only universe. Up until fairly recently, only monarchs had this enormous power over others—not merely decreeing what their subjects would do, but also when they would live or die. Some tyrants still have this power, and so does every one of us, at least over our dogs.

But if Merle could come and go as he wished, he'd no longer be my subject or my pet. If he could make his own decisions, he might decide that he didn't need me. Then again, he might love me for reasons other than my providing food and the right to take a pee. The door would change everything. In the Great Chain of Being—with God and angels on the top and rocks and dirt on the bottom—I, the person, would go down; he, the dog, would come up. I found the justice of Merle's cause hard to deny.

I bought the next-to-largest-size dog door, and the following day Merle watched a carpenter install it adjacent to the trailer's front door. When the man had left, I held open the flap and said, "Go ahead. Try it out."

We were standing outside in the snow. Merle ducked his head, peered into the trailer through the opening, and backed up cautiously. "I think a dog could get stuck in that thing," his look said, "and hurt himself seriously."

"Not a chance," I replied. "You're descended from wolves. They dig tunnels no wider than this for many feet to get to their dens. Go ahead." I gave him a little push, and he danced back. "Ha-ha-ha," he panted. "No way."

"Okay, watch," I said. Going down on my hands and knees, I turned sideways, squeezed my shoulders through the narrow opening, and crawled into the trailer. Holding open the flap, I looked back at him. He stared at me, wide-eyed.

"See, I'm in the house, and you're still out in the cold. Come on in."

He danced his feet anxiously, teetering on the edge of making a bold move.

But he wouldn't come. I stood and opened the front door. He bounded in.

"Watch me again." I crawled outside through the dog door and held open the flap for him. "Now you do it," I said.

He put his nose through the dog door, but he wasn't low enough and his head scraped the upper side of it. He jerked back reflexively, giving his head a sound knock. He yelped, more in surprise than in pain.

"Not to worry," I told him. "Just bend down a little farther."

Now he was spooked and hung back.

Standing, I opened the trailer's door and let him out. "Watch again," I told him.

I knelt and pushed open the flap with my head. Crawling into the trailer, I turned and held open the flap. "It's easy," I said. "Now you try."

Gingerly, he put his head into the opening, and I let down the flap. He paused, gauging the intent of the strange thing on his neck. Then in a rush of scrabbling paws he was through, extending his rear legs like some long-limbed wading bird taking flight. He burst into the living room and did a complete circle through the air without touching ground. Dancing his paws up and down in a gleeful patter, he woofed: "I did it! I did it!"

"Well done!" I shouted. "Once more."

I crawled back out the dog door, but this time lifted the flap only two inches—just enough for him to see my eyes under its lower edge.

"Come on," I enticed him. "Open it yourself."

He came forward, and, as he did so, I lowered the flap to its fully closed position. Nothing happened for a few seconds, but I could see the blurry shape of his head on the other side of the flap and hear his breathing as he smelled me. Then I saw his black nose emerge from beneath the flap's lower edge, followed by his snout and his golden-brown eyes, hanging between doubt and glee.

"Yes," I said, "You've got it. Come on through."

Out he leapt and gave an exuberant twirl in the snow.

Clapping my hands, I shouted, "Very good. Well done. In you go." I motioned to the door.

Like a cannon shot, he was through and into the house.

"Back out," I called and clapped.

And there he was, leaping from the door like a trained circus animal going through a hoop. But this was no parlor trick. He was grinning hugely at me, and with good reason.

Extending a hand toward his new entry, I said, "We did it. You have a door of your own."

As the winter took hold, we skied often. When I'd written all day and light was short, we'd leave directly from the cabin for a tour through the woods on cross-country skis. If we had a couple of hours to spare, we'd drive to the roadhead on the Gros Ventre River and ski-skate on the snowmobile road where we'd often see bighorn sheep. When we had a whole day, we'd drive up to Teton Pass, between the towns of Jackson and Victor, Idaho, with alpine touring skis in the car, bound for powder skiing on the high peaks.

As we began one of these excursions, I'd zip up my jacket and say, *"Vámonos, Señor,"* and gesture to his dog door.

Merle would give a faint wag of his tail and then wait until I opened the trailer's front door.

"Ya sabes que tienes puerta propia," I'd tell him as I opened the door of the trailer. You know, you now have a door of your own.

Another limp wag of his tail: *"Es para cuándo estás ocupado."* That's for when you're busy.

Of course, he wagged his tail in neither Spanish nor English, but in Doggish. I got his point.

Sighing, I'd motion for him to proceed.

He'd look up at me. "After you, please."

"Don't stand on ceremony, Sir," I'd proclaim. "After *you, please.*" And I'd motion him through the door once again.

"Oh, all right," he'd pant, "if you insist," and he'd walk out ahead of me.

At first I thought that he was acting in accordance with the way that wolves and domestic dogs have structured their worlds since time immemorial: deferring to the individual they consider dominant. In Merle's case, it appeared that he had compartmentalized his world into two domains: one in which he was dominant—the world of his friends Zula and Jack—and the domain of Ted and Merle, in which I was supposed to lead.

However, it soon became apparent that his decision-making was subtler than this. On a groomed track, when I was ski-skating, he'd lope at my side, as if we were equals. On the downhills, where my speed would increase dramatically as I tucked and schussed, he'd fall behind. Then, on the uphills, where I'd have to herring-bone, he'd be out in front again, laughing happily at my slowness.

In the backcountry, if the snow was below the height of his elbows, and light, he often chose to be in front, breaking trail. If the snow was deep, he let me break. Then, when it was time to ski downhill, he'd bound ahead. He quickly grasped, though, that he couldn't ski in front of me on anything but the most moderately inclined downhills—that no matter how fast he swam downhill through deep powder, I was faster on skis than he was on his paws and therefore I might inadvertently hit him. I only had to clip his butt once with the edge of my ski, and from then on he tucked himself in behind me.

Still, he wouldn't always follow in the deep furrow I left in powder snow. Rather, when the snow was light, he'd "ski" his own line, heading straight downhill and striking a vertical track through my S-shaped one, leaving what appeared to be a long string of dollar signs. At the bottom of the run, I'd turn and watch him, up to his neck and paddling languorously, a huge grin on his face as a billow of snow rolled in front of him. Riding this wave, he'd emerge slightly uphill of me, like a seal popping from the surf and onto the shore.

However, when the snow was heavy and I'd get far ahead of him, he'd bay at me in frustrated anguish, "I can't keep up! Slow down!" If I went out of sight, his cries would rise in pitch and finally reach a panicked crescendo, "You're gone! You're gone! I can't see you!"

At least I thought this was what he was hollering until a day when he demonstrated that he could be quite independent of me when he wanted to—that he was hardly a beta dog following his alpha human around.

I was with a couple of friends from Kelly and as we left the parking lot on the west side of Teton Pass we ran into Davie Agnew, a mutual friend from Idaho. A crusty, barrel-chested Scot and a renowned backcountry skier, Davie suggested that we join him and his companions for a tour to one of his secret spots. This was an invitation from a pioneer of skiing on the pass, and we agreed immediately, following him up to a ridge above Mail Cabin Creek and then down a series of undulating hogbacks that fell toward the Idaho state line. Each time we passed a bowl of untracked snow, I thought that Davie would surely stop and ski it. But he continued down the spine of the ridge, bypassing several magnificent high basins. Each time I paused at a bowl, Merle gazed at me with a quizzical expression: "Aren't we going to ski this? It looks great."

At the fourth basin, after Davie and the rest of the group had continued down the ridge, I gave Merle a shrug and said, "I guess not. Let's go."

I turned and skied off, expecting him to follow. But I heard no running paws. I stopped and looked back. He was staring into the bowl, his head cocked, an expression of longing on his face. Noticing that I had stopped, he looked at me and wagged his tail encouragingly. When I didn't move, he returned his gaze to the bowl. A moment later, without giving me another glance, he leapt off the ridgetop and began to ski the bowl himself—front legs extended, rear legs trailing behind him, turning left, then right, as he carved turns to the bottom of the valley. I watched, astounded.

Finally, several hundred feet down, the gradient leveled off and Merle came to a stop. Shaking himself, he turned and looked up at me with a panting grin and a whipping tail. "It's outrageous! You don't know what you're missing."

I slipped off the edge and figure-eighted my dog's turns.

"You know good snow, Señor!" I cried, coming up to him.

His tail beat so hard it slapped his ribs.

"And I won't believe you again, if you cry when I go out of sight." I shook my finger at him playfully. "You just want first tracks."

"Ha-ha-ha," he laughed.

"Sir, let me break trail up to the rim for you."

He fell in behind me. A half hour later, we caught the rest of the group, still making its way down through the forest. Davie never led us to his fabled cache of powder, so it was only Merle and I, thanks to him, who enjoyed decent turns that day.

Much as I loved skiing with Merle, I sometimes had to go without him. Dogs aren't allowed in the backcountry of Grand Teton National Park and sometimes I wanted to ski there—the peaks are higher than those on Teton Pass, the runs longer, there are fewer people, and it was closer to home. But just as Merle had figured out the difference between a shotgun and a rifle, so, too, had he learned to classify skis. Cross-country skis meant only a walk; skating skis meant a run on a groomed track; and alpine touring skis—wonders of wonders—meant powder skiing downhill.

Whenever I put these hefty skis in the car, his entire demeanor would change. Had he been a human, I'd have said that he'd drunk too many double espressos. His heart rate went up; he began to pant; his eyes became bright; his motions became rapid—head moving, paws going up and down. Let out of the car, he'd zoom along the snowbanks of the plowed-out parking lot, smelling urine spots, squirting them—pow, pow, pow—galloping back to me, and stamping his feet. "Not ready yet?"

"Not quite."

He'd throw himself onto the snow and rub his back before hurling himself upright. Shaking sinuously from nose to his tail, he'd pant, "Let's go! Let's go!"

"Are you finally ready?" I'd ask innocently.

He'd buck like a horse pricked by a burr. "Ready! I've been ready for hours!"

"Let's go, then!"

And up the trail he'd dash.

So whenever I put my alpine touring skis in the car, and then left him home, it was agony. His look would have caved the heart of a stone Buddha: shock, incredulity, disappointment. "I thought," his eyes would say as he stood on the porch, "that we were a team."

I would kneel by his side, put my arm around his shoulders, and say, "I'm sorry. I'm going to ski in the park. I love you, and I'll be back in a few hours. Then we can go for another ski."

My tone of voice only confused him: the familiar sounds of "I love you," full of sincerity, followed by my leaving him home.

"What is going on?" his somber look said as I drove away.

True to my word, I'd return in a few hours and we'd cross-country ski down the river. He enjoyed this, but it never matched powder skiing on Teton Pass, where his entire body language exclaimed, "This is life itself!"

Soon, though, I learned that he wasn't quite as shattered as he let on. Often, he wasn't at the trailer when I returned. His tracks in the snow revealed that he'd been in and out of his dog door several times—sometimes accompanied by the pawprints of Zula. What had they been up to? Discussing the dog politics of Kelly? Tearing up the trailer? The latter was never the case. At most, some water would be splattered around his bowl where he and Zula had drunk.

An hour or so later, I'd see him trotting up the lane, tail held high. A moment later, the flap on the dog door would slap and in he'd come with a bound. There was no frenzied leaping or barking at my return, no desperation to be let out because his bladder was bursting, only a cheerful "Hey, good to see you." I'd rub his inner ears gently with my thumbs, and he'd groan in pleasure, his jowls nestled in my palms.

Occasionally, though, I wouldn't even have time to fetch my other skis from the shed and take him for the little ski jaunt I had promised. *Slap!* would go his dog door, and he'd be gone, down the lane and into the heart of the village. It became apparent that he simply had come back to say "Hi" before returning to what he was doing—visiting, exploring, playing, conducting his own life. It gave me a great sense of relief that I could leave him now and then.

Nonetheless, seeing how much he enjoyed powder skiing, I'd go out of my way to plan routes in the national forest rather than in the national park so that he could come along. Often, a day in the backcountry entailed hours of climbing uphill—three, four, five thousand vertical feet—and miles of skiing downhill. Naturally, I expected him to be tuckered out. I was, and I was on skis while he was on his paws. The first time I realized that he was made of tougher stuff, we had gotten home to Kelly on a Sunday night and I had stopped at the office so I could check my appointment book. I fed Merle—he had bowls and kibble at both the trailer and the cabin—and then, from my desk, I heard the slap of his dog door.

A half hour later, I looked outside. Snow was falling heavily. I gave a shout, my voice muted by the wind. No Merle. I wanted to go up to the cabin, shower, eat, and get to bed. A bit annoyed at his disappearance, I opened a book and read for another half hour, finally giving up. Fetching a sleeping bag from the shed, I ate an energy bar from my ski pack, lay on the living room floor, and, tired from the long day of skiing, was asleep within a few minutes.

Perhaps an hour later, I was awakened by the slap of the dog door and saw Merle, standing just inside it, sniffing the air in his three-stage intake of breath, testing whether I was still here. Though his outline was very dim, I could sense his body language: a little tense, a little distressed. Had I left him and gone up to the cabin? At the fourth sniff of breath, he relaxed: Yes, Ted was right there. He walked over to my sleeping bag and ran his nose over my hair just to make sure. He then gave a tiny whine, more a hum, as if saying "Thank you for still being here," and nudged my face with his wet nose. I put an arm around his neck and said, "It's too stormy to go up."

He lay down and put his head next to mine on the throw pillow. I lifted the sleeping bag and put it over him.

"Where you been?"

"Phoooo," he exhaled, his lips lifting.

Resting a hand lightly on his neck, I thought about how little I really knew of his interests and energy level. He had skied all day, eaten dinner, and then spent another two hours walking around Kelly in a snowstorm. What would be the human equivalent of this last activity? Reading a book? Surfing the Web? Making phone calls? He'd been doing much the same thing—perhaps going to see Zula and Jack, noting where the deer were bedded, and what the breeze was carrying down from the mountains. He had been relaxing with the books of his world, interacting with his social circle.

Anthropomorphism is often maligned for ascribing human characteristics to animals who can't possibly know what we know. And there is some truth to this. I doubt Merle thought of the Big Bang when he gazed at the starry heaven. But the reverse—not ascribing volition to creatures who repeatedly display it—is also inaccurate. It leads to what poor translation always does: misunderstanding between cultures. Wrapped up in my needs, I had forgotten his. At the same time, he couldn't do whatever he pleased without letting me know that he'd be gone for a couple of hours.

The solution—since he was unable to discuss his plans with me, and, in fact, "plans" wasn't the right word for his quite literally following his nose—was to have the house and office located in one place. In this way our schedules could be somewhat independent of each other's. I had wanted to build a house for some time, and, as I scratched his ears, I began to think of the blueprints I had drafted and how I might revise them. Merle rubbed his forehead against my chin and gave a great contented sigh, followed by a sleepy yawn. And thus, like many mates, each in our own thoughts, only touching, and in silence, we ended the day.

CHAPTER 6

Growing Into Himself

M erle was almost two years old now—in human terms a teenager, and with many of the same characteristics. He could be full of himself one moment, frightened the next; his enthusiasm was high, his base of experience constantly expanding. He often surprised both of us by the ways in which he learned.

Take the day I first placed a pair of doggy panniers over his shoulders, thinking that he was now old enough to carry his own food. We were heading into the Wind River Mountains for the weekend, and the panniers contained four Ziploc bags, two of kibble and two of dog biscuits, divided equally so as to balance the load. He had watched me put gear and food into my own pack dozens of times before, so he certainly had a visual image of the process. And I had been careful to let him smell his food and the panniers before putting them on him. Yet, as I began to walk up the trail, he sat rooted to the spot, the look on his face clearly saying, "I am unable to follow you."

"Come on," I said. "Let's go."

"I told you," he whined plaintively, "I can't move."

I was perplexed. Dozens of experiments have been done with dogs who have watched other dogs do a variety of tasks—everything from finding narcotics to pulling sleds—and the results are conclusive: Dogs learn by observing other dogs, cutting the time it takes them to learn the same task not merely in half but by as much as fifteenfold. In one case, a group of seven-week-old puppies watched another group of dogs learn, by trial and error, to grasp a ribbon attached to a cart that was loaded with food. It took the demonstrators an average of eleven and a half minutes to figure out how to pull the food-laden cart into their cage. After five sessions, the observers were given a chance to do the same thing. They solved the problem in nine seconds. There's nothing surprising about this. Dogs have an inborn tendency to follow the lead of others in their group.

Elizabeth Marshall Thomas recounts an instance of such behavior in her book *The Social Lives of Dogs*. Thomas's son lived in Boulder, Colorado, and all his dogs ate once a day, in the evening. For some reason, they had developed the habit of eating lying down in front of their bowls. When one of these dogs—an Australian Shepherd and Chow cross named Pearl—came to live in Thomas's household in New Hampshire, she immediately noticed that her two companions, Sundog and Misty, ate standing up. She did not join them. True to her own pack's traditions, two thousand miles away in Boulder, she ate lying down. But the next morning, at breakfast, Pearl again noticed that Sundog and Misty ate standing up. "*The elders show the way*, says the dog law," Thomas comments, "and Pearl obeyed." Standing in front of her bowl, she ate like her new family. However, when dinnertime rolled around, Pearl reverted to eating lying down. For many months, until the memory of her family in Boulder faded, she ate both ways—standing at breakfast and lying down at dinner.

In a similar fashion to Pearl's new dog family, Merle exerted a powerful influence on his friends: Zula, Jack, and close to a dozen neighboring and visiting dogs. They learned to use his dog door simply by observing him. There was no need for him to illustrate the door's efficacy. He went through; they followed.

But when it came to watching me put on packs, observational learning didn't seem to apply. Had there been another dog accom-

panying us, wearing panniers, it would have been instructive to
see Merle's reaction. Lacking such a companion, I returned to him,
took off my pack, put it on slowly in front of him, and walked up
the trail. He still wouldn't follow, and his frustrated whine was perfectly comprehensible: "I told you. I am rooted to the earth."

Taking his leash from my pack, I went back to him and clipped
it to his collar. Though he didn't wander, I continued to take the
precaution of having him wear his collar, inscribed with his name
and phone number, while we were in the backcountry. I gently
tugged at him to follow. Uncertainly, his butt came off the ground
and he began to walk. And what a walk it was! He took a few fal-
tering steps, appearing that he might collapse under the weight of
the panniers. Then, after a few moments, he discovered that the
panniers weren't a crushing weight after all. His legs found their
gait. He began to speed up. Suddenly, he dashed ahead, ripping
the leash from my hand. Turning, he gave several woofs of incredulity: "I can walk! I can walk!"

"Of course you can walk."

A look of sheepishness crossed his face. He grasped that he
had psyched himself out—that the seeming weight of the panniers
had been in his head. His self-effacing grin was a marvel to behold.

I unclipped his leash, and up the trail he went, faster than
usual, I thought, as if to escape his own embarrassment.

That afternoon we reached a tarn nestled among the granite
walls of a high basin. I pitched my tent on a knoll, where a stand
of whitebark pine made a windbreak, and watched Merle, his panniers and collar removed, roll on his back and scratch. A moment
later, a marmot whistled, and Merle righted himself in an instant,
scanning the grassy field and glacial boulders that ran down to the
lake. His nose twitched, his ears perked, his tail stood erect.

The marmot whistled again, and Merle spotted him sitting on
a grassy mound. At a gallop, he reached the hole into which the
marmot had disappeared and began to dig furiously, dirt flying
between his rear legs, dust rising in a cloud. On and on he went,

looking up occasionally before resuming his furious excavation—
to no avail. After perhaps fifteen minutes, he gave up, walking to
a large boulder and climbing it from its sloping side. Then he stood
on its summit, inspecting every inch of the cirque before lying
down in a regal pose. Soon enough, another marmot whistled, and
Merle dashed off the boulder and began to dig. He did this twice
more—digging after a marmot, then lying on his rock—before returning to our camp, mouth, chest, and belly caked in dirt. He
stood in front of me, tail beating proudly, his shoulders thrown
back as if to say, "I am a dog in his kingdom!"

I had fetched a pot of water for dinner while he was occupied
with the marmots. He ambled over to it and drank half of it down,
leaving the remainder filled with dirt.

"Whoa, Señor!" I called out. "What's wrong with the lake?"

By way of an answer, he lay down with the pot between his
legs and finished it.

On the San Juan, he had drunk directly from the river, as he
had on all our other camping trips. Suddenly, on this trip, he had
decided that he wanted to drink from the pot in which I cooked
my food. Was this his way of expressing the time-honored sentiment of dogs the world over—that another dog's food or drink always tastes better? Whatever the case, from then on he would only
drink out of lakes and streams while we were hiking. Once we
reached camp, even if there was water a short distance away, he'd
wait to drink out of the pot. This was only the beginning of my
watching him turn into a character.

Not long thereafter, we took another backpacking trip into the
River of No Return Wilderness Area in central Idaho, accompanied by Benj and his then wife Deb. After several days of walking, we crossed the Middle Fork of the Salmon River and reached
a grassy airstrip, cut out of the forest, where we met the bush plane
that would carry us back to civilization. Even though Merle had
never been near a plane, he walked directly to it, accepting that
it was a different kind of car: It smelled of gas and oil; it was made

of metal; it had doors, windows, and seats; and Benj, Deb, and I got inside it along with our gear. He clambered in behind us and lay on our piled backpacks, between Benj and Deb, while I sat next to the pilot. As we rolled down the runway, I looked back and saw him totally at ease, his tongue lolling out of his mouth, his eyes pleasantly surveying left and right to the windows. His face wore the expression I had seen at the beginning of many a drive in the car: "Oh, how nice, we're off on another trip."

All this changed when the plane left the ground. Merle's lower jaw dropped and hung open. His head began to whip from side to side as he tried to look out each side of the aircraft simultaneously. His eyes became big and round, and he began to pant anxiously. He pushed his nose under Benj's hand and stared him in the face. I reached back and rested the palm of my hand on his shoulder. He looked at me fearfully, then, with a whine, back to the receding ground.

For the entire half-hour flight, he was on pins and needles, never taking his eyes from the windows, his body tense, saliva drooling from his tongue as he panted rapidly. And he wasn't a slobbery dog, and the cabin was anything but warm.

As we descended to Salmon and he watched the ground approach, his eyes filled with dread. When we rolled to a stop and the pilot opened the doors, he was out of the plane before any of us could move. The instant his paws touched the concrete, he put his nose to it and took a deep draught, as if to confirm what his eyes were telling him—that he was back on terra firma. Then he leapt into the air and barked at the top of his lungs. As Benj, Deb, and I exited the plane, he jumped at our faces, his feet barely touching the ground before he skipped into the air again, continuing to bark the whole time—not woofing or baying, but barking with joy: "We're alive! We're alive! We're on the ground and alive! We made it!"

On our River of No Return trip I also learned something more about Merle's past. One night, as we were camped by a lake, clouds covered the sky, and lightning began to flash. Soon it was snowing—heavy, wet snow in the middle of July. I was in my small, two-person tent, and Merle, as was his habit, was sleeping outside, by the zippered front door. No matter how much I cajoled him, he refused to come into the tent, and tonight was no different. Instead of joining me, he built oval-shaped nests in the duff.

These he designed with great care, excavating them with a different energy than he displayed when digging for marmots or ground squirrels. When digging out a rodent, he was feverishly excited. When excavating his bed, he was methodical and determined, taking it below grade several inches and then lying in it to test its shape. Inevitably he'd be dissatisfied. Standing, he'd dig some more, deepening the cavity here and there for his ribs and hips. As a last measure, he'd scratch out a hollow on one side into which he could snug his shoulder while laying his chin upon the nest's lip to gaze out at the world. I had never seen a dog so particular about his sleeping comfort, and on more than one occasion I had remarked, *"Tu es un chien vraiment méticuleux, Monsieur."*

In return, he would give me his put-upon look.

"You can come into the tent anytime you want," I'd tell him, holding open the tent door from where I was lying in my sleeping bag.

He'd look away with an air of mild irritation, indicating, "What good will it do me to be inside when I have to keep a lookout for bears?"

"I have pepper spray," I told him.

He'd hunch his shoulders and peer into the forest with a steady, sweeping gaze: "I must watch while you sleep."

And he did watch—all night. When I glanced out at him, he was staring intently into the darkness or dozing lightly, snapping awake at the slightest rustle. By dawn, he'd be haggard and have to catch naps throughout the day.

Now, in the middle of Idaho's River of No Return Wilderness, he lay in his nest as the sodden snow covered him.

"Come inside," I urged him gently.

As a reply, he huddled farther into his bed, which did little to protect him from the snow and wind.

Reaching out, I snagged his collar and pulled him toward the door. Flailing desperately, he twisted around, pulled his head out of the collar, and ran to the nearest tree, where he stared at me malevolently, as if I might have tried to drag him to his doom. He snorted at me, then began to dig a new nest directly under the shelter of the tree.

"Okay," I said, "I tried."

As the lightning continued to flash, I zipped down the tent door. The last I saw of him, he was casting dirt between his hind legs. In the morning, he looked totally played out, soaking wet and shivering from nose to tail as he stood by the front door of the tent, not uttering a sound except his polite little cluck, almost inaudible for the chattering of his teeth: "Could you please get up? You hung my food in a tree, and I'd like something to eat."

Two hours later, he was fine—fed and basking on a rock in the sunshine. But his behavior troubled me. What was it about the tent that scared him? And was his fear of it somehow connected to his having rejected the doghouse? I wondered if he had been confined in a small space as a young dog, and the experience had permanently scared him.

A few months later, on a trip in the Absaroka Mountains north of Jackson Hole, his fear rose again. We had made camp and eaten dinner when it began to snow. This storm was far worse than the one in Idaho. We were two thousand feet higher, at tree line, and it was September. Merle had dug a nest by the front door of the tent and huddled in it as the frigid wind blew over him.

"Come inside the tent," I said to him in a soothing tone, trying not to spook him as I stretched out my hand to grasp his collar.

He leapt to his feet.

"Merle," I said, lacing my voice with sweetness. "Please come inside."

He stood just out of reach.

"Come," I now ordered him.

That was it. Looking at me sternly, he turned his back and went to a nearby fir tree, under whose boughs he began to dig another sleeping spot.

Well, I wasn't going to freeze. I zipped the tent door closed and burrowed into my sleeping bag. About an hour later, I sensed him at the entrance. Opening it, I shone my headlamp outside. It was a wild scene: Snow blew horizontally; the trees lashed; the wind sounded like a runaway freight train; visibility was down to ten yards. Merle stood by the door, his fur plastered with snow, his eyelashes crusted with ice.

"Come inside," I said in my most entreating tone, and reached out my hand.

He slipped away, panting frantically. "I can't. I can't. But it's so cold out here."

And it was. My hand became numb and white as I reached for him, so I knew the wind-chill must have been about 30 below zero. Had Merle been alone, he'd have headed downhill into thick timber and shelter. But I was anchoring him to the spot. We were at an impasse: He wasn't going to leave without me, and I wasn't about to get out of the warm tent and move camp.

I slipped back inside and waited. Merle came closer, giving me a pleading look: "Do something, or let's leave."

I lunged, tackling him around his neck and shoulders. He yowled in terror, raking my chest and cheeks with his claws. I dragged him into the tent, snagging a hand through his collar, and twisting it so he couldn't escape. But as I zipped the door shut, he leapt against it, desperate to get out. I tackled him again, pinning him to the floor before wrapping my sleeping bag over him. He continued to struggle, yelping and crying out frantically.

"Easy, easy," I hummed to him. "Easy. It's all right. There's nothing to be afraid of."

I pulled the sleeping bag back from his head and saw his

mouth wrenched open, his teeth bared, as he hyperventilated. Petting his head, I leaned my mouth down to his ear and said, "Hey, hey, hey," softer and softer, placing my other hand on his chest and holding him.

"You're fine. I'm right here. There's nothing to be afraid of." I pushed my headlamp aside so that it wouldn't shine in his eyes, which were bugged out and darting wildly up to the low ceiling.

I began to massage him through the sleeping bag, rubbing it over him like a towel. I worked from his neck to his rump, steadily warming him as I murmured to him, "Oh, he's the pup of my dreams. I don't know where I'd find a better dog than this. He's simply the best." And then I began to sing, "I know a dog and his name is Merle. I know a dog and his name is Merle. I know a dog and his name is Merle. He's the best dog in the world." His rapid breathing began to slow, his tensed muscles relaxed, and his face took on a look of surprise—nothing bad was happening to him.

"See," I told him. "It's pretty nice in here, isn't it?"

A moment later, I felt his tail try to wag. But it was trapped beneath me. I continued to rub and fluff his fur, then I took off his collar, and got under the sleeping bag with him. Putting an arm under his head, I wrapped the sleeping bag over us.

"Better?" I looked him in the eye.

His tail thumped hard. Then he regarded me with a calm and tender expression before closing his eyes and putting his nose into my neck. He rubbed his forehead against my chin, back and forth several times, and gave a great, weary sigh, the kind I hadn't heard from him since the moment he had refused to get into the raft on the San Juan River—a sigh of being emotionally wrung out. He sighed again, this time with an air of peaceful letting go, of being protected. Pressing his knees against my belly and chest, he was asleep within a minute.

I lay there, staring at the ceiling of the tent as it shuddered in the wind and wondering what could have provoked such terror in him. Maybe someone had lured him into a tent and beaten him.

Perhaps he had raided a chicken coop and gotten stuck inside. I would never know. But unlike many dogs or people with embedded fears, his fear of tents vanished completely after that night.

In fact, it more than vanished. As darkness fell the next evening, I walked away from camp to brush my teeth, for the smell of toothpaste can attract grizzlies. Looking back to the clearing, I cast my eyes around the forest, but Merle was nowhere to be seen. I figured he was off doing his evening reconnaissance before settling into his nest. Shaking off my toothbrush, I walked back to the clearing, knelt at the door of the tent, and took off my boots. I heard a noise and looked inside.

"Ha-ha-ha."

Sprawled on my sleeping pad, Merle gave me the classic grin of the dog who's been caught in the act. His tail drummed with a mixture of delight and nervousness: "This is great! I hope you don't mind."

Laughing, I took off my boots and slid him off the pad, making some room for myself. He groaned melodramatically. I got under the sleeping bag. The next thing I knew, he was edging onto the pad.

"So, this is how I get paid back for curing you of your fear of tents?"

Pushing his snout under my hips, he shoved, trying to make some room for himself.

"Who's going to watch out for grizzly bears," I asked, "if you're sleeping in here?"

He squirmed up to my face, looked me in the eye, and by way of reply licked me on the mouth, just once: "I think we'll be fine. Just move over."

Among the many stories of how animals come to know their world, one of the most illuminating is that of Clever Hans, a sleek and stately horse—called by some an Arabian stallion, by others a Russian trotting horse—who was owned in the early 1900s by a retired instructor of mathematics named Wilhelm von Osten. Von

Osten, who lived in Berlin and was in his sixties, claimed that his horse could do addition, subtraction, multiplication, and division, as well as read, spell, and identify colors and musical tones.

Von Osten demonstrated the astounding abilities of his horse by asking him questions whose answers could be converted into a number that Hans would tap out with his right hoof. For example, if von Osten asked him, "What are the factors of twenty-eight?", Hans would tap out two, four, seven, fourteen, and twenty-eight. He could also nod his head to indicate "yes," shake his head back and forth for "no," and use his long nose to point in the directions of up, down, right, and left.

Clever Hans was soon the talk of the German capital and attracted the attention of the scientific community, whose members saw in his abilities what one of them called "the essential similarity between the human and the animal mind, which doctrine has been coming more and more into favor since the time of Darwin." One of those who was both impressed and puzzled by Hans's talents was Carl Stumpf, the director at the Psychological Institute of the University of Berlin. On September 12, 1904, Stumpf helped to convene a commission consisting of veterinarians, circus animal trainers, zoologists, physiologists, and psychologists. They all watched von Osten and Hans perform and came to the conclusion that the white-haired man—wearing a large, black slouch hat—wasn't giving the horse any cues or signs. Indeed, when other questioners replaced von Osten, Clever Hans still gave the correct responses to the questions he was posed. The commissioners unanimously agreed that no trickery was involved and that "this is a case . . . worthy of a serious and incisive investigation." Stumpf suggested to one of his colleagues at the institute, Oskar Pfungst, that Clever Hans would make an interesting study in "experimental animal and human psychology."

Pfungst proved thorough. In fact, the research he conducted has since been cited as a landmark in methodological sophistication, laying the groundwork for how future studies of animals would be conducted. He began by isolating Hans in a large tent in the courtyard of von Osten's apartment building, so that external distractions wouldn't influence Hans. He then recruited other individuals besides von Osten to ask the horse questions. By the end of the experiment, Hans was responding to as many as forty different questioners. Pfungst performed a large number of tests, to rule out chance, and varied the questioners, who sometimes knew the right answer and sometimes didn't. Sometimes they were deliberately given the wrong answer to see whether Hans could truly figure out the problems by himself. Last, Pfungst varied the distance between Hans and his questioners and even fitted the horse with blinders, so that he couldn't see who was talking to him.

Sadly, for all those thrilled by the seeming intelligence of the horse, his performance declined markedly when the questioners didn't know the right answers, or when they did but asked their questions while standing outside Hans's field of view. Pfungst concluded that both von Osten and the questioners must be giving Hans cues to the correct answers without realizing it.

Pfungst then carefully observed all the questioners, including himself, as they interacted with the horse. It wasn't long before he concluded that everyone to whom Clever Hans responded was giving the horse very subtle signs while he was striking the ground with his hooves and approaching the right answer. The questioner's body would subtly tense as Hans's hoofbeat approached the answer and then give an involuntary postural change when the horse reached it: a raising of the head, a twitching of an eyebrow, or even no more than the barest dilation of a nostril. At this moment, Hans would stop counting with his hoof. He was, it turned out, not mathematically gifted, but a master at reading the body language of people. As for Hans's shaking his head "yes" and "no," he was following the movement of his questioners' heads. As for indicating colored cloths, he was following the stare of his questioners' eye. When he couldn't see his questioners he not only failed to answer their questions, he also displayed great agitation.

Pfungst was not satisfied to stop here, though. He moved the experiment to his laboratory and, using himself in the role of Clever Hans, asked questioners standing close by him to think of a number between one and one hundred. He would then tap with his right hand and stop when he perceived that the questioner was giving him a subtle signal that he had arrived at the correct number. He was almost always right. None of the questioners was told the purpose of the experiment or what particular phenomena Pfungst was investigating, yet virtually all of them—twenty-three out of twenty-five—made the same involuntary raising of the head as the questioners of Clever Hans had, a movement Pfungst was able to graph by placing levers against the questioners' heads. These levers were in turn attached to pens that marked a smoked paper revolving on a drum. The graphs they produced were startling—the distances that the questioners moved their heads when giving a correct answer averaged only a millimeter. Pfungst later calculated that when von Osten interacted with Hans, he moved his head merely one-fifth of a millimeter, a movement slightly accentuated by the large brim of his slouch hat. That these distances were so tiny—in von Osten's case quite literally a hairbreadth—didn't matter. It was enough.

In this respect, neither man nor horse was exceptional. Both happened to be members of species, *Equus caballus* and *Homo sapiens*, whose ancestors had survived by interpreting subtle variations in the body language of their predators, minute distinctions that Pfungst described as "truly microscopic movements." Later psychologists would name this the "Clever Hans Effect," defining it, in the words of Robert Wozniak, a professor of psychology at Bryn Mawr College and interpreter of Pfungst's work, as "the fact that a subject's behavior may be influenced by subtle and unintentional cueing on the part of a questioner and that this cueing may reflect the experimenter's own expectations." In the case of Clever Hans, he had been trained to use his equine inheritance to an entertaining and lucrative end. People also use their inherited ability to read body language: Mind readers and poker players employ such skills every day.

Once, though, relying upon such skills meant the difference between life and death. In the late 1960s and early 1970s, Hans Kruuk, a zoologist from Oxford University, studied an original example of the Clever Hans Effect in one of the horse's wild cousins, the zebra of Tanzania's Serengeti National Park and Ngorongoro Crater. On some days, Kruuk found that the zebra would merely watch hyenas approach to within five or ten meters of them. On other days, the zebra would begin to flee when the hyenas were still over one hundred meters away. Kruuk wondered how the zebra could possibly know when hyenas were intent on hunting them and when it was safe to ignore them.

Part of the zebra's reaction, he discovered, was related to the size of the hyena pack. He observed that only one to three hyenas would typically hunt a herd of wildebeest. By contrast, the average size of a group of hyenas attacking a herd of zebra was 10.8 animals. The difference lay in how much harder zebra were to bring down than wildebeest.

Wildebeest also proved to be adept readers of hyenas. If they spied a large pack of them approaching, they wouldn't run. Experience had shown them that large packs of hyenas always bypassed them and targeted zebra. Obviously, both the zebra and wildebeest could count.

Yet zebra and wildebeest would sometimes watch a group of hyenas approaching—a group that was appropriately sized to hunt them—and not flee. There was something about the predator's gaze, and by extension its intentions, that both the zebra and wildebeest could read accurately.

Nearly sixty years before, Pfungst had described this process when he saw that Clever Hans produced the correct answers only when his questioners focused their minds on that answer. "The state required for a successful response," he observed, "was not the mere passive expectation that the horse would tap the number demanded of him nor the wish that he might tap it, but rather the determination that he should do it. An inward 'Thou shalt', as it were, was spoken to the horse."

Given Kruuk's findings, perhaps hyenas, by their very posture, can't help but give an "I am hunting you" signal to those zebra or wildebeest they want to eat. And the zebra and wildebeest read these infinitesimally fine changes in the hyenas' demeanor. The rewards for doing so are significant. Prey species save a great deal of energy by not running away prematurely. By running away when it's appropriate to do so, they stay alive. And predators watch their prey just as keenly. So much so that many herd animals—gazelles, pronghorn antelope, mule deer, even bison—will stot, bound with a stiff-legged gait, advertising to their predators that they're in such good condition that they can waste energy bouncing up and down. In effect, they're saying, "Don't bother chasing me."

Domestic dogs have also inherited this ability to read prey, predators, and the individuals in their pack. However, having lost the need both to catch food and to avoid becoming food, and rarely living in packs these days, dogs have transferred their body-reading skills to the most important figures in their lives— their people. Anyone who lives with a dog sees the skill employed daily. The dog knows when it will be walked, taken on a drive, or fed, even before its person makes a move toward leash, car, or fridge.

Not surprisingly, Merle, who walked on his own at all times of the day and night, had little cause to get excited when I reached for his leash. In fact, since he viewed any lead as confinement, he'd look at me circumspectly if I took his leash from the basket by the door, his brows pumping up and down with worry. *Could I possibly be thinking of leashing him in Kelly?* There was only one sad occasion upon which this happened—when I tied him to the wellhead so I could hose him down after he had rolled in cow poop. He disliked these baths, not so much because of the cold water (after all, he loved to swim), but, if his plaintive expression and sighs were any indication, because of the loss of his carefully applied perfume. Thus, only when he saw his leash go into my fanny pack would he spring up to join me.

As for tracking my motions toward the car, he was often already gone on his rounds when I'd leave for town. I'd whistle for him, and most of the time he'd appear within a few minutes. But sometimes he wouldn't, and I'd have to leave without him, only to see him angling toward me from some field, running full tilt. Sprinting up to my driver's-side window, he'd wear an anxious expression: "I heard you whistle! I did! Look down! I'm right here!"

Not infrequently, there'd be no sign of him, and I'd leave without him. Upon my return, he would berate me with baying yelps—"rar, rar, awoo!"—his voice rising higher and higher with annoyance as he explained that he had been busy and would have appeared shortly if I had only waited.

"He who snoozes loses," I'd reply. "I can't be at your beck and call. I waited for fifteen minutes and not only whistled but called you. I had an appointment to make."

"Ha-oof," he'd counter.

"Well, next time, I'll wait a little longer, and you can come a little quicker."

I'd begin to rub his ears, and, with trailing-off grumbles, he'd consent to my display of affection.

When it came to food, however, Merle left nothing to chance. Every day, at almost precisely 5:15 P.M., I'd hear the slap of his dog door. Instead of coming into my office to greet me and perhaps ask for a biscuit, as he did occasionally throughout the day, he'd lie down in the living room, within sight of both his bowls and me. If I hadn't fed him by 5:35 P.M., he'd walk directly to the corner of my desk and stand there, wagging his tail gently, right brow arched up, left down, indicating, "Sorry to bother you, but haven't you forgotten something?"

I had. Hands on the keyboard or phone to my ear, I had been totally immersed in what I was doing and hadn't made the slightest motion toward the pantry. So how was he able to read my body language?

Quite simply, he wasn't reading me. Unlike Clever Hans, or zebra and wildebeest, Merle had dispensed with observing my body language—at least in this case. Instead, like countless dogs the world over, he had created his own timekeeper.

Sometimes called a "biological clock" or an "internal clock," this timekeeper lies within the dog's hypothalamus, an area of the brain directly above the place where the optic nerves cross. Composed of about 20,000 neurons, the timekeeper is known as the suprachiasmatic nucleus. It takes in variations in the ambient light from the retina, then transmits this information to the pineal gland. The transmission is accomplished by a complex procedure during which genes encode proteins that, in turn, regulate the functions of the pineal gland's cells. Thus prompted, these cells secrete the hormone melatonin into the bloodstream, where it peaks at night and ebbs during the day, regulating sleep and wakefulness.

All told, these neurons, proteins, and hormones form a circadian system, one that is neither fully dependent on nor independent of the cycles of light and dark. In fact, animals can adjust their internal clocks to a new pattern regardless of when it occurs, so long as the pattern is sufficiently regular and, one might add, important to them. In the case of domestic dogs, it's the time kibble falls into their bowls. This may have been one of the reasons why Merle was so upset when I left him behind in Kelly. Since my departures were random, he couldn't set his clock.

Dogs aren't unique in having an internal clock. Species as different as fruit flies, humans, and birds have circadian rhythms, which don't have to be strictly a day long. (In Latin, "circadian" means "approximately a day.") Domestic dogs come into heat twice a year, and human females experience menstrual cycles around a twenty-eight-day period. Five-thirty in the afternoon, I should note, was hardly the time I would have chosen for Merle to eat, since I liked to eat between seven and eight o'clock at night.

It was his choice, a time he had decided upon independently of me during the first summer we were together. One day, he came to my desk as I was writing and stood with an imploring look and a wagging tail.

"What do you want?" I asked.

He looked at me silently; he broke into an energetic pant; he walked to his bowl. Well, nothing could be clearer. The next day at 5:30 P.M., the same: the imploring look, the excited pant, the walk to his bowl. And so on during the following days—always at 5:30. I got the message about when he preferred to eat dinner.

Some dog behaviorists might observe that it was Merle who had trained me, but this misses the point of how dogs and humans share a household in a give-and-take sort of way. As Brother Thomas, who began the German Shepherd breeding program at the New Skete monastery in upstate New York, once remarked, "We are to listen to a dog until we discover what is needed instead of imposing ourselves in the name of training."

Yet when I tried to follow Brother Thomas's advice and gave Merle control of his eating schedule, we had a meltdown. Shortly after he began to come to me at 5:30 P.M., I filled his bowl with a great mound of kibble, enough to see him through the next four days.

"There you go," I said. "It's up to you. Eat when you want and make it last."

He finished the entire bowl in under two minutes, gobbling it down voraciously, then licking his lips in satisfaction.

"That was supposed to last you four days," I said.

He gave me an expectant expression: "You mean that's it?"

Thinking that surely he would now spread out his eating, I refilled his bowl.

He finished every last nugget.

"I don't think this is going to work," I told him.

He wagged his tail enthusiastically: "Let's try."

"Maybe tomorrow," I replied.

No sooner had the words come out of my mouth than the phone rang. The delayed Fed Ex plane had arrived and my package was in town.

I picked up my car keys and said, "You want to come?"

With a huge meal in his stomach, Merle had lain down and looked like he was going to have a digestive nap.

He answered me with two thumps of the tail: "I don't think so. I am so comfortable here."

When I returned two hours later, I found him lying on his spine, his rear legs splayed, his fronts paws hanging limply over his chest, his breath coming in shallow gasps. His stomach bulged like a python's after it has swallowed a pig.

In an instant I saw what had happened. I had just opened a forty-pound bag of kibble and had given him two big bowls of it. Forgetting to empty the rest of the bag's contents into the plastic garbage pail where I stored his food, I had left the bag against the wall. Worse still, I had left it open. Merle had stuck his head in and eaten.

The bag was more than a quarter empty. Marveling at Merle's capacity to stuff himself, I put the bag on a scale. It weighed twenty-eight pounds. Merle had eaten twelve pounds of kibble over the space of three hours.

He now looked as if he were going to die. He didn't look in the least regretful, though. In fact, he wore a blissful smile.

"Merle." I leaned close to his ear, putting a hand gently on his belly. It was as tight as a drum.

He groaned painfully and opened his eyes. They were glassy. Faintly, he flopped his tail back and forth: "Let me die in peace."

A few moments later, he rolled onto his side and lay there panting. Then, he ponderously stood and squeezed through his dog door, his belly scraping its lower edge. He clumped across the porch and onto the grass, but he didn't get far. Heaving several times, he vomited up an enormous pile of kibble. Sniffing it, he wagged his tail appreciatively and glanced back at me. A

bigger wag of his tail: "That was so good." Then he headed over
the bridge toward Zula's yurt, perhaps to tell her that he had at
last fulfilled his life's dream: He had finally eaten as much as he
wanted.

Clearly, self-feeding was not going to work with Merle, an individual who had a history of starvation and the tendency of many
Labrador Retrievers to be chowhounds. It's a trait some interpreters
of dog behavior ascribe to the Labrador's early history, when it was
bred to retrieve fish in icy Canadian waters and subsist on whatever came its way. However, gorging preceded the breeding of
Labs and even the domestication of dogs. Wolves have been seen
to consume up to twenty-two pounds of meat at a feeding, and the
behavior is entirely practical. If you don't know when your next
meal might appear, it pays to eat as much as you can.

With this in mind, I thought about feeding Merle every four
days, but if his reaction the following day could be trusted, there'd
be no peace for me. At 5:30 P.M., he showed up at my desk, wagging his tail with its syncopated beat of entreaty: "Oh, please, it's
dinnertime! Oh, please, it's dinnertime!"

"You ate enough for two weeks yesterday," I said.

My tone of voice told him everything. His face fell.

He put his chin on my leg and stared up at me, his tail now
wagging so vigorously that his entire body shimmied.

"Sorry," I replied, "no dinner today. You want to eat like a wolf,
you can act like a wolf."

Looking crushed, he turned and lay down halfway between my
desk and his bowl.

Ten minutes later, he tried again, placing his chin on my thigh.
I told him to go lie down.

He asked to be fed at least a dozen times before we headed up
to the cabin, and even there he continued to plead. Finally, he
turned in, disgruntled, nose under tail, staring at me suspiciously,
trying to understand our falling-out.

He didn't ask to be fed again until five-thirty the next day, and

I relented. After all, he looked his old trim self. He inhaled his usual three-cup ration of food, and from then on we went back to a daily feeding schedule. In the meantime, I had discovered that Merle had oriented his internal clock to another reward, and that it had nothing to do with food.

From early on—in fact, from that first day on the San Juan River when he had answered his own echo—I knew that this was a dog who liked to sing. In Kelly, I quickly learned that it was impossible for anyone to play a guitar or a banjo around Merle without his sitting up, throwing his head back, shaping his mouth into a trumpet, and accompanying the musician with a litany of howls. He chimed in at weddings, at barbecues, and at impromptu jam sessions. He particularly reveled in birthday parties. At the very first note of "Happy Birthday," he would begin to yodel away, tail beating in happiness. He was often escorted outside, where he'd continue to sing by the door or an open window.

Thwarted in his attempts to sing along to live music, he turned his attention to the radio, but only certain tunes. One was the theme music for "All Things Considered," the National Public Radio news show. After a day of writing, I often did errands in town, and so we'd be in the car at 5:00 P.M., when the show comes on. As soon as Merle heard the first strains of the theme music, he'd throw back his head and begin to bay.

Soon I only had to reach toward the radio at 5:00 P.M. and he'd stand in the back of the car, wag his tail in anticipation, and burst into song as the first notes sounded in the car. Not long afterward, I noticed that he would get to his feet a couple of minutes before five and eagerly look from me to the dashboard. If I neglected to turn on the radio, he'd step forward and stare directly into my eyes. Up went one brow, down went the other, his head tilting significantly in a way that I had now been trained to interpret as "Excuse me, haven't you forgotten something?" I'd turn on the radio. Eyes bright with anticipation, he'd listen to the announcer recite the Wyoming Public Radio call letters, "This is KUWR Laramie-Cheyenne, 91.9, and KUWJ Jackson, 90.3." Then, the instant the first notes of "All Things Considered" sounded, he'd break into song. He had set another part of his internal clock to NPR.

After a while, he expanded his radio sing-alongs to Saturdays at noon, when "Riders Radio Theater" was broadcast. He learned the sequence of shows that preceded it: "Car Talk" and "The Ranch Breakfast Show," which we often listened to while driving the roads of Grand Teton and Yellowstone National Parks, looking for wildlife. When the latter show was drawing to a close, Merle would get to his feet and wait for the singing cowboy quartet, Riders in the Sky, to begin their opening theme—an unforgettable *"Ow-ow-ow, ow-ow-ow"* imitation of a coyote. As the first *"Ow"* sounded in the car, Merle would toss back his head, like an opera singer in the throes of an aria, and howl along.

Naturally, my observations weren't made under controlled scientific conditions. In some way I could have been subconsciously feeding Merle information that cued him as to when "Riders Radio Theater" was about to begin, just as Wilhelm von Osten did for Clever Hans. However, another observer corroborated my own sense—that it was the sequence of radio shows rather than what I was doing that gave Merle his cues. We were driving in Yellowstone National Park at the time, and my friend Kim Fadiman and I were excitedly discussing a bighorn lamb we had watched being born late the previous evening.

Suddenly Kim remarked, "Why is Merle standing and wagging his tail?"

I glanced into the rearview mirror and saw Merle looking to the dashboard.

"Oh," I said, "one of his favorite radio shows is about to begin."

I turned up the volume, which had been barely audible, and within a half minute came the *"ow-ow-ow"* of "Riders Radio Theater." Merle threw back his head and sang. Perhaps I had made some microscopic movement of my head or body while talking with Kim, and this had indicated to Merle that he should get ready to howl. Whatever the case, after several months of listening to "Riders Radio Theater," Merle didn't need the preceding shows or seemingly any cue from me to know when the show was about to begin. If we were in the car on Saturday morning, he'd look at the radio as the noon hour approached and wag his tail at me. I'd turn on the radio and out would come the singing cowboys and their coyote howls. Merle had set his singing clock on a weekly basis as well.

But no radio rendition of coyotes, no guitar or banjo music, not even a dozen human voices singing "Happy Birthday" could compare to what became Merle's enduringly favorite piece of music. The first time he heard it he was lying by the Christmas tree. As its opening bars sounded, he threw himself to his feet, eyes stunned with wonder and disbelief. Tossing back his head in the most energetic demonstration I had yet to see of his musical passion, he caroled along to the "Hallelujah Chorus" of Handel's *Messiah,* his mouth nearly coming unhinged. He did not stop: "King of kings, and lord of lords." "Yow, yow, yawoooo."

He accompanied every "And he shall reign forever and ever," every "Hallelujah," until the monumental final chords when— voice cracking and tail lashing so hard that I feared it might break off—he looked up at me with an angelic and spent expression, as if to say, "That is the most sublime music I have ever heard."

Some who have written on the subject of why dogs howl to music would note that Merle couldn't possibly have had a special affinity for the *Messiah.* Instead, they would say, dogs, like wolves, are merely howling along with their pack, and that the reason they often sound so dissonant is that, like wolves, they're modulating their voices to be slightly off-pitch from the voices around them. This may be true, but, if so, why then did Merle learn to sing on tune?

That he had learned to do so became apparent the first Christmas we joined the Kelly Carolers, an informal group of about thirty people who met for appetizers at one home, strolled around the village singing, and ended at another house for dinner. Dressed in big snow boots, bundled in down parkas, pulling children in sleds, and accompanied by a variety of the village's dogs, we stood at our neighbors' front doors and caroled.

Merle, I noticed, didn't immediately throw back his head and sing in his usual exuberant way. Instead, he kept his head lowered, directing his voice downward. His previous banishments must have made an impression upon him. Instead of howling raucously, he now picked up the first note of a carol, holding it in a low croon, like a shy bass singer unsure of his voice and coasting along in the background. When he'd run out of breath, he'd pick up whatever note the group was singing. Reinforced—no one escorted him away—he kept going.

It was enlightening to see the looks other dogs gave him. One was curious, wagging her tail questioningly as if to say, "What are you doing?" One looked highly suspicious and skittered off. A third seemed aghast and bumped his shoulder into Merle, repeatedly trying to get him to stop. Merle ignored him. Only the first dog joined him, taking his lead and remaining low-key. No group howl ensued. The dogs seemed to be in agreement that this was a human songfest.

The dog who had started to howl tapered off. Intermittently, Merle kept caroling, going house to house with us, never raising his voice or lifting his muzzle to the sky. At home, only hours before, he had been bellowing out the "Hallelujah Chorus," but here, among a group of people, he was singing in moderation, even to our robust renditions of "Jingle Bells" and "Deck the Halls." This gave me pause for thought. If dogs are so hardwired, I wondered, why had he decided to modify his behavior? If dogs think that howling to music is no more than howling along with a pack of dogs, how had he come to accommodate the notion that different human groups had varying tolerances for dogs who wanted to sing with them? How had he come to think outside of the box?

Oskar Pfungst had chipped away at this very question, at least in regard to the horse. After noting that his experiment proved that Clever Hans was incapable of independent thought, Pfungst lamented the fact that horses had been dumbed down through domestication, their world reduced to dark narrow stalls—quite literally a box. "Presumably, however," he went on to reflect, "it might be possible, under conditions and with methods of instruction more in accord with the life-needs of the horse, to awaken in a fuller measure those mental activities which would be called into play to meet those needs."

The same can be said about how we meet the life-needs of dogs whose world has become no larger than an apartment or a fenced yard. These dogs aren't necessarily stupid, but they don't have the opportunity to get their minds out of their box. Given a more natural environment—daily walks in a nearby park with other dogs is often sufficient—they can become like humans exposed to a good liberal arts education: They learn the discipline of thinking as well as mannerly discourse with their peers.

Blessed with a large education from an early age, Merle seemed to quickly grasp the rewards of flexibility. In the case of his singing, he decided that if he was going to be part of a group that was doing something he enjoyed, he needed to change his tune. One might argue that this was a limited sort of flexibility, and that he was simply observing the traditions of his human pack— one member of which, myself, would allow him to sing at the top of his lungs at home, while others would shout at him to go away. Being a pack animal, he thus modified his behavior accordingly, very much like Elizabeth Marshall Thomas's dog Pearl, who chose to eat standing in the morning with her new pack and lying down at night in memory of her old one.

Yet when something didn't appeal to Merle, he would never follow another dog's lead. Despite his obvious Lab blood, and even though he watched countless dogs play toss and fetch, he wouldn't change his mind about retrieving. If you held a ball, a stick, or a retriever dummy under his nose, his expression would turn sweetly intractable. Pulling his head back from the proffered object, he'd stare at you with bright and challenging eyes, every ounce of him saying, "Thank you, but I'm not interested."

No matter how much you would try to cajole him, employing the usual kissy noises that attract dogs so well (they mimic the high-pitched squeaks of rodents), he remained unshaken in his belief that such games were exactly that—games. Instead, he applied himself to the real—the real, somehow, always being connected to filling his stomach. Why should he respond to a person's ersatz rodent noise, his logic seemed to go, when he could chase and kill real ground squirrels? Why should he fetch a retriever dummy when he could flush and kill real ruffed grouse?

I admired his integrity, though some of my friends found it disconcerting. One young couple, longing for some doggy energy in their lives, borrowed Merle for a day hike. A few hours later they returned him at arm's length. "He caught a grouse," the woman said, a little shocked, "and ate it whole, right in front of our eyes."

His experience with a shotgun going off over his head had apparently not put him off from this form of hunting. However, he never became fixated on birds, the way some highly bred Labs, Pointers, and Setters are. He stayed a generalist and an opportunist, both characteristics of wolves, coyotes, and jackals, wherever they're found.

One day in particular sticks out in my mind as illustrating how these two types of dogs conduct themselves. Merle and I were hiking with the embodiment of the canine specialist: a highly bred gun dog whose raison d'être was hunting upland birds. No one was carrying a gun on this late-summer afternoon, but this dog was nonetheless totally on-task, vacuuming the terrain ahead of us for grouse scent. Dashing this way and that, he went right by a patch of currants.

Merle stopped, twisted his head, and sniffed curiously. He had never smelled currants before. Wading into the patch, he carefully inspected an individual currant by taking several deep breaths of it. Cautiously, he pulled it from its stem with his front incisors and chewed it observantly—unlike how he gobbled food with which he was familiar. I stopped and watched him. Sensing no bitter taste, he glanced at me and gave his tail a wag of endorsement: "This is very good." He then proceeded to nip off currant after currant, something he did the rest of his life whenever he found a patch. He behaved just as a coyote would: curious about the world, loath to pass up anything edible, especially if it contained furaneol, ethyl maltol, and methyl maltol, three compounds found in fruits that most dogs find fragrant and intensely sweet. The relationship between such plants and dogs is symbiotic. The plant gets its seeds spread in the dog's feces; the dog gets some extra calories and a pleasurable taste.

Whether the flashy gun dog's focus on grouse rather than on currants was an example of one type of inheritance overriding another or his specialized training acting in a similar fashion, I cannot say. What soon became obvious to me was that the attributes of specialist and generalist dogs tended to reexpress themselves in people who write about dogs. Some writers see wild dogs as embodiments of general intelligence and adaptability; others perceive domestic dogs as humanity's triumph over unruly nature.

Michael Fox, the veterinarian, bioethicist, wolf researcher, and former vice president of the Humane Society of the United States, is firmly in the camp of the wild dogs. Here is his take on the all-around abilities of the wolf:

> The wolf's general alertness, its state of arousal, the exquisite sensitivity of its sense organs of hearing, smell, and sight, and its remarkable agility, dexterity, speed, and stamina

demonstrate the phenomenon of natural adaptation.... Anyone seeing a wolf move, in its long, open, effortless lope or racing at full speed, or twist and turn on one foot, will admire, if not envy, its agility and coordination. Mind and body are one, totally integrated, and few dogs can match the liquid movements, speed, and stamina of the wolf.

The biologist and sled dog trainer Raymond Coppinger and his wife, Lorna, are just as fervently on the side of the domestic dog:

Unlike the wolf—if we have seen one wolf, we basically have seen them all—dogs are continually interesting. Take any specific behavior and there is a breed of dog that can outperform any wolf. Compared with wolves, sled dogs can run farther, greyhounds can run faster, bloodhounds have a better sense of smell, borzois have more optical overlap and better depth perception. Some would contend that, cognitively speaking, the wolf is smarter. That may be, but we would propose that if it is so smart, why can't we teach one to herd sheep, or fetch a ball, or deliver a bird to hand, or guide a blind person through the crowded streets of a city?

Indeed, the Coppingers go so far as to say, "Any breed of dog behaves with much greater complexity than any wolf."

Having watched thousands of domestic dogs and hundreds of wild wolves—as well as a handful of dogs who, like Merle, have lived physically and psychologically somewhere between the two—I'm not sure that the Coppingers are right. Specialist dogs can be brilliant at their jobs or sports, but, as is the case with some human athletes, mathematicians, or artists, their highly developed skills can leave them unobservant. Data outside their purview doesn't register. And the more proficient they become, the harder it becomes for them to think outside of the box. They become idiot savants.

Merle never followed this narrow career path, and some of my friends thought that this was a loss both for him and for me. By allowing Merle to do what he wanted, they argued, I had wasted his life as a potentially good bird dog and squandered the enjoyment I would have gotten, watching him flush and retrieve.

On the other hand, I never tired of watching him scent elk, chase chiselers, and delicately pick currants with his incisors— all pastimes he chose for himself. Eventually, he enlarged his frugivorous tastes to raspberries and thimbleberries, munching them whenever they were ripe. Oddly, he never liked huckleberries, even when I offered him the plumpest and sweetest of them, freshly plucked from the vine. He would give them a single lick and pull back his head. I couldn't tell if it was their taste or their texture—smooth instead of wrinkled—that prompted his indifference. At home, he was just as unpredictable, eating apples and pears but not cantaloupe or bananas. He'd munch carrots enthusiastically and give broccoli an occasional try, yet shun all other vegetables. Though a generalist, he had his preferences. Eventually, he expressed them on most matters, including when he'd accompany me in the car.

At first, as is the case for most dogs, the novelty of a car ride trumped anything he was doing, and he'd never refuse to go along. It didn't take him long, however, to realize that he might end up sitting in the car while I ran errands or went to a meeting. Nonetheless, he continued to leap into the car joyfully, a perfect example of what Samuel Johnson called the "triumph of hope over experience." As he matured, though, he'd sit on the porch and watch what I took along. If I put my briefcase or canvas bag of library books onto the front seat, and nothing else went inside the car or onto its rooftop carrier—no hiking boots, mountain bike, or skis, indicating that this would be anything more than one of my boring trips to Jackson—he would likely stay put.

"Sure you don't want to come with me?" I'd ask.

He'd stand and give his tail an apologetic little wag, the way people will open their hands and duck their heads as they backpedal into an excuse.

"Okay," I'd say, "See you later. Have a good afternoon."

And as I drove off, I'd see him leave the porch and head into Kelly, where more engaging alternatives awaited him.

In this way—day by day, trip by trip, season by season—he became his own dog. At two years old, he had filled out to seventy pounds, but seemed larger—not in weight, but in presence. The pool of quiet that surrounded him—that collected air he had worn from the moment we met—had expanded into an aura of self-possession as he worked through his phobias, catalogued his likes and dislikes, and gathered experience.

And because he was tranquil, he drew people to him. Children especially liked to touch him, asking, "Where's his collar?"

"He only wears it sometimes," I'd answer.

"But why?" they'd persist.

"How would you like it if you had to wear a collar every minute of your life?"

They would consider this, their hands resting on his ruff as if sensing something magical and beyond their experience—a dog without a collar, a quiet dog, who didn't try to lick them but looked them gently in the eye.

Part of Merle's equanimity, I thought, might have been attributed to the fact that I'm a relatively calm person, and he was therefore reflecting my demeanor, just as so many domestic dogs reflect the personalities of their human companions. Part might also have been created by his having spent his puppyhood among Navajos, a dignified and reserved people. And part of his composure was most likely influenced by his hound genes, which he seemed to have inherited along with his Lab blood. A friend had shown me some photos of Redbone Coonhounds, and some of them could have been Merle's brothers and sisters, aside from their pendulous ears. The texture and color of Merle's coat and the coats of Redbone Coonhounds were similar; their longish snouts, longer than a Lab's, were a close match; and their bold stance and the upright curving position of their tails were all identical. Most of all, Merle's behavior and the behavior of Redbone Coonhounds ran very much along the same lines: instead of barking, baying; instead of retrieving, tracking; instead of submission, an independent streak that said in a dozen different ways, "I'm my own dog."

The largest contribution to Merle's personality, however, came from the experiences he had both enjoyed and endured during his youth. He must have been exposed to a large variety of people, dogs, wild animals, and situations before his socialization window closed at the age of about four and a half months. Up until this age puppies will become habituated to almost anything, and Merle took almost everything in stride except shotguns and firecrackers.

The life he then discovered in Kelly was equally diverse as well as authentic. Whether he was on his own or with other dogs, the activities he enjoyed were unstructured and self-motivated—he was able to undertake them, break them off, and resume them according to his own schedule. None of this would have happened to the same extent had he not had a door of his own: *su propia puerta, sa propre porte.* Say it in any language, it means the same thing to the dog who's using it: freedom.

The dog behaviorist Dr. Patricia McConnell speaks to this issue when she writes, "A large number of the behavioral problems that I see have their origin in boredom. Ironically the problem has gotten worse as we've taken more care of our dogs and stopped letting them run free." Without really thinking about it, I had followed her advice: I didn't take care of Merle; I allowed him to take care of himself. The result wasn't an unmanageable dog, but a steady one.

Others noticed who he had become and trusted him. When my friends Scott and April Landale's first daughter, Tessa, began to crawl, she immediately made her way to Merle, lying on a throw rug in their cabin. Scott and April said not a word, made not a move, only watched—letting the situation between the little girl and the dog evolve without any input of their own. When Tessa put her arms on Merle's head and began to tug at his ears, he inclined his head. When she crawled over his back, he half closed his eyes, as if forbearance of the young was something he knew all about.

I'll admit I held my breath as she grabbed his tail, for Merle, despite his poise, had one significant jitteriness. If you inadvertently trod on his paw or tail while he was dozing, however lightly, he'd leap to his feet and yowl in your face in the most accusing way imaginable, "You oaf! Be more careful!" And then he'd catch himself and look abashed. Perhaps he had been stepped upon between his eighth and tenth week of life, when puppies are particularly sensitive to developing chronic fears, and had never forgotten the trauma.

Tessa yanked on his tail, and Merle whipped his head around. But he didn't make a sound. He merely studied her neutrally and pulled his tail out of her grasp. I let out my breath. Then she slid along his flank, past his shoulder, and pulled herself up by his neck, which he bowed to her. She began to touch his nose and his lips, and he put his moist black nose on her curly blond hair, his nostrils dilating as they drank in her milky scent. She continued her exploration of him by forcing open his lips and looking at his long white teeth, her tiny fingers tracing their sharp edges. He moved not a millimeter, aware of the great delicacy that had been entrusted to his mouth. At last, Tessa grew tired. Curling herself on Merle's outstretched legs, she went to sleep, snuggled against his chest. He rested his chin over her back, and his eyes met mine and held them. "This," they surely said, "is someone to be very careful of."

Then he, too, closed his eyes and, with the young girl in his arms, followed her into sleep.

CHAPTER 7

Top Dog

Given the length of our commute between the cabin and the trailer, just a mile and a half, how much Merle enjoyed his first run of the day, and how peaceable the scenery was, I suspect that we might never have built a house of our own had two things not happened, one dramatic, the other insidious. The first involved a moose.

He was a great bull moose, with enormous polished antlers, and had been hanging around the cabin as the winter snows deepened, browsing the willow and making a daybed on the south side of the cabin, where he dozed in the heat reflected from the logs. One night, tired from skiing, I had fallen asleep shortly after showering, feeding Merle, and eating my own dinner.

A few hours later, I heard, "Uh." A moment later, another "uh." Then, after a few more seconds pause, still another "uh." The uhs were being uttered very diplomatically, the human equivalent of a whispered "Excuse me."

Merle was making his glottal stop by my bedside. It had become apparent that he preferred to use the glottal stop at night, as if it were a less obtrusive way of waking me up than the lisping cluck. I opened my eyes, and by the light of the moon—it was almost full—I saw him looking directly into my face from six inches away. As soon as he saw that I was awake, he quietly blew breath out of his nose, a tiny snort, which meant "Please, can you open the door. I want to go out."

I sighed. The bed was warm, and when I had looked at the thermometer at the front door before turning in, it had read twelve below zero. For about the six millionth time, I wished Merle had a dog door up here at the cabin. However, soon after installing his dog door at the trailer, I had asked my landlady if I could put one in the cabin, which would involve cutting an opening in the logs. Her long silence had given me my answer. "It was just a thought," I added quickly. "It's not really necessary." I didn't want to push her. She was the kindest of lessors, charging me a fraction of the going rate, and, with the place's views and privacy, I certainly didn't want to leave.

Yet within days of installing the dog door at my office, I had come to appreciate how it alleviated one of the more frustrating aspects of the dog–human relationship. I simply hadn't kept track of how many times each evening Merle wanted to go outside. Now that I was no longer being his doorman at the trailer, his need to come and go at the cabin seemed outrageous. It could be half a dozen times a night.

When I thought about it, though, what was there to interest him in the cabin? He didn't read. He didn't talk on the telephone. He didn't write letters. He didn't watch TV (not that there was one). He didn't have long discussions with me about the national debt or the Persian Gulf War. Most of what he considered important was outside. And there was always the question in the back of my mind, Did he really have to pee or take a dump?

I had reached a point in my relationship with my dog from which there was no going back. I had come to admit that he had a life of his own. At least I couldn't go back easily, and, if I tried, I'd have to resort to the "just" phrase, the phrase every privileged class has used when trying to protect its interests while disregarding those of whom it considers its inferiors: He's *just* a slave; she's *just* a woman; it's *just* a dog. But after witnessing firsthand the breadth of Merle's personality, I'd then have to deal with what the psychologists call "cognitive dissonance." More bluntly, I'd have a hard time looking at myself in the mirror.

I got up and let him out.

The moose was standing twenty feet from the front door.

By how Merle reacted at that precise moment, I believed he wanted to relieve himself. He looked down the path past the moose, as if trying to figure out how to get away from the house and by the great beast without wading through the deep snow that surrounded the path.

Of course, he simply might have wanted to go on a midnight walkabout, which he loved to do; but he had eaten an unusually late dinner because of our ski, and his gestalt—that somewhat tense, ever so faintly clenched way he held himself—said, "I need to take a dump."

I saw Merle running the problem over in his mind—glancing at the deep snow to the side of the path, and then gazing at the moose, directly on the path and not giving any indication that he was about to leave. Vapor clouds poured from the moose's nostrils as he breathed, and his back was covered with frost that sparkled in the moonlight. He was magnificent. But I didn't think Merle was appreciating the moose's massive beauty.

Being an unfenced dog, Merle was quite fastidious in his toilet habits, as are all unfenced dogs. In this respect, domestic dogs who have a choice in the matter pattern their behavior after a long line of wolf ancestors who defecated away from their dens. It was these wolves, according to Bruce Fogle, the British veterinarian and animal behaviorist, who "were more likely to raise offspring that didn't suffer from heavy loads of intestinal parasites."

Merle would no more have left a turd near the cabin or the trailer than a human would have shat in his own living room. Nor was it necessary for him to mark with urine near either structure.

After his very first anointing of the porch post of the trailer upon his arrival in Kelly, he had marked only the perimeter of the properties, letting other dogs know "This is where Merle lives."

I now figured that he was going through a double bind: He didn't want to soil his house, but he also didn't want the moose to trap him in the deep snow to the side of the path. Moose are famous for rearing back and striking dogs on the head with their sharp hooves, and most dogs don't survive the incident. In fact, in North America more humans are injured each year by moose than by bears. Merle certainly didn't know these figures, but he and I had been put to flight by enough angry moose while skiing for him to have an idea that this wasn't an animal to be toyed with.

Perhaps his bowels clouded his mind. Without any warning, he ran at the moose, making a soft plosive woof while simultaneously bouncing to a stop with his front paws, as if he were trying to shoo the great deer away. The moose, an easy twelve times larger than Merle, lowered his antlers and charged, which brought him off the path and into the cleared area in front of the cabin. Merle slipped left, dashing under the moose's pendulous nose, and fled down the empty path. A good forty feet away, he turned and woofed sharply at the moose: "Woof, woof, woof, woof," four times in an angry, wounded tone, as if to say, "I was just trying to get by you."

The moose didn't bother to give chase.

"Merle," I called from the front door, where I was standing naked. "Stay."

The moose turned, sized me up, and charged. Adrenaline kicked in—I stepped back—but not in time. Fortunately, architecture intervened. The cabin had a miniature porte cochere, a little peaked roof and two small walls that provided a bit of shelter over the entryway. The moose's antlers struck these two walls, arresting him in full stride, the cabin shaking from the blow. At the very same moment, I managed to slam the door in his face. It was a half-pane door, and the moose's nose creamed the window, leaving a round, wet smudge mark, the size of a salad plate, in its very center.

My heart was jackhammering against my ribs. The moose glared at me through the window, tried once again to come through the door, and was foiled by his tremendous antlers. Collecting himself, he stalked off. When I saw him enter the spruce on the other side of the small field in front of the house, I opened the door and called to Merle, who, after a minute or so, trotted back smartly, panting with exultation: "We showed that guy."

"You know, Sir," I told him, "if you want to die that way, you can, but don't take me with you."

"Ha-ha-ha," he replied, looking quite unperturbed about the whole affair. "Not even close."

Even after this near miss I didn't make the commitment to building my own house—one that, most certainly, would have a dog door. Unbeknownst to me, however, the cabin I was so fond of was pushing me away. A year or so after moving into it, I was constantly getting sick, mostly with a stuffed nose and congested lungs that hung on for days. I even developed exercise-induced asthma and had to use an inhaler so I could ski race.

The odd part about the whole syndrome was that when I'd leave on an assignment—giving Merle's care over to friends in Kelly who would come to the trailer and feed him, and take him for hikes and skis while I was gone—I'd get better. My stuffed nasal passages would clear, my lungs would become less twitchy, my chronic tiredness would disappear. I'd return to Wyoming, and within three days I'd be sick again.

The upshot was that I had developed an allergy to the cabin, specifically to the plicatic acid that its cedar logs were emitting, a characteristic of the wood which makes it a powerful natural insecticide. This same toxic property also makes it the bane of woodworkers in the Pacific Northwest, as well as thousands of puppies whose owners raise them on beds of cedar chips in the hopes of reducing fleas. The only solution for ailing woodworkers is to leave the industry; the wheezing puppies must be removed from their fragrant beds. Drugs are only palliatives. I, too, had no choice. I moved down to the trailer and once again began to draw up plans for a house—one that wouldn't contain a single plank of cedar.

By the early summer I had some floor plans and elevations drafted, and I began to help a friend fell some trees. A horse logger, he had found a stand of dead lodgepole pines south of Teton Pass, tall, magnificent trees, a foot in diameter and 130 years old. We dragged them from their mountainside with his team of draft horses and stacked them on the half acre of land Donald and Gladys Kent had sold me. A quarter of a mile across the field from the silver trailer, it had an unobstructed view of the entire Teton Range. Merle and I would sit on top of the neat, trapezoid-shaped pile of logs, eight feet high and sixty feet long, and watch the sun set over the mountains while I'd rearrange the layout of the house in my mind.

As darkness fell we'd make the four-hundred-yard walk across the field to the trailer, and I'd take out graph paper and a T-square and draw several new versions of the floor plan. The following morning, wearing a carpenter's tool belt loaded with hammer, nails, iron tent stakes, and a ball of orange surveyor cord, I'd walk back across the field to lay out the rooms. Sometimes Merle would start with me. Sometimes I'd begin the walk alone and halfway there I'd hear him come from wherever he'd been, crashing through the sage to join me.

After staking out one of the new floor plans, I'd erect mock windows that I nailed together from one-by-two-inch strips of lumber, placing them in the imaginary walls of the rooms and varying the size of their openings as we took in their views. Finally, I'd sit in the sage—amidst the tracks of bison, deer, moose, and coyotes, whose home it had been long before it had been mine—and visualize sitting in the great room, kitchen, or bedroom.

"What'dya think?" I asked Merle on just such a morning.

Lying next to me, he had his forelegs stretched out before him, his head erect, his reddish-gold coat shining in the sun. He gave a tentative wag of his tail: "I don't know why we're sitting in the sage, but, if that's what you want to do, I'll sit here for a while longer."

A few minutes later, he gave a bored yawn, flopped on his side, and put a dramatic curve in his back as he stretched out his front and rear legs to the very tips of his toes. Yawning once again, he turned on his back and let his rear legs fall open, his front paws hanging limply over his chest. With his head thrown back in the grass, he opened his mouth as if drinking in the sun.

I watched him, my eyes running over his deep chest, the concave hollow between his last ribs, and the sparse golden hair on his stomach, its pinkish skin scattered with brown freckles the size of pinto beans. The golden hair resumed its fullness on the inside of his thighs and where his scrotum once was. In his supine position, I could also see the lovely fronds of creamy fur between each of his toe pads, giving them an exotic, wintry look even in June. The pads themselves were gray, rough, and striated—finely grooved—like rocks carved by glaciers. His nails and dewclaws were clear and glossy except where they entered his hair, and there each wore a mahogany-colored band, suggestive of a raptor's cere. His front paws were larger than his hind ones, and beneath his tail the hair was almost straw-colored, ash blond instead of gold, the color of ripe wheat when beat upon by the noonday sun. I couldn't take my eyes from him. Innocent, graceful, and completely finished, he didn't have a trace of self-consciousness.

Looking at me out of the corner of his eye, he now squirmed, rubbing his back on the grass. In a puppy, especially if accompanied by trembling, this sort of behavior would imply "I'm far beneath you in status; you have nothing to fear from me." Older dogs also engage in this maneuver if they're afraid of another dog or a person. In fact, they'll even sometimes piddle on themselves to get the message across: "I am just a little puppy and harmless." The posture almost always works—virtually no dog will attack another dog who's lying on its back in the defenseless position of a youngster.

Older dogs who are in an easygoing relationship with their human will frequently adopt a variant of this position, exposing their bellies to their person as a token of their feeling safe and content as well as inviting a belly rub. Subordinate wolves who have a friendly relationship toward an alpha wolf will also act this way toward the more dominant animal.

Merle's behavior, though, didn't make it clear that this was what he was saying to me—that he viewed himself as subordinate. In fact, he reached out a paw and touched my arm: "Excuse me, haven't you forgotten something?"

I began to rub his chest, and he breathed deeply, extending his head deeper into the grass. As my hand came up to his throat and lingered, he scrunched his neck, making several rapid movements against my fingers, indicating, "Scratch higher, please." I ran my nails over the bottom of his jaw and his entire body melted in utter contentment. He let out a groan. I stopped—to test him. A few seconds later, he touched my hand with his paw: "Don't stop." I worked my fingers to the very tip of his chin where the golden hair met his black lips, and he extended his neck and head in a stretch of supreme pleasure while pressing his chin hard against my fingers.

Michael Fox has pointed out how captive wolves will solicit grooming from one of their pack mates in a similar way, the one being solicited licking the other around the genitals as well as "besnuffling" the other, as he says, "around the ears, eyes, neck, shoulder, and corners of the mouth." Sometimes it was actually the alpha wolf whom Fox observed soliciting attention from a subordinate; sometimes it was wolves of equal rank who groomed each other.

I had also witnessed similar behavior taking place between Merle and his friends. Merle would let both Zula and Jack nuzzle his stomach. And Zula had become his equal and Jack his subordinate, their ranks clearly distinguished by Merle's willingness to share his food with Zula but giving Jack a sound smack on the side of the head with his eyetooth and a vicious growl when the younger dog tried to nose into his bowl.

So I continued to ask myself: Did Merle consider himself equal, subordinate, or dominant to me—or could he be all three? The answer came to me over several years, and what I saw changed my entire understanding of the dog–human relationship. In the meantime, when it came to his dog–dog relationships, an event was about to occur that showed me that not only did he have a highly refined sense of what it meant to be top dog, but that he could also employ an enviable degree of wile to keep himself in that position.

Clapping my hands, I said, "Enough of this lollygagging, let's get to work."

He leapt to his feet, shook briskly from nose to tail, then watched attentively as I began to rearrange the dimensions of the orange surveyor cord. We heard a noise and looked up. A woman in her twenties was rollerblading down the road past our land. Athletically trim, she had short brown hair and was dressed in cut-off shorts and a tank top. A large, white German Shepherd was towing her along on the end of one of those retractable leads that hadn't made their appearance in Kelly before the arrival of this woman, since no one walked their dog on a leash. But there was a good reason this woman kept her dog on a lead. In the few short weeks since she, her white dog, her boyfriend, and another, standard-colored German Shepherd had moved to Kelly, the white Shepherd had sent four of the village's dogs to the vet with lacerations—or so I had heard.

I hadn't actually spoken with any of the injured dogs' humans, and, like many of the stories filtering through the village, it was hard to tell how many people had added their two cents to the stories in retelling them. Merle's and my experience with the white

Shepherd had been placid. When we had biked by the woman's house (I'll call her Ms. W. after her white dog), her two Shepherds had always been chained by the front door and seemed to be models of canine citizenship, not barking or making the slightest move toward us. Merle, however, had not gone to them in his usual friendly way. He had kept his distance, staring at them without breaking his stride.

How the white Shepherd could have inflicted all this damage while being chained and kept on a lead escaped me. We now discovered her method. The moment she saw Merle standing next to me in the sage, she changed direction, tore the lead from the woman's hand, and hurtled off the road toward us. Merle looked up, his tail erect and stiff.

Without a bark or growl—a sure indication that a dog means business—the Shepherd plowed into him and knocked him off his feet. They fell in a melee of biting and savage growling. I didn't hesitate. The white Shepherd had fifteen pounds on Merle, and had him pinned to the ground by his throat. I reared back and kicked her in the flank, the force of my kick sending her sprawling and yelping.

The woman started to scream, "Stop! You're killing my dog!"

I paid no attention to her. I had never seen a dog act so viciously. The white Shepherd displayed none of the ritualized fighting behavior that all the dogs I knew engaged in while taking each other on—slapping each other around the face with their eyeteeth and rising on their hind legs to grapple each other with their forelegs. This dog acted toward Merle the way Merle acted toward ground squirrels: Pin, bite, kill.

Taking no chances, I kicked her again before she could recover. Doubled over, she fled to the woman, who was still shouting at me that I was trying to kill her dog.

I knelt and put my arm protectively around Merle's shoulders, who was on his feet and bristling. His thick ruff had saved him, and, miraculously, he wasn't bleeding.

"You tried to kill my dog," the woman yelled again from the road.

"Your dog," I shouted back, "tried to kill my dog."

"Your dog," she shrieked, "isn't on a lead. That's against the law. No one here has their dogs on leashes. I don't understand it."

We were barking at each other like dogs.

"Excuse me," I said, trying to control my voice with sarcasm, though I was shaking with fear and rage. "My dog was on my property. He was standing by my side, when you lost control of your dog. She attacked him with no provocation and had him down on the ground by the throat. You want to make a case out of this?"

"Everyone here hates my dog," the woman shouted, and then she began to cry.

"She's beat up four dogs," I retorted. "Now five. You need to control her."

"I will, I will," the woman yelled at me. "I'm sorry, I'm sorry." Keeping the white Shepherd on a short lead, she skated off.

"Can you believe that?" I said to Merle.

He gave a halfhearted wag of his tail: "No, I can't."

As we went back to staking out the rooms, my mind was in turmoil. What, I asked myself, what was wrong with the white Shepherd? She had come into a peaceful hamlet where all the dogs got along and suddenly started beating them up. It was easy to say that she thought of herself as the top dog in Kelly, but relying on the timeworn notion of dominance to explain her problem didn't fully uncover what was going on. There are a lot of dominant dogs who don't rip other dogs apart, nor do most dominant wolves administer corporal punishment to subordinate pack members. It has even been shown that the longest-lived alpha wolves are benevolent leaders whose pack members cooperate harmoniously. In wolf society, a heavy paw—what might be called the Joseph Stalin approach to leadership—leads to acrimony, strife, and palace coups. Merle, who seemed to be well on his way to becoming the dominant dog in Kelly, never used such threats. His style was Bill Clinton's—an engaging aw-shucks, let's sit down and have some ribs and talk about this.

And although the white Shepherd seemed self-assured, she more than likely wasn't. In fact, the opposite was probably the case. The chances were good that her need to dominate others came not from being strong but from being weak—from being an underdog, a term that has come to be used with approbation in human sporting contests but in 1887 was coined to mean exactly what it says: the dog who found itself on the bottom during a dog-fight, who, having been beaten, was helpless and on the ground.

There are two varieties of this unhappy state. The first starts by a dog not getting what it wants, which breeds frustration. The second entails being victimized, which breeds fear. In both cases, the dog can react to its low status by acceptance or by becoming a poseur. If the poseur isn't checked, it can become a bully, sometimes a violent one.

The entire syndrome may have begun by the white Shepherd's having been removed from her mother and littermates before or during her primary socialization period, when she was three to five weeks old. It is during this time that puppies learn to play together and begin to understand the difference between biting for real and biting softly during sparring matches. As the dog behaviorist Steven R. Lindsay notes, "If they exceed a certain limit in how hard they bite or bite in the wrong place, the partner will either yelp and quit playing or retaliate by attacking them." Being penalized for biting roughly gives young dogs a sense of appropriate behavior and fair play.

However, the white Shepherd's case seemed additionally complex since it was obvious that, while chained in front of her house, she was well behaved. Only when walking with her person did she attack other dogs. More than likely, these attacks occurred because the white Shepherd felt compelled to protect Ms. W. This need was probably fostered by Ms. W. herself as she transmitted her own fears to her dog. Usually, people do this unconsciously by tightening on the lead when approaching other dogs or people as well as by changing the expression on their faces—widening the eyes or rounding the mouth, for instance, in the universal signs of apprehension that dogs can read so exquisitely. Perhaps Ms. W., like thousands of people, had gotten a big dog on purpose—a dog of a breed with a genetic predisposition toward aggressive behavior—in the hope that it would protect her. To be fair, such dogs almost never become aggressive without the proper reinforcement, the human rewarding their first lunges and barks at other dogs and humans with a "Good dog." Just as often, the reward can be more subtle: the dog not getting a check by voice or, if that doesn't work, by leash, so that it learns that its aggressive behavior will be permitted. Tragically, the more fearful the person is, and the less the dog is checked, the more ingrained becomes its aggression.

When I replayed the incident, I realized that Ms. W. had made no attempt whatsoever to call her attacking Shepherd back. She didn't sing out, "No!" or "Heel!" as her dog raced toward Merle. And perhaps it wouldn't have done any good. The white Shepherd, like many aggressive dogs, probably hadn't been trained to obey the basic commands of no, sit, come, and stay.

The situation I now found myself in was uncomfortable. One of the most refreshing aspects of living in Kelly was that people left each other alone. Even the most eccentric of us (and there was eccentricity aplenty) could live as we wished. Yet the white Shepherd was dangerous, and if Ms. W. wanted to live in the village, or, for that matter, anywhere with other dogs and people, it might be helpful if someone spoke to her about working with her dog. She could begin by gently introducing the Shepherd to other dogs—at a safe distance—while maintaining control over her with something more than a retractable lead. She could use the sort of halter collar that fits around a dog's head. A muzzle also might save a lot of strife. If the Shepherd didn't lunge, she could reward her with a kind word and perhaps a treat. If these measures weren't successful, fluoxetine, the canid version of Prozac, might help. The association between aggressive behavior and abnormal brain chemistry has been well documented, and a serotonin reuptake inhibitor might calm the Shepherd and make her more receptive to training. I really didn't want to be the someone who spoke to Ms. W., but if the white Shepherd eventually killed a dog, especially my dog, I'd feel awful.

Later that day, while Merle was off on his own business, I walked over to Ms. W.'s house and tried to explain how she might help her Shepherd without broaching the subject of the possible causes of the dog's aggression: You're a fearful person, and your fears have created a monster. We stood at her front door, her two Shepherds locked inside, the white one growling menacingly. Ms. W. said that the white Shepherd was "really a very loving and affectionate dog," but had a "few problems." She said that she was "working on them with her," and that I shouldn't worry because she was "always on her chain." From now on, she'd keep her under a "tight leash" when walking. She said that she was sorry about a dozen times.

Though I wasn't sleeping in the cabin, I still cooked there, sleeping outside, under the stars, with Merle by my side. On the very day that Merle had been attacked by the white Shepherd, I had redrawn the floor plan, filled out an application for a construction loan, and revised an article for an upcoming deadline. Hungry and preoccupied, I left the trailer with Merle in the early evening, biking down the dirt lane and turning onto the potholed blacktop. In an instant, I realized that we had to go by the white Shepherd's house. In fact, I could see her in the distance, chained by the front door with her companion.

Merle was trotting by my side, and for a moment I considered turning around and biking home the long way through the field, across our land, down the main road of the village, and finally over to the river—almost a mile out of our way. It seemed unnecessary.

Merle wasn't a fighter, and I trusted him to stay by my side. He had always trotted by the white Shepherd's house, and, previous to this morning's incident, he had never been in a fight. He was larger than all the females in the village except her, and any uncut males who were his own size didn't view him as a threat since he was neutered. When they tried to mount him, he neither fought them nor stood for their displays of dominance. Instead, he slipped his butt away from them and met them chest to chest.

His reaction now took me by surprise. As we approached the house, the hair on Merle's back stood up like an electrified Mohawk, and his breath began to rasp.

Before I could react, he broke into a gallop and dashed across the lawn toward the two Shepherds, fangs bared and growling viciously.

"Merle," I bellowed. "No!"

The white Shepherd leapt to her feet and tore out to meet him. My only thought was "She's going to rip his head off."

Merle knew better. He skidded to a stop just as she was jerked backward by her chain and crashed in a heap. Somehow, he had calculated the precise length of her tether. Bouncing to her feet, she lunged at him. To no avail.

Dancing his front paws up and down, Merle pattered eighteen inches from her slavering jaws. His snarl was gone. His lips were down. "Ha-ha-ha!" he panted. "Ha-ha-ha!" Had he been a child, he would have been taunting, "Nya-nya-nya-nya-nya."

This totally undid the white Shepherd. Her barks rose into one long hysterical shriek of rage. Foam flew from her mouth. Hideous, she surged against her chain, choking herself as Merle continued his little dance in front of her, laughing in her face. The other Shepherd had stood, but remained behind the white Shepherd, watching.

"Merle," I shouted at the top of my lungs, fearing that she'd tear her chain from the logs. "Come! Come now!"

He whipped around and followed me as I rode off.

Trotting by my side, he panted jubilantly, wagging his tail from side to side like a medieval soldier waving a campaign banner.

"You are so bad!" I cried. But I couldn't hold back my laughter. "Way bad."

He stepped gaily, and his eyes sparkled at me: "Got her."

How had he known how long her chain was—known so exactly that he had charged to within a foot and a half of her? The only thing I could think of was that while on his rounds he had seen her stretch the chain to its full extent, had marked that place on her lawn, had filed that distance away in his mind, and then used it to his advantage. His revenge was straight out of Che Guevara's manual: Know the terrain; hit the enemy at its weakest; never use brute strength. He was now so full of himself, he was bursting at the seams.

"You be careful, Sir," I warned him. "What if she hadn't been on her chain?"

He tossed his head at me: "Don't sweat it, Ted. I got it wired."

In this he was mistaken.

In late April, a couple of weeks before our horses arrived, I went over to Idaho and bought an old but serviceable four-horse trailer and a used, three-quarter-ton pickup truck to pull it. I had always taken delivery of leased horses at the trailhead and returned them at the same place. Now, wanting to keep the horses in Kelly and do a variety of pack trips over the summer, I needed a rig.

I held open the door of the pickup, and Merle jumped onto the front seat as if he had been doing it his entire life. Puffed up and holding himself erect, he sat with electric anticipation as I fastened a specially made dog seat belt around his shoulders and chest. When I got behind the wheel, he sat even taller, holding my eyes, as if to say, "Guess what? I'm a big dog now. In fact, I'm as tall as you." Clearly, sitting in the front seat of the truck with me—

instead of behind me in the back of the Datsun, and more recently our new Subaru—had given him increased status.

Within minutes, he let me know this in no uncertain terms. Without any apparent motion, he somehow maneuvered himself across the front seat so that his left haunch was pressed against my right thigh. Staring straight ahead, he leaned against me until he had pushed me against the door.

"Sir," I said, laughing and pushing him across the seat. "What gives?"

Five minutes later, he was back at it, leaning against me and staring straight ahead with a proud and arrogant expression. I pushed him away again, and, sure enough, within minutes, he inched across the seat until his full weight was bearing on me.

Evidently, sitting in the front seat with me, our heads at equal height, had given him license to change our status—leaning against another animal is one way in which both wolves and dogs express dominance.

"Okay, enough of this," I told him, pushing him firmly away and pointing a finger directly at him while looking him straight in the eye. "None of this one-upmanship. You lie right down there." I pointed to the opposite side of the bench seat.

Raising his snout, he glanced away and laughed, "Ha-ha-ha." Then he lay down, wriggling his butt so that the base of his tail just grazed my thigh. Turning his head, he gave me a quizzical over-the-shoulder look: "Is that okay?"

"Touching's fine," I told him, "but no pushing."

He gave me another panty laugh, and down the road we went in our new blue pickup.

The four horses lived in a corral that I had built near our pile of house logs. Merle had been quite intrigued by the corral's erection, for ever since watching the building of his doghouse, and the installation of his dog door, he had gotten the impression that a nail belt and tools had something to do with him. The doghouse had not been much fun, but clearly the dog door had been a triumph. So he followed my spiking the rails and bucks together, just as he had watched my staking out our new home's dimensions.

When the four horses arrived, it suddenly all made sense to him: Ted using his nail belt and tools meant a corral, and that equaled horses. In an instant, he was like a commoner before royalty. He gazed up at the horses with adoration; he followed them around, smelling their legs and avoiding their kicks; within minutes, he rolled in their poop, wearing the goofy expression cats adopt when they've buried their nose in catnip. He was in seventh heaven, and more so when we went riding, which was about every afternoon.

But instead of trailing me, as he did when we hiked, he immediately trotted in front of the horse I was riding, a sorrel quarter horse named Tinker. Tail erect, head swiveling left and right, Merle led us down the trail, letting everyone know that he was in charge. To test him, I clucked Tinker into a trot and went by him. Immediately, Merle loped into a gallop and took the lead. This was so unlike him that I dismounted, tethered Tinker to a sage bush, and began to hike. Without hesitation, Merle dropped behind me. I returned to Tinker, mounted, put him into a walk, and Merle dashed in front of us and led once again. Apparently, he had his own notions of our little family's hierarchy: Ted on ground, Merle follows; Ted on horse, Merle leads.

One June evening we were proceeding in this fashion—Merle ahead, Tinker and I behind him—deep into the prairie that lies between Kelly and the Snake River. Merle climbed a slight rise and stopped short, his gaze on something in the distance. Tinker took a few more steps, and we were able to see what had caught Merle's attention. Twenty yards off, a half dozen bison glanced up from their grazing and turned toward us.

We advanced to Merle's right side, and the three of us stared at the huge shaggy animals. They were shedding their winter coats and the black fur hung from their shoulders in ropy tatters.

Merle and Tinker continued to watch the bison with excitement. Then Merle glanced up at me with a longing expression. Tinker read his energy and turned his ears back, the way a horse does when he's waiting for direction. I don't know why I did it, but I did. I clucked my tongue, and Tinker and Merle both shot forward.

The bison grunted and wheeled. We closed the gap and galloped among them, hooves thundering, the air sharp with wooly musk. Merle streaked ahead, his mouth open in utter glee as he pulled abreast of the lead bison and matched him stride for stride.

Finally, reason prevailed. I pulled on the reins, whistled to Merle, and the three of us slowed, the bison cantering off and leaving us blowing. Tinker tossed his head the way horses do when they're charged up and playful, and Merle sent me an ecstatic grin: "At last, you came to your senses!" And in the world of horses and dogs, just for an instant, I had.

These were childish days. The dawn came early, the dusk was long, the valley green from the warm spring rains. In the heat of the afternoon, Merle and I would walk to the Gros Ventre River and jump off the big eddy rock. Side by side, we'd float down the emerald channel, both of us dog-paddling and smiling at each other in the easiness of the current. Sometimes I'd come up behind him and put my arms around his chest, and sometimes he'd swim up my back and hang his paws on my shoulders. Just before the waterfall, we'd angle to shore and shake ourselves off on the rocky beach. Spying a stick, I'd pick it up and rear it over my head to test him.

He'd look at me with his head cocked, not cringing in the least, in fact staring at me placidly, with an expression that said, "I'm over those puppyhood fears. I'm a big dog now."

I'd toss the stick into the water, and he'd give it his cool appraisal and look back at me, one brow going up, the other down, signifying, "That doesn't mean I'll fetch. That's for other dogs."

In August, Benj and I rode the Continental Divide from Jackson Hole to the border of Yellowstone National Park, riding at twelve thousand feet across the Buffalo Plateau and dropping into the head of unnamed drainages to camp. Hour after hour, Merle led us across the high tundra, occasionally disappearing over a hill, only to reappear ten or fifteen minutes later on an escarpment ahead of us, where he'd look down and laugh at our slowness.

For a week we rode under the blue sky, picketing the horses in the late afternoons and letting them graze as we lay on our saddle blankets with a switch of grass in our teeth, our noses filled with the pungent scent of horses and the fragrance of lupine.

After a few days, time collapsed and my life started anew, tasting like my first kiss with a sixteen-year-old girl who had never taken a sip of coffee or drunk wine or smoked a cigarette. The purple lupine was from that time, and the pine-filled air was from that time, and my reddish-gold dog was from that time, lying with his head upon my chest, paws twitching, as he led our horses through his dreams.

Back in Kelly, on writing days, we'd often walk in the afternoon, especially when I was having problems with the piece I was working on. I'd whistle for Merle, and we'd saunter down the river road while I'd ponder where the piece might go, ruminating on its difficulties "like a camel," as Henry David Thoreau once noted in his great essay on walking. It was also in this essay that Thoreau recounted an anecdote about William Wordsworth. A visitor asked the poet's servant if he might see her master's study. "Here is his library," the servant replied, "but his study is out of doors."

I couldn't help but think that the same was true of myself— that much of my study was done outside, and that it was Merle who helped me to read the books of that library. He had shown me how to smell the wind; he had taught me the importance of getting down on all fours and putting my nose into the ground; now, he demonstrated how to read between the lines.

We were tracking some pronghorn antelope, and Merle kept smelling the prints and lifting his nose, smelling the prints and lifting his nose, as if following a scent that oscillated. Putting my own nose to the spoor, I could detect nothing. Yet later, when we found the herd and I shot one of the antelope, I put my nose directly on her hooves. The result was startling: The cleft in her back hooves smelled far more strongly of pronghorn—that tangy mix of herbivore and sage—than did her front hooves. Since then, every antelope whose hooves I've smelled, smelled exactly this way, and not one person to whom I've recounted this observation has ever said, "I knew that." Nor has any book I've read mentioned it. But Merle knew it, as no doubt countless wolves and coyotes have known it—"known" meaning "experienced." And I learned it by watching him.

On just such a post-writing day we were walking down the river road—I thinking about some intractable paragraphs, Merle loping ahead, deep in his world of odors. Curiously, when we walked in and around Kelly, as opposed to the backcountry, he always led, as if this were his territory and he was leading an apprentice around. To our right was an irrigation ditch, overgrown with tall summer grass, and beyond it stretched a mowed field of alfalfa, used to feed the horses and longhorns on the neighboring Teton Valley Ranch.

Suddenly, Merle's nose whipped right. In the same motion, he leapt into the ditch. Out popped a coyote, Merle in hot pursuit. The coyote glanced over its shoulder and adopted the disdainful lope that coyotes have when being chased by dogs: "You catch me? Right." Perhaps it was the coyote's obvious contempt for him, or the memory of the coyote pack beating him up, that sent Merle into a startling burst of speed. The coyote must have heard him coming. It looked back and its eyes bugged out—Merle was a stride away. The coyote began to run in panic; Merle kept apace; and I watched in silence. This was a score to be settled without any interference from me.

A moment later Merle surged upon the coyote, striking it on its left hip with his right shoulder and knocking it off its feet. That's all he did. As the coyote regained its footing and fled with its tail stuck between its legs, Merle turned and sprinted back to me, cleared the irrigation ditch in a bound, landed on the road where I stood in amazement, and began to turn circles in the air, barking in wild paroxysms of glee. I hadn't heard him bark since getting off the bush plane in Salmon, Idaho. But this was a special occasion. He had finally counted coup on the coyotes, and in one of the most elemental ways that dogs can show their dominance—by pushing aside another dog with a blow of the shoulder or the hip.

I knelt by him and stroked my hands over his head while he stared into the field where the coyote had disappeared. Eyes aglow, he pulsed with elation.

"You *are* a big dog now!" I exclaimed.

The truth of these words became apparent over the next few days as Merle's demeanor changed. He had always been friendly to the other dogs in Kelly, smelling their butts as they smelled his, wagging his tail, and romping with them. But I now noticed that he took on magisterial airs with those dogs who tried to fawn over him. As they licked his lips, whined, and groveled for attention, he inflated his posture, tail stiff and arced over his back, and gazed into the distance. Giving them only a few seconds of his time, he walked on.

"You have certainly become the grandee, Señor," I told him.

Holding his head high, he pranced ahead.

At least with his very good friends, Zula and Jack, he remained unchanged, though I did notice that the three of them no longer tore in frantic circles after each other. Occasionally, they burst into a small game of chase and chew, but the high energy of their puppyhood was gone.

I was also happy to see that Merle's lording it over some of the village dogs didn't extend to any of his people—at least the adults. With children, he became more bold. From an early age, in fact when she was still in her high chair, Tessa had fed Merle tidbits, putting her entire hand in his mouth and allowing him to gently remove the food from her fingers. I had never seen him try to steal food from her or anyone else, but this now changed.

He was sitting next to one of Tessa's friends, a tow-headed four-year-old boy named Petey, who, along with Tessa and some other children, was watching the rodeo in Jackson. The children's eyes were fixed on the barrel racing while Merle gazed serenely into the distance, the epitome of canine sobriety, a being for whom the rodeo, even with its horses and manure smells, presented no attraction.

This was a façade, and it wouldn't be his last.

The moment Petey absentmindedly let his ice-cream cone dangle from his hand, Merle leaned toward him without moving a paw, and, with a quiet roll of his tongue, whisked the scoop of vanilla ice cream from the cone with such finesse that Petey never knew it was gone. Swallowing his treat, Merle drifted back to his studied pose, the guardian watching over his children.

A moment later, Petey raised his ice-cream cone to his mouth and found nothing. "Waaaa!" He burst into tears, and Merle glanced this way and that with a startled look on his face: "What?! What happened? Is everything all right? What can I do?"

This ability to feign disinterest while plotting a stratagem became one of his trademarks. Lying on the porch of the trailer, for instance, he'd ignore our neighbor's semi-captive raven, who was free to fly around Kelly. The bird would perch on our trailer's roof, cawing down at Merle. Chin on his paws, studying the aspens, Merle would affect deafness: "Raven? What raven?" On and on the raven would caw. Finally, unable to goad Merle into a response, the bird would swoop down and hit Merle with his wing.

Like a coiled spring, Merle would leap into the air, snapping his
jaws at the raven, who, equally clever, hovered just out of reach
and flew off low and slow enough that Merle could chase beneath
it, losing his gravitas and barking wildly in frustration—the third
time I had heard him bark.

And, of course, there was still the white Shepherd to be reckoned with—or the memory of her. As we drove by her house in
the car, Merle would stand in the back of the Subaru, the hair on
his spine on end, growling deep in his throat while staring daggers
at her front door. But she was never outside, though her companion sometimes was, and I finally assumed that Ms. W. had gotten
rid of the troublesome dog.

We took to biking by her house again, and Merle would begin
to pant violently as her cabin hove into view. But he never left my
side—never even made so much as a dart toward the other Shepherd. One afternoon, though, as we came around the bend, I spied
the white Shepherd herself, reposing on the grass in front of her
house, her companion alongside her.

Stopping, I grabbed the ruff of Merle's neck, for he had already
begun to speed up. He bolted from my grasp—ignoring my
shouted "No!"—and flew at the white Shepherd. She launched
herself at him, her teeth finding empty air as he arced within a foot
of her and her chain jerked her backwards. Snarling ferociously,
she lunged at him again. He turned around and executed a light
two-step patter with his paws, staying just beyond her reach. Before I could shout "Come!" he whirled and raced to my side, tail
beating as he laughed his head off.

Obviously, counting coup on the coyote hadn't distorted his
sense of reality. The white Shepherd wasn't someone he was going
to take on *diente a diente*.

"What can I say, Señor?" I shouted at him. "What can I say
about you?"

He bucked up and down with glee.

CHAPTER 8

The Gray Cat

By the time I found a bank willing to give me a construction loan, fall had arrived and the building season was over. We moved completely out of the cabin and into the trailer and resigned ourselves to starting the house next spring—or at least I did, since Merle seemed quite content with our new sleeping arrangements. I rolled out a pad and blankets on the living-room floor near the woodstove—the back bedroom was like a freezer—and Merle curled himself next to me.

We were soon joined by someone else. He had the smoothest pewter-gray fur and a stunning white tuxedo bib, four white paws, and intelligent yellow-green eyes. A stray cat, he had adopted one of the women who lived in the yurts, and he knew Merle and me from the time this woman and I had been seeing each other. Merle and I had spent quite a bit of time at his place, but the cat had never come to the trailer before.

When the woman left town, leaving the cat behind to fend for himself, he wandered over to the trailer and came through the dog door as if he knew exactly where he was heading. Looking a bit wan and undernourished, he went to Merle's empty bowl and sniffed it before giving it several licks of his pink tongue. Then he curled his tail around his paws and sent me an imploring look: "I'd eat dog food if you had it."

Feeling sorry for him, I gave him a cup of Merle's kibble while Merle, ten feet off, head between his paws, watched the cat eat, one brow going up, the other down, expressing his doubts about what was happening—he had a grave suspicion of cats. Finished eating, the cat walked over to Merle, who visibly tightened. When the cat had tried to make friends with him on previous occasions, Merle would have nothing of it, backing away from him, his face creased with acute worry, his eyes never leaving the cat's white paws and their concealed claws. But, in Merle's favor, it must be said that he never chased the cat or acted aggressively toward him.

The cat now touched noses with Merle as Merle held his breath. Then the cat began to tenderly lick Merle's right ear.

"We can't kick him out after that," I said to Merle.

Ignoring the cat's overtures, Merle stood and walked to his dog door. Looking over his shoulder, he cast me a look that said, "You're not really going to invite him in here, are you?"

The gray cat watched Merle leave before coming over to me and doing figure eights around my feet. I picked him up. Despite his lack of food, he must have weighed fifteen pounds. He turned in my arms. Settling himself neatly, he stared at me with his yellow-green eyes and began to purr.

Although he was a male, he had been called Roxy by the young children of his former owner. The name simply wouldn't do.

"Gray Cat," I said, capitalizing his coloration with my voice and turning it into a name. "I know it's not a fancy name, but we don't stand on ceremony here. Can you live with it?"

I put him down and went back to my desk. About an hour later, I heard the dog door slap. After taking a few more minutes to finish the paragraph I was working on, I turned around and had my answer. Merle and Gray Cat were sleeping butt to butt on the living-room couch.

The differences between cats and dogs have probably been noted since cats began to live with people in Jericho and Cyprus about seven thousand years ago: how cats are solitary and dogs social, and how cats share our homes but never lose their wildness whereas dogs become almost totally domesticated. As the archaeo-zoologist Juliet Clutton-Brock writes, "By their offerings of food, affection, and comfort humans persuade cats to share the same core area of their home range." In the case of Gray Cat, the persuasion went the other way: It was he who wooed us. Although I had had three cats before him, as well as two dogs, this was a novel situation—never before had I lived with a cat and a dog at the same time. It was now instructive to see how these two souls interacted with each other and with me.

When the first October snow fell, Merle burst out of his dog door, threw himself on his back, and rubbed in ecstasy on the cold white fluff. A minute later, Gray Cat lifted the flap of the dog door (now also the cat door) and peered out at the white landscape with a look of horror. Not believing his own eyes, he reached his paw to the snowy porch and immediately shook it off as if he had touched a toxic substance. He whirled and gave me a despairing look: "No! Winter's back!" He sprang upon the couch and curled himself into a ball.

Since he had no litter box, he was, at last, forced outside. If it was snowing and windy, he'd dash back within a minute, grimacing dramatically while he shook snow from his back. But if it was sunny, he'd actually sit on one of the porch rails. Fluffing up his fur until he looked like an enormous gray owl, he would send disapproving looks at Merle and me roughhousing in the snow. That's putting it mildly. Our clubbiness and never-flagging camaraderie disgusted him. However, I believed that Gray Cat secretly envied our friendship and wanted to join our team, for on many an afternoon, as Merle and I began our walk to the post office, he would meow enthusiastically and pad after us. After only two hundred feet, though, a look of doubt would cross his face, a sort of crushing knowledge that he was going against eons of cat evolution—cats like to slink and hide rather than march along. Poor Gray Cat;

he would sit down and look at us plaintively, almost as if saying, "I tried, guys, I really did." And then he'd turn and make his slow way back to the trailer.

Sometimes, when the February weather grew warm, he'd slip outside and hunt among the cottonwoods, looking for rodents under the snow. Once or twice I tried to follow him, but he'd stop and turn, his eyes glaring at me and saying, "I don't want you along. Can't a cat have some privacy?"

Merle, on the other hand, was always pleased to have me track him down, his body language saying, "Great, you found me. Let's go!"

In a similar fashion, their reactions to my writing were totally different. Merle would come into my office, lay his chin on my thigh, and, by wagging his tail steadily, ask if I was ready to do something fun. When the answer was "not yet," he'd return outside and find something with which to divert himself. Gray Cat, by contrast, found being a writer's cat to his liking. He would jump on my desk and lie in the sun, just beyond the keyboard, occasionally putting his paw on my fingers to stop their tapping. Then he'd glide onto my lap while I was reading and bask in my stroking him. And, of course, each night he would sleep with us in the blankets on the floor, which, I gathered, did not count as clubbiness, but just a good snuggle.

We broke ground in April, and before the backhoe came, Merle and I walked over to our land and sat in the sagebrush where the house would rise. In the skiff of new snow lay bison prints. The animals had come through the previous evening and stopped to graze on the newly sprouted grass. This I took as a good omen, and I made a promise: I'd restore the native grasses around the house so the bison would still come and graze. Merle stuffed his nose into a print, blew out a snort, and looked at me with a wagging tail: "Ah, bison."

It took about a month to dig the hole, lay the foundation, and drill a well. All this involved big machinery—earth movers, cement-mixing trucks, the drilling rig—and even though Merle went to the construction site with me each day, he didn't like the noise, standing off a ways and bounding joyously through the sage when we left.

All this changed when the four-man log crew arrived and we put on our nail belts. Nose to the subfloor, Merle padded around the newly laid plywood, which stood several feet above grade. Walking to its edge, he adopted a heroic pose, staring across Kelly with a satisfied air. The house gave him a vantage above the sage.

As we scribed and laid each log in place, he smelled them, and when the interior walls went up he inspected each room. Many dogs don't normally like to climb stairs, especially exposed ones, but as soon as we had put up a skeleton staircase, with narrow treads and no risers—an airy affair even for people—Merle scrambled up it. I had gone to the great room for a Skil Saw and heard his pant from the balcony above. He was looking down at me, lashing his tail and grinning from ear to ear: "This is so cool."

He followed the electrician around. He pushed his nose into the plumber's toolbox. Mid-morning, when I'd have to return to writing, he wouldn't follow me to the trailer; rather, he stayed on with the crew. Sometimes, at the end of the day, the crew long gone, I'd wander over to see what progress had been made, and I'd find him walking around the house as if he were tallying the day's work. Occasionally, I even found him sleeping on the deck.

He had no bed at the construction site. He wasn't fed there. His dog friends lived across the field. Yet he became fascinated by the house. I wondered if he sensed my emotional investment in the project and had taken ownership of it as well. Perhaps he saw the house as an enlargement of our territory. Or maybe it was simply interesting: the smells of the new materials; our riding around in the pickup truck; the different people who came to work on the house; and the sense that here was something fresh and engrossing to explore.

That dogs may crave this sort of stimulation is not a notion we often entertain. Yet their wild cousins, wolves, can lope dozens of miles in a day, investigating from river bottom to ridge crest, and a pack will set off on an excursion of a couple of hundred miles, only to return a few weeks later to where they began their odyssey. All the while, these animals are watching, scenting, and learning new country. They're engaged, and it was clear that Merle was, too.

If he had an inkling that this might be our new home, it was sealed on the day we installed his new dog doors—one in the front door and, several feet beyond it, one in the interior door of the mudroom. No sooner had I tightened the final through-bolt and stood up, extending a hand to the outer door, than he charged through it and without pausing leapt through the inner one as well—slap, slap. Turning to greet me as I came in, he wriggled with delight and gave me a throaty pant: "Yes, home, sweet home."

The roof went up. The windows came. We stained and chinked the logs. Often, I made it up as I went along, redrawing a detail at night and bringing it over to the log crew the following morning. Luckily, the architect whom I had engaged to do the detailed drawings lived just down the road in Kelly, and sometimes when I couldn't figure out how many stairs were needed to reach the second floor or whether a log would carry a structural load, I'd bike my quick sketches over to his house, and he'd redraw them.

On just such a day, I had ridden some sketches over to him and he had drawn a few variations of the new porch I had visualized. None was exactly what I had in mind, and I decided to fetch a book from the trailer, which had a photograph of what I wanted. Jumping on my bike, I said, "I'll be back in a minute."

Off I went, Merle loping at my side. The architect lived about two hundreds yards down the road from the white Shepherd's house, but I was no longer concerned about her. Her house had been vacant for days.

I saw their cars first, in the driveway, then the two Shepherds themselves, lounging before the front step of the house.

We were still fifty yards off when Merle broke into a sprint. The white Shepherd saw him coming and hurtled out to meet him. This time she wasn't on her chain.

Merle didn't stop or hesitate. He must have known that stopping was pointless. They met halfway across her lawn, going full-tilt, and she bowled Merle over, her momentum carrying her several feet beyond him. He sprang up as she turned and began to savage her around the neck. She roared and bit him back.

I jumped off my bike as Ms. W's boyfriend raced from the house. We each grabbed a dog's tail—I, Merle; he, the white Shepherd—and pulled them apart. Snarling, they tried to get at each other, and we dragged them off, calling to each other, "I'm sorry. I'm sorry."

Holding on to Merle's ruff, I escorted him around the bend and gave him a quick glance—nothing damaged. Jumping on my bike, I said, "Come on, let's go."

He looked back down the road.

"Don't even think about it," I told him.

He wagged his tail hopefully. "No way. Let's go." I began to pedal, and he followed me to the trailer. As I tried to find the book, Merle drank some water and lay down in the middle of the living room.

"Okay," I said, "let's take the long way."

Stiffly, he got to his feet and it was then that I noticed he was lying in a pool of blood.

Dropping the book, I knelt by him and parted the hair on his shoulder. The white Shepherd had slashed him down to the scapula.

"Oh, Merle," I moaned. "That looks really bad."

He regarded me stoically. I ran to the bathroom, got some compresses, and began to apply pressure. Picking him up, so he wouldn't have to walk and open the wound further, I put him in the car and drove to the vet.

Several stitches later, we drove back through Kelly and by the white Shepherd's house. Merle jumped up and growled menacingly.

"Hey," I said, "you won. Look."

The white Shepherd, her standard-colored companion, and the two cars were gone. The shades were drawn, the house deserted.

Still, every time we rode by the white Shepherd's house, whether in the car or by bike, Merle would pant hoarsely, his hair standing on end, his eyes blazing.

When this had happened a half dozen times, I stopped and straddled my bike. "Look, Señor," I told him, "she is really gone. I saw a For Rent sign at the post office. Go ahead and take a look." I motioned with my hand to the front door.

Gingerly, he crossed the lawn and smelled where the white Shepherd had lain on the grass, the stone steps leading to the lintel, and the front door itself. He glanced back at me and a slow smile crossed his face: "Yep, she's gone."

Then he raised his leg and peed on the steps. Scratching mightily, he cast dirt against the door.

He trotted smartly to my side and off we went. He didn't pant in triumph or wag his tail jubilantly. Instead, his face wore a satisfied look of accomplishment. Perhaps, I thought, he hadn't been far off the mark when he had told me, "Don't sweat it, Ted, I got it wired." The white Shepherd had left, peace had returned to the world of Kelly's dogs, and he was never in another dogfight as long as he lived.

On the day the floor finishers put the final coat of polyurethane on the pine floors, I walked over from the trailer to have a look. During the months in which the house had been built, many people had stopped by and walked through the house, since it wasn't every day a new log home went up in Kelly. To prevent such visitors from inadvertently stepping on the newly finished floors, I had asked the floor finishers to lock the sliding doors to the deck and the front door when they left. But I had forgotten to mention the dog door.

Opening the front door, I saw a line of dog prints, each print with its four toes and large central pad pressed deeply into the still tacky polyurethane. The line of prints walked to the wood stove, stopped, did a cloverleaf to the main window of the great room and looked outside, then walked back across the room and into the hallway. When I raised my eyes, there was Merle, standing on the balcony above the great room, his head between two balusters as he grinned down at me and wagged his tail with great enthusiasm: "This looks terrific."

I sighed. "Come on down, please," I said, gesturing to him with a curled index finger. He whirled and I heard him bounding down the stairs. Across the great room he ran, leaving another set of tracks.

"Ah, Sir," I said, kneeling before him and giving him a pet as he stuck his head against my chest. "I'm glad it meets with your approval."

Several days later, when the floor had fully dried, the floor finishers returned. They resanded and refinished the great room, the hall, the stairs, and the balcony—all of the balcony, that is, except the corner where Merle had stood, looking down at me and wagging his tail. I had asked them to leave his pawprints there. Years later, they're still there, overlooking the house he helped to build.

By October, I'd gone through my budget and had to let the carpenters go. I did the rest of the finish work myself: the kitchen counters and cabinets, the daybed in the alcove, the mudroom, the balustrade for the stairs going to the second floor. On Halloween evening, I took off my nail belt, put some wood on the fire, opened a beer, and pulled a chair in front of the stove's blazing window. Merle lay at my feet. The house glowed around us, and he turned on his back and looked up at me out of the corner of his eye. Thump-thump-thump went his tail.

"Yep," I agreed. "We done good."

The only thing remaining was to bring what little furniture we had in the trailer, as well as Gray Cat, over to the new place. A couple of pickup truckloads moved all my kitchen stuff, the couch, and my books.

It was now the first week in November and it had been snowing heavily for several days. Putting on leather gloves and a stout canvas jacket, I went back for Gray Cat. I had learned the hard way—on visits to the vet for Gray Cat's inoculations—that he hated to ride in vehicles. My hands and arms bore the scars of his anger.

As I carried him from the trailer, and he spied the truck, he began to struggle and claw at me. I hustled him into the cab, and the moment I released him he launched himself against the window, bouncing off of it. I marveled that he hadn't broken his neck. He then set to yowling at the top of his lungs, as if he were being drawn and quartered.

At the new house, I bundled him into my arms as he screeched and scratched me. Hurrying him across the porch and through the mudroom, I deposited him in the great room before the toasty woodstove.

He looked around—up to the twenty-foot-high ridge log, to the beckoning alcove with its brightly colored throw and fluffy pillows, to the kitchen, to his bowls that I had put out, and he turned, walked directly to the front door, and, slap-slap, left.

I ran after him. Plodding through the deep drifts, he was heading across the field to the trailer.

"Gray Cat," I called.

He looked back at me, eyes burning with hatred.

I went inside and watched him from the great room's large picture window.

"Can you believe that cat?" I said to Merle.

Merle gazed out the window where I had pointed.

Gray Cat, looking like Dr. Zhivago trying to find Lara, was disappearing into the wind-whipped snow.

The next day I tried to bring him over again. The results were the same: He fled the house and plodded across the drifts, back to what he considered home.

I shut off the heat at the trailer and gave him no food. I let three days go by and went back. He was curled in the corner of the trailer's living room. The place was freezing, and he looked weak and malnourished.

"Gray Cat," I said, "please come to the new house. There is nothing here. It's over."

I picked him up. The instant we stepped outside and he saw the truck, he fought me. I got him over to the new house and held him in my arms as I walked him around, showing him his bowls full of cat chow and water. When I let him down, he streaked out the cat door.

Running after him, I pleaded, "Gray Cat."

He ignored me, plowing through the drifts with an intensity that was hard to misread: "I would rather die in the trailer than live here."

So be it.

Seven and a half hours later, just as it was getting dark at four-thirty in the afternoon, I heard a meow, or thought I did. I gave it no mind. Shortly, there came another meow and another.

Coming downstairs, I saw Gray Cat sitting on the back deck in front of the sliding glass door. I looked at him, and he looked directly at me. There was no humility in his expression. His expression said, "Open the door."

Why he hadn't gone around to the cat door was an interesting question. It meant another fifty yards of travel through the deep snow, and perhaps Gray Cat was tired of playing Dr. Zhivago.

I slid open the door and he walked in, glancing left, right, and up to the ceiling with the attitude of a discriminating buyer of high-end objects. Spying the alcove, he walked directly to it, sprang onto the daybed, turned to face Merle and me, lay down, took another glance around the great room, and began to lick his paws with a weary air that implied, "Well, this will have to do."

"Gray Cat," I told him, "you are a piece of work."

Unperturbed, he raised his head and stared at me. There was no apology in his eyes, no attempt at ingratiation. Every molecule of him said, "Just remember, I am not that dog."

CHAPTER 9

Estrogen Clouds

We kept a bachelor household, it's true; but it was hardly monkish. Merle had always welcomed female guests at the trailer, and our new location on the main road provided him with an expanded social network. There was Josie, a round and jolly chocolate Lab. There was Boone, a spry little Border Collie. There was Emmy, a soulful Golden Retriever. And, of course, there was his old flame, Zula, who made the trek across the field. But since all of them were neutered, nothing came of their friendship except exuberant play.

Gray Cat, on the other hand, wanted nothing to do with his own kind, male or female. He was a being about whom Charles Dickens's description of Ebenezer Scrooge seemed apt: "secret, and self-contained, and solitary as an oyster." Sans balls—and as far as I could tell sans any passions besides hunting and snoozing—he left on his nightly forays, only to return at daybreak with the occasional offering of the tail end of a rodent at my bedside to show what he had been about. Cool and careful as a sniper, he never came home with a tattered ear or gashed forehead, some wound of honor demonstrating that he'd been in a territorial or mating fray.

As for me, I carried only one major wound of the latter sort, and it had healed well. In fact, it seemed to have occurred in another lifetime. If I caught the whiff of estrogen blowing my way, I had no reservations about raising my nose and following, which, at least at the trailer, led to some amusing moments.

Since I had no bed, my loves and I often found ourselves on the floor. There we'd be, going at it, when suddenly we'd feel a third party thrusting away behind us.

Breaking into laughter, one woman said, "Do you do *everything* with your dog?"

"Excuse me, Sir," I told Merle. "Could you find someplace else to go?"

Grumpily, he curled up in the corner.

Building a house with an actual bed thus conveyed some advantages to my love life, for Merle wouldn't climb on the bed without an invitation. The trailer, though, had given me a significant insight into my dog: Neutered or not, the only thing missing from his libido was the proper stimulus.

It took me by no surprise, then, when I spied him solicitously guiding a little white-and-black dog toward the house one fine spring morning, his eyes star-struck, his tongue lolling out of his mouth in lustful appreciation of her perfume.

He came through the dog door first, and the wee dog, a Jack Russell Terrier, vaulted in after him. They began to cavort around each other, and without further ado Merle crouched over her and attempted to copulate with her, an attempt that was somewhat hindered by the vast difference in their sizes. Merle had a profound erection, though, and, if his avid thrusts in the right area could be trusted, he appeared to know what he was doing.

His behavior, despite not having his testicles, wasn't that unusual. Contrary to popular myth, castration—especially castration after a dog has matured—doesn't always affect his personality or his ability to work. It may make him more willing to accept authority from humans, but in many cases it doesn't prevent him from mounting and mating with bitches in heat, who appear to show no preference between cut and uncut dogs, as was being demonstrated by Ms. Jack Russell, who seemed to be thoroughly enjoying herself.

When she and Merle separated, she jumped up, placed her paws on his shoulders, and energetically licked his neck, ears, and cheeks. Merle looked at her adoringly.

Walking over to them, I fingered her leather collar. On its brass nameplate was written "Shayla." Why Merle was so interested in her became immediately obvious. She was bleeding and most definitely in heat.

"Quite the catch," I told Merle, who happily wagged his tail.

I gave them each a dog biscuit and they devoured their treats before romping around the great room. They soon chased each other out the dog door and rolled on the grass before taking turns mounting each other. Shayla, of course, couldn't mount Merle while he was standing, so he lay down, and she thrust at his rear end before racing around to his nose and mounting his head.

After about an hour of such antics, they lay on their sides, exhausted, their paws touching. Ten minutes later, they sprang up and went at it again. Several more hours went by.

Watching Merle, I had to wonder at the reasoning of the person who had castrated him. Perhaps the person had bought in to the standard line of animal welfare organizations across the land, which is "Don't have unwanted puppies. Spay and neuter your dogs." And given that about two to four million dogs are euthanized each year in the United States and Canada alone, this reasoning is impossible to fault.

But there are other ways to achieve the same end. If you have a male dog and you don't want him to become a dad, a laparoscopic vasectomy is a less invasive procedure than castration and an equally effective form of birth control. Most traditional vets, though, don't support vasectomies. They argue for castration because it eliminates roaming, which may save a dog from being hit by a car.

Castration, some vets claim, also reduces the incidence of testicular cancer, hernias, and prostate problems.

Likewise for female dogs. Vets routinely recommend spaying
(the complete removal of ovaries and uterus) over tubal ligation
(tying the tubes) or a hysterectomy (the removal of the uterus), both
of which will prevent pregnancy and are far less demanding sur-
geries. The rationale for spaying is very similar to that used for
males. With the elimination of bloody discharge and odors, the dog
owner has a sanitary animal who doesn't attract male dogs. With
her roaming urges reduced, the bitch will stay home and out of
traffic. She's also protected from mammary, ovarian, and uterine
cancer by the loss of her reproductive organs.

However, in rural places, where there is little traffic, it seems
hard to justify castration or spaying simply to protect a dog from
the occasional car. Unless the dog is confined at all times, it will
probably roam—that is the nature of dogs. As for preventing yet-
to-arise diseases in our dogs, few of us—female or male—would
willingly part with our own ovaries or testes to prevent a condition
that may never appear. We'd rather keep our sex intact and address any problems when they arise, such as testicular cancer,
which is quite treatable in both dogs and humans. Indeed, some
vets believe that castrating dogs predisposes them to prostate
cancers.

Do our dogs feel similarly? Do they miss being sexed? These
are hard questions to answer, but we can think of them in this way:
If we were neutered before sexual maturity, we probably wouldn't
miss what we didn't know. So may it be with our dogs.

The more practical question to address, particularly for male
dogs, concerns the efficacy of castration. Does it actually change
unwanted behavior—roaming, mounting, urine marking in the
house, and aggression toward other male dogs, the very sorts of
behaviors that cause people to give up their dogs to shelters where
they are subsequently euthanized? Timing seems to be key. In general, the earlier castration is done, the greater the likelihood of

success, since the unwanted behaviors have yet to be established. Once such behaviors have been learned, they're far more difficult to eradicate, as was shown by a study done at the University of California Davis Center for Companion Animal Health. There, fifty-seven dogs were neutered for ongoing behavioral problems. Their behavior was then monitored over a five-year period. For the first three problems—roaming, mounting, and urine marking in the house—only 25 to 40 percent of the dogs showed any resolution. With aggression toward other dogs, one of the most common reasons cited by dog owners for castrating their animal, resolution of the problem was even lower: Only 10 to 15 percent of dogs who lost their balls also lost their desire to fight other males.

Merle was a case in point: Castration had done nothing toward reducing his love of roaming. Whether it had reduced his willingness to fight other male dogs I couldn't say, since he never fought with any dog except the white Shepherd. Nor could I say whether he would have been a less loveable dog had he been entire. If his reaction to Shayla could be trusted, castration hadn't done a thing to cool his ardor for bitches in heat.

And this posed a dilemma for me, albeit one more theoretical than practical. I was certain, having watched the huge affection between Zula and Merle that, had they not been sterilized, they would have mated. Chances are that their offspring would have been swift, beautiful creatures with a lot of their parents' energy and even temperaments. If Zula's humans would have welcomed the litter so would I, and I'm sure that we'd have seen to it that every puppy got a good home.

As for the hypothetical offspring between Merle and Shayla, I wasn't as enthusiastic, for I like the Jack Russell personality less than that of the Vizsla. Yet Merle and Shayla were smitten with each other. It was also probable that, given Kelly's dog population, Merle hadn't been the first dog who had come knocking at Shayla's door. In other words, Shayla had chosen him, which is fairly common: Bitches can be quite discriminating, choosing only one dog among many suitors. In fact, lying on the wood floor of the great room while gazing deeply into each other's eyes, Merle and Shayla gave all appearances of being not only in a state of lust but also in a state of love.

Some readers might find this observation suspect and put it down to my being one of those dog owners who can't differentiate between their own emotions and those of their dogs. However, Konrad Lorenz, who won a Nobel Prize in 1973 for his work on the organization of social behavior in animals, often spoke of his Greylag geese "falling in love." Occasionally, his colleagues took him to task for being anthropomorphic, and he would reply, "It is the accurate term for a real phenomenon for which there is no other name. I consider the term appropriate to any species, if that is in fact what they do."

You've probably guessed where this discussion is going: Being an advocate of dogs having as much freedom as possible, I found myself hoisted on my own petard. I was willing to let Merle roam around Kelly and love whomever he desired, but I would have been more inclined to welcome his pups with Zula than those with Shayla. This was two-faced, I knew, but how many of us have breathed a secret sigh of relief when a close friend leaves off what we consider an inappropriate romance and marries someone else?

By late afternoon, Merle could barely stand up. He lay under the great room's picture window, sides heaving, glassy-eyed, played out. Indefatigable, Shayla pranced around him. When she could rouse Merle to no further efforts, she tried to mount his head. He growled a warning. She continued to hump and thrust. His growls grew deeper. Undeterred, she continued to bang his snout like a little jackhammer. He erupted, roaring in annoyance and smacking her with the side of his snout, sending her flying several feet across the room.

Then he dropped his head on the floor and looked at her with a pleading expression: "I've got nothing left. Please leave me alone."

She came over and sniffed his head. He growled again; she turned and perkily trotted out the sliding glass door, back to the yurts from where she had come.

Unlike domestic dogs, who are highly opportunistic when it comes to sex, wild wolves are quite monogamous. The male and female of an alpha pair breed exclusively with each other until one or the other dies. For a long time, these basics of lupine social life weren't known. It was assumed that when more than one female in a pack had pups, it was the dominant male who was the father of both litters, for such behavior had been observed in captive wolves. However, recent genetic studies done in Minnesota and Alaska show that such infidelities don't take place in the wild. Instead, the fathers of the nondominant female's pups are immigrants who have been taken in by the pack or transient wolves who risk death or mauling to breed with her when she comes into heat. Thus, even though the opportunity to dabble exists for the alpha male, faithfulness is the norm.

It was a norm that I, too, strove for, though I found myself far more successful at emulating Merle's behavior than that of a wild wolf. To be fair, I wasn't a complete dog, as the saying goes, but was serially monogamous. The reasons that my relationships didn't last were as varied as the women whom I dated: I wanted a family and they didn't; I was taken by the outdoors and they felt lukewarm about it; I liked Wyoming, and they thought that their state was the place to live. But underlying these reasons was the one I found difficult to bring up as the true cause for our relationships not working: My heart simply hadn't opened as it had the night when Merle walked into my life and said, "I am yours."

I know what you're thinking—this guy's pathetic; it's a dog, for Christ's sake. But, hey, the dog and I were still together after five years, and I hadn't gotten past one year with anyone else.

There was one woman, however, about whom I felt differently. I kept running into her on top of Signal Mountain, outside the Kelly

post office, and at dinner parties thrown by mutual friends. We
would start chatting and, an hour and a half later, would discover
that our errands had slipped away unnoticed or that our food had
grown cold. It was obvious that both of us liked to talk, yet our conversations were different from those we shared with others. They
immediately found deep topics: what was right work; how one found
such a calling; how landscape affected a person's spiritual well-
being; how much we cherished these mountains but also our families far away; how, someday, we wanted to have families of our own;
and, most tellingly, why we found it easier to talk with dogs—she
would kneel and put her arms around Merle—than with some
people. She was a great lover of dogs and had been since girlhood.

This woman, whose name was Allison, worked only four miles
up the road, at the Teton Science School, and we might have become a couple had it not been for the disparity in our ages and
heights: She was seventeen years younger than I and five inches
taller, a Nordic goddess whose regal bearing was softened by trop-
ical green eyes and a small inward lean of her two front teeth,
which gave her an air of mischief. Given how much we had in common, I saw little reason to fret over our public image—the tall
young woman, the short older man—but she did. And so nothing
ever came of our talks except the feeling that our souls had known
each other for a very long time. At this juncture, fate intervened.
Allison moved away—back to the Midwest, where her family
owned a chain of department stores to which she believed she
owed some allegiance.

I hadn't thought of her in a couple of years, and then, on a
cold, snowy February night, I walked into Dornan's, the bar that
perches above the Snake River at the entrance to Grand Teton National Park in Moose. And there she was, sitting at the bar, drinking a glass of wine and listening to a bluegrass band. She gave me
a smile that could not be faked—a thousand watts of joy at seeing me. We talked until the place closed and then, since I had car-
pooled over, she gave me a ride home. It was so cold that the stars

vibrated in the heaven, and so did the car. After not seeing each other for a couple of years, the air felt electric with possibility.

We went to dinner the next day; we went to the movies; we skied on Teton Pass. Then she went back to Nebraska, and we began telephoning each other—three-hour talks during which all we wanted to do was be in each other's arms. On Memorial Day weekend, I flew to Omaha to visit her. Other than going downtown to eat, we never got out of bed. About halfway through that weekend, I looked in the bathroom mirror and thought, "You look just like your dog."

A month later, Merle and I went for an extended stay. In the interim, Allison had gotten a Golden Retriever puppy, a tiny ball of floppy ears and sparkling, dark eyes named Brower, partly because he had brow markings and partly after David Brower, the famous conservationist, whom she admired.

But because she had to work in her family's store each day, Allison was forced to leave Brower at home in an oversize wire crate. When we arrived, he reminded me of seltzer bursting from a bottle. He raced out the front door and stopped dead as he saw the big golden dog emerge from the Subaru. Open-mouthed, he stared at Merle, not knowing quite what to do. Merle held his tail erect and gave it an encouraging little wag—he had immediately read both Allison's and my energy about this little dog. That was all Brower needed. He bounded toward him, squirming every square inch of himself as he tried to lick Merle's lips.

Merle gave the little guy a few sniffs before holding his head high, ignoring his frolicking with the imperious bearing he used on all dogs he considered his underlings.

"Merle," I told him, "be nice. You two are going to know each other for a long, long time."

This was no idle prediction.

When I had come to Nebraska, it wasn't with the idea that I'd be on vacation. I was finishing a book, and Allison had her duties at the store. Unlike her, however, I could stay at home with the dogs and write. This was nothing novel for Merle, but for Brower it was a revelation—no more life in the crate, a new human for company, and a big friendly dog to play with.

I had worried that Merle would be standoffish to the little pup, but this wasn't the case. In fact, he took to his new role as mentor with enthusiasm, escorting Brower around the yard, excavating interesting smells with a poke of his paw, sniffing, then allowing Brower to sniff. Merle would raise his leg, squirt, and scrape, and Brower, not old enough to raise his leg, would squat. On they'd go: the big dog demonstrating, the little dog watching and copying.

I had also been concerned that Merle might go into one of his urban funks, the first appearance of which had made itself known when I had taken him on a book tour and we had stayed at a friend's home in Boulder, Colorado. Merle had lain with his head between his paws, staring at me while I talked on the phone and typed on my laptop, his weary look saying, "This is the most boring day of my life."

"I'm sorry," I told him. "We're in downtown Boulder. There are leash laws. You can't just roam around. Give me an hour, and we'll go for a walk." By way of an answer, he gave a great sigh, indicating, "Have I told you that this is the most boring day of my life?"

"Yes, you did tell me that," I replied. "Let me finish this and we can take a walk." The drama queen, he fell onto his side, letting his head drop to the floor with a disgruntled thunk. He gave another tremendous sigh, his entire rib cage expanding and collapsing. Holding my eye, his penetrating gaze repeated, "By the way, have I mentioned to you that this is the most boring day of my entire life?"

But suburban Omaha wasn't downtown Boulder. Allison's large fenced yard was overhung with oak trees, and they were filled with squirrels. Few other situations, I think, could have pleased Merle more at this time in his life, for he had become jaded with hunting ground squirrels around Kelly. In fact, he had begun to chase them half-heartedly, as if they no longer presented him with much of a challenge. And this may have been true, since he had become enormously adept at catching them.

Instead, he had set his sights on more difficult game: the red squirrels who lived in the conifer forests where we often hiked. Preyed upon by swift and stealthy pine martens, red squirrels have evolved into super-vigilant and exquisitely agile creatures who, at the slightest hint of danger, leap through the branches to safety. Merle would dash beneath their aerial getaways and stand on his hind feet, forefeet extended up the trunk of an evergreen as he gazed at the chattering little animals. Turning, he would give me the most wistful look: "If I could catch a tree squirrel, my life would be complete."

Now, his wish had been granted. Allison's yard was crawling with tree squirrels. They were gray instead of red, but color didn't seem to matter. Merle took one look at the backyard, raised a paw, and went into stalk mode.

I had set up a makeshift desk on the patio and wrote as he hunted, and Brower, the keen aspirant, watched his every move, bounding in at the last second to foil Merle's stalks. The third time he did this, Merle growled at him horrifically, striking him on the side of the head and seeming to maul him with bared teeth, by all appearances inflicting a mortal wound. But, of course, adult dogs regularly reprimand their puppies in this way, never even scratching them. Brower got the message. He threw himself on his back at Merle's feet, pumping his paws in the air and whining for forgiveness.

Merle gave him his "Oh, my god, puppies!" look, which sent Brower into a greater effort to placate him.

By midday it was time to call a break from writing and hunting squirrels. I put Brower on his leash, and, letting Merle walk on his own but keeping his lead in hand, we walked through the leafy streets toward a nearby park. As we strolled, we passed dogs behind fences who ran at us, hackles raised, barking at the top of their lungs. Apoplectic, they dashed back and forth on their side of the fence as Merle stared at them with incredulity. Glancing up at me, he sent me a look that could only be interpreted as "Poor sons of bitches."

"Now, now, Señor," I told him. "Don't be mean. What dog lives like you?"

"Ha-ha-ha," he panted, not deigning to give the dogs behind the fences another glance, which drove them wild.

None of this was lost on Brower. Initially terrified of the dogs who rushed at us, he soon adopted Merle's royal indifference. Years later, when Brower had grown into an uncut male who was the top dog wherever he went, I thought that some of his personality had been molded on those Omaha streets. In fact, the only male he ever deferred to was Merle himself, to whom he always acted like a nephew whose uncle has been a teacher and a friend.

Sometimes, on those humid Midwestern afternoons, when I couldn't write another word, we'd lie in the grass under the oak trees, Brower stretched out on one side of me, Merle on the other. Brower, who hadn't been confined in his crate since our arrival, would gaze into my eyes with a look of supreme gratitude that said, "Ted, man, you saved my life!" He'd lick my mouth, and I'd rough up his head, and Merle would put a steadying paw on my arm while sending me a look of ownership: "Excuse me. Just remember who the main dog is."

Main dog or not, he and Brower got brushed together and fed together and walked together, and, on more than one occasion, as Allison and I would look up from our love-soaked panting, we'd see Merle and Brower, both sitting by our bedside, tails wagging enthusiastically, just the way a pack of wolves watches their alpha pair mate.

She'd giggle and say, "My poor innocent puppy has been corrupted by you two."

Then one day, as Brower sat by my side on the patio, Merle spied a squirrel hopping a little too far from its oak tree. He rose and began to creep toward it in slow motion. The squirrel, who had now seen quite a bit of Merle, gave him a nonchalant look: "Here we go again." Merle sprinted. The squirrel whirled and bolted around the right side of the oak—its standard escape tactic. But apparently Merle had learned from his unsuccessful attempts. He dashed around the trunk to the left, meeting the squirrel head-on as it came around the back side of the tree.

The squirrel, who was glancing over its shoulder to where it expected Merle to be, squealed in surprise and leapt upward. Merle jumped and plucked it from the bark in one motion. As he landed, he flipped the squirrel into the air, catching it with a snap of his jaws. He shook it once and pranced toward us like the king of the world. Barking ecstatically, Brower rushed out to greet him. Merle dropped the squirrel in front of his protégé and sent me an enormous look of satisfaction: "Tree squirrel, at last! Did it!"

Which is exactly how I felt, holding Allison in my arms, our dogs lying at the foot of our bed: After years of searching, I had found the woman with whom I wanted to be.

CHAPTER 10

At Home in the Arms of the Country

When Merle and I left Omaha that summer, we started in the dawn and drove all through the hot day, seven hundred miles across the Great Plains before turning north at Rock Springs and climbing onto the vast open steppes that lie west of the Wind River Mountains. For another hundred miles we drove alongside their breaking crest of granite before entering the canyon of the Hoback River and winding under its redrock cliffs, the peaks rising higher and higher until we came into Jackson Hole and saw the Tetons welcoming us with open arms.

It was there, as we turned onto the Gros Ventre River road, that Merle, who had been reclining on his green bed, stood and began to wag his tail in anticipation. He rested his chin on my shoulder, pressing his cheek against my ear for the next seven miles up the river. When we turned off the main road he let out a deep, heartfelt pant, as if he'd been holding it the entire day: "HAAAA!" "Home!"

It being summer, it was still light. He ate his kibble and slap-slap, was gone through his dog doors and into the heart of the village, eager to make his rounds. No matter what kind of interesting or boring trip we'd return from, this became our standard routine upon arriving home: I would open my mail and check phone messages, and Merle would go off to check his.

I quickly learned not to expect him back soon, and the longer we had been gone, the longer he stayed out. He might return at eleven or midnight or even two A.M.; there was simply no telling. I'd wake to find him on his blankets in the corner of my room or, if it was summer, he might be downstairs on the wood floor, directly in the middle of the great room where the breeze flowed from the deck doors to the front doors, both wide open. If it was winter, he might be on the dedicated quadruped couch—the one I had moved from the trailer and which now sat opposite the newer, human couch. Almost always, Gray Cat would be there with him, butt to butt. In the spring or the fall, I'd often find Merle on the front porch, near its step, chin resting on his crossed paws, shoulders humped while the sleet covered him. I'd open the front door and call, "Hey, come on in." He'd look up, give me a sleepy glance, and put his head back down with a relaxed and contented air that seemed to say, "This is too splendid. You should come out as well."

Watching him enjoy what, to me, was perfectly wretched weather, I assumed that here was a dog who couldn't be tempted by creature comforts. But I had forgotten his love of sleeping on my pad in the tent, which should have been a clue as to the multiple facets of his character. Our new home soon let him express them. I'd come home and discover that he had taken a pillow from the alcove and carried it upstairs, leaving it on the floor near my bed. The pillows were never chewed, and I wondered what he did with them until one day I found one of the throw rugs in the great room bunched into an elaborate bed, just like the nests he dug in the dirt. The impression of his body had been left in its folds, and one of the alcove's pillows lay exactly where his head had lain.

"*Monsieur,*" I told him, extending a hand to his lair, "*pour un chien qui aime bien la vie au grand air, tu aimes aussi le confort.*" For a dog who likes the outdoors so much, you also like your comforts.

This was too much French for him. He wagged his tail heartily, implying, "It was a very good snooze."

"Are you getting so old," I asked him, massaging his neck, "that you need a pillow to rest your head?"

He leaned against my legs and groaned in pleasure as I massaged all his favorite spots. It wasn't that he was getting old—he was only five; it was that, as he had matured, he had grown ever less inclined to distinguish between the world of people and the world of dogs. In fact, I had watched him become more perplexed and, occasionally, even distressed when he saw dogs being treated like dogs—chained, fenced, or crated. When we went to a house that wasn't dog friendly, and he had to wait outside while I paid my visit, a wounded look would cross his face.

It was clear that, in his mind, the major taxonomic lines dividing species weren't those that separated humans and canids, but rather those between "us" (dogs and people) and "them" (wildlife). He had further classified wildlife into species that he could chase with impunity (squirrels and coyotes) and those that could never be chased (moose, deer, elk, bighorn sheep, and bison), although on that evening when I'd lost my mind and come to my senses, I'd made an unforgettable exception for bison. Finally, there was Gray Cat, as well as the other cats of Kelly, who were given their own species designation between "us" and "them." Like hot weather and cities, cats simply had to be respected and endured.

Merle's ordering of the world, it was plain to see, mirrored my own, which was hardly surprising since I had raised him. There were some important distinctions, however. I had no interest in chasing squirrels, and I was quite fond of coyotes. I also really liked cats, a habit that Merle found bewildering. From his corner of the bedroom, he would watch Gray Cat wake me by putting a paw on my face. As soon as I'd open my eyes, Gray Cat would begin to meow loudly: "I'm out of food. I'm starving."

"How's our big hungry puss?" I'd reply, scratching his cheeks and making him purr.

Raising his head from his bed, Merle would give me the most disgusted of looks: "You're letting that cat get away with murder."

Despite his feelings about the feline world, Merle always acted politely toward cats, as he did to all people: no pushy greetings, no jumping, licking, or barking. If some people were uncomfortable with having even this well-behaved dog close to them, I would only have to give a small flick of my index finger, indicating that he should leave, and he'd pad off and lie down. His refined social skills led more than one person to comment, "He doesn't act like a dog. He . . . he's almost like a person." What they really wanted to say was that he was like a diplomat from a strange land, one who displayed some odd foreign manners but who nonetheless spoke the lingua franca well. Groping for words, one individual said, "I mean, when I'm around you two, I sometimes wonder who's the person and who's the dog." Then she backpedaled, adding, "I'm sorry. I didn't mean to offend you."

"Not at all," I told her. "In fact, that's one of the nicest compliments I've ever been paid."

I was totally sincere. Her observation meant that, in the space of only four years together, Merle and I had worked our way back to the time when people and animals "spoke the same language," as one old Inuit song recounts.

By the fall, it became obvious that Allison had had a change of heart. Being groomed for the CEO position in her family's business had been a heady prospect, but a life of pantyhose and power suits hadn't translated into her calling. She missed the mountains, she missed skiing, and we missed each other. She and Brower moved to Kelly, into a log house across the field from Merle and me.

In Omaha, as a way of dampening her guilt over leaving Brower home all day, she had bought him every sort of toy: rawhide chews, pig ears, balls, stuffed animals. But no gift seemed to lift his spirits more than the one she gave him when they moved to Wyoming—a door of his own.

He would leave their home, making his way under the cottonwoods, and come into my view as he galloped through the sage. Although he and Merle now weighed the same, about seventy pounds, Brower had turned into a taller and rangier dog, as well as one who was paler gold in color. He had a great feathery tail, and it would stream behind him as he'd execute a sideways drift around our south deck, tear across the north porch, claws clattering, and slap-slap, explode through the dog doors and burst across the great room as if we hadn't seen each other in months. As was more often the case, I had just left his and Allison's house early that morning, or he had left ours with her. He'd leap up to greet me, paws on my shoulders, smooching my face while panting ecstatically, "Ted, man, old buddy! It is fabulous to see you! This is the best!" And it was. His time was his own; his life was his own; Omaha, the fenced yard, the leash, and the crate were gone.

Merle would look up from the couch, one brow raised to indicate, "Ah, youth is here."

Before I could say, "Down, Brower," he'd spy Merle on the couch and rush to him. "Merle, Merle, Merle!" he'd pant in wild happiness. "How's it going? Let's do something!"

Keeping his hind end on the couch, Merle would put his front paws on the floor and do a dignified stretch, wagging his elevated tail in a reserved greeting.

Brower, kissing him all over the face, would be unable to stand another moment's delay: "Oh, come on! Let's go, let's go, let's go!"

And without waiting, he'd rush out the dog door, followed by Merle. I could see them go down the road, side by side, tails waving like the plumes of two courtiers. The first time they set off like this, I couldn't help but follow at a distance.

No more than two hundred yards down the road, Merle stopped

at the creek and waded through it, as he did most mornings. "Here's the creek," he seemed to say. "This spot has excellent wading. You can find frogs here." A little farther on, he turned right and went across the main road into the field where the cutting horse instructor kept his training sheep. Merle paused fifty feet from the pen. The cutting horse instructor hated dogs bothering his livestock. "Those are the sheep pens," Merle seemed to say by his direct glance at them. "Great smells. Don't even think of trying to get in there." He turned and recrossed the road. "Over here, I have visiting rights to these rabbits. Very interesting viewing." Merle and Brower stood in front of one of our neighbor's hutches. "Again," Merle seemed to say by his immovable stance a few feet from the hutch, "leave them alone." From there, he led Brower to the one-lane bridge over the Gros Ventre, where they paused and looked upriver. "On your left, you'll see waterfowl and trout in the pools, but if you cross the bridge, we'll be in big game country. Keep an eye out; we might see some elk on those hillsides." Merle gave the hillside, where we'd often seen elk, a long surveying look. He wagged his tail: "Now that's something a dog can get excited about."

Of course, Merle spoke not a word to Brower—not a bark, not a woof, not a whine—but his face was a labile study in conversation, just as the faces of wolves are when they hunt in a pack and "speak" to each other with a leading motion of their eyes, snouts, and ears. One has only to have attempted communicating with a fellow human being while observing shy wildlife to note how effective this sort of nonverbal communication is. "They went that way; they're standing right there; let's crawl ahead for a better view" can all be said by moving the eyes, brows, and head. And one doesn't have to go to the outdoors to know this. "I love you beyond measure, you light up the world, I will stand by you to the end" have been said with nothing but the eyes—both between people, and between dogs and people—for a long, long time.

I left them to their ramblings, and several hours later they burst back through the dog doors, huge grins on their faces, their Kelly tour complete.

Now there were four of us to ski or walk in the afternoons, and Brower, the exuberant youngster, would tear off dry branches from fallen logs and bear them along proudly. He was enormously strong and occasionally would manage to rip off a branch some ten feet long. We then had to step smartly, or he'd wipe us out at the knees as he pranced by our sides.

Merle would look at me and roll his eyes: "Oh, my god, are we really friends with that dog?"

We often walked to the river, where I would throw sticks into the Gros Ventre for Brower and he'd swim out to retrieve them. Merle watched these games with studied aloofness, his entire body language implying, "This is beneath me."

It was on perhaps our fourth or fifth walk, after I had thrown a stick for Brower and praised him lavishly upon his retrieving it, that Merle sat down in front of me, his eyes riveted on mine and brightly lit with some obvious scheme.

"What's up?" I asked him.

He shivered slightly, as he always did when excited. I suddenly understood. His eyes were telling me, "I can do that."

"Why don't you hold Brower a second," I asked Allison.

Presenting the stick in front of Merle's nose, I said, "Are you really going to retrieve?"

He shook in readiness.

"All right, let's see what you can do."

I flung the stick into the river, and Merle, defying four years of nonretrieving history, leapt into the water, swam downstream, grasped the stick in his jaws, paddled to shore, ran to me, and dropped it at my feet with a nonchalant toss.

"I am stunned," I told him. "What gives?"

"Ha-ha-ha," he panted. "No big deal."

I threw the stick again and he retrieved it, throwing it at my feet in the same careless way.

One more time I launched the stick into the river, but this time Merle sat there without moving.

"Go ahead," I said, "get it."

He looked at the stick, he looked at me, and he actually sighed. Not hiding his reluctance, he walked into the water, swam downriver, and retrieved the stick. Walking up to me, he flung it at my feet with an "enough of this nonsense" toss of his head.

When I threw the stick a fourth time, he simply watched it float away.

"Fetch," I told him. "Go get it."

He turned to me with one of the most expressive looks I've ever seen on a dog or, for that matter, a human. His head was cocked to the side with wry indulgence, and his eyes hung on mine with tender reproach: "I showed you I can do this, but it's really not my game."

"Let Brower go," I said, and Allison released him.

He hit the water, swam downstream, and fetched the stick. Merle watched him without moving.

Allison then held Brower and I tossed the stick for Merle, wanting to see if what we were witnessing was some form of dominance expressing itself—if Merle had decided not to let his one-time pupil steal the show. His reaction now demonstrated otherwise. He looked at the stick, floating away; he looked at me; and his eyes said, as they always had, "Sorry, I don't fetch." Evidently, he had wanted to show me that his stand on retrieving was not a lack of proficiency but a lack of desire. This wasn't the last time he'd make such a statement.

In his intriguing book *Dogs Never Lie About Love,* Jeffrey Moussaieff Masson remarks that dogs are never paralyzed by the need to judge and to compare. They don't dwell on the fact that today's walk isn't as nice as yesterday's, or this forest isn't as interesting as the one they were in last week. Dogs have no favorite walks, only people do, writes Masson, adding that dogs love all walks. "They love being wherever they are. The reason, and it is a great lesson, is no doubt that they are perfectly content to be who they are, without torturing themselves with alternatives: They love being dogs."

Not so with Merle. He preferred our walks on the hills above Kelly to the one along the river. He preferred downhill skiing on Teton Pass to touring up the Gros Ventre. And if we were in cities he preferred walking on grass, in parks, to pavement. That he genuinely preferred some places over others was not hard to decipher: His exuberant body language expressed his enthusiasm over those places he enjoyed; his less-than-exuberant body language showed that other places were just ordinary. At times, he could show that he was truly displeased with a place, sulking with his head between his paws in some suburban home while his eyes said, "Can't we get out of here?"

I'd then take him for a walk, and, instead of being in love with where he was, he'd express the very opposite. Walking the streets of Boulder, Helena, Bozeman, or Missoula, for instance, he'd sniff along the curbs, lawns, and trees, and his body posture would say, "Nope." He'd go a bit farther, sniff, and indicate, "Nope." A little farther on, his lackadaisical body language would imply, "Nope, still not what I want." But when we got to a park where many other dogs had walked, he'd immediately perk up: "Ah, at last, something interesting to smell."

Still, when all was said and done, he loved his home best. Returning from one of these suburban strolls, he'd go directly to our car, stand by its rear door, and wag his tail at me hopefully: "Please, can't we go home?"

"We're here," I'd say, "try to enjoy it."

The immediate drooping of his head gave new meaning to the word "hangdog."

Was he reading my energy? I don't think so, for in some of these places I was having a high old time, visiting with friends I saw intermittently, eating great food, drinking good wine, and talking late into the night about politics and books. In the midst of such uplifting conversations, Merle would pad to my side and put his chin on my thigh. His body would move steadily with his imploring tail, his eyes saying, "Isn't it time to go home yet?" I'd let him out, and he'd walk directly to our car, stand at the door, and once again give me that longing look: "When can we go home?"

This was not a dog who lived in the delightfulness of the present or who had no ability to compare. What he had accumulated was a large data set, one that had allowed him to define "home" not only as Kelly, but as all those places where he could be a dog in the way that he had come to understand dogdom: his time at his disposal and lots of room to roam.

As often as possible, we joined him in these places. In the summer we hiked, in the winter we skied, disappearing into the backcountry and following routes others didn't travel. On some remote knob, overlooking an empty valley, we'd stop for lunch—Brower and Allison, Merle and me—she and I sitting on our packs, the dogs eating their biscuits while we ate our sandwiches. At such moments we could have been the first people to have ventured into North America, moving down the spine of the Rockies with our packs and our dogs. The sky was quiet, the forest private. We were alone and peaceful in a way that it is ever harder to be alone and peaceful: the outside world not gone, but out of sight and out of mind.

The dogs, I thought, helped us appreciate these moments. Lying in the grass and staring down at some distant valley, they would gaze without moving, not mesmerized by the distance but brought to rest by it. Even if we put a hand between their shoulders and gave them a scratch, they wouldn't budge from their

tranquil reflection. Leaving our hands upon them, we'd soon feel
the quiet of the place coming up through their bodies, as if they
had become conduits for stillness.

Some of these places we returned to over and over again because of their long views, or their ancient trees, or because the in-
cline of a particular slope was perfect for skiing. Like all those
people who have believed themselves the first to happen upon a
scene, we named these special places, especially our favorite ski
runs: The White Goddess; Winter Magic; Hidden Peak; and Puppies' Powder, the latter for how our dogs bounded after us, their ears
flapping like the wings of birds. There was also Merle's Delight,
named for the time we skied a steep and narrow gully, the snow so
light it resembled air-driven spume as it sprayed over our shoulders.
Reaching the creek bottom, we looked back and saw Merle, up to
his neck in powder, his head gold, his pink tongue laughing, as he
surfed a moving wave of snow down into the cold gray dusk.

The town of Jackson seemed especially distant in these winter months, and if we didn't turn on the radio our sense of isolation was complete. There was nothing beyond our windows except
the snow and the mountains and the Milky Way. This was hardly
a lonely feeling. Instead, the country seemed big and protective,
the way our parents once felt when there was nothing beyond the
comfort of their arms.

It was during this time that Allison got a job. Financially, she
didn't need one, but she didn't like being unemployed while listening for her calling—it went against her work ethic. So she
worked at the Teton Valley Hospital, on the other side of Teton
Pass, in Driggs, Idaho, developing outreach programs for seniors.
The fifty-mile commute meant an early-morning departure from
Kelly, and she rose to an alarm, something I hadn't done for years,
relying instead on my subconscious to let me know when it was
time to get up and write. This could be 3:30 in the morning; it
could be 7:30. Thus, at least when Merle and I slept alone at our

house, he had no set human routine upon which to pattern his. Sometimes he was around when I opened my eyes; sometimes he wasn't; and sometimes we awoke together.

"Bonjour, Monsieur," I'd say, looking over to the corner of the bedroom where he slept on his pile of folded blankets, *"la journée de travail commence."* The workday begins.

If he had been out most of the night, tending to his affairs, and it was still dark, as it often was in the winter when I got up early, he'd give me a pained expression as I lit my bedside lamp. He'd put his paws over his eyes and bury his head in the folds of his blankets. "Your workday begins," he'd groan, making an "awwwrrr" sound deep in his throat, "mine is just getting over."

"You are such a boulevardier, Sir," I would tease him. "Did you close down Kelly's night spots?"

He'd yawn and go back to sleep as I washed up and fixed breakfast.

But by first light, I'd hear his claws on the wooden stairs, and he'd pad softly into my office, greeting me at my desk by laying his chin on my thigh, his tail moving his body in a slow undulation: "Hmm, so good to see you now that I'm awake." Then he'd be gone, pushing powerfully through the driveway's deep snow or, if it was summer, his paws moving in that tireless, sun-dappled trot, his reddish coat aglow. Watching him—five years old, perhaps like many dogs his size, halfway through his allotted years— I sometimes recalled A. E. Housman's lines, in which he laments the too-quick passing of youth:

> With rue my heart is laden
>   For golden friends I had,
> For many a rose-lipt maiden
>   And many a lightfoot lad.

Numerous people who saw Merle at such moments, his gold fur rippling in the sun, his eyes bright and clear, his paws trotting lightly, would exclaim, "Oh, what a beautiful dog!" If they were hunters, they might remark, "That is one good-looking bird dog. You ought to come—" And they'd extend an invitation to come hunting on their ranch or farm.

"Thank you," I'd reply, "but Merle hates bird hunting. He's an elk dog."

"Oh, you just haven't trained him right," the more persistent would tell me. "He's got bird genes for sure." And they'd mention some trainer they knew down in Texas or in the Dakotas who had taken charge of their dog and "turned him into a near field champion." They'd give me his phone number and once again invite me to come hunting with them.

I never followed up on these invitations—I didn't want to embarrass Merle in front of dogs who were near field champions, nor could I imagine shipping him off to some faraway trainer who would rejigger his brain with a shock collar. Besides, even though it would have been nice to have had pheasants and partridges to eat, we were wealthy in elk and antelope meat, the freezer shelves stacked with white packages. The root cellar was full of potatoes and carrots from the garden; the pantry gleamed with glass jars of tomatoes and peaches. Under the porch were six cords of firewood. We felt rich from the land and rich with each other: Our two dogs and we were a family.

Sometimes, though, Merle would get a little sulky because of how much time I was spending with Allison—not that he wasn't always nearby. Obviously, though, she now had command of the bed, and when he came into our bedroom he'd give us a dispirited look before padding glumly to his pile of blankets.

Allison, who was highly attuned to both dogs' and humans' feelings, decided to make up for how she had diverted my affections from him. She bought him an L. L. Bean dog bed, one of those plush, green, round, top-of-the-line ones, with his name inscribed in gold script along its edge: *Merle*. No more folded blankets for him or moving his rather thin, bottom-of-the-line L. L. Bean bed from the car. She brought the new bed over from her home and presented it to him, and he gave it an exploratory sniff before lying down upon it with several appreciative thwacks of his tail and a sidelong glance at me that put me on notice: "See, this woman knows how to treat a dog."

The round bed became Merle's favorite, and no one else could use it—not Brower, and especially not Gray Cat, both of whom Merle now looked upon with a certain amount of distrust since they had become fast friends upon their very first meeting, an event that I believe astounded them as much as it surprised Allison, Merle, and me.

Brower had come into the great room, and Gray Cat had raised his back up to his full height while hissing a warning. Brower, who was quite fearless, had leaned close and wagged his tail vigorously. Gray Cat gave him an experienced once-over—he had seen every manner of dog and could size them up in an instant. He deflated himself and allowed the young dog to approach. Gently, they touched noses. Whatever was communicated in that first sniff was enough. Gray Cat turned and bounded away playfully, instigating a chase. Brower leapt after him. Sprinting, Gray Cat suddenly did a forward somersault, coming up under Brower's belly and clawing wildly at him. Brower stood with a happy grin on his face, as if this violent scratching were just what he needed. Then he fell on Gray Cat, who squirted out sideways, but not in panic. Instead, he lay on his side and allowed Brower to catch him in his jaws. Going limp, Gray Cat half closed his eyes in ecstasy as Brower chewed him gently.

This became their little dance. Every time Brower came over to our house, and Gray Cat happened to be there, they touched noses and began their chase. Over and over, they'd dash across the great room, Gray Cat somersaulting forward to come up under Brower's belly, claws bared. In the meantime, Merle watched from his couch, one brow going up, the other down, with a look of deep concern that said, "Brower, you will never know, my friend, until it's too late, if that cat can really be trusted."

Despite his misgivings about Gray Cat, Merle nonetheless slept with him on the dedicated quadruped couch. But that was as far as he would go. Once, when he found Gray Cat on his green bed, he lay down a few feet off and stared at him, as if the force of his gaze would wake him. And within a few moments, it did. Gray Cat opened one eye, saw Merle, and with studied indifference got up, stretched, and appeared to remember something he had to do. Walking by Merle without looking at him, he padded down the stairs. Merle rose and went directly to his bed, sniffing it all over before lying down with several snorts, as if to clear his nostrils of cat smell.

The only other member of the household whom he'd allow on his bed was me. I'd lay down behind him, and he'd thump his tail and wriggle his back against my chest, asking for a scratch.

Sometimes we'd sleep hours together in this way, waking up to see the stars in the skylight or ravens walking over it in the dawn. Once, a flock of trumpeter swans flashed by in the sunrise, brilliantly white and honking.

Most nights, though, I slept in my bed and he on his. He now actually preferred sleeping on it, for if I'd extend a hand to my bed he'd give it an appraising look before discounting it and walking to his own. There he would begin a conscientious manicure of his fur, removing any mud or dirt. When he was done, and I was done reading, I'd ask, "Time for sleep?" And he'd beat his tail in reply.

I'd reach for the light and say, "Good night, my bonnie boy, and may flights of elk sing thee to thy rest."

Thwack-thwack-thwack went his tail: "You, too."

And the last thing each of us saw, as the light went out, was each other's eyes.

On the weekends, when Allison didn't have to go to work and the roads were closed because of drifted snow, we'd lie abed in the morning. The dogs, having let themselves out for a pee, had returned, and each slept in his corner of the bedroom, the snow melting on his fur, filling the room with damp dog smell.

With their sleeping breaths in the background, we'd lie in each other's arms and I'd listen to Allison talk about becoming a psychotherapist. It was the calling that had finally beckoned to her, a natural extension, she said, of her interest in why some families were happy and others weren't, and why some people moved through life with optimism and others faltered and fell. I would talk about my writing, about whether a piece was working, and sometimes I'd read her passages from it and she'd point out flaws I hadn't seen. Then we'd discuss our friends' lives—who among them had strong marriages and who weak, and why; who was foolish and who wise, and how they might improve their lot—laughing until our stomachs ached and we had tears in our eyes, as only a couple can laugh when, in the privacy of their bedroom, they allow themselves the liberty of believing they have a handle on things.

We called this sort of discussion our "A & C"—analysis and commentary—and we would always extend it to our own relationship, whose major rough spot was our differing views on intimacy. I wanted more closeness; she wanted more space. Finally, we managed to reach an accord: She would keep her house and I mine, and if we had children they'd commute between our two places by a breezeway across the field. It was our standing joke, our way of dealing with the fact that she wasn't ready to commit, even though many of her close friends had married and were starting families. But her reluctance, I finally realized, was deep-seated and might never go away. I was an older, self-made man, and she was a young princess. In the language of dogs, I was a mongrel, and she was holding out for a pup with papers.

On some mornings, though, as the stove crackled and the snow fell, our different backgrounds and what we looked like together when we stood side by side—the tall woman, the short man—vanished, as did my pursuit of her and her retreat. Then there was only the warmth of the house, and Merle and Brower yipping in their dreams, and she and I under the covers, while the mountains loomed close and held us tight.

CHAPTER 11

The Problem of Me

I always wondered what Brower and Merle thought as they lay in our bedroom, listening to Ali and me talk: whether they had the same emotional regard for us as we had for them; whether they could plan and reason; and whether they had that ultimate test of consciousness—the sense that one's unique combination of physical body and beliefs equals this being called *me.*

As far as I could tell, neither dog paid much attention to these enduring questions concerning the differences between the animal and human mind. Rather, each of them dealt—in quite different ways—with the more vexing issue of Allison and me leaving Kelly without warning. For long periods of time, we'd do exciting things with them, treat them with great affection, and then we'd disappear, not to come back into their lives for days and sometimes weeks at a time.

Since I never saw Brower in the places Allison left him when she traveled—the kennel and doggy camp, the latter allowing him to run and play with other dogs—I can't say what his reaction was to being separated from her. I think it was much like the one he displayed when she left him with Merle and me. By all appearances, he had a fun-filled time skiing, hiking, and camping with us, as well as being Merle's sidekick in Kelly. As Allison observed, "When he's with the guys he forgets all about me." And there was some truth to this statement. When he was with us, he didn't go back to his place to see if Allison had returned.

Merle, on the other hand, was a more attached and anxious soul, always ruminating on the problem of me—the man who had rescued him from his hardscrabble life in the desert but periodically deserted him. If I left him at the Landales', he would walk the five miles down to Kelly, looking for me. If I tried to leave him home when I left on an assignment, he would follow me—but in a way that demonstrated that he could draw logical inferences about how best to foil my departure.

We were still at the trailer when I first noticed his ability to reason in this way. I had packed my laptop, camera, and duffel as Merle watched with growing concern. When I put these articles together—and made no move to fill a Ziploc bag with his kibble— it was an almost certain sign that he was to be left at home. His suspicions were confirmed when I knelt and said, "I'm going to be gone for only two nights. Scott will come down this afternoon and pick you up so you can spend a couple of days with Tessa. That'll be fun."

He hung his head in misery.

After refilling his water bowl, I left him on the porch, his tail at half mast, wagging a slow dirge.

To get out of Kelly from the trailer, I had to drive east on our potholed lane, whereupon reaching the Gros Ventre River I turned left on the main road through the village. Coming to the Grand Teton National Park road, I turned again, now heading west, and eventually passed the tiny one-room post office that stood on the edge of Kelly proper. Although I had driven a mile from where I had started, I was only three hundred yards from the trailer, having executed three sides of a quadrilateral around Kelly's central field.

And there was Merle—sitting on the shoulder of the road, looking directly at me as I drove toward him, his tail wagging hopefully.

Slowing the car, I reflected on how he had figured out a way to intercept me. Several times each week, he and I walked from the trailer to the post office to get the mail, and he had driven out of Kelly with me hundreds of times in the car. But from his perspective, two feet off the ground, the route he needed to travel so as to meet me on the park road couldn't be seen. Sagebrush higher than his head, cottonwood trees, and scattered homes interrupted his line of sight. Consequently, he must have inferred where I was going, and where I would end up, and correlated this information with all the possible choices open to him. In other words, he must have created a mental map of the landscape upon which he had plotted our trajectories. Instead of giving chase to the car (as he did after I had driven off and he belatedly came to my whistle), he had taken the short side of the quadrilateral. His reasoning seemed to be that my leaving him behind showed not an unwillingness to take him along, but a temporary failure of eyesight. Surely, if I saw him on the road in front of me as I left Kelly, I would change my mind. Unfortunately, that wasn't an option. I was flying.

I got out of the car, knelt, and put my arms around him. "You are quite the clever dog," I told him.

Wag-wag-wag went his tail, but not too robustly, since my tone of voice wasn't promising.

I kissed him on the head and rubbed his ears. He groaned in pleasure. "I'm sorry," I said. "I love you, but I'm getting on a plane, and I'll be in a city for two days. I assure you, you will have a better time with Tessa, Scott, and April at the ranch."

He put his head against my chest: "I won't have a better time with them than with you."

"Okay, my lad, I have to go."

I kissed him again and left him on the shoulder of the road, looking forlornly at the rear end of the car as I drove away.

Merle, I suspect, had no idea that he had acted cleverly in cutting me off at the pass. He was simply using the same navigational skills that wolves and many other wild animals use when, after having explored their home range, they can strike out from any point and make a beeline home.

Many preliterate hunting-gathering cultures not only saw this kind of pragmatic behavior exhibited by animals on a daily basis, they also noticed that animals displayed a rich array of human emotions. These observations led them to believe that animal consciousness and human consciousness were so alike that, as one Arctic culture put it, "In the very earliest time when both people and animals lived on earth a person could become an animal if he wanted to and an animal could become a human being. Sometimes they were people and sometimes animals and there was no difference."

This smooth interchangeability was steadily eroded, however, as an increasing number of people began to make their living by herding and farming. Wildlife became an enemy, killing livestock and eating crops, and humans began to erect fences to protect their property from the wild. Some of these fences were actual ones, like corrals, and some were symbolic, like the Jewish faith's sanctioning human dominion over all of Earth's creatures, and, later, the Christian faith's decreeing that humans had souls but animals didn't.

The rationalists of the seventeenth century, spearheaded by the mathematician and philosopher René Descartes, increased the separation between people and animals when they described animals as mere machines that were incapable of feeling. As one of Descartes's disciples, Nicolas de Malebranche, wrote:

> [I]n animals, there is neither intelligence nor souls as ordinarily meant. They eat without pleasure, cry without pain, grow without knowing it; they desire nothing, fear nothing, know nothing: and if they act in a manner that demonstrates intelligence, it is because God, having made them in order to preserve them, made their bodies in such a way that they mechanically avoid what is capable of destroying them.

Such sentiments made animals the targets of vivisectionists who wanted to study their internal workings. As a result, countless dogs met pitiless ends on dissecting tables, and some scholars and scientists raised their voices in protest. The Cambridge philosopher Henry More, for example, called Descartes's view of animals an "utterly destructive and murderous idea." The Scottish philosopher David Hume wrote that "no truth appears to me more evident, than that beasts are endow'd with thought and reason as well as men." And Charles Darwin, as I've noted, passionately believed that animals had much the same emotional and mental complement as people.

Their voices, and others, led to the animal protection movement in the 1800s and the creation of animal protection societies in Europe and North America, the first being the Society for the Prevention of Cruelty to Animals, founded in London in 1824. But bettering the lives of "dumb animals," as they were called even by those who were trying to protect them, didn't necessarily translate into the belief that animals and people shared the same consciousness. By the middle of the twentieth century the views of men like Hume and Darwin had been eclipsed by a tide of experimental evidence that seemed to show that animals were, at best, trial-and-error learners who were incapable of reasoning. The man most responsible for setting this trend in motion was the late-nineteenth-century British psychologist Conwy Lloyd Morgan, who happened to be very fond of dogs.

One of the classic problems Morgan analyzed was nearly the same one I describe above—in which Merle, wanting to go with me, used reason to cut me off at the pass. But Morgan, looking at the same evidence, came to a different conclusion. In his illustration, a dog chases a rabbit along some curved shrubbery each morning only to see the rabbit disappear into a drain. After a few days of such unsuccessful chase, the dog starts the rabbit but, instead of pursuing it along the curve of the shrubbery, goes directly to the drain and catches the bunny.

According to Morgan, the dog's success didn't mean that it had reasoned, "If I take the shorter route"—in effect the chord of a circle—"I'll beat the rabbit to its hole." Not at all. The dog had simply associated the rabbit with the drain by what Morgan called "sense-experience." He went on to caution that "in no case may we interpret an action as the outcome of the exercise of a higher psychical faculty, if it can be interpreted as the outcome of the exercise of one which stands lower in the psychological scale."

This maxim, which is known as Morgan's Canon, has profoundly influenced how scientists, and eventually modern dog trainers, have viewed the minds of animals. At its heart is the concept of Occam's razor or the law of parsimony, which states that when two theories compete to explain an unknown phenomenon we should err on the side of the simpler explanation.

Yet Merle refused to act simply. If I blocked his dog door because it was below zero outside, he wouldn't stand outside it, waiting to be let in. He'd come to the sliding glass doors of my office and pant, "Hey there, open the door." If he came home from his rounds and found that I was gone but the car was still in the drive, he wouldn't stay home, waiting for me. Canvassing Kelly, he'd find me, appearing as surely as if I had left him a note as to where I was. And I knew that he did this because I could read his tracks in the newly fallen snow—entering his dog door, leaving melted pawprints in my office and our upstairs bedroom, then exiting the house to head across the village. I began to think that he was acting like many self-actualized members of a human partnership: He cherished his independence, but he also loved his partner. And he began to show me this in a surprising way.

When I'd awake, I'd find a bone by my bedside, always placed between my bed and the bathroom door so I couldn't miss stepping over it as I made my way to the john. And it was not any bone, but always and without fail a large beef bone, with the meat and gristle still on it, and sometimes a bit of dirt, as if it had been freshly dug up. Merle would be standing by the bedroom door, looking at me with bright and expectant eyes, his head cocked, as if to say, "See what I brought you."

I never discovered who in Kelly gave Merle these bones, though I asked around. What I did find curious was that the bones, other than being coated with his saliva, were quite untouched. The other curious factor to be considered was that he never brought me elk, deer, or antelope bones, all of which he found around Kelly and two of which, elk and antelope bones, I gave him regularly. Only beef bones.

What did this mean? Did he view beef bones as special because he got them infrequently? Did he understand that I owned lots of elk and antelope bones and was thus rich in them? Was bringing me a beef bone his way of saying, "I could have eaten this special treat myself, but I saved it for you because I love you, and you might like it"?

Unlike Gray Cat, who ate the choicest parts of his mice and left me the tails, Merle was leaving me what he valued most. And he was sticking around to watch my reaction. I never saw Gray Cat do that.

I therefore always made a great fuss over the bones Merle left me, for I was touched by this thoughtfulness. Here was my dog giving me more than affection, loyalty, and devotion by the look in his eyes, his body pressed to mine, and his tracking me down when he found that I was gone. It appeared that he had moved into the realm where we operate when we offer symbols of our affection.

No matter how many times I tried to explain his behavior by employing Morgan's Canon, I couldn't. If he were simply seeing me as his pup and was replaying the hardwired behavior of an adult wolf who brings food back to the den for its young, why not bring me one of the bones I gave him, or one of the elk or deer bones he found at other people's homes after they butchered animals, or, easiest of all, why not regurgitate some of his kibble? Why beef bones? It seemed that the complex explanation was really the simplest: He was giving me something I didn't have; he was giving me a gift.

I responded in kind. I licked and gnawed at his bones a bit before trying to hand them back to him. His reaction was always the same—he wouldn't take them. In fact, he would draw back his head in surprise, his look saying, "No, no, that's for you." This from a dog who adored bones and would chew them for hours, manipulating them in his paws and sucking their ends with his eyes closed in rapture.

I'd carry the bone into the bathroom and, after washing up, would take it downstairs and place it directly in front of his dog door. He'd watch me with a bit of chagrin—"You don't know what you're missing"—and then he'd pick it up, and slap-slap, head outside, where he'd lie on the porch and chew it into something that resembled a seashell that has been tossed by the waves until it is smooth and round and polished.

Undoubtedly, Morgan and most of the researchers who followed his lead into the twentieth century would have found these two anecdotes—claiming to show reason and emotion in dogs—thin gruel. These men increasingly relied on controlled experiments done in the laboratory and, pulling their chins, would have said, "Interesting examples of reasoning and emotion in animals, Mr. Kerasote. Now show us some proof."

In 1932, that's exactly what Edward Tolman did. A psychologist at the University of California, he used an experiment designed by one of his graduate students, H. C. Blodgett, to argue that animals retained memories of their territory and could make informed decisions based on this information. Hungry rats were allowed to run through a maze for six days, but without any food reward. On the seventh day they found food at the end of the maze and, within two trials, were completing the maze as quickly, and with as few errors, as the control rats who had gotten food every day.

Tolman concluded that the first group of rats had learned the twists and turns of the maze while wandering around freely. He called this process "latent learning" and coined the term "cognitive map" for the mental geography that rats, dogs, and people assimilate in their travels and then retain so as to help them get economically from place to place. It was this very sort of mental map, Tolman would say, that Merle used when he cut me off at the pass.

I also believe that because Merle wandered extensively and had the opportunity to build ever larger cognitive maps—in all senses of the term—he was able to make a leap of the canine mind and bring me beef bones as tokens of his affection. A bold statement, it's true, but I'm willing to give him the benefit of the doubt, as I imagine Tolman's contemporary, Robert Yerkes, would, if he were alive today.

A Harvard psychologist who co-founded the *Journal of Animal Behavior* in the early 1900s, Yerkes stood out from his colleagues in that he understood an animal's behavior to be a window into its subjective experience: If you bring someone beef bones over a period of eight years to the exclusion of other bones that are readily available, it's more than chance; it's likely that you're saying something by this action. In a time when most psychologists believed that animals led impoverished mental lives, Yerkes sided with Darwin when he wrote, "There is no question, in the mind of the person who really knows animals, that the higher vertebrates possess a great variety of sense qualities and feelings. . . . Of emotions, sentiments, associations, memory images, ideas, and even certain forms of judgement there are noteworthy evidences, and the more liberal among psychologists are at present inclined to believe that at least some animals, among them the dog and horse, the raccoon and cat, experience conscious complexes which are much like ours."

Such liberal views, however, remained in the minority during the early part of the twentieth century, and not without reason. In the late 1800s, the Russian physiologist Ivan Pavlov had graphically demonstrated that if you showed a dog food and rang a bell while it salivated, it would soon salivate when the bell was sounded, even in the absence of food. Following Pavlov's lead, many animal researchers designed stimulus-response experiments, forgetting that even though a conditioned response could be readily produced in their subjects, these animals were in fact complex beings who might act differently in a natural environment where stimuli are never experienced in a vacuum, but against a background of other interacting stimuli. The result of relying mainly on laboratory observation was that animals came to be seen as simplistic creatures, influenced predominantly by positive and negative reinforcements like food and electrical shocks.

It was the American psychologist John Watson who subsequently applied this view of animals to the social arena. If controllers could manipulate enough stimuli, his reasoning went, they could control the entirety of their subjects' lives. This notion would lead to profoundly tragic consequences for millions of people in the Soviet Union and China, but Watson was unable to foresee its political implications when he wrote, "Give me a dozen healthy infants, well-formed, and my own specified world to bring them up in and I'll guarantee to take any one at random and train him to become any type of specialist I might select—doctor, lawyer, artist, merchant chief and, yes, even beggar-man and thief, regardless of his talents, penchants, tendencies, abilities, vocations, and race of his ancestors."

In the 1930s, the Harvard psychologist B. F. Skinner then took equal portions of Pavlov and Watson and combined them with his own laboratory experiments—trials of positive reinforcement with which he taught pigeons to play toy pianos and discriminate between playing cards—to produce the science of behaviorism. As Skinner enthusiastically reported, his techniques made "it possible to shape an animal's behavior as a sculptor shapes a lump of clay."

Skinner was both a meticulous scientist and a great popularizer of his lab work. Not stopping with rats and pigeons, he gave the public an easy way to train their dogs when he invented clicker training, using an inexpensive device that makes a cricket-like sound and substitutes for the human voice saying "good dog" or "yes." In this way, the clicker gives the dog a precise, unvarying cue that it has executed the correct behavior and that a reward or reinforcement will follow. And the reinforcement worked both ways. People enjoyed clicker training because it was easy and got results.

Skinner became controversial, however, when he made the case that animals perform their conditioned responses in a "purely mechanical" fashion, without really knowing what they're doing. He then extended this notion to human beings. The world of introspection, he claimed, was "vastly overrated" and wasn't an essential part of the fields of behavior or medicine. When *Beyond Freedom and Dignity* was published, its very title made the hairs of libertarians stand on end. Their suspicions of Skinner's totalitarian tendencies only increased when he approvingly quoted one of Jean-Jacques Rousseau's most chilling passages from *Émile:*

> Let [the child] believe that he is always in control, though it is always you [the teacher] who really controls. There is no subjugation so perfect as that which keeps the appearance of freedom, for in that way one captures volition itself. The poor baby, knowing nothing, able to do nothing, having learned nothing, is he not at your mercy? Can you not arrange everything in the world which surrounds him? Can you not influence him as you wish? His work, his play, his pleasures, his pains, are not all these in your hands and without his knowing? Doubtless he ought to do only what he wants; but he ought to want to do only what you want him to do; he ought not to take a step which you have not foreseen; he ought not to open his mouth without your knowing what he will say.

Substitute the word "dog" for "baby" and it's not hard to see why dog trainers eagerly adopted Skinner's methods. After all, who doesn't want an obedient dog? And unlike babies, do we really need to worry about a domestic animal being subjugated? The word "domestic" implies that condition.

Today, the language of Rousseau and Skinner can be found in a variety of dog-training manuals. As Kevin Behan writes in his book *Natural Dog Training*, "To Master a dog, we must be decisive and control everything that the dog learns so the dog will have no opportunity but to learn what we want him to." Not only should everything be managed, Behan continues, but the dog should also have "absolutely no unsupervised freedom."

Jean Donaldson, in *The Culture Clash: A Revolutionary New Way of Understanding the Relationship Between Humans and Domestic Dogs,* is just as clear about the role humans should play in this ancient relationship: "You have control of your dog's access to everything he wants in life: food, the outside world, attention, other dogs, smells on the ground, play opportunities." She advises micro-managing every detail of a dog's life down to training it to eliminate on command. Why do we need to oversee dogs in this fashion? Because, she answers, they have "little, smoothish lemon brains," not at all like the "convoluted, melon brains" that allow humans to think.

George Orwell warned of the perils of this sort of control in his novel *1984* (published in 1949), but few dog trainers have worried about becoming Big Brother to their dogs, especially when Skinner's methods—clicking for the correctly executed behavior followed by a treat—have produced hundreds of thousands of spit-and-polish dogs: field dogs, service dogs, and the family pet. Yet the nagging question remains: Does controlling a dog's life through micro-managing its behavior short-circuit its ability to think on its own?

During the 1930s, Professor E. G. Sarris of the University of Hamburg investigated this issue by doing a series of innovative experiments with a dog named Argos. A male of Pinscher, Spitz, and Dachshund descent, Argos was twenty-three months old when Sarris began his experiments, suspending a piece of meat by a string high enough above the dog so that he couldn't reach it, even with a great leap. Close by were wagons with little and big boxes on them. Once Sarris showed Argos that the wagons could be towed by loops, the dog quickly realized that the wagon with the bigger box needed to be towed under the meat in order for him to stand on it and grasp the meat. Sarris made the problems harder and harder, putting obstacles in front of the wagon, which Argos needed to remove one by one so that he could roll the wagon under the meat. In addition, Sarris hid the wagon a dozen feet from the meat. Argos would run around in widening circles, searching for it, and, when he found it, pull it into position so he could stand on it and retrieve his prize.

According to the animal behaviorist Marian Stamp Dawkins, whose book *Through Our Eyes Only?* is one of the more compelling explanations of animal consciousness, Argos's actions demonstrated the two attributes of thinking. "The first," she writes, "is that the thinker should have some sort of internal representation of the world in his, her, or its head. This means that it does not just respond to the stimuli immediately surrounding it but carries a memory of things that were there in the past but are now gone or are out of sight. The second is that something is done to that representation to enable the true thinker to work out what would happen under new circumstances—for example, if everything were turned upside down or one element were changed."

Sarris did further experiments, trying to ascertain the extent of a dog's internal representation of the world. After chaining Argos and some of his kennel mates in place, he showed them a piece of meat attached to a string. Then he tossed the meat out of reach. The loose end of the string was left within their grasp, however. One dog, Phryne, tried to reach the meat by lunging, soon gave up, and yawned with "an expression of helplessness." Another, Ares, became frustrated, barked wildly, and bit at his chain. Both Niki and Argos initially lunged at the meat a few times before becoming quiet and studying the string. Within forty-eight seconds, each used the string to tow the meat toward them. When the tests were repeated, Argos and Niki reeled in the meat within four seconds of seeing it.

Sarris then showed them the meat at the end of the string before tossing the meat over a wall. Both Niki and Argos pulled it in. Sarris proceeded to lengthen the string to five, ten, fifteen, twenty, and forty meters so as to see how far—both in distance and time—the dog's internal representation of "meat at the end of the string" extended. Niki was able to retrieve the meat when it was fifteen meters out, but Argos truly shone. Even when the meat was forty meters away, he pulled it in.

Sarris's conclusion from these experiments was the opposite of the one reached by his contemporaries, Watson and Skinner. There are real differences in "temperament and intelligence," he wrote, that predispose individuals to certain activities. In other words, despite positive reinforcement, you can't train any child to become an artist or any pigeon to play the piano—at least not well—as the American behaviorists claimed. Dog training expert Steven R. Lindsay emphasizes this concept when he advises dog owners to ask themselves whether the dog under their care, "given a choice, would likely select the career being chosen for it."

Sarris's experiments also showed him that "a widening of the dog's *'Umwelt'* was possible." The German word *Umwelt* means "environment," but Sarris used it in the sense of "the surrounding world of the dog, which it is capable of understanding." Key to such an expanded understanding of the world was giving dogs the time and space to work through problems on their own. What they needed was less control, not more.

———

One autumn day I saw firsthand where allowing a dog to make its own decisions on a regular basis might lead. Merle and I were traveling in the high mountains east of Yellowstone National Park, trying out two llamas as pack animals instead of horses. One of the llamas, its coat brown and white, was doing a workmanlike job of carrying our camp and food onto the Continental Divide. The other llama constantly wanted to sit down. And there are few creatures—maybe a camel—who can be more stubborn than a llama when it puts its mind to something. This llama, colored black and white, could not be cajoled; he could not be pulled; he could not be prodded.

There we were, halted several miles from camp, on a high barren ridge in one of the more remote spots in the Lower Forty-eight, the sky becoming roiled with storm clouds, and the second llama refused to move. More. He lowered himself to the ground and folded his feet calmly beneath him as if he might wait a decade before the whim to move crossed his mind again.

He was dallied to the first llama's packsaddle, so I figured if I got the first llama moving, the second might follow. I clucked the first llama into a walk; the second sat firm. The result was that the first llama's packsaddle was nearly torn off. Of course, this was nothing new—to a lesser degree, it had been happening all day. But whereas the first llama had previously become annoyed, stomping his feet, he now became infuriated. He turned and spit into the second llama's face. Placidly, the second llama gazed into the distance as a mix of phlegm and masticated vegetation dripped down his cheeks.

In the meantime, Merle had been watching the unfolding of this little drama from a sitting position a dozen feet off to the side, his head twisting intently from the first llama to the second and then to me, pulling, pushing, and exhorting the stubborn beast in no uncertain terms to get to his feet. The next thing I knew, Merle was rushing at the second llama, woofing at him while lunging menacingly at his forequarters, as he had done to the bison and the moose. All to no effect. The llama stared beyond Merle into some ethereal distance where men and dogs and good pack llamas were not troubling him.

Merle tried the woof-and-lunge maneuver once more—nothing. Turning, he seemed to give up and walk away, putting on an air of nonchalance as he ambled behind the llama. Then, without warning, he darted at the llama's rear and sank his teeth into his butt. No nip—this was an honest-to-goodness bite. The llama leapt to his feet and lunged forward, running into the first llama, who began to trot up the trail.

In this way—Merle following the second llama and worrying his heels each time he slowed—we got to camp. Arriving at tree line in the next valley, I picketed the llamas and looked at Merle.

"Thanks," I said gratefully. "I didn't think you had any Heeler in you."

He panted happily, wagging his tail in the half-mast position that I had come to learn meant "I think it's time to eat." And it made me wonder if, back there on the trail, Merle had worked out that getting to camp meant eating and had prudentially decided to take matters into his own hands or, more accurately, his own teeth. Perhaps he had read my frustration with the llama and interpreted it as a call for assistance.

Whatever his motives, his actions impressed me. He had seen a problem that neither I nor the other llama could solve, and—just like Argos using the right-sized box—had thought outside of the box, coming up with a solution that worked. His ability to solve our dilemma in an elegant way—and without any reinforcement from me—was unlike any behavior I had witnessed in a dog, a creature who normally is just along for the ride and, like a child, isn't expected to use its brain.

So who is right? Are dogs mere trial-and-error learners, stimulus-response machines, who respond to clickers and dog biscuits? Are their brains accurately portrayed as "lemons," with all the negative connotations the word implies? Or might their brains be very much like ours, quite capable of reasoning and emotion, yet with a crucial difference?

According to the animal scientist Temple Grandin this difference lies in the frontal lobes of the cerebral cortex, the convoluted gray matter that covers the rest of the brain like a helmet. People have big frontal lobes that help process raw data into abstractions. Dogs have smaller ones and lack the ability to make such generalizations. However, as humans evolved big frontal lobes and dogs didn't, humans lost the ability to discriminate the tiny individual details of the world while dogs retained it. Autistic people, like dogs, also have this ability because, as Grandin points out, their frontal lobes receive "bad input." And she should know. An autistic person herself, she has turned what is usually thought of as a handicap into a gift, interpreting animal behavior as few have been able to do. Acting as a consultant to the meat industry, she has designed one-third of all the livestock-handling facilities in the United States so that animals can move through them with less stress.

To illustrate what seeing the world in vivid detail means, she describes how a dangling chain, a dark shadow on the floor, or a bright reflection on a metal bar can all cause cattle to balk as they move through a livestock plant. Such sensitivity to tiny objects and noises is what autistic people also report. They say that they can see the flicker of fluorescent lighting or hear the hum of electric wires in the wall. People who aren't autistic miss these details and see only the big picture. They "see what they're expecting to see," Grandin writes. "New things just don't register."

It was no surprise to me, then, that Merle froze at the sight of the first life-size bronze statue of an elk he encountered and immediately began to stalk it. He was simply reacting to the is-ness of the world. Until he found out differently, an elk was an elk was an elk. This constant attention to detail must have stood him in good stead when he was a pup roaming the desert along the San

Juan River—if you notice every potential source of food, you won't starve. Now, as a grown dog, he went into a crouch thirty feet from the bronze elk, but I could see that he was growing suspicious, his body language expressing doubt. Extending his nose forward, he sniffed and crawled forward. At fifteen feet, he suddenly sagged with the knowledge that he'd been fooled and turned to me with a look that said, "Why didn't you tell me?" He never stalked that particular elk again, but if he saw a statue of another elk in another place—and also happened to be upwind of it so he couldn't smell it—he'd stalk it. In his mind, all new statues of elk had to be considered real until proven otherwise.

Did being fooled in this way make him a lemon brain? I doubt it. It meant that he processed the world differently from humans. The result was that he and I became a highly effective team. As Grandin points out, "Dog brains and human brains specialized: humans took over the planning and organizing tasks, and dogs took over the sensory tasks. Dogs and people coevolved and became even better partners, allies, and friends."

The important thing to remember, she adds, is that evolution didn't get rid of our smaller, interior brain—the one all mammals share and which houses emotion—while our larger, more modern cerebral cortex was developing over it. Nor, for that matter, was our very ancient reptilian brain discarded. Every one of us still has the equivalent of a reptilian brain in our brain stem, which takes care of our basic life-support functions such as breathing. This interconnected, three-part brain structure—what the neuro-physiologist Paul D. MacLean calls "the triune brain"—is why people so often act like dogs and dogs act like people: Parts of both our brains are the same.

This is also the reason why dogs can display what contemporary biologists have termed "Machiavellian intelligence." Another name for this sort of intelligence is "calculating reason," a concept that can be defined as the ability to work out what to do in constantly changing social situations, especially when other members of your community possess the same skill. Put simply, this means that dogs can lie.

For many years I found this impossible to believe. I was certain that Merle was incapable of any falsity, his heart an open book. How could anyone, I thought, who persisted in taking the world at face value—deceived by statues of elk—be anything else than who he was? I had read Jeffrey Moussaieff Masson's *Dogs Never Lie About Love,* and had nodded my head in agreement when he wrote, "Dogs do not lie to you about how they feel because they cannot lie about feelings. . . . Nobody has ever seen a sad dog pretending to be happy, or a happy dog pretending to be sad."

Then one day I left on another assignment. We were at the new house, and as I loaded the car Merle stood on the front porch with his head slung low in despair, his eyes liquid and plaintive: "I thought we were a team. I thought we'd never part. You're leaving me again."

I petted him, told him I loved him a half dozen times, and I'd be back in three days. Scott would pass by after work and pick him up so he could stay at the ranch. I drove off, watching him stand on the porch, his entire posture wounded to the core. I got slightly beyond the post office—he had realized after several more attempts at running to the P.O. that I wouldn't take him along—and it was here that I discovered that I had forgotten my wallet. I drove back. Only two minutes had elapsed since I had left him, and there he was, not on the front porch, but trotting jauntily toward the village, his tail high and wagging in that eager way he had when he set off on his rounds.

If he were truly someone who could not practice deceit or lie about his feelings, one might have said that he was simply being a dog: a being who was totally immersed in the moment. Two minutes before, he had been sad at my departure. Now, heading down the road—out to snag a biscuit, chase some ground squirrels, or see his friends—he was happy. He lived utterly in the present. But his behavior in the next few moments belied this notion.

His ears went back—he had heard the familiar sound of the Subaru's engine—and, as he wheeled, his expression went from happy expectation at what he would find in the village to startled surprise at my return. His face then took on a look of sheepishness.

He approached my car with his head and shoulders lowered, his tail wagging hard, but held far below the horizontal, which he only did when he had been caught at something he ought not to be doing, like exploring empty elk wrappers in the trash. He was clearly embarrassed. I stopped the car, and he came up to the door, grinning hugely at me, the corners of his lips pulled back in the classic pose of a submissive dog. "Ha-ha-ha," he panted. "You're back! What a surprise!"

"You, Sir," I said, wagging a playful finger at him, "are a faker."

"Ha-ha-ha," he continued to pant, and now he began to whine, a plaintive little protest: "I really do miss you when you're gone. I really do. But—"

"I know, I know," I finished for him. "A dog's got his own life. And you, Sir, have an especially rich one. 'I thought we were a team. I thought we'd never part. You're leaving me again.' You should be on stage, Señor."

"Oowoo." His whine turned into a woof of protest. "I do miss you. I really do."

"I know you do." I laughed, scratching his ears.

I fetched my wallet, petted him again, and got in the car. He watched me drive off. He no longer looked chastised. He wore a fatalistic expression, like someone who has been caught in the act and who realizes that he has no defenses whatsoever. His MO had been discovered: He wasn't quite as downtrodden when I left as he had tried to make me believe. In short, he had been milking me for sympathy.

When I tried to apply Morgan's Canon to explain Merle's behavior, the result was unsatisfactory. Merle did not go from sad to happy and remain happy at my return, which would be the response expected from a dog who lives in the moment, is overjoyed to see his person return, and has no calculating reason. Instead, he became flustered and embarrassed. To fully appreciate what was happening during our interchange, it's important to note that Merle had never before greeted me in the fashion I've described. Either he was overjoyed to see me or he bayed in frustration, signifying that I had stayed away too long. Embarrassment had never been part of his repertoire. Why? I had never before immediately returned once I had left on a trip.

Most of us act the very same way when we've been caught dissimulating. Clearly, the principle of parsimony doesn't always explain what our dogs are doing. Their behavior can be as complex as ours, and when it is—when they operate from the parts of their brains that function in a similar way to the human brain—their actions deserve an equally complex explanation.

The work of the veterinarian Nicholas Dodman, the head of the Animal Behavior Department at the Tufts University School of Veterinary Medicine, has substantiated this idea. Dodman has pioneered the treatment of depression, anxiety, and obsessive-compulsive disorder in dogs with the very same psychotropic drugs that have been so successful in treating these disorders in humans. "In my practice," he says, "I work on the basic principle that pets are as emotionally invested as we are, experiencing anger, fear, boredom, loneliness, jealousy, and other sophisticated emotions. Acting on this firm belief, I am able to diagnose and explain behaviors to myself and to owners. . . . The very success of pharmacologic treatments . . . is testimony to the basic similarity between the mental processes of humans and nonhuman animals."

I continued to wonder, however, if a similarity between the mental processes of human and nonhuman animals necessarily implies that dogs have the ultimate hallmark of consciousness—self-awareness. Do dogs know, staring at themselves in a mirror, that *this* body, containing *these* thoughts, is *me*?

Watching Merle pass by the mirror in my bedroom, I doubted it. The mirror was tall and narrow, by my closet door, in a place that Merle rarely went. The few times I saw him pass it, he glanced at his reflection without giving any apparent recognition that the dog facing him was himself. In fact, he completely ignored his image in the mirror, as do most dogs and most other animals except chimpanzees and dolphins.

Occasionally, researchers have seen a dog, parrot, or monkey interact with its reflection, but with the sort of greeting gestures that indicate that it considers its reflection another member of its species and not itself. When, after a while, the animal doesn't get the expected response, it ignores its reflection until the mirror is moved to a different location, and then it repeats its social interaction as if the reflection were a new animal.

Experiments with chimpanzees and dolphins, however, show that when a mark is placed on their bodies in a location that they can't see without a mirror, they use the mirror to investigate the mark. In the case of chimps, they will touch the mark with their fingers and then inspect and even sometimes smell their fingers. One dolphin, who had a mark placed on his tongue, immediately swam to the mirror and opened and closed his mouth as he examined the mark—behavior he had never exhibited before. Researchers have therefore concluded that only chimpanzees and dolphins have the same sort of self-recognition that we do.

I remembered, though, how Merle had recognized the echo of the howling dog on the San Juan River as his own voice and responded to it with a tail whose excited wagging clearly stated, "That's me!" Could a dog have acoustic but not visual recognition of himself? Now and again, I puzzled over this question.

Then one day I went to get some physical therapy for a pulled muscle in my back. The practitioner, a sports trainer named Jen

Fuller, was a great fan of Merle's and said he was welcome to come along to her studio. As we entered, I noticed that one wall was entirely mirrored. Merle noticed it, too. He turned his head and watched the man and the dog walking across the carpeted room side by side.

Merle stopped dead and looked sharply up at me; then he looked back to the mirrored wall and gazed at my reflection. His mouth parted slightly and he cocked his head quizzically. I was obviously standing beside him, but I was also standing alongside that dog in the mirror. He next stared at Jen's reflection and then to the woman herself, standing a few feet from me. He glanced to me, then back to my reflection. I raised my hand, and he saw my reflection raise its hand. Leaning forward, he gazed with intense concentration at the man and dog in the mirror and tentatively wagged his tail. The reflection of the dog wagged its tail.

As if the rug had been pulled out from beneath him, Merle sat down. He turned his head up to me in wonder; he looked back to the mirror; then he looked back to me. He began to wag his tail with considerable vigor.

"I get it," his expression said. "I see who I am."

The big mirror, taking in the entire room and all its occupants, had apparently let him see himself alongside people whom he recognized from the real world. It had provided him with the necessary context to understand what a reflection was. Suddenly, that reddish-gold dog in the mirror wasn't some strange, odorless, two-dimensional dog to be ignored, but the dog who walked with Ted. He had an identity. He was *Merle*. To paraphrase Descartes, who will more than likely turn over in his grave hearing his famous words recast so as to describe the mind of a dog, "I see myself within my world and therefore I am."

What Merle did next corroborated my translation. He walked to the mirror and lay down before it, facing his own reflection. As Jen and I began to discuss my exercise routine, he turned his head left and right, raising his chin and watching how his reflection did exactly what he did. He showed none of the behavior typical of his interaction with other dogs—no smelling, no posturing, no tail flagging. He was intently studying different views of himself, as he had never done before.

"That's you," I said encouragingly.

He wagged his tail very hard.

From that day on, every time we visited Jen's studio, Merle would first say hello to her, then he'd lie in front of the mirror as she and I talked over my exercises. He'd turn his head this way and that, studying himself first head-on and then in profile. If his body language could be trusted, not only did he know who he was, he continued to be pleased with his image. And the next time he passed by the bedroom mirror, he walked directly to his reflection and gave himself a look, his wagging tail proclaiming, "Yep, that's me."

CHAPTER 12

The Mayor of Kelly

I called Merle by many names in addition to his own: Ski Dog, Señor, Monsieur, the pup of my dreams, Sir. Sometimes, when he was looking very royal on his dedicated quadruped couch, I would joke with him, *"Ah, le roi des chiens,"* oh, king of dogs, and, alerted by my tone of voice that I was pulling his tail, he'd look away and ignore me.

Others called him Merley, Mooey, Moo-Moo, Merlster, Mooward The Pooward, Love Sponge, Golden One, and Merle The Pearl. But of all the nicknames he received, none was so widely used as The Mayor.

It's hard to say who first appointed him to the office, although the honor may go to Arthur King, a short, convivial man who owned the spread on which Scott and April lived. Handsomely retired and with free time on his hands, he perhaps saw a kindred soul in Merle. Arthur liked to linger at the post office, telling stories of his horses, dogs, and grandchildren, and consequently often ran into Merle, who, just as often, went to the P.O. to socialize with other Kellyites as they came to get their mail.

"And how's the mayor today?" Arthur would say, leaning over his ample middle to greet Merle face to face.

Taking an appreciative sniff of Arthur's trouser cuffs, redolent of horse corrals and Springer Spaniels, Merle would give a hearty wag of his tail: "Better now, Arthur."

It was our new house, however—near the junction of the park road and the only road into the village—that was the springboard that launched Merle's political career. Everyone had to pass by our drive to get into or out of Kelly, and Merle, in between making his thrice-daily inspection tours around the village, would lie by the entrance to our drive, greeting cars as they went by.

Standing, he'd peer into the vehicle's driver-side window and give his tail a wag: "Hey, good morning, how are you? Lovely day, isn't it?" And he'd often be there in the late afternoon when people returned. He'd rise from the warm tarmac and walk in front of an approaching car, so it had to slow down. Proceeding to the window, he would say, "Welcome back."

Nothing pleased him more than to have two cars stop at the same time, each going in opposite directions, both drivers leaning out of their windows to give him a pat on the head.

"You are a traffic stopper, Sir," I'd tell him when he'd trot back inside.

He'd do a little two-step with his paws: "Just keeping in touch with my constituents."

Of these he soon had many, a large percentage of them female, whom he'd visit in a clockwise direction, making a great circle route around the village, like some 747 dropping off packages of good cheer and taking on fuel for the next leg of its journey.

His first stop was the Kents', across the road from us. He'd slip under their buckrail fence, go to their side door, and stand on his hind legs, front paws hanging limply while he peered through their kitchen window to where Gladys and Donald were having their morning coffee. I'd see the door open and in he'd go.

About a half hour later, out he'd come, trotting around the back of their log cabin, to emerge from their far drive and head south down the main road. His next stop was at Eric Moore's. A songwriter,

Eric liked to compose on his guitar while sitting on his front steps. Merle would join him there, and they'd have a sing-along. Later, Eric named one of his CDs *Song Dog,* after the coyotes who lived around Kelly, but also after Merle, who is pictured in the album's cover pamphlet, standing next to Eric's shoulder, both their heads close together, mouths open as they croon to the sky.

A woman named Jill Oja lived in the same house, and she'd often collect the surrounding dogs, taking them like a pied piper for a long walk by the river. If Merle couldn't find a song or a walk with his friends, he'd proceed to the eastern side of Kelly, where he'd visit Beverly Wood and her collection of horses, mules, and Golden Retrievers. Like Gladys, Beverly was always a soft touch for a biscuit.

From Beverly's Merle would circle south and west along the banks of the Gros Ventre River, stopping in to visit whomever he'd find at home. Eventually, he'd pass our old trailer and meander around it, taking in its scents. From our new house there was an unimpeded view of where we had lived, four hundred yards across the field, and I could sometimes catch a glimpse of him through my binoculars, zigzagging around the porch, smelling, speeding up, and slowing down to give a spot half a minute or more of deep consideration.

More than likely, these spots were where moose had bedded during the night or a coyote had left its mark, but I always wondered if the smells of his past persisted even though Zula had moved away with her family, Jack had been shot for chasing cattle, and his successor, Jack Two, had been hit and killed while chasing a snowmobile trailer in front of the post office.

Whatever the case, Merle would lift his head and his eyes would slowly refocus as if returning from a long ways off. Then, squaring his shoulders, he'd set a speedy course for the western boundary of Kelly, where Lucille Garretson's cabin stood. A stooped and elderly bookkeeper, she worked the night shift at Snow King Resort in Jackson and rose just about the time Merle passed by for a mid-morning treat. From there he'd go to the post office and finally come home, having completed his first circum-ambulation of the village for the day.

Soon, though, Merle was paying the price of his ambitions, as do a lot of politicians. He began to put on weight, his torso and belly getting rounder and rounder until some people, instead of calling him "Mr. Mayor," began to call him "The Sausage."

I couldn't understand how a few biscuits here and there could be making Merle into a balloon, so I began to follow him. Merle, however, would have nothing of it. Unlike when we took a walk around the village together, and he would lead, if he saw me try-ing to follow him at a distance, he'd stop, trot back to me, and wait for me to set the route. If I tried to follow him secretly, he always seemed to spy me out and would come up to me with a "gosh, great to see you" look on his face.

"Go ahead," I'd say, motioning for him to proceed.

"Ha-ha-ha," he'd pant and sit down. "You lead, please."

I had to leave the house far behind him, scuttling here and there for cover like some burglar before I discovered what he was about. Gladys was feeding him all sorts of kitchen scraps—left-over casseroles and bread—and the number of people he hit up for a dog biscuit was truly phenomenal. It was Lucille, though, who was pushing him over the top. She was feeding him a daily ration of grilled chicken breasts and filet mignon stuffed with Roquefort cheese that the chef at the Snow King Resort was giving her.

I printed a sign—"Please do not feed me. The extra weight is bad for my joints and heart"—and hung it around his neck. He gave me the most put-out look: "You gotta be kidding. Me, *moi*, the dog who does not wear a collar, wear this?"

"You can't control yourself, Monsieur," I told him. "This is the price."

It did little good. Merle's constituents and he were in a co-dependent relationship, especially the old ladies. I went to each one and impressed upon them that they had to stop feeding Merle

or I would keep him home—no more visits. This threat worked
with everyone except Lucille, who said she'd try but she didn't
think she'd be able to stop feeding him.

"He looks so irresistible," she said.

"He's milking you," I said.

"I can't refuse him," she answered.

It was at this time that Allison got a shock collar for Brower. She
was finding it difficult to get him to come consistently, and he also
was jumping on people when he greeted them. I thought long and
hard about trying it on Merle, hating the thought of shocking him
but fast running out of alternatives to stop his bingeing. He was
hanging out at Lucille's for a good part of the day, either sitting
expectantly on her front step or parking himself there for a nap.
I'd be leaving for a bike ride or a hike, activities he enjoyed, and
after calling for ten minutes I'd have to go over to her place and
fetch him. Even after seeing me in biking shorts or hiking boots,
he wasn't terribly excited to leave, and I found myself reflecting
on something that B. F. Skinner once said: "The fundamental mistake made by all those who choose weak methods of control is to
assume that the balance of control is left to the individual, when
in fact it is left to other conditions."

In the past, the other conditions that Merle had been exposed
to while he wandered around Kelly had been healthy. They had
made him a well-rounded dog. Now, some of these conditions were
making him well rounded in a way that was guaranteed to shorten
his life. When at last I blocked his dog door and refused to let him
leave the house without me, he'd come to my desk at ten-minute
intervals, asking to be let out, doing his little dance with his front
paws and panting excitedly.

Obviously, the problem we faced was founded upon freedom.
Confine the dog and you can control every calorie it consumes. To
be fair, what was happening to Merle was just as much a human
problem as a canine one. Eating as much as possible works for a

Merle and I met on the San Juan River, Utah, on the night of April 21, 1991.
He was a thin, ten-month-old pup, surviving on his own in the desert.

(Photo by Ted Kerasote)

Floating down the San Juan River, Merle loved to lie on the cooler and watch the canyons go by. Here he is with our friend Benj Sinclair.

(Photo by Ted Kerasote)

Two of Merle's earliest and best friends in Kelly were Zula, a Vizsla, and Jack, a Border Collie.

(Photo by Ted Kerasote)

Merle knew Tessa Landale from the time she was born, guarded and played with her, and took tidbits gently from her fingers. *(Photo by Ted Kerasote)*

Merle and I spent hundreds of days in the backcountry. On one of these trips we hiked the length of the Pariah River, through Utah and Arizona. As always, we'd stop for a moment of "eyes locked together." *(Photo by Allison von Maur)*

Merle gets in a last few turns before the snows melts. He loved to "ski," sliding down the snow like an otter with front and rear legs outstretched.

(Photo by Ted Kerasote)

Merle scouts for elk with Scott Landale and Eric Stone, high in the Gros Ventre Mountains east of Jackson Hole.

(Photo by Ted Kerasote)

Merle scents the air for the invisible and airborne trails of elk.
(Photo by Ted Kerasote)

Merle met Brower, a young Golden Retriever, in 1995 and became his mentor. They remained friends for the rest of their lives.
(Photo by Ted Kerasote)

Brower, Merle, and I climbed many of the peaks in the Gros Ventre Mountains east of Jackson Hole.

(Photo by Allison von Maur)

One of Merle's favorite pastimes was to help Kelly songwriter Eric Moore compose a new song.

(Photo by Chuck Manners)

When Merle died, I buried him on our land, near the prayer flags, his spirit always close.

(Photo by Mayo Lykes)

One of Merle's favorite hikes and skis was Snow King Mountain, above the town of Jackson, Wyoming, where he could meet and greet his many canine and human friends. Behind him lie Jackson Hole and Grand Teton and Yellowstone national parks. *(Photo by Ted Kerasote)*

wolf or a dog who, like Merle, gets a lot of exercise and finds the occasional windfall of a carcass or a casserole. It doesn't work when someone indulges a dog's hardwired tendency to eat as much as it can. In short, if Merle was going to keep his freedom, I had to change my neighbor's behavior as much as I needed to change my dog's. I borrowed Brower's shock collar.

It had an orange neckband and a small black transmitting box with two prongs that made contact with the dog's neck. The prongs were interchangeable and color-coded. Green gave the biggest shock. Yellow, orange, red, and brown prongs gave lesser shocks in descending order. Brower would respond only to the green prongs, exhibiting no more than a sudden flinch, as if to say, "Oh, yeah, I remember—don't jump on people." Given Merle's history with guns, I wasn't sure that starting him out on green was the best of ideas. So I tested the collar on myself and almost jumped through the roof at the shock. My admiration of Brower's stoicism went up markedly. I used the red prong on Merle.

When I put the collar on him, he gave me a disgusted look and tried to study the contraption by craning his neck and peering out of the bottom of his eyes.

"Enjoy yourself," I told him and went to my desk. Ten seconds later, I heard the dog door slap.

After about an hour, I took the transmitter, put my bike and some dog biscuits in the car, and drove over to Lucille's, where I found him—sure enough—sitting on her step, staring at her front door with hypnotic intensity. "Open the door, Lucille," his gaze commanded. "Open the door."

Stepping out of the car, I yelled, "No," and shocked him.

He yowled a high-pitched bay and whirled to face me.

"No," I said again.

He ran toward me. I opened the door of the car and he leapt in. I took the collar off, gave him a biscuit, and said, "Thank you. How about we go for a bike ride."

The next morning, however, he was back at Lucille's.

I drove over, shocked him again, and he yowled just as pitifully. This time he didn't come right away.

"Come," I called. "Come, please!" And he ran to the car, jumped in, and we went for a hike.

But filet mignon stuffed with Roquefort cheese is a powerful reinforcement. The following morning I found him at Lucille's just as before. This time, he only had to see my car pull up before he started yowling at me. And instead of coming to the car, he ran across the field toward our house before I had a chance to shock him.

"What are you doing?" asked Lucille, opening her door.

I told her.

"That's awful," she said.

"You can continue to feed him," I told her, "and he'll keep getting shocked."

"This doesn't make me happy," she said.

"I'm not exactly thrilled by it, either," I replied. "Don't you understand that you're killing my dog with what you're feeding him? It's like giving crack to a kid. And if I have to keep him home to keep him away from you, he'll be really unhappy. Please, can't you stop?"

Her sharp gray face became a mask of conflicted emotions.

"How about we make a deal," I offered. "If he comes by here, you can feed him one biscuit a day—one small biscuit."

She thought about this.

"I'll even buy them for you, the kind he likes."

She looked at the ground. "You don't have to do that," she said, and without another word shuffled inside.

I drove home and found Merle lying on the dedicated quadruped couch.

"Are we done with Lucille's?" I asked.

He gave the tip of his tail the tiniest of wags.

I took off the collar and petted him. "It's for your own good, you know."

We had a few days of respite; then I noticed him leave the house and head directly across the field toward Lucille's cabin. I called him back and put on the shock collar. He gave me a grievous expression.

"Your choice," I told him. "You can go over there and you'll get shocked. This is nonnegotiable."

"Ha-ha-ha," he panted, "okay," and without missing a beat he turned and walked out to the main road, where he trotted south, toward the opposite end of the village from Lucille's. I waited about two hours before walking to the post office and along the buckrail fence to Lucille's, almost certain that he had tried to fake me out. Of course, he was there.

"No!" I shouted, shocking him.

His voice rose in a heart-rending series of bays and howls. "Why are you doing this to me? Why?"

I shocked him again, shouting, "No!"

Then I started to walk home. A minute later, I turned my head and caught sight of him, following about fifty yards behind me. When I got to the house, I waited for him. Tail low, he came up to me.

"Good," I said, removing the collar and handing him a biscuit. He took it without interest, opened his mouth, and let it drop to his feet.

"I'm sorry," I said, "that biscuits, and elk and antelope, are no longer good enough for you. You can go live with Lucille and be her dog if you want. I'm sure you'll get to do a lot of skiing and mountain biking and hunting with her."

He stared at me.

I shrugged my shoulders. "Go ahead," I said, extending a hand across the field. "See you later."

I walked inside, shutting the sliding screen door behind me. From my office, I watched him look across the field, first toward Lucille's, then toward the main road, where he would normally begin his rounds. He lowered his head and sniffed at the dog

biscuit. Picking it up, he ate it perfunctorily. A minute later, I
heard the dog door slap and his paws come across the pine floor.
I heard him drink some water then pad to the middle of the great
room, where he lay down with a disgruntled sigh.

For the next two days I kept an eagle eye on him. He made his
rounds to the south and came home directly across the field without going toward Lucille's. Then, on a warm sunny afternoon, I saw
him begin to meander through the sage, smelling here and there
as if he had no particular destination in mind and were simply following his nose wherever it led him. But he was going west.

I opened the sliding glass doors and stood on the deck.
Whistling sharply, I held the shock collar aloft, letting it dangle
from my fingers.

He turned. I raised the collar higher.

"No, no, no," I said.

He glanced in the direction of Lucille's cabin.

"No," I repeated.

For a good five seconds, we remained in this standoff, then he
walked to the deck and lay down, glumly putting his chin on his
outstretched paws.

"Well done," I said, dropping the shock collar by his side.
Going to the fridge, I got him an elk bone that I had defrosted for
this moment. When I brought it out to him, he took it softly from
my hand, put it down on the deck next to him, and laid his chin
back on his paws. I left him to his sulk.

About an hour later, as he was working on the bone, I went
outside, sat down next to him, and put an arm over his shoulder.
He dropped the bone and put his chin on my thigh.

"Are we done with Lucille?" I asked.

He gave his tail two thumps on the deck: "I'll try."

He really did. It also helped that his pitiful howling had had its
effect on Lucille. She stopped feeding him. Periodically, I'd wander over to her house, but he was never there. Much as I hated to

admit it, my experience with the shock collar bore out the experimental evidence of many studies, which has shown intense punishment to be effective in reducing unwanted behavior to zero while positive reinforcement gets only marginal results. Even more important to note, the behavior eliminated by punishment doesn't return, as it often does when positive reinforcement has been tried.

There is a difference, though, between this sort of punishment and the sort that becomes abuse, creating stressed and permanently cowed dogs. Steven R. Lindsay, who has trained dogs for the U.S. Army, notes three commonsense checks that a dog owner can use to differentiate between pain that is inflicted beneficially and that which turns into cruelty. Punishment, says Lindsay, that is unpredictable, uncontrollable, and inescapable is abuse. None of these conditions applied to Merle or, for that matter, Lucille.

Within a few months, he was back to seventy pounds, slim and lithe, and no one was calling him "The Sausage." He kept to the south and east sides of Kelly, spending more time with people who had their own dogs and who knew intuitively that the way into a dog's heart is never through its stomach but through activity and affection, a concept whose truth was verified by John Paul Scott and John Fuller during their massive study *Genetics and the Social Behavior of the Dog.* Dogs who were hand fed by attendants immediately lost interest in their keepers if they were shown no affection. On the other hand, dogs became attached to people who lavished affection upon them even when these people did not feed them. As Scott and Fuller wrote, "[A] puppy does not automatically love you because you feed it."

Lucille learned this the hard way. She later told me that Merle would not come into her house, nor would he let her pet him. "I'd get so mad at him," she said in exasperation, "but finally"—her thin face softened—"he let me pet him, just on the head, and only occasionally."

It was at this point in Merle's long tenure as mayor that the dogs of Kelly faced a crisis. The dogcatcher began to visit the village. This was unprecedented, for even though Kelly was in Grand Teton National Park, the park's leash laws had never been enforced within the village's boundaries. Since the village's dogs were well behaved, and the village was off the main tourist routes, the dogs were given dispensation by the park—unstated, of course—to roam freely.

Most of us suspected that the sudden appearance of the dogcatcher had been initiated by the cutting horse instructor, who was tired of a few ill-mannered dogs bothering his training sheep. In short order, numerous dogs were picked up, and their owners had to drive to Jackson and bail them out of the pound. Several dogs were caught repeatedly. Somehow, Merle glided through these months without being nabbed, and one morning I finally saw how he did it.

Only a minute or so after he had left on his rounds, I went to the shed to fetch some tools. He was trotting south, tail high, head erect, looking briskly left and right. At that very moment, I heard tires rumble over the cattle guard at the entrance to the village. So did Merle. His ears went back and he glanced over his shoulder. The white truck of the dogcatcher was coming down the main road. Without breaking stride, Merle faded left—faded being exactly what happened. Without giving any indication that he was alarmed, he simply angled into the tall grass by the side of the road and disappeared as if the golden field had swallowed his golden body.

His instant reaction to the dogcatcher's truck made me suspect that he had seen the man capture other dogs and put them in the truck's enclosed rear compartment. I didn't think that he himself had had a confrontation with the man and escaped, because several people in the village had mentioned watching Merle spy the dogcatcher at a distance. When they had looked for Merle the next moment, he had simply vanished.

His behavior seemed to be another demonstration that animals can learn by observing other animals and then apply what they've seen to themselves without any direct positive or negative reinforcement. In other words, the training is in the watching, not in the doing. I've described several instances of dogs learning in this fashion in previous chapters—dogs watching other dogs pull sleds and then imitating them; a dog watching other dogs eat and then mimicking their stance in front of their bowls; and Merle watching Brower retrieve and then doing it himself.

Karen Pryor, the psychologist who was responsible for popularizing clicker training after Skinner invented it, also tells a story of observational learning on the part of two porpoises, Malia and Hou, whom she trained to perform at Hawaii's Sea Life Park and Oceanic Institute. Each porpoise had her own act—back jumps, fetching rings underwater while blindfolded, aerial corkscrews—which each performed separately from the other. One day, however, both porpoises had trouble from the start; everything they did was a little rough and mistimed. Nevertheless, they managed to perform all their tricks, including difficult ones, like the high hoop jump, that had taken Pryor weeks to train.

When the show was finished, Pryor was left scratching her head at what had gone wrong. Then her assistant came up to her and said, "We got the animals mixed up. Someone put Malia in Hou's holding tank and Hou in Malia's. . . . They look so much alike now, I just never thought of that."

Remarkably, each porpoise had done the other's routine so well that Pryor assumed that they knew their acts by heart and were merely having a bad day. Without any reinforcements—no tossed fish, no whistles, no clickers—the two porpoises had learned each other's acts simply by watching each other perform.

Pryor saw this as a leap of the imagination on the part of Hou and Malia—what she called "insight." Wolfgang Köhler, one of the fathers of Gestalt psychology, agreed and used the same word, insight, for the phenomenon of animals having a eureka experience. He added that the animal suddenly sees the "structure of a situation" in a different light.

What intrigued me most about the dogs of Kelly, with respect to the dogcatcher, was why those who allowed themselves to be repeatedly caught never had such an insightful moment. Were they unable to remember what happened to them after they were put inside the dogcatcher's truck, or did they find their stay in the Jackson Hole Animal Shelter pleasant? Temple Grandin points out that "nervous animals investigate their environments more, learn more, and get smarter in the process." Perhaps the dogs who were repeatedly caught were so placid—so highly domesticated—that the stress of being confined in the pound didn't bother them. An unflappable Holstein cow fits this description perfectly.

Merle, and those other dogs who were never caught, could hardly be said to be nervous—far from it—so perhaps a better description of their ability to avoid danger is "cautiously suspicious." In times gone by, if you lacked this trait you were quickly eliminated from the population by predators. But even the most cautious of animals occasionally makes a mistake. Merle made his as he walked from Donald's and Gladys's house to our own, across the school bus turnout where a variety of repair trucks parked during the day, their drivers sitting in their cabs and making phone calls. Merle walked in front of one of these parked trucks. Later, when I reflected on the incident, it occurred to me that his recognition of the dogcatcher's vehicle must have been primarily acoustic rather than visual. The door of the truck opened. Nothing unusual in this—many of these service people gave him biscuits. The dogcatcher stepped out and nabbed him.

I've often questioned why the dogcatcher, a stocky and unsmiling man, walked Merle across the road to my office door instead of taking him directly to the pound. Perhaps it had something to do with Merle's having become a well-known dog by this time, not only in Kelly but also in Jackson, a result of his house sitters taking him with them when they went into town.

Weeks later, I'd be hiking along some trail with Merle and people whom I didn't know would stop us. Merle and these people would greet each other warmly, then the people would introduce themselves by saying, "We've never met you, but Merle has spent a couple of days at our house," or "We've hiked Snow King with Merle," or, the topper, "We went shopping with Merle in Idaho Falls." Perhaps the dogcatcher had some sense that hauling such a well-liked dog to the lockup without a second chance might be bad PR.

He held Merle by a collar that he had slipped over his head. Panting frantically, Merle looked desperate. Right then, I was pretty sure that he and the dogcatcher hadn't gone shopping together in The Falls. I slid open the glass door and immediately took the collar off Merle's neck. He sprang inside.

"Thank you," I told the dogcatcher, trying to keep my voice pleasant despite my anger at him for disrupting Kelly's dog paradise. Then, unable to control myself, I added, "But he knows the way home on his own."

We looked at each other.

The dogcatcher said, "You know dogs aren't supposed to be unleashed."

I took a breath. For whatever his reasons, the dogcatcher had spared Merle some time in the pound and saved me a trip to town as well as the fine.

"I know," I said, deciding not to argue, "and I appreciate your bringing him home. That was kind of you."

Perhaps I had surprised him. He didn't say another word. So I nodded and slid the glass door closed respectfully. The dogcatcher walked to his truck.

Turning to Merle, I said, "How do you do it, Sir?"

"Ha-ha-ha," he panted gleefully, pumping his paws up and down at his escape. "That was a close one!"

He was a hard dog to treat like a dog, even, I suppose, for the dogcatcher.

A few more weeks went by, the white truck of the dogcatcher cruising the village every other day. Then, suddenly, he was never seen again. The cutting horse instructor may have stopped complaining, or perhaps the county finally got the message from Kelly's angry dog owners: Since we lived in the park, let the park's policy about dogs prevail. It was both a simple and a fair one: No trouble from the dogs, no need to leash them.

CHAPTER 13

The Alpha Pair

Like all couples, Merle and I had to make compromises. Most often, at least in the summer, they were about fishing.

Taking a fly rod from the shed, I'd ask him, "Want to come?"

In return he'd give me a long-suffering look that I had come to know well. That slender cane in my hand meant that nothing exciting was about to happen. We'd walk to the river—good enough—and then I would proceed to stand in the water, walking, if you could call it that, upstream at a pace that would try the patience of a snail.

And all this to catch a trout. The first time I caught one in his presence, and he picked it off the shoreline, he dropped it immediately, holding his mouth open and gagging, "Ugh." He sent me a look of complete disgust: "May such slime never touch my mouth again." Turning, he immediately went to the river and had a long drink.

Despite his dislike of trout—at least ungrilled ones—he would come along with me, pausing to smell the flowers and gaze at birds flying across the sky, while sending me beseeching looks: "We could go on a nice hike, you know." Then, at the river, he'd wait on the bank as I cast, sighing intermittently, his entire slumped posture saying, "Have I told you how bored I am yet?"

One hour was his limit. Then he'd wag his tail slightly, as if to say, "I've paid my dues. See you at home." And off he'd go.

In the winter, it was my turn to be patient. After I had skied a slope and had stopped to put on my skins for the ascent, he'd come swooping by me, laughing and ignoring my "Hey, this is where we're stopping. Merle!" Down, down, down, he'd continue, finally halting where the gradient left off. Tail whipping feverishly, he'd indicate, "Oh, my god! You don't know what you're missing. Come on down!" Of course, he wouldn't make the slightest effort to climb back up, for he'd learned the hard way that he'd only flounder in snow that light and deep. He'd wait for me to ski down to him and break the uptrail. I hadn't wanted to descend that far because my energy for breaking trail wasn't limitless and I had other slopes in mind to ski that day. But he wanted to ski more of *this* slope, and so I obliged him.

Then there were those days when he wouldn't come when I called him. Instead, he'd look at me from afar and wag his tail with ever-increasing intensity, meaning "It's you, my friend, not I, who should come. I've found something fascinating, and I think you'll enjoy it."

Some dog owners would look upon this sort of behavior as an act of flagrant disobedience and wouldn't tolerate it, but I saw it as my being affiliated with a dog who knew as much about the country and its animals as I did, sometimes more. By listening to him, I frequently learned things I never would have known. Walking to where he was, I'd see wolf sign, bear sign, weasel prints, perhaps a hidden grouse, or elk in the distance.

Once, coming up to him, I found him standing over a line of superimposed prints in the snow. A wolf had been tracking an elk, placing its paws precisely in the elk's deeper hoofprints, and thus saving energy. Merle swished his tail at me: "Pretty interesting, eh?" Another time, as we hurried down a trail, a forest fire not far behind us, he stopped and stared to the right. I looked behind us to the smoke-covered sky. He didn't move when I kept going, raising his eyebrows at me with that look of "better pay attention." I followed his gaze, and there, not sixty feet from the trail, stood a large black grizzly bear, his front paws balanced on a log, his rear ones on the ground, as he stared at us intently. As soon as the bear saw my gaze fall upon him, he turned so slowly that it appeared he might be melting. Oozing over the log behind him, he quickened his pace and vanished in the tangled deadfall. Looking down, I met Merle's eyes and he gave me the patient look that a parent gives a child: "See, you almost missed that."

The most unforgettable instance of Merle's disobedience opening a new horizon for both of us came around the summer solstice. Tinker had been in the corral for a couple of days and I at my desk, and both of us were itching for a gallop. We headed into the great prairie northwest of Kelly with Merle leading the way. I let Tinker have his head and he took us on a canter of a couple of miles, stopping finally to blow and graze. Removing his bridle, I lay on my back, looking at the dusking sky and breathing in the fresh smell of the new grass. Shortly, I felt Merle snuggle against my side and put his chin on my chest. Then we both fell asleep.

I awoke with a sense of being watched. Thirty yards off sat a coyote, gazing at us. I met the coyote's eyes and instead of fleeing, it walked closer, not in a straight line but in an arc, first away, then closer, until it was twenty yards off.

At that moment Merle awoke, instantly spied the coyote, and hurtled toward it. The coyote turned and fled.

"Merle, no!" I shouted, thinking that the coyote might lead him toward a waiting pack.

Both of them vanished over a small rise.

I called Tinker, bridled him, and rode after Merle. Within two hundred yards, we found him. Trotting toward us, he was trailed by two coyotes, only thirty feet behind him. The three dogs seemed easy with each other, as if all the animosity between the two species had been laid to rest. A moment later they proved it. Merle turned and followed the coyotes, not chasing them in anger but in play.

The coyotes loped off, then reversed course and followed Merle. He set off with a little hop and a shake of his head, as if to say, "This is amazing! Who would have believed it—playing with coyotes!" Within a hundred yards, he made a lazy circle back upon the coyotes and bounded after them as they sauntered off, exhibiting the same sort of body language: "This is fun! Playing with a dog!"

I could not help but join in. Clucking Tinker into a trot, we followed them a ways only to have the two coyotes turn around and chase us. Round and round we went, circling under the darkening sky, horse, dog, man, and coyotes playing until the stars came out and the coyotes set a course for the mountains, their quickened pace saying, "Bye-bye for now."

I leaned off my saddle and said to Merle, "Well, does this mean you've reached a détente with these two coyotes, or with all coyotes?"

Wag-wag-wag went his tail: "Let's wait and see."

These, then, were some of the times I was quite pleased to have a dog who didn't always respond to "Merle, come!" There were other times, though, when I wasn't so pleased. I would go to where he stood only to find nothing—no tracks, no poop, not a sign of wildlife, at least none that I could discern. But, obviously, whatever he had scented was important to him.

Of course, when I knew perfect obedience was necessary—as in downtown Seattle—I took no chances and kept him on a leash. Could I have trained him so that no matter the circumstances he would have immediately answered my call? I believe I could have, for it's the rare individual who can't be reinforced to follow simple commands even though one may not be able to turn him into a rocket scientist as John Watson claimed. But such training—which would have made my commands into absolute law—inevitably would have changed Merle's and my relationship. We would have become the sort of dog–human couple that millions of dog owners aspire to: an alpha human giving orders to a subordinate dog, orders that must always be obeyed.

This model has been said to mimic the pack structure of wolves—a hierarchical one in which an alpha individual runs the show—and is thus recommended by countless dog trainers as a natural way to produce happy dogs and harmony in the home. I would agree that being an alpha to your dog is one way to enforce order. I doubt, however, that it always produces the happiest of dogs or, if we were to examine the situation objectively, real harmony. In fact, what it often produces is a simmering conflict between the social ambitions of the maturing dog and the human who believes that the dog sincerely welcomes staying a perpetual child. When the dog then goes ballistic—chewing furniture, peeing on the carpet, barking, or engaging in power struggles with its human—dog experts offer a variety of reasons for the sudden appearance of these dysfunctional behaviors: The dog is bored, it needs more exercise, it's anxious, or it's trying to be the dominant individual in the relationship and needs to be put in its place; if he's an uncut dog, castrate him. Daily exercise with other dogs can certainly help to reduce these sorts of dysfunctional behaviors, but—and this may say a lot about the blinders we wear—no one ever makes the suggestion that something natural is going on. The dog wants not dominance, but equality. No one ever makes this suggestion because it sounds preposterous. After all, it's only a dog, right? And the dog's genetic ancestor, the wolf, puts its subordinates in their place all the time. The only problem with basing dog training on wolf society is that many of our notions about how wolves live have recently been overturned. In short, wolves live more egalitarian lives than any of us suspected.

One reason why this aspect of wolf society has remained unknown is that much of our knowledge about wolves has been based on watching captive packs in zoos. As David Mech, one of the world's most experienced wolf biologists, has commented, "Attempting to apply information about the behavior of assemblages of unrelated captive wolves to the familial structure of natural packs has resulted in considerable confusion. Such an approach is analogous to trying to draw inferences about human family dynamics by studying humans in refugee camps. The concept of the alpha wolf as a 'top dog' ruling a group of similar-aged compatriots is particularly misleading."

Mech was one of several biologists who, at the end of the twentieth century, began to watch wild wolves in a different way. On Ellesmere Island, he was able to habituate a pack to his presence and study their behavior over several generations from a distance of only a few feet. And, in Yellowstone National Park, every Canadian wolf released during the reintroduction program of 1995–1996 wore a radio collar, as did a majority of their offspring in the ensuing decade. These collars have allowed park biologists to track and to watch wolves from the air on a daily basis without disturbing them.

Such intimate observations have added depth and complexity to our traditional views of wolf society, in particular the idea that wolf packs are rigidly hierarchical. Instead, researchers have seen alpha male and alpha female wolves sharing *leadership*—making decisions on a relatively equal basis about where to hunt, what to hunt, and when to move the pack. Douglas Smith, the head of the Yellowstone Wolf Project, also recounts how in captivity alpha wolves eat first, then beta wolves, and so on down the pecking order. "But in the wild," he says, "we've never observed anything like that." Instead, he's photographed nine wolves eating an elk they had just killed while the alpha male slept to the side. In another instance, he's seen an alpha female having to force her way into the kill between her offspring.

Smith also likes to point out that the long-standing persecution of wolves has destroyed their natural pack structure and left us with the false impression that wolf society is typically composed of an alpha male, an alpha female, and their pups of the year— what he calls "the simple pack." However, when wolves have been protected, "multi-generational packs" have developed. "These," he says, "have a deep bench." In addition to having an alpha male and female, and their subordinate pups of the year, multi-generational packs contain two-, three-, and four-year-old wolves who are no longer completely subordinate to their parents. "These older, non-alpha wolves know what they're doing," he explains. "They're experienced and can lead, kill, and defend the pack, and they do."

What's even more fascinating, according to Smith, is that there are many times when the wolves in a pack will be unable to agree on what to do. "When that happens," he says, "everybody usually does what the alphas are doing—most of the time. But if some wolves don't want to go along with the alphas, nothing happens to them. They just go off in a different way. But try and breed with the wrong wolf," he adds, "like an alpha's mate, you will get your ass kicked. This suggests to me that wolf society has an organized structure but also has free will."

Furthermore, it's important to note that even though the alpha male and female are dominant over their particular sex group, the younger female wolves deferring to the alpha female and the younger male wolves deferring to the alpha male, these relationships aren't static. Wolf families develop just like human ones: When children mature they, too, get to lead. In other words, rank is neither innate nor molded early. Instead, as Mech has written, "All young wolves are potential breeders and ... when they do breed they automatically become alphas."

In this regard, submission can be seen in an entirely different light. It's a passage, not an enduring characteristic, and it serves a useful purpose. Juveniles that behave solicitously are more likely to gain access to food defended by adults. This enhances their nutritional condition and gives them a better chance, when they disperse, to form their own packs and become alphas. Submission is also necessary for survival—someone needs to coordinate group hunting. But as the cultural anthropologist Constance Perin has noted, "The 'submissiveness' of dogs below the 'top dog' signals more their location and cooperative role in this food-getting system than it does 'being dominated.'" She goes on to say that dogs' relationships with people mirror their relationships to littermates, who, in the wild, are "contemporaries."

Scott and Fuller said something similar in their study on the social behavior of dogs, noting how such equal footing can be achieved as dogs and humans interact: "When socialized to people, both dogs and wolves transfer to human beings the social relationships which they would normally develop with their own kind insofar as this is permitted by their owners."

These social relationships, wolf researchers have now seen, are far more complex, dynamic, and shifting than that of a dominant individual laying down the law for subordinates. However, most dog owners, having heard the mantra of "be a strong alpha" for so long, quite understandably reproduce a pack structure that's dysfunctionally skewed toward dominance rather than cooperation. One of the best examples of the strife such a pack faces was demonstrated in Yellowstone's Lamar Valley from 1997 to 2000. During these years, the alpha female of the Druid Pack, Wolf 40, ruled over the other females of the pack with an iron paw, constantly harassing and even savaging them. Given their subordinate behavior, one would have thought that none of them had any leadership potential whatsoever. Yet, on a night after which Number 40 gave a particularly ferocious mauling to Wolf 42, the tide turned for this aggressive leader. The badly mauled wolf, along with several other subordinate wolves, ganged up on the matriarch and killed her. Wolf 42 then stepped into the role of alpha female, but with one crucial difference: Her personality was the antithesis of her predecessor's. Gentle and magnanimous, she raised Wolf 40's pups in addition to her own and also welcomed the low-ranking Wolf 106 and her pups into the pack's den. Under Wolf 42's leadership, Wolf 106 blossomed. She became the finest hunter in the Druid Pack and eventually the leader of her own pack, the Geode Creek Pack, where she, too, instituted a benevolent reign.

Such bloody confrontations rarely occur between humans and dogs. Rather, by a thousand different cuts—our control of ingress, egress, food, water, elimination, and fun—we reduce dogs to a state of quiet capitulation, a softened version of the Stockholm Syndrome, named after the Norrmalmstorg bank robbery of 1973, during which two ex-convicts held four bank employees hostage for five days. The victims became emotionally attached to their captors and subsequently defended them after they were freed from their ordeal. Two of the women even became engaged to two of the robbers.

The incident provoked a great deal of social research bent on discovering whether the reaction of the hostages was a freak incident or an example of a pervasive social condition. The latter proved to be the case, and the hallmarks of the syndrome—a powerful individual's coercing a captive into submission, and even the demonstration of affection—have now been identified in cases of dependent children, battered wives, prostitutes, prisoners of war, and victims of hijackings.

Obviously, most dog owners don't intend to harm their dogs in this way. The opposite is the case. If the $15 billion Americans spent on dog food alone in 2004 is any indication, most dog owners do their best to give their dogs happy and healthy lives. Yet it's difficult not to concede that virtually all dogs remain captives. Indeed, the activities they enjoy—roaming, seeing other dogs, and exploring interesting odors—are constantly thwarted by the demands of modern civilization and training methods that have been designed to bring about what one dog trainer, echoing the words of numerous others, has called "the reversal of millions of years of evolution and genetic propensity." Is the loyalty people then receive from their dogs true devotion, or the numbed reaction of captives to captors?

To begin to answer this question, consider just one in-vogue training method—crating. Dog experts of all persuasions counsel confining both puppies and adult dogs in crates to toilet train the young dog quickly (a dog doesn't like to soil its sleeping quarters) as well as to keep adult dogs calm. Jon Katz goes so far as to say that "dogs are den animals" and that a crate "approximates the dim, cozy den that a dog would inhabit in the wild." He adds that "left out in the wild, almost every dog would seek out a space very much like a crate and voluntarily make it his headquarters."

Such claims need to be put into perspective. The researchers who studied feral dogs in central Italy, for instance, didn't see "almost every dog" seeking out a den. What they discovered was that only females and their pups used them. The same holds true for wild wolf packs—only the alpha female regularly occupies a den, and then only during the period in which she gives birth and is nursing. Even her mate will only occasionally enter the den. The other wolves in a pack don't seek out shelter. They sleep in the open, or beneath underbrush if it's very stormy.

Yet, on occasion, domestic dogs do build dens. Elizabeth Marshall Thomas recounts how her dogs, when confined to an expansive pen next to her house, created a den large enough for four of them by digging into the side of a hill. They undertook this lengthy excavation despite her having provided them with what she calls "substantial shelters," some of them outfitted with small doors and filled with hay and cedar shavings. She suggests that her dogs made their own den because of the need of group-living mammals to create a spot that acts as a meeting place and focuses the group's energies and attention. In addition, she points out that the den had its practical side in the muggy and buggy climate of Virginia: It had a constant temperature as well as protection from mosquitoes, sun, and wind. Nonetheless, Thomas observed that when all four of her dogs occupied the den, only the last dog to enter its narrow tunnel stayed voluntarily. It would emerge "calm and refreshed" from its nap while the rest of the dogs, whose free exit had been blocked, popped out looking "very agitated." Thomas then goes on to say something telling. The calmest moments her dogs experienced weren't when they were in the den, but when she and they lay outside together, gazing from a hilltop to the forest below.

Merle also seemed his most serene while watching distant landscapes from high overlooks. As for dens, he took his lead from wolves. In the thirteen years I traveled with him in the backcountry—from Arizona's canyons to the Canadian Rockies—the only shelter I saw him seek out was that of streams when it got really hot and evergreens when it was snowing hard. He scraped out a nest beneath them and let himself be covered by the falling snow—just like a wolf.

He also acted like a wolf in his making our house into a gathering place, what wolf biologists call a "rendezvous" or a "loafing site"—the place a wolf pack locates near the female's den and that they use to congregate, snooze, chat, and generally hang out. Free to come and go as he wished, Merle brought at least a dozen other dogs to the house. These dozen dogs were the ones I actually saw. Ranging in age from year-old pups to senior citizens, they were Labs, Golden Retrievers, Australian Shepherds, Border Collies, Vizslas, Terriers, German Shepherds, and a variety of mongrels.

Not once did I find the furniture chewed or shoes or clothing destroyed, though these were readily available and I was gone for hours. Returning, I'd find the dogs asleep on the deck or on the great room floor, as relaxed as if they had been drugged. And they *had* been drugged—by endorphins, fresh air, and the grass under their paws.

This view of domestic dogs sees them as responsible individuals, even when not confined. In fact, it bases good behavior on freedom. It also understands dogs as maturing over time and becoming self-actualized adults—just like their lupine ancestors, who may not reach full adulthood, which is quite distinct from sexual maturity, until they are five years old. It embraces the idea that older dogs have wisdom and can teach younger dogs how to behave with decorum. It trusts the dog.

An increasingly widespread understanding of dogs, however, sees them as wolves, but only as infant ones—individuals who have been permanently halted by domestication in the stage of puppyhood. Unsuited to making decisions on their own, these are exactly the sort of animals who crave our direction and must be periodically crated for their own peace of mind as well as ours.

This line of reasoning can be both self-serving and self-fulfilling. Consider the findings of researchers at Loránd Eötvös University in Budapest. They asked dog–human couples to perform a variety of problem-solving tasks. Dogs who had a strong dependent relationship on their humans performed more poorly at solving the problems than those who didn't. In fact, the more the dog fulfilled the role of a child substitute for its human, the more dependent it became.

I was determined not to go down this road with Merle and received support from the work of Karen Pryor. Despite being the foremost advocate of clicker training since Skinner, she also cautions, "Nobody needs to control or be controlled by cues and signals all the time; living creatures are not a bunch of machines."

The more I listened to trainers like her, the more Merle's ability to call his own shots continued to surprised me. It shouldn't have. According to Pryor, you get what you shape. Reinforce automaton-like behavior and you get a robot. Reinforce creativity, inventiveness, and open-ended decision-making, and you get a dog who's closer to being your peer. But watch out. You also get a dog who may put you in your place, and by this I don't mean vie with you for dominance. Rather, as your dog becomes more self-actualized, he may hold up the mirror for you, and the face you see can be humbling.

This issue might never have arisen in Merle's and my relationship had it not been for Ralph Yaeger. Ralph lived in Helena, Montana, with his wife, two young boys, and a Golden Retriever named Scout. Ralph was tall, affable, and handsome—Christopher Reeve as Superman—and Scout was frumpy, opinionated, and a little over-weight, the canine version of Gertrude Stein. Ralph worked for a nonprofit organization whose mission was to promote ethical hunting, and, having read my work on the subject and met me at a wildlife conference, he invited me to serve on its board and to come bird hunting with him. Both invitations might have fallen on deaf ears had we not thought so similarly about the place of hunting in modern life.

For us, hunting wasn't a sport. It was a way to be intimate with nature, that intimacy providing us with wild, unprocessed food, free from pesticides and hormones, and with the bonus of having been produced without the addition of great quantities of fossil fuel. In addition, hunting provided us with an ever-scarcer relationship in a world of cities, factory farms, and agribusiness—direct responsibility for taking the lives that sustained us, lives that even vegans indirectly take as the growing and harvesting of organic produce kills deer, birds, snakes, rodents, and insects.

We lived close to the animals we ate, we knew their habits, and that knowledge deepened our thanks to them and the land that made them. Our thanks also went out to our dogs, for it was they, and particularly their noses, that helped us make wild meat a steady diet.

Two of Ralph's and Scout's hunting companions were a Helena fireman named Bill Orsello and his Golden Retriever, Eli. It was they who clinched my decision to take Merle bird hunting. Bill tended to think about hunting along the same lines as Ralph and I, and both he and Eli were big guys with gentle dispositions. Unlike Bill, however, who was a powerhouse of activity, Eli was laid-back, just as inclined to sit on the tailgate of Bill's truck, looking at the sky with a dreamy expression on his face, as he was to set off hunting.

I thought that if any two people and any two dogs could cajole Merle into giving bird hunting one more try, these two could. I was right—at least about Merle's liking them. He took to them immediately, for Ralph and Bill were tender in their greetings, and Eli and Scout made a big fuss over this new Wyoming visitor, breathing in his exotic, elky smell with extreme interest. In turn, Merle smelled the birdiness they wore in their fur—pheasants, sharptail grouse, Hungarian partridge, ducks, and geese. Within a half minute of meeting each other, the three dogs were wagging their tails in perfect time.

The acid test, though, came when we loaded the shotguns in Bill's truck. I had put mine, cased, in the roof carrier of the Subaru on the drive up, so Merle wouldn't see it, but Bill used this moment to show me his favorite gun. Merle took one look at it and dropped his head in dismay: "Oh, no! So this is why Ted brought me here."

Eli and Scout, however, began to wag their tails at the sight of the shotgun, and this confused Merle. Shotguns were bad news, weren't they?

Peer pressure at last carried the day. When Eli and Scout jumped into Bill's truck and I extended a hand to the tailgate, Merle sighed and climbed aboard, lying between Eli and Scout, his flanks pressed to theirs as if they were his security blankets. They in turn pressed against him soothingly as if to say, "Nothing to worry about, ol' buddy. This is going to be fun."

From Helena we drove up the Missouri River to Great Falls, then east to Lewistown, where the mountains rise like archipelagos from the plains. In the valley where Ralph was born, we began walking through rows of cut wheat, Merle following leerily behind me and watching Scout and Eli with great attention as they crisscrossed through the standing brush at the edge of the fields.

Eli flushed the first pheasant, its long tail streaming as it cackled and flew over the willows. At the bang of Bill's shotgun, Merle flinched, ducked, and began to pant in panic. I was certain he would run away, but he surprised me. Seeing Eli retrieve the bird, he rushed to him and ran protectively by his side, casting worried looks at him, as if he might have been hurt by the shot.

When Eli gave Bill the bird, Merle sat next to the bigger dog, his head turning from his newfound friend to Bill with some perplexity. Apparently, no one had been hurt, and Eli seemed to be enjoying himself.

Scout flushed the next pheasant, Ralph brought it down, and Merle, having loosened up a bit, rushed in and put his nose in the bird's purple and green feathers as Scout handed it over. Taking a big sniff, he immediately grabbed the bird from Ralph's hand and tried to eat it. Now this was the part of bird hunting he could understand!

"No, no, Merle," Ralph said, laughing and taking the bird back. "You have to wait until we grill them."

Ralph put the bird in his game vest, and Merle stood on his hind legs to give the canvas pouch a long smell. Dropping to all fours, he wagged his tail happily.

I was elated. Just letting Merle be with these dogs—watching them bird hunt without any pressure on him to perform—appeared to be a natural and effortless way of getting him to overcome his bad history with firearms. All might have gone well had Eli not vaulted a small stream a few minutes later, lost his footing, and fallen off the bank. Landing on his butt, he began to cry out in pain. Using only his front legs, he clawed his way up to the field, dragging his rear end—paralyzed, it seemed, from the waist down.

Merle leapt over the stream, rushed to Eli, and began to whine in dismay. Pushing him with his snout, he jumped up and down, crying out and giving every indication of saying, "Oh, Eli! You're hurt! You're hurt! Please stand up!"

Bill rushed to Eli, but Merle intervened, protecting the big Golden Retriever with his body while trying to push Bill away.

"Merle!" Bill shouted, his voice rising in fear. Eli, it seemed, had become a paraplegic. Bill shoved Merle off, and I grabbed him.

Carefully, Bill began to explore Eli's hindquarters. "I can't feel anything broken," he said. "Let me give him some massage."

He worked his fingers along Eli's spine as I held on to Merle, who was whining and trying to lunge toward Eli.

Suddenly, without warning, Eli stood up and walked out of Bill's hands. I released Merle and he ran to Eli, dancing around him joyfully and pressing his nose into his neck while calling little endearments to his friend.

Padding along, Eli rubbed flanks with Merle, breathing deeply but quietly, like some big football player who has had the wind knocked out of him: "Hey, Merle, it was nuthin'."

Scout, who had remained unflappable during the entire incident, who in fact had been nosing here and there, was already trailing the next bird. We took another tack through the mown wheat, but seeing Eli injured had rattled Merle's nerves. As Scout flushed a pheasant and Ralph shot, Merle jigged sideways from the blast. Not watching where he was going, he stepped onto a sharply mown-off willow at the edge of the field. Yowling in pain—perhaps he thought he'd been shot—he held his paw in the air and began to sprint toward the truck.

"Merle," I called. "Come."

He tossed me a scornful look: "Not on your life."

I followed him to the dirt road where the truck was parked and found him lying by the vehicle.

"Are you okay?" I asked.

His body language remained guarded.

I examined his injured paw, and it appeared fine. I petted him and told him he had done a great job. He continued to stare ahead and didn't wag his tail. Opening the tailgate, I let him jump in the truck, where he stayed even when the others returned for lunch, his head between his paws, his eyes moving nervously between us as we talked.

When we got ready to set off on the afternoon's hunt, Merle finally raised his head.

"You can stay here if you want," I told him.

"Ha-ha-ha," he panted, at last showing some emotion. "I think I will."

He glanced down at Eli and Scout, wagging their tails at him.

"Up to you," I said. "Don't let them change your mind."

He slapped his tail against the bed of the pickup, but he didn't budge.

"Okay," I told him. "Hold down the fort and we'll see you later."

And, three hours later, there he was, wagging his tail at our return.

I was so certain that this experience had put him off bird hunting permanently that I considered leaving him home the next time Ralph invited us to Montana. But Ralph said that Merle could stay in the truck while we hunted, enjoying Scout's and Eli's company in Helena and at the motel in Choteau. This sounded like a fine idea—both of us getting our needs met—and all went according to plan until we arrived at the farm where we were going to hunt. Instead of staying in the truck, as I had expected, Merle leapt out with Scout and Eli and rushed to greet Ri and Purdey. Two black Labs, male and female, they belonged to Eric and Angie Grove, who also were from Helena. Along with them was Dinsdale, the male black Lab of one of Eric and Angie's friends.

After discussing how we'd spread out across the barley fields, we began to load our shotguns. It was then that I discovered that Merle was gone.

I cast my eyes to the horizon—long rows of stubble, cottonwood trees, the distant mountains of the Montana Front dusted with snow. But my dog was nowhere to be seen. Puzzled, I looked under the truck. A moment later, I heard a knocking coming from above my head. When I peered into the camper shell, I found Merle curled in the very back corner of the pickup's bed, shaking violently with his nose under his tail. Our loading the shotguns must have undone him.

"Oh, Sir," I said gently, crawling on my hands and knees to him. "Are you having a flashback?"

His answer was to shake harder.

"Listen," I said in a soft voice as I petted him, "I'm going to leave the hatch of the shell open. You stay right here, and we'll be back in a few hours."

I closed the tailgate, left the back window up, and we set off through the mown barley. We hadn't gone three minutes down the field, though, when I heard the sound of flying paws. Up tore Merle, breathing hard.

"Ha-ha-ha," he panted sheepishly at me. "I got a hold of myself. I got a grip. I'm ready to go now."

I rubbed his shoulders and he rushed away from me, joining the five other dogs, who mobbed him happily.

He had gotten a grip. He ran among Eli, Scout, Ri, Purdey, and Dinsdale, following them as they flushed and retrieved, never doing any of the work himself, but appearing to have a wonderful time by staying as far from the guns as possible.

Was his fear of guns cured for good? Hardly.

As we loaded the shotguns the next morning I found him cowering in the same corner of the pickup truck. I left the hatch open and left the decision to stay or come up to him. A few minutes after our departure, he came running across the field to join us, just as sheepish as the previous day and just as excited to join the other dogs. He spent the entire day loping among them, never once flushing or retrieving a bird on his own.

The following day everyone except Eric and me had to go to work. The two of us drove to a ranch that overlooked the Missouri River, and there Ri swept over the steep hills like an Olympian athlete, flushing coveys of sharptail grouse and Hungarian partridge while ignoring Merle completely. Not quite. Occasionally, he'd look back at Merle, padding along in the rear, with an expression that said, "Wow, you really are a duffer, aren't you."

About mid-morning, Ri and Eric took the upper line around a shelterbelt of willow, and Merle and I went along their lower flank. I was surprised to see that, with no other dog or person present, Merle moved up to my side, even slightly ahead of me, and began to scan the terrain alertly. He seemed relaxed, with an easiness in his shoulders and a suppleness in his gait that I hadn't seen the entire weekend or during our first hunt near Lewistown. If anything, he had the looks and the behavior of a classic bird dog, and in a moment proved it.

His head did a 90-degree swivel uphill. He sniffed twice and bolted into the willows. Two seconds later, a large pheasant burst from the trees and soared overhead. I swung up the shotgun, seeing in my peripheral vision Merle running beneath the pheasant and tracking him. I fired. The pheasant arced from the sky and bounced on the grass.

Merle sprinted directly to the bird and picked him up in one grab, as if he had been doing it his entire life. Then he trotted back to me smartly and sat before me in a perfect imitation of the other dogs' retrieving style.

I was thrilled and overwhelmed. Without any reinforcement—except that of seeing his peers hunt—he had learned every detail of flushing and retrieving and hadn't been spooked in the least by the report of the gun. Bursting with pride, I held out my hand to receive this, his first bird.

But instead of presenting the pheasant to my hand as the other dogs had done for their humans, he spit it at my feet.

There was no mistaking the scorn in his gesture. He held himself erect and looked at me with enormous defiance.

I reached down and tried to pet him, but he pulled back his head from my hand, his posture not softening in the least. Ramrod straight and with every muscle tense, he fixed me with blazing eyes.

"See," they said, "I can do this. I just don't want to."

Up until this point in my life, virtually all the dogs I had run into had pleased me. A very few—two, in fact—had frightened me. Many had made me laugh. A couple had made me cry. One— this one sitting before me—had made me feel ashamed on the day I had hit him for chasing cattle. Dozens of dogs had filled me with love. No dog, until today, had managed to humble me.

"I understand," I told him.

He stared at me hard.

"I get it," I said. "You really hate bird hunting."

And as I spoke these words, I recalled the day I had showed him how to walk around a bison, and he had exclaimed, "I get it, don't mess with bison." Today he was doing the instructing.

Picking up the pheasant, I took a moment to send some thoughts its way before slipping the bird into the pouch of my vest. Then I broke the shotgun and laid it over my shoulder.

Merle eyed it soberly.

"Let's go," I said, extending my hand for him to lead. "After you. We're done with this."

He held my eyes a moment longer as if to gauge my sincerity. Then he turned and, with his head and tail held high—not giving his happy pant, his little jig, or any indication that he was anything but dead serious about what he had just told me—he trotted quickly toward the truck.

A few days later, back in Kelly, the incident took on deeper meaning when I had occasion to take my rifle from the shed to go elk hunting. Without any hesitation, Merle followed me to the car, wagging his tail enthusiastically. I opened the door and he bounded in. When I got behind the steering wheel and turned the key, he laid his head on my shoulder and pressed his cheek against mine, nudging me a couple of times. I looked in the rearview mirror and saw his eyes, eagerly staring into mine. His tail was wagging very hard, saying, "See, my friend, I still like elk hunting."

And he always did, helping me to find dozens of elk as well as antelope over the years. But take out that shotgun, and he'd sit on the porch. I accepted his decision about the place bird hunting would have in our lives. Actually, I did a little better than that. I respected it. Perhaps, had I been a smarter or more caring man, I might have learned this lesson from a human partner. But I learned it from my dog: At a certain point you need to acknowledge that your partner knows more about what makes him or her happy than you do. Stepping back, you let that partner be.

CHAPTER 14

White Muzzle

Over the next year, I tried to apply what Merle had taught me about giving one's partner space to my relationship with Allison. But the analogy failed one critical test: Merle wanted to live with me and Allison didn't.

We persevered, though, trying to work through our rough spots: sharing the dishwashing fifty-fifty; using first her car, then mine; and negotiating a happy medium on sleep and sex. But of course these weren't the real issues.

Eventually, we went our separate ways, and she found someone else—someone who she thought would be more compatible with her needs. To her credit, she was blisteringly honest about what these were. Even though no one could foretell the future, she said, she didn't want to take care of a husband in his old age, and the new man was younger than I. Just as important, he played better for the folks back home.

This was valuable information to have. Despite the fact that we had a lot in common, more than either of us had experienced in any other relationship, it was clear that I'd been barking up the wrong tree. In response, I, too, found someone else, actually several others, none of whom seemed quite right, as anyone not embroiled in the hurt and anger of being rejected could have predicted.

The dogs rode through this confused time with nary a raised eyebrow. Brower still galloped across the field, did a sideways drift around the deck, and burst through the dog doors to skid into my office with undiminished excitement: "Ted, man! Where ya been? I haven't seen you in ages!" And when Allison would stop at my front door—to ask how I was and to say she missed doing things with me, her face a mask of ambivalence and mixed messages—Merle would lean against her knee and swish his tail with a heartfelt gesture he used with no one else: "Oh, I've missed you. How I've missed you." Unlike me, he didn't then segue into an endless series of whys—why, if we remain so close, if we can converse so intimately, can you not be with me?

His attitude proved instructive—care for her, but let her go—and his consolation was far better than that which came from the therapist whom Allison and I hired to facilitate our protracted separation. Merle would come into my office and lay his chin on my thigh, not asking for water, a biscuit, or for me to accompany him on a hike. He'd move his tail so that it undulated his body, his soft, comforting motion washing up my leg and into my heart. He had no hands to hold it, but he did so every day.

I'd put my hand on his head and feel my frustration ebb away, my blood pressure go down—just like all the books say happens when a dog touches us—and, simultaneously, I'd feel him go easy under my hands, the soothing going back and forth, wordlessly but strong: *I am here. So am I. I am glad. Me too.*

The behavior he displayed when I was absent also helped me to recover. His favorite house sitter, an observant young woman named Jen Carroll, who doted upon Merle and whom he cared for greatly, would tell me that after a few days of my being absent Merle would leave on his rounds, but before setting off would sit in the middle of the road and howl mournfully. Then, having had a good cry about my being gone, he'd collect himself and get on with his life, proceeding south into the village, with head and tail erect.

This behavior was also a gloss on the received wisdom that dogs are unable to tell time. Living in a blissful state without clocks or calendars, they supposedly have no concept as to whether their person has stepped out to get a newspaper for five minutes or headed to the South Seas for five weeks. But clearly this wasn't the case for Merle. He would let several days elapse after I had left, remaining hopeful all the while that I'd return. When that didn't happen, he'd give vent to his feelings of being abandoned and begin to howl on the road.

His greetings upon my return also showed me that even though he didn't tell time as we did, he knew the difference between my being gone a short time and a long one. If I was gone just a few days he'd welcome me ecstatically when I pulled into the drive, his tail going round and round like a helicopter's rotor, his front feet dancing with joy, his entire body wriggling in anticipation. But if I stayed away a couple of weeks or a month, when I stepped out of the taxi with my gear, he'd plant his front paws several yards from me and howl bitterly: "Wow, that was a long time! Do you even remember me? What were you doing without me?" If I tried to pet him, he'd back off and continue to bay at me angrily. I'd crouch in front of him and beckon to him by patting my palms against my chest. "Oh, *pobrecito perrito*," I'd croon. Oh, you poor doggy. "Come here. I missed you lots."

He'd finally step toward me, put his head into my chest, and let me rub his back while he continued to yip his remonstrations.

Then I'd say, "Oh, yes, yes, yes, yes, yes, I know you were lonely. But I also remember the time when you were *so, so* sad when I left and two minutes later you had forgotten me."

"Yar-yar-yar," he'd yip. "Yeah, yeah, yeah. But I still miss you."

He'd continue to voice his complaints with little high-pitched yelps, but they'd soon fade into contented groans as I'd put my nose against the top of his head and kiss him, saying, "Oh, how I missed you!"

Shouldering my pack, I'd head inside. Panting, "Ha-ha-ha, ha-ha-ha," he'd begin to dance around me: "Okay, see, I'm over it."

He was one of the best examples of how to deal with disappointment and ride through anger, for it was apparent that he had no interest in his emotions becoming him. He clung to them for an instant, the way our mountains clung to their weather, then let them roll over him and fade away.

Sometime during these roiled months—it happened so subtly I couldn't say on what day I noticed it—Merle's muzzle lost its reddish-golden hue and became creamy. On closer examination, I saw that the individual hairs had begun to turn white.

"Sir," I said. "You appear to have become middle-aged."

He didn't seem to notice. Staring at himself in Jen Fuller's big mirror, he continued to cock his head this way and that, admiring himself. Nor could I see—other than in his graying face—that the passing of the years had affected him in any way. He could still lope alongside my mountain bike for hours at a time and put in an enormous day in the peaks around the house, ascending and descending ten thousand vertical feet while covering eighteen horizontal miles through the snow. Nor had he cut back on his political duties. He still made his three circumambulations of the village each day, stopping in to see his constituents, his determined trot between visits saying, "I am a very busy dog. I have things to do and people to see." And at the end of his workday, he still had enough energy to tear mad circles around me if I tucked in my head like a turtle, opened my eyes wide, and tried to grab him. If I put some country-western music on the CD player and tapped my chest with my palms, he'd stand on his hind legs, put his front paws on my shoulders, and we'd dance around the great room together while he panted, "This is fun!" Sometimes, he'd even come and find me if some bluegrass music began to play on the radio, jumping off the dedicated quadruped couch, trotting into the office, wagging his tail, and pumping his paws up and down, indicating, "Let's dance."

It was at these times, and only at these times—standing face to face—that he would lick me. Perhaps this was because he felt somewhat vulnerable after a minute on his hind legs, or maybe he was simply imitating human kissing, which he'd certainly seen enough of. Whatever the case, he'd often give me a big smooch with his tongue.

Gray Cat, still on the couch, would look at us with bored disdain. He'd be even more put out when his buddy Brower came over. Instead of starting an immediate game of chase and somersault with him, Brower would leap up at me and plead, "Me too! Dance with me too!"

I'd move Merle's paws to my left shoulder, pat my chest, and let Brower put his paws on my right one. With an arm around each dog, I'd coast them around the room.

Occasionally, as I was reading on the deck an hour later with Merle lying on one side of me and Brower on the other, the phone would ring. It would be Allison, asking, "Is my dog over there?"

"He's reading with Merle and me on the deck," I'd reply. "We were just dancing."

"Could you please send him home."

"I can try, but I don't think he'll leave."

I could hear her sigh, and then she'd say, "The power of the guys."

"It's the Omaha connection, you know. He never forgets."

By her silence, I could tell that my subtext had jabbed her, as I had intended.

"No, he doesn't," she'd say, her voice carrying sadness about how things had turned out and frustration with me for bringing up a tired subject. "I'll pick him up on my way into town."

Since Brower never forgot what we had shared, and because he continued to visit often, forcing Allison to fetch him, she and I went through many variations of this conversation, teasing apart the endless strands of who we had been as a couple and who we might become. One might say that it had been our dogs who had cemented us together romantically and our dogs who helped us to reshape ourselves into enduring friends. And if it was Brower who was primarily responsible for Allison and me talking about our past, it was Merle, with his newly minted white muzzle—his newfound expression of debonair worldliness and kindly wisdom—who helped me to slide into the future.

On more than one occasion, he and I would be walking in town, and a woman coming the other way would spy Merle, catch my eye, and angle toward us.

"Oh, what a beautiful dog you are!" she'd say, kneeling in front of him and putting her arms around his neck. "So distinguished and so gentle. And look at those eyes."

Moving her arms down his back, she'd rub her fingers through his fur, and I'd give Merle a scratch as well—she and I now talking about him and dogs in general—the woman's hands and my hands coasting by each other while carefully avoiding any contact, for it was clear what was happening: We were petting Merle so as not to touch each other so soon after meeting.

Merle would look at me out of the tops of his eyes, feeling what was going on and also smelling it, the air heavy with pheromones. "Here we go again, my friend," his glance would say. I'd wink at him, meaning "I owe you big time," and I did, for he continued to be a chick magnet.

Yes, this was one of the primary ways I healed. I wanted to be told by someone I found attractive that I was still attractive. I wanted to be able to make plans with someone for Friday night, for the weekend, so as not to feel like some transoceanic sailor, alone in his cockpit, with nothing before him but the empty sea. More often than not, I couldn't find anyone to fulfill this role; but there was always Merle.

Without telling a soul where we were going, we'd set off into the backcountry, following our noses to some remote lake or valley that neither of us had ever seen. And even though some of the books I read during this time pointed out that my wilderness trips were just as much an escape as my getting involved with new women, that I was avoiding sitting with my pain, I found my mountain journeys the sweetest of balms, camped there in the high pines with my dog, the stars above whispering their eternal comfort, a small reminder that the poet Mary Oliver has translated better than anyone:

> You do not have to be good.
> You do not have to walk on your knees
> for a hundred miles through the desert, repenting.
> You only have to let the soft animal of your body
>   love what it loves.

I'd wrap my arms around Merle's shoulders and bury my nose in his ruff, smelling his crisp, sweet odor, like roasted nuts with a hint of lanolin. "Oh, you smell good!" I'd say. And he'd stuff his nose against my chest, breathing in deeply and shuddering on the exhale while thumping his tail: "Oh, you smell good, too!"

In this way, holding him, I let go of her.

Then, in the spring of his eighth year, he began to limp badly, walking with an abnormal gait known as a "head nod." He'd let his head drop as his sound forelimb, the right one, would strike the ground; he'd lift his head as the opposite leg—the sore left one—made contact. The odd, jerky motion was his way of trying to reduce the weight he was putting on his injured leg. I couldn't recollect an instance of his recently falling or even stumbling, but trauma wasn't the issue; it was overuse. All those fast downhills while we were mountain biking had finally caught up to him, taking their toll on his shoulders and elbows. His vet prescribed Rimadyl, a nonsteroidal anti-inflammatory drug, and the termination of his mountain biking career.

I could sympathize. My career as a marathoner had recently ended after too many years of long-distance runs compounded by carrying heavy packs in steep terrain. X-rays of my neck, lower back, knees, and ankles showed bone spurs, compressed cartilage, and bulged discs. In fact, Merle and I were now exactly the same age—forty-eight—according to one dog–human age comparison in which the first two years of a dog's life equal twenty-four years in human years, and then each subsequent year of the dog's life equals four years for the human. Another, more recent, study also discounts the traditional notion that one year of a dog's life equals seven human years. It factors in a dog's weight and breed to calculate its age in human terms. According to this study, Merle would have been about fifty-six.

Whatever the case, we'd get up in the morning and take our glucosamine sulfate-chondroitin capsules together, his in a canine form called Cosequin. After consulting with the local alternative veterinarian, Marybeth Minter, I also added fish oil, vitamins C and E, and coenzyme Q-10 to Merle's diet. She said that the fish oil, with its omega-3 fatty acids, was a natural anti-inflammatory agent. The vitamin C would bolster his immune system; the vitamin E would improve his coat; and the coenzyme Q-10 was an antioxidant that helped to slow the aging process. My doctor had recommended exactly the same regimen for me.

"*Voilà, Monsieur,*" I'd say to him as I opened our various bottles at the kitchen counter, "*on prend nos vitamines ensemble.*" Let's take our vitamins together.

I'd swallow mine in one go with a glass of water. He wouldn't abide the canine equivalent—vitamins added to his kibble. He'd unerringly work his tongue around the capsules, and I'd find them in the bottom of his bowl. I couldn't imagine giving him four pills each morning the way I had given him medicine in the past—putting my hand over his muzzle, pressing in his lips with my thumb and forefinger until his lips were under his teeth (few dogs will bite their own lips), then inserting a pill to the very back of his tongue and closing his mouth quickly while immediately holding his nose up to the sky and softly stroking his throat.

After giving it a bit of thought, I knew the answer. Merle loved fat of all kinds. I dabbed each of his pills in a tiny smear of butter, and he lapped them from my hands like candy.

Even without any mountain biking, however, and with all these supplements supposedly helping his joints, his head bob didn't go away. By the middle of the summer, I was concerned enough to make an appointment with an orthopedic surgeon from the Veterinary Medical Center at Colorado State University in Fort Collins, who visited Jackson Hole once a month. A bright, quietly competent man named Erick Egger, he watched Merle walk, manipulated his legs, and talked about osteoarthritis complicated by the possibility of a fragmented coronoid process, a bit of bone and cartilage that breaks off in a dog's elbow and which is often difficult to identify on X-ray, as was the case with Merle when X-rays of his left elbow had been inconclusive. Erick now suggested keeping Merle on his supplements and not allowing him to run. If he continued to have problems, I could bring him down to CSU for a bone scan, a technique that injects a low-level dose of radioactivity into the dog's bloodstream. Accumulating quickly in the dog's bones, it can then be photographed with a special camera. The resulting images are similar to X-rays, but—displaying white "hot spots" that indicate areas of osteoarthritis—can be a better diagnostic tool in determining the source of a dog's lameness. Erick then added something that made my heart stop: Merle's lameness could also be caused by a nerve root tumor, which was usually fatal.

Over the summer I kept Merle to a walk—at least when he was with me. Some of our walks were long, twelve to fifteen miles, but they were still walks. When we went mountain biking, I'd brake throughout the downhill sections, keeping him at a slow trot, my efforts evoking the most curious looks from him: "What is wrong with you, Ted?"

"It's not me," I replied. "It's you. You're lame."

"Ha!" he shot back. "It's nothing. Let 'er rip!"

Like most dogs, and some people, he had a trait that didn't help him take care of himself: He had the ability to press on through severe pain. Not once, through months of limping, did he complain.

By October he wasn't significantly better, and we made the long drive from Jackson Hole to Fort Collins, where another team of specialists watched his gait and x-rayed his entire body to discount the possibility of the nerve root tumor or any other form of cancer that would appear on the films. The two hours I walked around the campus with Merle awaiting the results were some of the longest in my memory.

Finally, when the time was up, I left him in the car and went to the waiting room where Paul Cuddon, a tall canine neurologist in a white lab coat, greeted me. He spoke with an Australian accent and had been extremely gentle while giving Merle a physical exam. He must have seen the look on my face, because he got to the point right away. "He's fine—no cancer." Then, motioning to a light box on which he had placed Merle's X-rays, he added, "But when was your dog shot?"

"What?"

"He's carrying a bullet in his right shoulder. It's lying right behind the ridge of the scapula."

He pointed to the X-ray, but he didn't have to. The small-caliber bullet was as clear as day, its nose slightly flattened from the impact.

"I don't know when he was shot," I said, and went on to explain how Merle and I had met on the San Juan River. "There wasn't a trace of a wound, and he could walk fine. In fact, he's always been a fantastic runner."

"Then he must have been shot very early on when he was a pup," Paul said, "and the wound healed with no permanent damage. The bullet's not his problem, and I wouldn't recommend taking it out. It's encapsulated and not causing him any discomfort.

But I think we need to go to a bone scan to find out what's bothering him."

"Okay," I agreed, "let's do it." Then, staring at the X-ray, I added, "Well, at least I know why he doesn't like guns."

Paul blinked. "I should say so."

Since Merle's urine would be radioactive, he had to stay at the facility overnight. I handed his leash to a technician and as the man walked him down the corridor toward the lab, Merle kept turning toward me and tugging at the leash with a look of dazed incomprehension. It was the first night since we had been together that he was kenneled.

Twenty-four hours later, I met him at the end of the same corridor. He was padding along quietly, but when he saw me, he ripped the lead out of the technician's hand and ran toward me as I kneeled with open arms. Mobbing me, he began a wild dance of jubilation, moaning and woofing and panting, "Oh, I am so glad to see you! I thought I'd never see you again! We're back together! We're back! We're back!"

A middle-aged woman, who had been filling out an admissions form in the chair next to mine, looked up and said, "That brings tears to my eyes."

"Mine too," I said, not using a figure of speech.

A few minutes later, Merle and I were seated in a consulting room with Paul. On the light box was a full-body view of Merle's skeleton. Standing in front of the bone scan, Paul pointed out the hot spots along Merle's spine and in his elbows. The left elbow was particularly "hot," very white, and Paul said that the attending radiologist had concurred with Erick Egger's diagnosis of a problem with the left medial coronoid process.

Later, when we saw Erick, he looked at the bone scans and suggested arthroscopic surgery to clean up the joint. He, too, read my expression in an instant. "Take your time," he added. "This isn't an emergency."

I said I would. It wasn't that I didn't trust Erick—his reputation was gold-clad, as was Paul's; it was the feeling I had that I should be patient and give Merle time to heal on his own.

We went back to Jackson Hole and I put Merle on a new kibble with extra supplements and vitamins. I bought him natural dog biscuits. And I had Marybeth start acupuncture treatments. These she did at our home, for she made house calls in the old style of a family doc, carrying her black leather bag with its medical supplies and seemingly endless store of ostrich jerky that she used to distract her patients into compliance. Before she'd even open the bag to take out her stethoscope, Merle would run his nose along the top of the bag, his tail waving in happy arcs: "I smell something yummy in there."

After having his strip of jerky, he'd stand calmly in the middle of the great room while Marybeth—dressed in jeans and hiking boots, her glossy brown hair pulled back in a ponytail—put needles in his head, elbows, and spine. I'd sit before him, rubbing his chest, and she'd attach the needles to a small battery-charged device that provided electrical stimulation. When he was all hooked up I'd get him to lie on his side, and I'd recline by his outstretched paws and put a hand on his chest to keep him calm. It was hardly necessary, for he so liked Marybeth and how the acupuncture felt that he was soon sleeping. His deep breathing relaxed me and I, too, dozed off, waking twenty minutes later as Marybeth began to remove the needles.

She also showed me how to give Merle a full-body massage and manipulate his legs through a range of therapeutic motion. When I'd break for lunch, I'd whistle him up if he wasn't inside and get him to lie in the middle of the great room. Kneeling over him, I'd begin by massaging his neck, saying, *"C'est très important, Monsieur, pour un chien athlétique comme toi, d'avoir un massage tous les jours."* It's very important for an athletic dog like you to have a massage each day.

Groaning in pleasure, he'd stretch to the tip of his toes and scrunch his neck under my hands, asking me to press harder. I'd say, "And now let's do those problematic elbows." After massaging them, I'd go to his back, saying, "And now your back, and those ribs, your hips, your knees, and finally each and every toe."

He'd shudder with delight and let out a huge sigh. "Oh, that feels so good!"

Rolling him to his other side, I'd repeat the massage, ending by placing him on his back and rubbing my hands from his chest to his belly.

"*Voilà*," I'd announce, clapping my hands, "*c'est fini.*" We're finished.

I'd step away, and he'd dart out a paw to catch my leg. Opening an eye, he'd hold mine: "Really? Are we finished so soon?"

"Yes, Sir," I told him. "I have to go back to work, or else how will I pay for that high-priced kibble and dog biscuits you're eating?"

All these treatments—acupuncture, massage, and supplements—may sound a little woo-woo, but are endorsed by those vets at the cutting edge of their profession. The American Veterinary Medical Association, for instance, is a proponent of acupuncture, stating, "Veterinary AP (acupuncture) and acutherapy are considered an integral part of veterinary medicine. These techniques should be regarded as surgical and/or medical procedures under state veterinary practice acts."

Dr. Kurt Schulz, who teaches at the School of Veterinary Medicine at the University of California, Davis, and is the lead author of the extremely helpful book *The Pet Lover's Guide to Canine Arthritis & Joint Problems*, also endorses massage therapy for dogs, as well as the use of "nutraceuticals"—a newly minted term that refers to "naturally occurring products that are eaten to improve health."

And there was Marybeth, who simply by watching Merle suggested to me that his thyroid levels might be low. Sure enough, a blood test showed that she was right, and she prescribed a drug called Soloxine to bring his production of thyroxin back to normal.

By early December, Merle was walking without any head bob and sliding downhill through the new powder as if he had never had a joint problem in his life. I was certain that two of our oldest known therapies—time and tenderness—had worked their magic along with prescription drugs, supplements, acupuncture, and massage. The coming of winter had also helped, the cooler weather invigorating him to an astonishing degree, which should have come as no surprise since older dogs have a more difficult time at thermoregulation and use more energy when they're hot.

"Ski Dog!" I exclaimed as he popped out of the snow above me, his tail lashing in glee. "You are restored."

"Ha!" he panted. "I feel like my old self."

"You look like it," I added, "except for your white face."

Diplomat that he was, he didn't mention the white streak in my forelock. He gave me his biggest grin and leaned his shoulder against my leg. We were getting older together.

CHAPTER 15

What Do Dogs Want?

One cold winter afternoon, as Merle ran along the frozen shores of Yellowstone Lake, he found a nest of pigeons. He grabbed the mother bird and shook her, the chicks peeping, as I yelled at him to leave her alone. He dropped her, and we took a few steps toward a spring where some splashing made me think that otters were playing among the rocks.

Suddenly I found myself in ankle-deep, shin-deep, then knee-deep water, the bottom falling away, the ice I had been walking on sinking fast and leaving no land. Waist-deep in the freezing water, I turned around and grabbed for the solid shore, but it was gone, everything around me moving like a river. Turning, I searched for Merle and found him swimming behind me, his eyes worried. Glancing ahead to where the frozen lake had been, I saw only wide gray water, wide as the sea, with icebergs tumbling over a horizon toward which we were now being swept. When I looked around for Merle, there he was, swimming strongly by my side, his face steady and calm.

Wrenching myself awake, I saw his chin on the edge of the bed, his deep brown eyes staring into mine, his tail moving back and forth inquiringly: "Are you all right?"

Putting my hand on his head and bringing my nose to his, I said, "Just that old swept-away dream."

He increased his tail's tempo: "I'm right here."

I held my hands against his cheeks, feeling his steady comfort, like a living rosary, a connection to gravity and ground. Perhaps that's why, in my dreams, he was so often beside me as I was swept off by forces beyond my control. And in those dreams, he was always young and so was I.

In the waking world, of course, we were not. But though we were getting older, we were far from our dotage. In fact, for a couple of years after we saw Paul Cuddon and Erick Egger at the CSU Veterinary Medical Center, Merle seemed not to age at all. Marybeth Minter periodically gave him acupuncture; I gave him his daily massages and supplements; and he ate a specially formulated senior kibble along with frequent additions of elk and antelope meat and their bones. His weight stayed at seventy pounds, and the worst that happened to him during this time was that he occasionally had bad breath.

"Sir," I'd say, recoiling from his panting, "you could clean copper pans with that. I'm sorry. I haven't been giving you enough bones. Here, let me get you one."

Within a day or two of his gnawing on an elk or antelope femur, the bones would have worked their magic, scraping off the accumulated plaque while also changing the chemistry of his digestion. I could safely plant a kiss on the end of his nose without thinking of buying a gas mask. However, the opposite didn't hold true for him. If I offered him a kiss within an hour or two of brushing my teeth, he'd back away with a pained expression. And if I tried to brush his teeth, no matter what flavor of dog toothpaste I used, he'd wear the same pained look and flick his tongue in and out as he tried to rid himself of what he obviously considered an unpleasant taste. After half a dozen trials with a variety of toothpastes, we stuck to nature's dentifrice—bones—for his oral hygiene.

The memory of toothpaste lasted, however, and there were times that I thought he actually dreamt of it. As he slept on the dedicated quadruped couch, I could see him flicking his tongue over his incisors, his face wearing that same mildly disgusted look as his feet twitched and his eyes darted in REM sleep. On other occasions when he was dreaming, he'd emit little yelps, his paws running faster and faster, and I'd wonder if he was chasing Zula or a bison. Sometimes his dreams seemed to be full of the white Shepherd, for he'd growl angrily and draw back his lips as if tearing into her. Once in a while, though, his growls turned fearful, as if he were being chased by some great beast, a grizzly bear perhaps, or an ancient canid enemy looming in his subconscious, who I could barely conjure. Maybe it was even the person who first beat him or fired the bullet into his shoulder.

There were also times I saw him dreaming peacefully, his paws moving languorously, his face calm, and I wondered if he was dreaming of us, as I often dreamt of us, not being swept away, but walking or lying in a green meadow whose beginning and end could not be seen. Or maybe he was dreaming of Shayla, as I often dreamt of my loves.

I thought it significant that he always had his most violent dreams on the dedicated quadruped couch and his most idyllic ones upstairs on his plush, green L. L. Bean bed in the corner of our room. Perhaps his worst nightmares were not of some mythic short-faced bear or angry shepherd on the Navajo Nation, but of Gray Cat himself, finally emerging from deep cover and unleashing his claws.

Now and then as Merle and I walked or skied up Snow King—the ski area that looms over Jackson—we'd see Allison and Brower. She had moved away from Kelly, to the other side of the valley, and we ran into each other less frequently—a blessing, we both realized. Brower, of course, didn't think so, and he'd greet both Merle and me ecstatically before falling in by Merle's side as we began walking up the ski hill, Allison and I talking about where our lives were taking us—she had gone to graduate school and had become a psychotherapist; I was writing more books and fewer magazine articles. Perking their ears, the dogs listened to us while matching each other stride for stride. Brower would look at Merle out of the corner of his eye and say, "See, I'm a big dog now." And Merle, matching his pace, would return the look, replying, "That's true, but I can still keep up."

At the parking lot, I'd open the back door of our Subaru, and Merle and Brower would both jump in. Allison would call Brower to come, but he'd refuse to go with her, lifting his head and laughing, all the while retreating farther and farther into the car, which she took as his taunting her, but I translated as "Why don't you come with us so we can all be together? That's what I want."

Of course, I wouldn't say this. The time for saying such things was over—at least from me.

She'd have to drag him out by his collar as he'd dig in his front paws. Scooting him into her Toyota, she'd say, "It never stops. The power of the guys." There was no edge in her voice, though, and I'd answer, laughing, "We smell like elk."

She'd laugh, too, and we'd give each other a hug and go our separate ways.

Then, in Merle's tenth year, he developed what his vets called "an elongated soft palate," which made him wheeze with heavy exertion. We'd be walking up some trail in the dark, hoping to find an elk, and as the trail steepened, he'd begin to pant with a raspy intake of breath that was audible for hundreds of yards.

Surgery was one of the recommended treatments, but I wasn't convinced that this was the best course of action to take, especially because he was otherwise healthy. I elected to see what would happen if I didn't push him so hard uphill. I began to leave him home when I thought the chances of finding an elk were high and I would need to move quickly and quietly. As I had expected, there were some heart-rending scenes at the car, his tail wagging lower and lower and finally stopping in mute disappointment when it became obvious that I wasn't going to take him. The crushed look on his face said it all: "I can't believe you would do this to me."

"Do you want to eat elk?" I'd ask him quietly. "We're not going to get an elk if they hear us coming. If I get one, I'll come right back for you."

He'd meet me at the car when I'd return, his mayoral rounds suspended for the morning, and immediately smell my boots. If they bore no sign of elk, the introspective look on his face would turn to one of faint remonstrance: "See, this is what comes of leaving me behind." On the other hand, if my boots were smeared with blood, he'd begin to cavort in ecstasy, dancing his paws up and down while he woofed congratulations at me: "You did it! You got one! Let's go!" And he'd leap into the car and rush up the trail ahead of me, panting heroically and coming upon the carcass with eager looks in every direction. Running his nose over the elk and breathing in her scent, he'd lick her neck and spine before scribing larger and larger circles around her, his nose to the duff as he pieced together what had happened.

"Oh, yes, they walked from over there." Sniff, sniff, sniff. "And here is where you came from." Sniff, sniff, sniff. "Then she fell by that log, ran to this side of the clearing, and the rest of the elk ran off that way." He'd look up happily, reliving the morning, his tail wagging in steady approbation: "Well done!" I have seen wolves, lagging behind in the hunt, give their successful pack mates who have pulled down the elk a similar greeting.

His eyesight, too, remained as sharp as ever. Walking along a high ridge in the summer, he'd stop suddenly and gaze into the distance. At these moments, the very tips of his golden hairs took on a vibratory quality, the rims of his nostrils dilating, his ears pricking forward in minute attentive contractions. I could see his heart beating in the blood vessel that wrapped over his Achilles' tendon, his entire focus captured in those taut, poised lines of hind legs, haunches, and pulled-in stomach. Raising my binoculars, I'd see an elk three-quarters of a mile off.

"Good spot!" I'd exclaim.

"Ha!" he'd exhale and wag his tail hard: "You bet."

Sometimes at the end of one of these days, after we had made a large loop across several ridges and valleys, we'd find ourselves descending a hanging drainage that neither of us had been in before. Since we hadn't walked up the drainage, there was no scent to lead him back to where we had started; since we were below tree line, we had no glimpse of the mountains to orient us. Yet, as if he had a GPS in his head, he'd take the right direction home.

Watching him move so confidently through the country, I couldn't help but think of a story Barry Lopez recounts in *Of Wolves and Men*. "An old Nunamiut man was asked," writes Lopez, "who, at the end of his life, knew more about the mountains and foothills of the Brooks Range near Anaktuvuk, an old man or an old wolf? Where and when to hunt, how to survive a blizzard or a year when the caribou didn't come? After a pause the man said, 'The same. They know the same.'"

That's how I felt about Merle and me in our corner of Wyoming. We knew the same, the same. About some things—what animals crossed the village at night, the life of its dogs, and the routine of some of its people—he knew far more than I.

When Merle and I had seen Erick Egger in Colorado, one of the last things I had asked him was "How long might Merle live?" He cast a glance at Merle, as if he might be taking stock of everything he knew about his physical condition and the life expectancy of certain breeds of dogs. "I bet you get six more years out of him," he said.

Merle was eight when Erick gave us this estimate, and I, thinking that fourteen was a long ways off, tucked this information into the farthest corner of my mind, like a balloon payment that I had no desire to reflect on. For three years I didn't. Then, jumping into the front seat of Scott Landale's pickup truck, Merle missed his footing, fell backward onto his butt, and broke his tail. I was away on an assignment, and for the first time in my life I had an inkling of what it feels like when you leave your child in the care of the best of friends, and she or he is hurt. Not that the Landales could have done anything to prevent the accident, nor would I have done anything different had it been my truck. Merle had always made the leap from the ground to the front seat of a pickup truck handily. This time he missed. He was eleven.

Merle's tail now had a crook in it, near its base, and it took a long time to heal. To speed his recovery, I massaged him twice a day and he'd groan more deeply than usual, giving his tail not the old, hard, steady thump-thump-thump but a more measured one—thump-pause, thump-pause, thump-pause. And instead of closing his eyes in sleepy pleasure during his massage, he'd hold my gaze with a look of studied feedback: "Oh, you're getting close to the spot that hurts. Yow!" His eyes would start. "You sure found it. Yes, yes, do exactly what you're doing."

Then, just when I thought he was getting better, he began to wet his bed. Getting up on that fateful morning, he looked at the wet spot with dismal perplexity, his shoulders hunched, his tail drooping, as if he had let himself down.

"Not to worry," I said, kneeling by him, with an arm over his back, though I was worried myself, "we'll just pop that in the washing machine."

I called Marybeth, who stopped by in the afternoon and examined him, getting him to wince as she ran her fingers over his back.

"I don't think the incontinence is from old age," she said. "The nerves to his bladder may have been affected when he fell on his sacrum."

This ever-lengthening chain of medical problems left me feeling low. It seemed that Merle and I had both just been forty-eight years old, not even middle-aged by my lights, and in the ensuing three years, given the more rapid aging of dogs, he had become sixty, or even seventy-one, if one accepted the data of the more recent study, and was now showing it. At least he was an athletic senior, I thought, who was compliant in doing what was necessary to restore his health.

Marybeth gave him several acupuncture treatments over the course of the next two weeks and prescribed two Chinese herb formulas designed to help his kidneys and immune system. Each morning he was now taking eight different vitamins, supplements, and prescription meds, and, true to his being a very particular dog, he quite suddenly no longer wanted his pills dabbed in butter. In fact, he would spit them out. I was at a loss for a substitute, a convenient spread to make the pills palatable, but he solved the problem for me. As I fixed my toast one morning, he came into the kitchen and stood by my side while wagging his tail with interest. I had smeared tahini—roasted sesame butter—on the bread and was licking my fingers. By his steady gaze, I could tell he wanted a taste. I held out a finger to him and he cleaned it avidly. Though I had been using tahini for years, he had never expressed the slightest interest in it. Dipping one of his pills in the jar, I offered it to him. Slurp. It was gone. And so butter was out and tahini in.

I also took him to an Idaho chiropractor and homeopath, Jim Davis, who accepted dogs as patients. He adjusted Merle's sacrum and lumbar spine, and after only one visit Merle was walking with less stiffness. A repeat visit gave him even more relief.

As I stretched the following morning on the throw rug next to my bed, working on my own stiff back, I could hear him coming rapidly up the stairs. Spying me on the floor, he grinned—he always took great pleasure in seeing me at his level—and came over to touch noses with me. I reached up and rubbed his ruff, saying, "You took those stairs like you were a pup."

He beat his tail in steady agreement. His bed-wetting had tapered off with the acupuncture treatments, and the only lingering effects of his fall seemed to be the fall of his tail. He could no longer hold it perfectly erect, arched high over his back—his flag and symbol of authority. Instead, it stuck out at about a fifty-degree angle, and I could tell by the subtle expression on his face—mild confusion mixed with annoyance—that his inability to use his tail to signal his status bothered him. He soon devised a way to compensate for the loss, however. Instead of marching right by dogs he considered his subordinates, as he used to do, with his tail high and softly waving, he now paused and gave them a chance to smell his lips, redolent of elk and antelope. I had always thought that size and demeanor alone had given him status, but I now realized that it was also how he smelled, his very being giving off the scent of canine wealth: fresh meat and bones. However, allowing these dogs to carefully inspect his mouth caused some of them to respond in the time-honored fashion of have-nots. They would immediately turn and head for our land in hopes of grabbing the bone Merle had just been chewing.

"Ah, Sir," I said, turning and kneeling before him, "isn't this getting old a bitch?" Then, realizing what I'd said, I added, "Maybe that'd be just right for you."

Rocking back, he put his paws on my shoulders and looked me in the eye. I placed my index fingers in his ears and softly rubbed their interiors in gentle circles, a massage that never failed to make him go limp with contentment. His lower jaw sagged and his soft, deep pants made his lips flutter like the wings of a butterfly. Bringing my hands to his shoulders, I gave him a squeeze and said, "Oh, you are still a handsome dude."

"Ha-ha-ha," he panted, lifting his head to grin at me, one brow going up, the other down, though now their motion was not so visible since his face had grown so white.

The alchemy of aging knows no favorites. Just as Merle recovered from his injury, a mass appeared on Brower's upper jaw, under his right lip and near his nose. When it didn't go away, Allison had it biopsied, and it turned out to be a malignant fibrosarcoma, a cancerous tumor that is often fatal if it shows up in a dog's mouth. Brower was six.

The tumor continued to grow rapidly, presenting Allison with two choices: Let the tumor grow until it prevented Brower from eating or try surgery to remove it. Unfortunately, because of the tumor's tentacle-like formation, the surgery would entail removing half of Brower's snout.

She told me all this as we sat on the deck one evening, Merle and Brower off in the sagebrush beyond the three prayer flags, the tall white banners just moving in the breeze. I had brought them home from Nepal, where such banners can be seen outside Buddhist monasteries, the homes of Sherpas, and on high mountain passes. Imprinted with blessings, the flags cast their good tidings downwind, in this case toward the house.

Only the dogs' tails were visible in the sagebrush, Brower's tail high, Merle's a little lower, the two courtiers still.

"What would you do?" she asked me.

Watching our dogs, she had stopped crying. I watched them a moment longer, touched that she had come to ask my advice as well as by the unexpected course of things. So long ago, I had wanted a bird dog, and I had found Merle. So long ago, I had wanted a wife, and I had found this friend.

I watched the dogs a moment longer before saying, "I think I'd do the surgery. Brower's not going to care what he looks like, and it might save his life."

She began to cry again, the sort of tears that go far beyond the subject at hand. "He is such a beautiful dog," she said.

"He is," I agreed, but I knew what she meant—that even though Brower wouldn't care what he looked like, she would, a beautiful woman who took such pride in how things looked.

A few seconds later, I knew I had been right, for she fixed her eyes on him, bounding through the sage, and said, "This seems like a test just made for me."

After doing more research and consulting another specialist, she came to a decision. She brought Brower over to the house to take some photographs of him and me playing on the deck—the last photographs of the two of us when he still had his face. The growth on his upper jaw had begun to disfigure his lip into a painful-looking snarl. When Allison drove away toward Colorado for his surgery, I stood on the deck with Merle and watched her car go down the park road. She had her arm extended out her window, reaching aloft as she waved good-bye. In the rear window, Brower stood, laughing at us, his ears flapping in the wind.

A few weeks later, he burst through the dog doors, leapt into my arms, and put his paws on my shoulders. "Ted, man!" he panted. "It's great to see you! I can't tell you what I've been through!" And for the first time in his life he looked intimidated, not without reason.

The results of his surgery were horrific. The top half of his snout was gone, cut off cleanly in front of his eyes, his two lower canines sticking into empty space around his tongue, the twin holes of his nasal passages opening and closing within a wall of pink flesh as he breathed.

Though I had internally gasped, I hugged his shoulders and gave him a kiss on the side of the head. "Browse!" I cried. "It is so good to see you too!"

Tearing my eyes from his amputation, I saw that the rest of him was still whole, the perfect Golden Retriever, slim with feathery ears and tail, his brown eyes now turning merrier as he saw Merle coming over to take a perfunctory sniff of his nose. The expression on Merle's face remained absolutely matter-of-fact: "Hmm, Brower's missing half his snout. Let's head down to the creek."

Out the dog door they flew, and that was that. Brower did not hide or spiral into depression. He did not stop hiking, skiing, and tearing off branches from fallen trees. He continued to mount any uncut dogs he could find. Despite the loss of half his snout, he didn't change his behavior or his optimistic outlook on the world. He was a lesson for all of us.

As was the Gray Cat, who went missing shortly before Brower came home. Months before, he had begun to limp and pick at his food. When he didn't come around in a few days, I took him to the vet, who ran some tests and diagnosed him with diabetes. We put him on a low-calorie diet and I would call him twice a day to the refrigerator, where I kept his insulin. *"Chat Gris, viens ici, s'il te plaît, pour ta médecine."* He'd stand calmly at my feet while I slipped the needle into a fold of skin between his shoulders. *"Ah, comme ton ami, Merle, tu es un patient très accommodant."* Like your friend, Merle, you are a very compliant patient. And indeed he was except when it came to his new diet, which he settled into grudgingly.

"I'm sorry," I'd say as he sniffed his food and left it untouched. "You are of an age, Sir, that you can no longer be choosy."

But when he regained his mobility, he chose to be choosy, slipping out the two cat doors—slap-slap—and heading into the dusky sagebrush, green eyes wide as he searched for rodents. He brought back a mouse tail in the morning, and I told him, "Gray Cat, you're not as fast as you once were. Are you sure you want to go out there at night?"

That night, when he discovered that I had blocked his door, he told me that he did. He came to my bed and caterwauled in my face: "Ted! Open the door. Oh, Ted! Open the door." I turned away from him and he stomped over my shoulders. Putting a paw on my face, he cried again: "Did you hear me? Open the door."

Merle—who wasn't happy either to have found the door plugged—looked up from his bed with a sour expression: "That insufferable cat."

And so I let Gray Cat out, and we had peace. One day a few months later, he didn't come back. In the morning I searched in wider and wider circles around the house, finding no evidence of any struggle, which led me to believe that he had been grabbed on the fly by a coyote and carried off. Over the next few weeks, when I'd hear a coyote yip into song, I'd think of Gray Cat and console myself with the fact that he would have had it no other way, that for eleven years he had been a night hunter just like the coyotes, Great Horned Owls, and mountain lions among whom he slipped so fearlessly.

One day, though, as the afternoon sunlight fell on my desk, his going the way he wanted to—off by himself, an outdoor cat—did not buoy my spirits. I missed his soft gray sprawl on my lap and his putting a paw on my fingers as I typed. Getting up, I walked into the great room and said to Merle, "Don't you miss Gray Cat?"

Lounging across the entire length of the dedicated quadruped couch, his chin comfortably on its arm, he didn't appear to be giving much thought to our old buddy. Up went one white brow, down went the other. He glanced around. "Gray Cat? I haven't seen him for quite a while."

"You are a hard-hearted soul," I told him.

He blew out a breath: "Phoooo."

Although Gray Cat's disappearance left him indifferent, it did serve to increase his affection toward me. Coming through his door, he'd spy me lying on the human couch, reading. In the past, there would have been a good chance that Gray Cat would be curled on my belly, and Merle would have sent him a jaundiced stare before going to the opposite couch, reserved for the four-legged members of the household. Now, he would immediately come to me, put his chin on my hip, nosing me hard as he wagged his tail: "Oh, this is so nice! Just the two of us." Then he'd go to his couch, lie down, and stare at me with the utmost contentment: "This is the best. You and me."

His obvious pleasure in having me all to himself made me think of the question that Elizabeth Marshall Thomas poses in her book *The Hidden Life of Dogs:* "What do dogs want?"

She answers that "they want each other," going on to say that "human beings are merely a cynomorphic substitute" and that "dogs who live in each other's company are calm and pragmatic" without the desperate, even hysterical need to communicate their feelings and observations to humans.

Thomas is certainly right about some dogs. But in thirteen years of living with Merle, I saw another aspect of dog behavior. When I was working at my desk, for instance, Merle spent most of his time outside with other dogs and also with a large cross section of our human neighbors. Even when I went to town, he would often choose to stay in Kelly and conduct his own affairs. Discounting his longstanding issues with shotguns and firecrackers, and his understandable dislike of having his paws or tail stepped on, he was as calm and pragmatic a dog as one could wish for. Nonetheless, he would become instantly and boundlessly excited if he saw me getting ready to go elk hunting or powder skiing. This wasn't hysteria. It was the passion of someone who knew what he liked. At these moments there wasn't a dog on the planet who could quell his enthusiasm for being with me. Yet take away these two activities—hunting big, tasty animals and floating down through the winter landscape—would Merle have liked me so much? I doubt it.

What do dogs want, then? The company of dogs, or the company of people? For many dogs who have the freedom to be themselves, both. Dogs with choices exercise their individual tastes, picking dogs or people, depending on which group meets their needs at a particular moment. Such behavior destroys the illusion that a dog's love is unconditional, but so what? Our love—at least a significant part of it—is conditional, just like theirs. We prefer to be with those who respect our selfhood, who do interesting things, and who smell right.

During the next year, after Merle's back healed and we returned to a more normal level of activity, my dog—now approaching perhaps seventy-seven in human years—reminded me of the legendary Norwegian cross-country skier Jackrabbit Johannsen. Born in 1875, Johannsen was an early champion of long, slow distance training and the health benefits of aerobic exercise. After coming to North America in 1899, he scouted and cut many of the cross-country ski trails still enjoyed in the eastern United States and Canada and, well into his sixties, skied thousands of miles each winter. He lived until 111 and could still be found skiing every day into his early 100s, his own life proving an elegant testimonial to what he had preached.

Following Jackrabbit's tracks, we climbed and descended the powder of Teton Pass; we ski-skated in the Absarokas; and we skinned up Snow King in the dawn before work. It became ever more obvious that Merle was a cold-weather creature, his hoarse, asthmatic panting nearly vanishing in the winter. At the summit of Snow King, he would fling himself upside down in polar joy and rub his back across the snow while his paws kneaded the frigid air. Spine massaged, he'd jump upright and stand on the edge of the mountain, his face rimed with frost, as he stared over Jackson Hole sprawling north to Yellowstone.

As I'd begin my preparations for the downhill run, he'd trot to my side and watch me intently while his tail carved the air. After folding my skins, tightening my boot buckles, clamping down my heels, cinching the drawstrings on my gloves, and putting on my goggles, I'd ask in my habitual pre-ski banter, "Well, Sir, are you finally ready?"

"Ready?" he'd snort, stomping his paws. "I've been ready for five minutes!"

"Let's go, then!"

And down the catwalk we'd fly—well, not quite. I would do many turns, checking my speed, so as to keep his pace at a trot and not molest his joints.

We'd be back at the house just as the sun rose, and I'd put out his breakfast. After showering, I'd come downstairs and find him lying in front of the woodstove, his eyes on me as I began to cook my own breakfast. Each time I'd meet his glance, he'd slap his tail hard on the pine boards several times, which was hardly his typical behavior when he'd already been fed and I was cooking something as repulsive to him as oatmeal. No, those tail thwacks had nothing to do with food. They meant, "Oh, what a great ski that was!"

"It was indeed," I'd reply.

Finally, he'd close his eyes and have a half-hour nap—a recent concession to his age—before heading out the door for his rounds.

Perhaps the most intriguing aspect of living with Merle during these years, as he went from a mature dog to an older one, was watching him change two long-standing behaviors. The first involved his bones.

Like most dogs, he would guard his bones from other dogs who might be on the prowl. Spying such a dog walking on the road, Merle would stop chewing, hold the bone still in his mouth, and level an armor-piercing stare at the passerby: "I see you watching me. Don't even think about it." Since possession is close to 100 percent of the law in the dog world, he never had a problem.

His glowering at dogs on the road was fine with me—it was like having an alarm system on one's car—but I didn't want him to act this way toward people. So from early on I had trained him not to be possessive of his food by hand-feeding him, then closing my hand over the offering. Soon, I could hand him the juiciest of bones and a moment later hold out my hand and say, "Please give that to me." He'd drop it in my palm. "Thank you," I'd say, examining it. "This is a lovely bone." And I'd hand it back to him. In this way, he learned that a bone would always end up being his, and perhaps this was one reason why he felt comfortable leaving his beef bones by my bed.

As Merle became older, however, and he realized that bones weren't a scarce resource, I began to notice that instead of chewing every last vestige of flavor from them before letting them out of his sight, he would clean them of meat and gristle, gnawing on them for perhaps an hour, before leaving them in the grass and climbing onto the deck for a digestive nap.

Now, one could say that Merle was no longer gnawing his bones into powder because his teeth were failing. But even though some of them were worn, the eagerness with which he attacked his bones in the first hour of acquiring them demonstrated that he was feeling no pain. What would often happen next was confirmation that his behavior vis-à-vis bones had changed.

If the wind happened to be blowing from the north—from our house toward the village—one of the neighboring dogs would soon appear and cast an appraising eye over the scene. Did Merle send the dog an ominous stare and rush to protect his bone? Never. Lifting his head, he would calmly meet the other dog's gaze, his composed body language saying, "Yes, I am done with that bone over there. You can have it if you wish." And thus assured, the dog would trot up, take the bone in its mouth, and head back to its own land.

Having watched this interchange take place between Merle and eight different dogs, over several years, I was reminded of the behavior of coastal brown bears whom I had photographed in Alaska. With an endless supply of salmon in the rivers at their feet, they will catch a fish, bring it to shore, and high-grade it, eating only the roe and the brains, which contain more fat than the flesh. They then walk off and leave the rest of the carcass for smaller bears.

In the age-old debate over whether nature or nurture is the most important factor in determining an individual's character, the behavior of brown bears with respect to abundant salmon and Merle's behavior with respect to seemingly endless bones are examples of how a change in the environment—an increased richness in the food supply—can alter what appears to be hardwired behavior. Brown bears who live far from salmon streams do not readily give up food to other bears. Likewise, most dogs do not easily give up still succulent bones to other dogs.

What might then be said concerning the true nature of brown bears and dogs? Simply this: Given the right stimuli, their nature is plastic, even through old age.

The neurologist Antonio Damasio touches upon this issue in his book *Descartes' Error,* where he describes how some of our genes can't unfold their potential until they have been modified by experience. As he puts it, "What happens among cells, as development unfolds, actually controls, in part, the expression of the genes that regulate development in the first place. As far as one can tell, then, many structural specifics are determined by genes, but another large number can be determined only by the activity of the living organism itself, as it develops and continuously changes throughout its life span."

The second behavior that Merle changed in his older years had to do with bird hunting. One fall afternoon as I walked from the shed to the car with my shotgun, he fell in by my side, wagging his tail.

Astonished, I held out the shotgun to him and said, "I'm going grouse hunting. See, it's the shotgun."

"I can see it's the shotgun," said his steadily wagging tail.

Though I could see that his tail wasn't wagging as enthusiastically as it did when he saw the elk rifle, it was wagging nonetheless, indicating, "I want to come with you."

"Merle," I replied, "let me get this straight. You can see the shotgun. You can see me wearing my bird-hunting vest, and you can smell it. And you still want to go with me?"

Wag-wag-wag went his tail.

"Okay. You never cease to amaze me."

I opened the door of the Subaru and he jumped in. When we got to the trailhead, he loped ahead of me, looking this way and that, smelling here and there, noting what he usually noted: "Oh, just a robin. Hmm, badger hole. Oops, coyote there." Up went his leg, quick squirt, scrape, scrape, "ha-ha-ha." Obviously, he was not concerned with finding grouse, and we found none.

The following afternoon was no different. He asked to come along; we had a pleasant stroll through the aspen, and never saw a grouse. But on the third afternoon, not fifteen minutes from the roadhead, a grouse flushed before us in a noisy blur of wings. The boom of the shotgun resounded through the forest. Merle watched the bird fall into some thick underbrush with complete disinterest.

I wondered if he had gone slowly deaf, managing to compensate for his loss of hearing, and I hadn't noticed it. If he couldn't hear the sound of gunfire, perhaps his main reason for not going bird hunting had vanished. He was slightly ahead of me and in the quietest undertone I said, "Merle."

Instantly his ears snapped toward me. He turned his head. "Yes?"

Not deaf.

I went to the alders into which the grouse had fallen and tried to force my way in. The thicket was almost impenetrable.

"Could you please give me a hand," I said, "and get that bird."

He gave me an uncooperative look.

"Go in there," I said again. "You're not above eating grouse when I grill them. Come on now, get that bird for us."

"Ha!" he panted, laughing at me. "You know I don't fetch."

"I do know that. But since you came along, you could be useful. Please." I motioned once again to the underbrush, and his body posture slumped into grudging agreement: "Okay—for you."

Taking his time, he pushed into the dense alders. I heard some thrashing, and ten seconds later he emerged with the grouse in his mouth and tossed it at my feet.

"Well done, Señor!" I cried, and clapped my hands.

He was a sucker for applause.

"Ha-ha-ha," he panted. "I guess it wasn't that bad."

From that day on, he went bird hunting with me, at least most of the time. Occasionally, when I took the shotgun from the shed, he'd look at it and say, "You know, I think I'll stay home today." And he would. Did that mean he wouldn't go the next time? Not at all. Sometimes, in fact, he would even flush grouse. But did that mean he would retrieve them? Never willingly, and then only in thick underbrush. I would have to ask him several times to "please get that bird" before he'd fetch it, bringing it to me as if he were Sisyphus himself condemned to retrieve grouse for eternity.

What had caused him to change his mind about going bird hunting? Since I wasn't taking him elk hunting as often, had he decided that spending time with me was worth the cost of being around the noise of a shotgun? Was he tired of his mayoral duties and wanting a break from them?

I can no more say why he changed his mind about bird hunting than I can say why he decided to prefer tahini to butter for taking his vitamins. Or why, after a year, tahini no longer appealed to him, and he would take his vitamins only if smeared with Lamaderm dog food. Or why one day, when on a sudden lark I put a bandana around his neck as we went out the door to a party, he accepted it with jovial prancing. Was it that I was dressed in party clothes, and he knew we were heading someplace with music, people he liked, and tidbits to scarf? Why, then, even when he knew we were going elk hunting and was beside himself with joy, would he grow instantly sober when I put on his red collar? Was it because the red collar had come upon the heels of the choke collar and would be forever associated with his loss of chasing cattle? From that party on—and he was a party animal—bandanas joined dog panniers as meaning fun.

And so what do dogs want? They want what they want when they want it. Just like us.

CHAPTER 16

A Looser Leash

During these later years of Merle's life I went to the Alps each spring to write about ski mountaineering. I always made a point of stopping in Chamonix, the small French city that lies at the foot of Mont Blanc, for as Kelly felt like home, so, too, did the Chamonix Valley. Great white pillows of glaciers, capped by granite spires, rise twelve thousand feet above the birch trees and violets. The ski routes are long and elegant. The food—bread, cheese, wine, fruit, coffee—still has a rich handmade taste, and there are plenty of cafés where I'd sit and gaze up to peaks I had just climbed. But what makes Chamonix so special is its dogs.

On any given day, two dozen or so free-roaming dogs occupy the central square of Chamonix, the Place Jacques Balmat, as well as the surrounding cobblestone streets. This is particularly remarkable because Chamonix, despite its quaint atmosphere, is hardly a village. Ten thousand people live in the valley, and its population swells to 100,000 during the summer tourist season. Vehicular traffic is heavy. A superhighway comes up the valley from Geneva, skirts along the edge of town, and heads through the Mont Blanc tunnel to Italy. In the other direction, a major mountain pass connects the Chamonix Valley to the autobahn that runs through the Rhône Valley in Switzerland. And in between—among apartment buildings, boutiques, restaurants, and throngs of people—the dogs play, snooze, go into and out of cafés, and occasionally jump into the central plaza's fountain to bathe. Then each night they disappear.

Like Kelly, Chamonix had a canine mayor, a black Newfoundland in the prime of his life whom I could see from my hotel balcony each dawn as he trotted briskly down the bike path along the Arve River, his body language saying, just as Merle's did, "I have things to do and people to see."

During the day, when I strolled through the central plaza, I would see him passing in the opposite direction, returning from his rounds of the city and maintaining his position, as did Merle, not with pushiness or aggression, but with quiet good cheer and diplomacy. Pausing to greet his constituents, he'd give them about ten seconds of his time—"*Je suis content de vous voir,*" It's good to see you, sniff-sniff—and then proceed on his way.

The first afternoon I met him, I was dressed in a T-shirt and shorts, for the May weather was warm. I had seen him weaving among the pedestrians, too preoccupied with his mayoral duties to stop and socialize with mere tourists. But as he came by me at a trot, his head turned. He slowed and stopped. Standing still, I cupped my palm for him. He took a sniff and let his wet black nose drift to my thigh. He inhaled deeply and his eyes went soft, his posture changing from hurried efficiency to reflection. Lifting his warm brown eyes, he met my gaze.

"*Bonjour, Monsieur.*" His rear end swayed in a greeting. "*Votre odeur m'intrigue.*" Your smell intrigues me. "*Le cerf, peut-être?*" Deer, perhaps?

"Very good," I replied. "*Nous avons les cerfs aussi où j'habite.*" We also have deer where I live.

The Mayor of Chamonix took another appraising breath of my leg and let out a small sigh: "*Ah, Monsieur, j'aimerais bien rester plus longtemps et vous connaître, mais comme vous voyez je suis un chien très occupé.* " I would like to stay a little longer and get to know you, but as you can see I'm a very busy dog.

Raising his shoulders, he gave me one more look: *"Alors, au revoir et à bientôt, j'espère."* Good-bye then, and see you soon.

And with that he hurried off, touched noses with several dogs around the fountain, and headed toward the river.

Anyone who lives in a city, including many French people, will at this point be puzzled—loose dogs among thousands of pedestrians, a great Newfoundland with the run of the city? What about leash laws? Poop laws? Health laws? Yes, the French attitude about dogs is very liberal—well-behaved dogs on a leash are still allowed to accompany their humans into many a restaurant—yet the Chamonix example is a bit extreme, even for France. After all, there is a national law mandating that unleashed dogs be within earshot of their humans and under their immediate control.

I, too, was puzzled by Chamonix's toleration of so many free-roaming dogs, and one day I set out to discover how the situation had come about. I interviewed the chief of police, two veterinarians who practice in the heart of the valley, and the head of the local branch of the *Société Protectrice des Animaux*, an animal-welfare organization that was founded in 1845 and is the French equivalent of the Royal Society for the Prevention of Cruelty to Animals and the ASPCA.

First off, I was told, none of the dogs were strays. As I could see, all the dogs wore collars; all belonged to people. Some were owned by shopkeepers whose places of business surround the Place Jacques Balmat; others lived farther off, in residential areas on the hillsides above town. They were walked by their people in the morning or let loose to do their business in their yards and the greenbelt near their homes. Then, on their own, they proceeded downtown to spend the day with their friends. And, as was apparent from walking downtown, the dogs had mastered the art of pooping at home or in the woods—the streets were clean of dog droppings.

Along the river paths, however, where people frequently walked their dogs for the purpose of having them do their business, poop-bag dispensers had been erected. The chief of police, a darkly handsome man in a trim blue uniform named Gérard Frau, also told me that he hoped that sand pits could be installed at strategic locations in town to make it easier for dog owners to find locations where their dogs could relieve themselves in a sanitary way.

More important in facilitating easy relations between free-roaming dogs and humans, he felt, was France's 1999 law prohibiting the importation and breeding of dangerous dogs such as Pit and Staffordshire Bull Terriers. Unfortunately, this law was being increasingly flouted, with the result that more people were being attacked. In Chamonix, however, he couldn't recall a single instance of a pedestrian being bitten by a free-roaming dog.

What about enforcing the law requiring that off-leash dogs be within one hundred meters of their human or within earshot? I asked. He gave a Gallic shrug of his shoulders and said, "With everything else going on in Chamonix, that's not high on my list of priorities."

One of the veterinarians with whom I spoke, Dr. Franck Miallier, a fresh-faced man with widely set blue eyes, concurred with the chief of police's take on dog bites. "The bites I see," he said, "happen within the family. In fact, there are hardly any dog bites from the free-roaming dogs because they're so well-socialized."

Dr. Valerie Hermann, who practices several kilometers upriver from Dr. Miallier, agreed with him. A short, commanding woman with brilliant golden hair, she used virtually the same words as Dr. Miallier: "The dogs are so well socialized to people, we don't see bites."

Absence of injury, however, doesn't necessarily mean that people are happy about sharing their space with free-roaming dogs. Yet in a couple of days of canvassing opinion on the square, I found that people weren't troubled by the dogs. They all said much the same thing: The dogs were mannerly; they didn't beg, bark, or whine; and so what if they strolled among pedestrians? A bartender at La Potinière, an open-air restaurant on the plaza, spoke for many when she said, "It's just not a problem. No one complains."

The only person who voiced a somewhat different sentiment was a handsome, middle-aged woman walking across the square with her husband and a small white poodle. I asked them, "Why do you keep your dog on a leash when everyone else lets theirs wander?"

"Oh," said the woman, "we are from Dijon, and unleashed dogs would never be tolerated there." She pursed her lips and exhaled the small puff of air with which the French express their disapproval: *"phoo."* It sounded remarkably like the noise Merle made when he disagreed with me.

"Mais, c'est Chamonix," the woman added. But this is Chamonix. *"Chacun ici fait grand cas de la liberté."* Everyone here makes a big deal about freedom.

This notion was reiterated by Dr. Hermann, who, with a twinkle in her eye, told me, "Chamonix is the capital of skiing and alpinism. It's the free spirit. The people are running free, their children run free, the dogs run free."

Significantly, everyone with whom I spoke ignored one of the most crucial factors in the city's toleration of free-roaming dogs: No automobiles are permitted in the very center of town; it's a pedestrian mall. In the narrow cobblestone streets that lead to the plaza, motorists can't go much above fifteen miles per hour. In this way, in the heart of a busy city, both dogs and people enjoyed what Merle and I and our neighbors enjoyed in our small village: a place devoted to people and animals instead of to cars.

———

Although the special circumstances surrounding Chamonix's toleration of free-roaming dogs can't be readily duplicated in other urban centers (at least not without changing some cultural attitudes), there are important lessons to be learned from this small city in the French Alps. Foremost is the fact that thousands of pedestrians intermingle with off-leash dogs without being bitten or even bothered. The Chamonix experience thus goes against the grain of how other urban centers, as well as towns, have tried to protect pedestrians from dogs—by keeping the dogs on a very short leash. This is certainly wise legislation when it comes to streets congested with automobiles, but it is counterproductive when applied with a broad brush, making all city and suburban parks off-limits to dogs who are within voice control of their humans while enjoying some off-leash play. As Temple Grandin has noted, "[L]eash laws may be short-circuiting some core principle of animal behavior in the wild."

I suspect that this principle has a lot to do with the fact that all of us need to meet and then get to know other members of our species in an unconstrained way. To appreciate what this means to a dog, try this thought experiment.

Put a collar around your neck, attached to a six-foot lead. At the other end of the lead is a dog who is at least twice and perhaps four to thirty times your size. Now go to a party and try to talk with another human being while your dog pulls at you, barks at you, and, through the leash that connects the two of you, transmits its annoyance, impatience, hurry, and concern. Is it any wonder that there are so many neurotic dogs?

More and more animal-welfare organizations are trying to make this point. The San Francisco SPCA, concerned that off-leash dog privileges might be curtailed in Golden Gate National Recreation Area because of the public's fear of dogs, has been one of the most outspoken, saying in an official position paper, "Off-leash areas are essential to the well-being of dogs. Regular off-leash play makes for healthy, well-adjusted dogs. It burns off pent-up energy, builds confidence, improves a dog's social skills and helps prevent aggression. Conversely, limiting dog play results in under-socialized, under-exercised, under-stimulated dogs and often leads to behavior problems."

On the other side of the continent, in New York City, a dog-advocacy group named FIDO has said the same thing: "FIDO believes that dogs need off-leash time to exercise and to play with other dogs in order to be healthy and well-socialized."

This sort of talk makes more than a few non–dog owners nervous. They watch TV newscasts of gruesome dog maulings, especially of children, or read about them in the newspaper, and the reports often make reference to the increasing number of dog bites, and may even cite the most recent data available from the Centers for Disease Control, showing that 4.7 million dog bites occurred in the United States in 1994.

At first glance, this sounds like a national disaster. Do we really need any more dogs, especially unleashed ones? Aren't organizations like the SPCA and FIDO simply looking out for the interests of their members, who want their dogs to have as much freedom as possible? Or does one of the principal contentions of these groups, that off-leash dogs are not a threat to public safety, have some merit? One person who has tried to answer these questions is the science and education writer Linda S. Shore, who has done the most comprehensive review of dog bites in North America ever compiled, using data from The Laboratory Centre for Disease Control, a branch of the Canadian national health agency, as well as from the U.S. Centers for Disease Control.

The most significant piece of information to come out of her review confirms the experience in Chamonix. The majority of dog bites (65 percent in Canada and 75 percent in the United States) do not happen to pedestrians who encounter an off-leash dog in a public place. Rather, most dog bites occur within the home to a family member who knows the dog. In fact, only 1.1 percent of all the dog bites surveyed in Canada occurred in public parks, sports, or recreation areas. (The same information was not available from the CDC.)

Shore's research into emergency room visits also puts the danger of dog bites into perspective. Only 1.3 percent of all people admitted to an ER in the United States were treated for a dog bite. One's chances of going to the ER for having fallen down, been cut by a knife in one's own kitchen, crashed one's car or bicycle, fallen victim to overexertion, gotten burned while cooking dinner, had a foreign object fly into one's eye, or cut off a toe in the lawn mower are all far greater than having been bitten by a dog. The only accidents lower than dog bites in the national ER admission statistics are poisoning, suffocating, and walking into another pedestrian.

This data is especially relevant when viewed alongside the recent work of animal behaviorists. Innumerable case studies have shown that the large increase in dysfunctional canine behavior, especially aggression, is a direct result of more and more dogs living solitary lives. Supervised free-roaming dogs aren't a threat to public safety; unsocialized ones are. These are the very sort of dogs who, spending their lives in solitary confinement from their own kind—often in a suburban yard—bark their heads off at passersby, make life hell for the mail carrier, and act aggressively toward other dogs and people when they meet them face to face. Such sequestered dogs may have their own dog door, but if the door leads to no more than a lawn and a fence, the dog has merely been put in a bigger crate.

The ultimate truth of living with a dog is the same as that of living with a person you care about: It takes time. And in this respect, many urban dogs may have more fulfilling lives than their suburban counterparts. Their humans, being urban people and not so wedded to automobiles, walk, and when they walk they take their dogs with them. If they have access to a park with hours devoted to off-leash recreation, both person and dog get what most of us need, if not every day, then close to every day: access to a reasonable amount of green space, safety from cars, exercise, and good conversation with our own kind.

These four criteria are worth keeping in mind when one's local parks department is about to turn yet another grassy field—open to free play—into softball diamonds. Likewise, these four criteria can be used as discussion points in the ever more frequent debates over whether a last piece of farmland, adjacent to a growing suburban center, should be kept as open space or turned into a shopping mall.

It may be no accident that as these criteria, especially space, have decreased, depression has increased in both humans and dogs. Research done on the entire adult Swedish population has demonstrated a strong correlation between the stresses of urban living and the incidence of depression and psychosis. As a society, we have elected to treat this neurochemical change in our brains with psychotropic drugs—antidepressants—a wide-ranging experiment in treating symptoms, not causes, and one whose long-term biological and social consequences can hardly be foreseen.

Some of the short-term ones can be. Dr. Nicholas Dodman, the pioneer of treating depressed dogs with antidepressants, advises his clients that "without environmental enrichment . . . pharmacological treatment . . . will be less likely to succeed." His advice cuts across the species line.

The next time I visited Chamonix, the Newfie was gone, his office occupied by a happy-go-lucky dog of about seventy pounds, a curly-haired fellow, brown-and-black and of indeterminate ancestry. Not standing on his dignity, as had the Newfie, he bounded toward me, took in my smells, and gave me a frolicsome bow, bending low over his outstretched legs while wagging his tail with great enthusiasm. Instead of saying that he was *"un chien très occupé,"* a very busy dog, and hurrying on, he said, *"J'ai vraiment chaud,"* I'm really hot, and leapt into the fountain for a swim.

CHAPTER 17

The First Passing

The golden hair on Merle's elbows steadily disappeared and was replaced by calluses. Small warts grew on his back and benign fatty tumors—lipomas—over his ribs. His warm brown eyes took on a bluish cast, an increased density in the cellular structure of the central portion of the lens, called nuclear sclerosis, which makes the eyes of older dogs reflect light differently but doesn't markedly affect their vision. And his hearing slowly waned until I could stand behind him and say his name—not in an undertone but quite loudly—and get no response. Yet if I'd clap my hands or whistle, he'd instantly turn, for he was still able to hear these particular frequencies. Distant passersby, watching me on the deck, clapping my hands and whistling, must have thought, "Well, it's happened. He's finally gone mad."

His energy went up and down. Sometimes he could lope alongside me as I ski-skated; sometimes his back end became seized up and all he could do was walk slowly. His right rear leg began to atrophy, the paw turning inward, another result of his fall from the truck—the nerve that supplied his leg had been pinched. He could no longer stand on his hind legs and dance with me. Instead, as I two-stepped in front of him, he'd circle me arthritically and pump his paws up and down. Then he lost his voice. He was barely able to croak along to the "Hallelujah Chorus." Soon, I would return from a trip and he wouldn't chew me out with baying cries, though his lashing tail would say, "Gosh, I missed you."

All of these geriatric changes paled when Brower's cancer returned. A bulge the size of an apricot pit began to distend the wall of his snout beneath his right eye. It grew to the size of a golf ball, a peach, and then, over the period of a year, into a cracked and monstrous bulge the size of a fist that left blood in the snow when he scraped it.

Of course, he was still skiing with Allison. And dancing when he stopped by the house. And hiking up Snow King, where people, unable to bear the sight of him, would later confide to me, "Why doesn't Allison put that dog down?" Instead, she put him on her Christmas card, sitting next to him with her arm around his shoulder as they both smiled into the camera. The rest of his body was still that of the perfect Golden Retriever and so was his spirit, as he displayed on the first of June when, for old time's sake, he, Allison, Merle, and I climbed the Sleeping Indian, whose summit rises a mile above Kelly to 11,200 feet.

Brower pranced along the tundra, Merle galloping behind him, stiff but game, and watching them I thought, "I hope I can move that way if I'm terminally ill or I'm eighty-three. And at this altitude, no less." It was Merle's birthday—the day I had made his birthday, not knowing what day he was actually born. He was thirteen, and it was his twelfth time up the mountain.

We sat on the summit together, the dogs eating their traditional biscuits, we eating our traditional cookies, and all of us gazing at the mountains stretching away as far as we could see. On the way down, only a mile from the roadhead, I took a vaulting jump over a tree that had fallen across the trail. A moment later, I heard a dull thud behind me, followed by Merle's howls. He had also jumped the tree and had come crashing down to earth.

He lay on his side, wailing and appearing paralyzed. It was the first vocalization I'd heard from him in months. Talking to him softly—"Hang in there, Merlster, hang in there"—I felt him all over. Nothing seemed broken, and I helped him to his feet. Incredibly stiff, he managed to hobble to the trailhead, where I had to lift him into the car. By the time we got home, I had to carry him inside.

The next day an X-ray showed a lumbosacral subluxation. In layman's terms, he'd thrown out his back, which, in fact, was what he had been baying, "My back, my back, oh, my back!" Painkillers and muscle relaxants got him mobile, and more chiropractic work from Jim Davis put him on the mend. But as he was recuperating over the next two weeks, a man with six dogs—Rhodesian Ridgebacks, Golden Retrievers, and mixed breeds—moved in across the field from us. One day, as Merle was hobbling outside for a call of nature, they rushed him. He wagged his tail—"Good to meet you, welcome to the neighborhood"—and I'll always remember the expression on his face as they swarmed over him. It wasn't fear or anger, it was "This is uncalled for." One of the pack, a nervous, mean-spirited dog, bit Merle twice on the shoulder. Within days, the bites swelled into infected hematomas, and Merle had a high fever. The vet put him on antibiotics and again he slowly improved, resuming his mayoral duties only to have the local deer herd chase him across the field, the bucks with their antlers down. Only the quick intervention of one of our neighbors saved him from being gored.

I kept him inside and began to walk with him, slowly building up his strength. A week after his fever subsided, I helped him into the car and we drove to the Hoback River, where I left him on the grassy bank as I waded across the channel, casting upstream. Occasionally, I looked back to see him resting contentedly and snapping at flies. The next time I glanced up, he was swimming across the river, the current sweeping him downstream toward some rapids. His eyes expressed not the slightest dismay, only a steady intent on the bank beyond me, which he reached handily. Emerging from the water, he shook himself off and sent me the smuggest of expressions: "You see. I'm feeling better."

"Merle, you gave me a heart attack."

"Ha-ha-ha," he replied. "No big deal."

He walked along the bank, watching me fish and examining the trout I caught with an analytical expression: "Well, I guess this is important to you."

We meandered about a half mile upstream and when it was time to go back across, I said, "You think you can make it?"

Eyes half closed, he swished his tail—"of course"—and followed me into the water, swimming through the swift current by my side. On the other side, he bounded out and shook himself exuberantly, giving the tip of his tail a smart little tap in the air. My aging dog was back.

Three weeks later, as I was writing at my desk, I heard him sit up from the floor of the great room. He took several steps toward the dog door, setting off on his third tour of the village, when he fell down and began to thrash. I sprinted from my office and found him flopping on his side, his right leg collapsing beneath him each time he tried to struggle to his feet. Each time he fell, he slammed his head onto the floor. Grabbing him, I put my arms around him and held him close to me. His eyes were wild and afraid, as if something terrible had happened to him. "Easy, easy," I said. "I'm right here." He was breathing hard and fast.

When I steadied him, he could barely walk and kept falling to his right side. When he tried to shake his head, he fell over. The vet who had been taking care of him along with Marybeth Minter, a lanky young man named Theo Schuff, examined him an hour later, his blue eyes behind his gold-rimmed spectacles concerned and tender as he said, "You've been through it the last few months, haven't you, partner?"

"Ha-ha," Merle panted tiredly, "tell me about it."

"Well, we're going to get you fixed up," Theo replied, helping him swallow another round of painkillers and muscle relaxants. Rubbing the back of his neck, Theo told me that Merle might have vestibular disease, a condition that affects the inner ear and throws off a dog's perception of its body's position relative to the earth. It could be caused by an infection in the middle ear or by lesions in the brain, but its prognosis was good—a full recovery in a week or two. Merle should have complete rest and, if I wanted the expert's opinion, I should take him back to Colorado to see the neurologist Paul Cuddon.

I made the trip, and Paul's diagnosis was that Merle might actually have had a stroke. He had lost his proprioception in his right rear leg; the blink reflex of his right eye was blown; and when he'd reach for a biscuit, he'd miss it by two inches. An MRI would tell for sure.

Upon our return to Wyoming, I scheduled one at the hospital, but one delay followed another since humans get first crack at the machine, which having been down for a while was now backed up with a waiting list. We waited, and I continued to take Merle with me wherever I went, letting him out of the car to walk a few yards at his favorite spots—the base of Snow King, the Cache Creek trail, the start of our old mountain-bike route at Shadow Mountain.

Some of the people who saw him during this time were merciless in their comments, as if they were talking about no more than an old car that needed to be junked. "He's sure gotten decrepit," one friend told me. "Wow, is he ever over the hill," said another. And several came right out and said it: "Have you thought about putting him down?"

I was glad I wasn't their dog.

As we drove back to Kelly, Merle would lie as he always had—in the rear of the Subaru, its seats folded down so he had the entire cargo area to himself—his head erect and turning to watch the scenery go by.

"How you doing?" I'd ask, taking a quick glance at him.

"Just fine," his bright eyes would reply, "riding around in the car with you."

We began his physical therapy by walking from the porch to the road, a distance of about a hundred feet. When he was able to do that without stumbling, we began going to the creek, which was the usual start of his rounds, a distance of three hundred yards, there and back. Then we went to the post office—a round trip of eight hundred yards. Then to the river, a little more than a mile.

Jim Davis gave him several spinal adjustments during these weeks and mixed up a homeopathic stroke-healing formula that I added to Merle's food. And as Merle's appointments at the hospital for his MRI continued to be cancelled for human patients, some sort of healing took place. His balance returned, and so did his blink reflex. He stopped missing his biscuit. He was able to shake his head and not fall over. Perhaps it had been vestibular disease after all; but dogs, like humans, also recover from strokes.

By September we managed to repeat the first grouse walk we had ever done together, the one he had fled as a pup after I shot over his head, a three-mile round trip. In a few days we followed it with our river loop, the one on which he had counted coup on the coyote, five miles—all our walks done in the early morning, for it was clear that if we went out in the heat of the day his back legs would seize up and collapse.

On our third time along the river loop, Merle spied a bison and broke into a trot. The bison didn't move and Merle stopped a good distance from it, looking back at me with a grinning pant: "You know, that felt pretty good."

A mile farther on, the herd of deer that had chased him spotted us and bounced off. Forgetting all his training, he ran after them, but stopped when he was thirty yards from them. The deer stopped as well and stared at him with bored expressions that said, "You are an old harmless dog, and if you get any closer we'll take you out again." He returned their glance and raised the ante by wagging his tail sharply and standing taller: "I could catch you if I wanted to, but I don't chase deer."

He turned his head to me with one of the most gratified smiles I have ever seen on a dog: "Yeah, I can still do this stuff." And to prove it, he trotted proudly along the road, his form trim and economical, tail washing the air at a 50-degree angle. When a red squirrel dashed in front of him, he sprinted after it, sending it up a tree, where he stared after it with glowing eyes.

Upon reaching the porch, I knelt in front of him and gripped his shoulders. He rocked back on his haunches and we looked at each other for a long time. Then he dropped his head and pushed its crown directly against my chest.

"You are the best," I said, putting my mouth on his ear.

His tail broomed the planks. Then he raised his head and laid his cheek against mine.

The recovery was deceptive, or, rather, I was unable to put what was happening into perspective: He was recovering his strength and his agility, but never to their former states. When October came around and I was loading an overnight backpack to go elk hunting, he glided between my legs and leaned against my inner thigh. He made no sound, only took a huge breath and let it out with a heartfelt sigh that said it all: "I don't see my dog panniers. Once, they would have been the first thing you took out. Once, you wouldn't have left me behind."

I rubbed his inner ears, and he clicked his teeth—chatter, chatter, chatter—meaning, "Oh, that feels good, but please don't leave me."

And this time I couldn't, though a few hours later I was regretting it. He was flagging in the heat and beginning to limp as we made our way up the very ridge that we had sat upon a decade before, where he had nudged my shoulder and said, "Look behind us, elk are walking right there."

I debated whether to press on into the next valley, unable to decide if I was trying to make him happy or denying what was happening. If he was so stiff that he couldn't walk tomorrow, I doubted that I could carry his seventy pounds to the roadhead.

I made the decision for us. "How 'bout we walk down now," I suggested pleasantly, "while we still can?"

He could hardly answer. The sun blared down on us, and he panted.

I gave him a few minutes to recover, my arm around his shoulders, he leaning into me. As we had done since we first met, we sat and gazed over the country.

Finally, we headed down, his hind end collapsing under him as he wove drunkenly. Then, either a new batch of endorphins kicked in or the horse-to-the-barn syndrome began. He picked up his pace and at the bottom of the ridge was going along smartly as we entered the shade of the conifers. A creek burbled. Across a meadow the Tetons stood. Not a cloud in the sky.

But his right leg was turned in ominously and this time I knew that he would no longer recover, at least not enough to be able to come to these high places with me. The thought crippled me in midstride. Kneeling, I wrapped my arms around him, my eyes stinging with tears. He gave me a puzzled look. What could be wrong with me? We had just been walking along so nicely. "Ha-ha-ha," he panted mildly: "It's not that bad, Ted. There have been other times we haven't found elk."

I laughed and rubbed his ears between my hands. Standing, I said, "Lead on, Sir, lead on." And down the trail he gimped, and into the cold weather he trotted. When the snow fell, he squared his shoulders and pushed his way out the dog door, extending first one and then the other hind leg behind him in his elongated stretch. Tok, tok, tok, his claws sounded on the porch, and once in the driveway he gave himself a snow bath, putting his head under the new powder, and shaking it back and forth as he emerged. Washed and ready, he set off down the road, trotting rapidly, his mayoral duties before him.

The change in him was miraculous, but I had no illusions. I simply enjoyed each day, listening for him to return from his rounds and pad into my office. Putting his chin on my knee, he'd say, "Are you still working? Very good. Let me have a little nap until you're done." And he'd go to the dedicated quadruped couch

and slowly—front paws up, one hind leg up, second hind leg up—
lever himself onto its comfort.

Then, in the afternoon, we'd ski for five miles along the river
road, he trotting by my side, nose cleaving the cold air, eyes bright,
tail waving. "Ha-ha-ha," he'd pant at me. "What a great ski!"

"What a great ski," I'd say back. "What a great ski!"

But no physical therapy or winter weather could help Brower. He
grew steadily weaker despite Allison feeding him elk, organic
chicken, and every natural remedy in Marybeth Minter's ample
medicine bag. His surgeons said that nothing further could be
done for him and that his first surgery had bought him his time—
two and a half more years—and he had used it well, enjoying
every minute. Eventually, his kidneys began to fail, and Allison
had to rehydrate him with an IV. His tongue had been pushed out
the side of his mouth by the tumor's growth, his right eye was
squinted closed, and he began to have trouble breathing.

On a January afternoon she called me, asking if Merle and I
would like to come over and celebrate Brower's ninth birthday—
two months prematurely, she knew, but she doubted he would
make it until March. In fact, the end was probably days away.

We arrived a little after seven, and Brower came out his dog
door to greet us, the right side of his face a horrible mass of distorted tissue, hard scab, and oozing sores that smelled like a rot-
ting carcass. The disease seemed designed by an ironic god. The
rest of him was as glossy, golden, and robust as ever.

Allison had ordered pizza and we took it to the great room,
where a fire was going. We sat on the floor and I petted Brower,
crooning, "Browse, do you know you're the best?"

"I know that," said his wagging tail.

"Merle," I called, "come on in and join us." But he wouldn't.
He remained standing at the edge of the great room, watching us
despondently.

Allison mentioned that Brower had rallied in the afternoon and eaten a bunch of elk and chicken. We didn't have much of an appetite, however, and put our pizza aside to pet Brower as he lay between our outstretched legs. The smell of his tumor was strong.

She began to cry, wondering out loud if it was finally time to euthanize him. His white blood cell count had gone through the roof, and his breathing had become labored. I remained silent. I couldn't answer.

She had given Brower some Tylenol laced with codeine before we had come, and he grew sleepy with the drug and our petting. Putting his chin on one of his stuffed animals, he closed his eyes. Unlike Merle, he had no inhibitions about squeaky toys.

Merle had finally lain on his belly, his chin on his paws, one brow going up, the other down, as he watched Allison with sober concentration. Then he, too, closed his eyes. Allison continued to cry, and I put my arms around her—two people, their dogs, and the life they had once shared, now reaching its end.

After a bit, she collected herself and said, "I need to give him some fluid."

She brought the IV bag and stuck the needle into Brower's neck. He sat on my lap while the bag drained, a pouch growing under his hide, and I petted him, saying, "Browse, what a pup you are, what a champ," and he closed his eyes and fell asleep in my arms.

When Merle and I went to leave, Brower tried to stand and put his paws on my chest, but he didn't have the strength. There was a glint in his eye, however, and he followed us outside. When I opened the rear door of the Subaru, he hopped in before I could help Merle up, and no amount of cajoling by Allison or me could get him out. He laughed at us, standing beside Merle, who was now also grinning.

The somber mood of the house had been forgotten. We were in the Subaru, the eternal door to fun and play.

Allison had to crawl into the car and pull Brower out.

"The power of the guys," she said, half laughing, half crying. And then she added, "He loves you so much."

She hugged me and said she would call when she decided that it was time. Then she hurried inside. Brower remained in the driveway, lit by the garage light, clouds of frosty breath rising from his bulbous snout. His left eye, the one still open, held my eyes. I sent him a good-night smooch, and he pricked his ears.

In the morning, Merle wouldn't move from his bed. I went over to him, put a hand on his shoulder, and the instant I touched him, he yelped in what I thought was pain. He tried to stand, but seemed enfeebled, whereas yesterday he had been running in the snow. His head hung listlessly; his ears drooped; his eyes were sunken. And then I understood.

Kneeling, I picked him up and carried him down the stairs, taking him outside, where he limped only three feet from the deck to pee. After making his crippled way back into the house, he ate his vitamins, but no breakfast. I brought his bed downstairs to the great room, put it in front of the fire, and he lay down as if it were he, not Brower, who was dying.

Lying before him, I rubbed his ears, and, making my voice playful, said, "Oh, he's a pup. He's a pup and a half. He's a pup and seven-eighths. He's a double pup. He's the best pup in the world." But my old ditty, which had made him wiggle with delight so many times, could do nothing to raise his spirits this morning.

He looked at me with utter sadness. He had smelled what was in the air.

Allison called the following morning, saying that the time had come. Brower's tumor was badly infected; its growth couldn't be controlled; he was ever more uncomfortable. Marybeth would euthanize him that afternoon, but I could come by earlier to spend some time with him and a few friends who would be there to bid him good-bye.

I left Merle home even though he had recovered somewhat, coming down the stairs on his own and walking to the post office with me.

"Ha!" he exclaimed in the cold January air. "I've gotten a grip."

Nevertheless, I felt that watching Brower die wasn't what he needed.

I brought Brower a last antelope bone, and, abandoning his ragged, stuffed bear and rawhide chews, he set to it with loving concentration.

Allison had invited four friends, two men, two women, and we sat in the great room around Brower, the fire going, the Tetons soaring beyond the windows. We ate cheese and crackers, drank wine and beer, and watched him work on his bone.

Marybeth arrived with her tackle box of drugs, and Allison said that perhaps it was time to say good-bye. She knelt before Brower, telling him at great length how much she loved him and would miss him, and the two women mentioned how Brower had been a model of good cheer in adversity.

I offered a poem. One day last winter, I explained, Brower had noticed that Allison had begun to cry when she had seen him leave blood in the snow from his tumor. When they had gotten home from skiing, he had written this poem, and asked me to translate it for him, and send it to Allison, which I had, and now I wanted to read it for them.

"Do not cry for me," it began. "I have lived each day like it was my first, I never know that there will be a last." It went on to say that "I have run and chased and laughed, I have smelled girl dogs and horse poop and rotten meat. I have eaten bad fish and fresh elk—mmm." It said that "I have skied great peaks and listened to coyotes and wolves," and "if I have been sad, it has never been for me, only for you when you have been low." It concluded by saying that "I am the happiest of creatures—a golden dog of yours." And for this reason, "Do not cry for me. But you can cry, and I will be there. For I know one thing—I am first in your heart. Which is why I always sleep the utter peace of always seeing you."

The sky had turned a deep cold blue; cloud tufts hung over the mountains. Brower went from person to person, getting pets and hugs, and worked on his bone. Allison began to waver, saying, "He seems so vital. How can I put him down?"

Marybeth said she could make room in her schedule tomorrow, and I said I could return any time.

So Allison postponed, walking around, unable to sit, seeming to grow more gaunt and hollow-eyed by the minute. Brower stood between my legs, and I held my face on his back, and we just felt each other. At last, he became very tired and went to his bed. But after smelling it carefully, he continued to the hearth, where Allison had lit several white votive candles. Giving them a sniff, he lay on his belly before them and closed his eyes. She got his teddy bear and put it between his paws, and he rested his chin on it, his ears splayed out over his elbows. He breathed softly, the breath hissing through the now tiny opening of his nasal passage. He looked content and at peace.

Allison turned to Marybeth and asked if the injection was ready. Marybeth said it was, so Allison knelt by him, and Brower, without any prompting, rolled on his left side and put his head on the floor, his legs outstretched. Marybeth gave him the injection in his ruff.

Kneeling next to Allison, I touched Brower's leg, and he opened his left eye a moment, looked at me, lifted his paw, and placed it in my hand. I clasped it with both of mine, and he closed his eye and began to breathe deeply.

Allison had her face pressed to his neck, telling him that she loved him and would never forget him. Up until this moment, the afternoon had seemed well scripted, everyone sad but behaving nicely. Then an abysmal moan came from her, a sound that I did not believe Allison capable of, a sound so awful in its grief that I had heard it only once before. It was the sound that the mother of my six-year-old friend had made when, on our way home from school, he had been hit by a car and killed. The sound of irreplaceable loss. There would be other dogs for Allison, but not the dog with whom she had set out on her own and become an adult.

She reached out and clasped my hand. When she let go, I put my face on Brower's cheek and whispered into his ear, "You fly on, Browse. Thank you"—the words I next spoke took me by surprise. "Thank you," I whispered, "for scarring my floor."

I laughed to myself, remembering how he had run through the two dog doors—slap, slap—and had torn across my new pine floor, greeting me ecstatically and leaving scratches everywhere with his nails. I had complained to Allison, and she had said, "You don't have to let him in." I had considered it, but not for long. After all, it was just a floor.

He continued to breathe, a whistling, grating breath, and I wondered how long it would take for him to die. Then Marybeth said to Allison, "Whenever you're ready." And I realized that she had only given him a sedative and still had to administer the lethal injection.

Allison covered Brower for many minutes, talking to him so no one else could hear. Still, I held his paw. At last, she took a scissors and clipped some hair from his chest, stomach, and tail. Then, she nodded.

Marybeth shaved a bit of his hock, the electric clipper making a jarring noise. A moment later, she injected the solution. Brower's tail lifted high in the air and fell to the ground. Allison began to weep convulsively, and we all put our hands on her back, though I still held Brower's paw in one hand, feeling his rough pads and the lovely filaments of fur between them.

Who knows how long we sat there. It grew dark. And finally we let go.

CHAPTER 18

Through the Door

Merle skied through the winter, not the deep powder, but flat tracking. At the end of March his back end weakened, both hind legs splaying, so he could barely start on his rounds. He made it to Gladys's across the road and no farther. I knew he must be hurting, because dog poop began to accumulate in the plowed driveway.

He also began to slip on the pine stairs to our bedroom, so I stapled outdoor carpeting to the treads. The added traction helped him for a while, but coming upstairs soon proved too difficult. I moved his bed downstairs, under the great room's large picture window, directly next to the dedicated quadruped couch, which he could not mount either. In fact, he had begun to refuse my help in getting onto it, and he wasn't being proud. It hurt too much when he got off.

At night, I'd look down at him from the balcony, just drinking him in, lying on his green bed. He was still long and golden, still trim, only his face white, and I would marvel at how our dogs manage to stay so beautiful into their old age while most of us do not. I would stand on the pawprints he had left in the polyurethane nine years before—when he had looked down at our newly finished house and exclaimed, "This looks great!"—and I'd say, very loudly, "Goodnight, Merle. Sweet dreams, pup of my dreams."

He'd look up, hold my eye, and thump his tail: "You too."

Then I'd shut off the light.

On the last day of April I woke at 2:45 A.M., hearing him dreaming. His dream seemed more violent than usual, and I walked out of the bedroom door, turned on the light, and stood on the balcony. He lay half off his bed, running in his sleep. I went back to my bed, but shortly heard him walking around the great room, stumbling and bumping into furniture.

Hurrying downstairs, I found him disoriented, walking constantly to the right, slamming into the walls, and getting stuck in corners. He was very agitated. Kneeling behind him, I put my arms around him and held him to my chest as he panted and looked around fearfully.

"I'm right here," I said. "I'm right here."

But he didn't respond. He was displaying some of the same symptoms of the previous summer—lack of coordination, falling to one side, circling, his head tilted to the right, and also nystagmus, a back-and-forth motion of the eyes. But now there was something so profoundly disorganized about him that I couldn't wait until morning to seek help. I called Marybeth. She drove over and gave Merle some homeopathic tablets, but he remained agitated and disoriented. She suggested calling Theo after the clinic opened and getting his opinion.

Settling Merle on his bed, I sat by him until he fell asleep at five. Then I went upstairs and dozed. Shortly, I was astonished to see him standing by my bedside, stomping his feet, panting, and asking to go out. Though he hadn't climbed the stairs in a month, there he was.

I helped him downstairs and let him out—he seemed unable to navigate the dog door—and he peed and had a difficult, protracted bowel movement, leaving a trail behind him.

After I guided him to his bed, he fell asleep while I caught a few minutes of shut-eye on the couch. When he awoke, he gave me his usual happy smile—"Hey, good to see you, where's my breakfast?" I put some kibble in his bowl, and he walked normally into the hallway between the great room and my office, where his bowls sat, and polished off his meal.

"Phew," I thought. "He's back."

But as he returned to the great room, he suddenly curled his head to his left side as if trying to bite his hip, his lips snarling fiercely. He dropped to the floor, his limbs jerking, his eyes bulging and straining. Then he grew quiet and stared vacantly.

Sitting by him, I called Theo Schuff, and he advised me to keep Merle quiet and bring him in that afternoon. In a calm voice he told me that seizures weren't fatal and could be controlled. I put the phone down and sat by Merle, my hand on his shoulder. Despite Theo's assurance, I felt that this was no ordinary illness. Under my hand, I could feel Merle changing states and slipping away. Picking up the phone again, I made a couple of calls and wiped my schedule clean, cancelling a radio interview and my date that evening. They no longer seemed important.

Twenty minutes later, Merle surged to his feet and wandered to his bowls, knocking them over and spilling water across the floor. Without stopping, he bounced off the wall, caroming here and there, and staggered toward his dog door, only to get stuck in the corner. Turning back into the great room, he collapsed on the floor, howling softly, his body clasped in a tight U. Then his lips went back in that terrible snarl and he foamed at the mouth as he writhed across the floor.

When he had quieted, I picked him up, put him on his bed, and lay with him. Not ten minutes later, he lifted his head and looked me in the eye, seeming to snap out of where he had been. His look said, "Help me."

"I wish I could," I replied, "but you'll have to ride this through. Remember when I had benign positional vertigo a few years ago, just like you're having, and I was bumping into the walls? Was that ever no fun!"

He moaned at me, not pleading, but saying, "This is so strange."

We lay there for an hour. Then he rolled to his feet and walked drunkenly to the glass doors. I let him out. He walked across the deck and onto the grass, falling several times as he made his way to the clump of aspen trees at the corner of the deck, where he lay down on his belly in their shade. Looking at the Tetons, he panted softly. The breeze ruffled his fur and for the first time since the previous day, he looked happy.

In a while, he stood and began walking toward the road.

"Are you okay?" I called from the deck, where I had been watching him.

"Ha!" he exclaimed. "I think so."

Going down the drive, he turned right and started south on his mayoral rounds. Following him, I stopped him within fifty yards.

"I don't think this is a good idea," I told him. "How about taking a day off?"

"Ha-ha-ha," he replied. "I'm fine."

"Are you sure? You're weaving a bit. Come on, let's go back home." I turned him around and walked with him to the deck and into the house, where I sealed the dog door.

Then I went upstairs and took a shower, and when I came down, I found him taking a dump in the middle of the great room. I cleaned it up and as I did he had another seizure, foaming at the mouth and peeing on himself. A few minutes later, he curled into that horrible U-shape and began to bark plaintively—this from the dog who almost never barked.

Calling Theo, I described what was happening and he told me to come right in.

I was there twenty minutes later. Theo started an IV with saline and prednisone, a steroid, and suggested that an MRI might tell us what was going on.

I said, "Let's do it," and he called the hospital, which had an opening at five. To keep Merle quiet in the meantime, we moved him to an oversize crate padded with blankets. As soon as the door closed behind him, however, he began to thrash and moan, trying to get out. Tim Gwilliam, the other vet in the clinic, who had taken care of Merle before Theo had joined the staff, came into the room and suggested that I run some errands with Merle until our MRI appointment. Being in the car with me, he said, might calm him.

It did. As soon as I carried him into the Subaru, he relaxed and went to sleep. But a couple of hours later, just as I pulled into the clinic's parking lot, he seized again. Running into the office, I found Theo, and he hurried out with his medical bag. Merle looked awful, gnashing his teeth against his lips as bloody saliva flew from his mouth.

Both of us climbed into the back of the car and held him.

"Do you want to go on with this?" Theo asked.

For a moment, I didn't understand him. Then I realized what he had meant.

"I'm not putting him down," I said, "until I know what's wrong with him."

"You bet," Theo answered. "Let's wait for the MRI."

When Merle finished convulsing, he opened his eyes and looked at us lucidly.

"I think he might want to pee," said Theo.

We carried him out of the car, but when he tried to take a few steps his legs tangled and he fell helplessly to his side. Kneeling, I picked him up and pressed him against my chest. He began to bark loudly, on and on without pause. Putting my mouth against his head, I said, "Easy, easy."

For the first time in our life together, I couldn't translate what he was saying. I didn't know if he was suffering. I felt powerless to help him, and I suddenly understood why so many of us put our dogs to sleep. It's legal, and we cannot stand their pain. I closed my eyes and held my dog, trying to hold on to what I knew—his feel, his smell. But I didn't have a clue as to what he was telling me.

We took him inside, Theo gave him an opiate, and he finally calmed down.

A few minutes later, Allison walked through the door. After Brower's death, she had told me that if I needed support when Merle's time came to call her. It was our agreement—while our dogs were alive, we'd be there for each other.

Blond hair in a ponytail, she knelt by Merle and touched his ears. "Oh, my beautiful boy," she said, "you have the softest ears in the world." Then she began to weep.

An hour later, along with Theo, she helped me to carry Merle into the MRI wing of the hospital and onto a gurney, where an attendant draped him in a white sheet and wheeled him into a glass-walled room. We made small talk while waiting, the conversation circling back to dogs—the ones we had, the ones we had known—and how it seemed unfair that parrots and turtles lived so long. It got us through the forty-five-minute-long procedure, and then the radiologist came out with films in his hand. He pointed to a bright spot on Merle's right frontal lobe and said, "That's inflammation and swelling. It could be a stroke or a viral infection. I don't see a tumor."

I felt my body collapse with relief.

It was only momentary. At home Merle became inconsolable, moaning, circling, fouling his bed, upon which I had laid towels, and howling mournfully. At least I now had a better idea of what he was saying, for I had called Paul Cuddon, who had told me that Merle's vocalizations were involuntary and due to his cerebrum being disorganized from the seizure. He was not in pain. Paul had then suggested that I keep Merle on the prednisone, to reduce the swelling in his brain, and add a dose of potassium bromide, which would control the seizures. He asked that I Fed Ex him the MRIs.

At 2:00 A.M., Merle was still pacing and howling, and I called Theo again, who told me to bring him in. When we got to the clinic, he put Merle on an IV since he still wasn't drinking, and mixed up the anti-seizure formula according to Paul's directions. Merle quieted after a shot of Valium, but when we got home, he wanted to go outside. I followed him around the aspen trees as he repeatedly fell and regained his balance. Guiding him inside, I led him to his bed, but he fought me, moaning and circling. Unable to calm him and overwhelmed by a feeling of helplessness, I finally put my arms around him and laid my mouth directly on his ear.

"Merle!" I shouted.

I felt a tiny pause in his agitation.

"I know a dog and his name is Merle," I began to sing, trying not to break into tears. "I know a dog and his name is Merle. I know a dog and his name is Merle. He's the best dog in the world."

"Ha!" he panted loudly. "Ha!" he panted again as the rigidity went from his body and he sank into my arms and slowly onto his bed, where I lay behind him and held him against my chest. Then, for the first time in twenty-six hours, both of us fell dead asleep.

This was a Friday. During the rest of the weekend I gave Merle his drugs, mixing the potassium bromide solution into balls of elk, which he wolfed, and holding his bowl of kibble before him so he could nibble at the kernels. Every few hours, he crapped on his towel-covered bed, or if he managed to rise and go to his dog door he didn't reach it in time and left a trail across the great room. But as the potassium bromide and prednisone took effect, he began to sleep soundly. I found something rote and physical to do—stacking firewood—that kept me within earshot of him. On Sunday afternoon, as I was working, he wandered outside on his own and lay in the grass, watching me.

I had called the Landales and they stopped by—Scott and April, and their two daughters, Tessa, nine, and Eliza, five. They lay in the grass next to Merle and petted him.

"He doesn't look that bad," said April, a matter-of-fact New Englander whose brassy auburn hair matched her optimism. "Remember, girls, when you would ride on Merle's back? What a strong dog he was!"

"And gentle," Eliza said.

"Very gentle," April agreed.

Tessa, having grown into a coltish, freckle-faced girl, slipped off to their car, where she stood, blinking.

Scott had never been a man of many words and still wasn't. Tall, with reddish-blond hair and athletically built, he almost always spoke in a subdued tone as if to minimize his physical presence. Yet he could let out great whoops of glee and surprise, and I think that's why he and Merle got along so well together—tonally, they were kindred souls.

Merle had hunted with Scott almost as much as he had with me, and I had often seen the two of them face to face—Merle sitting, Scott kneeling—as they touched noses. Now, Scott put his hand on Merle's shoulder and said only two words, "Merley, Merley."

Eliza leaned close to Merle and asked, "Is he having sayzures?"

"Not right now," I said. "Maybe they're finally over."

She reached down to pet him and a reflective look crossed her face. Glancing up, she said, "This must be very sad for you."

By Monday Merle's seizures were over. Going in and out by himself—I left the doors of the house open—he meandered through the long grass along the edge of the mowed firebreak. Again and again, he returned to the clump of aspen at the corner of the deck, where he lay with his mouth open to the breeze while he watched the Tetons. It had become his favorite spot: soft grass, shady trees, a big view.

Paul Cuddon called in the afternoon, saying that he had received the MRIs and what they showed wasn't typical of a masslike brain tumor. He didn't think it was a stroke, either. It could be encephalitis or a glial cancer, a diffuse type of brain tumor that didn't shift the brain within the skull. The prognosis for the infection was reasonable with vigilant treatment. The prognosis for a glial tumor wasn't. Radiation and chemo would only buy time. He suggested a spinal tap to find out which it might be.

With a few calls to Theo and M. J. Forman, another vet in town who had done quite a few spinal taps, I arranged for Merle to have one on Thursday. Then I finished stacking the firewood and by dusk took off my boots on the north porch. Putting my feet in the cool grass, I hung my head between my knees, as tired as I could remember ever feeling. I don't know how long I sat there, but I suddenly felt a wet nose touch my bare shoulder—I must have fallen asleep and didn't hear Merle come across the grass. He had walked around the house from his spot under the aspens and found me. I raised my head, and he placed his cheek against my jaw and leaned into me. I put my arm around his shoulder, and he let out a great sigh—"HAAAA"—giving me a look of complete trust and thanks.

We did the spinal tap on Thursday morning, and I asked to help in the operating room, something not often allowed when the people you love are undergoing surgery. But M. J.—a blond woman with a bouncy disposition—was fine with my being there. A vet tech shaved the crown of Merle's head and gave him anesthesia; Theo held Merle's nose down to his chest, exposing the occipital crest; and M. J. worked the four-inch-long needle into the back of Merle's skull where the spinal cord met his brain, joking, "Now you're going to see my hands shake." I didn't see them move a hair.

It wasn't only the delicacy of the procedure that made her try to interject some humor into the morning. Everyone knew what was at stake: White blood cells in the spinal fluid meant an infection and a potential cure; no white blood cells meant the glial tumor and difficult choices ahead. I stood with my hands on Merle's hips and watched thirty-seven drops of clear spinal fluid drip out of the needle's barrel into a glass vial—M. J. counted them.

After Merle woke from the anesthesia, M.J. and I walked him in front of the clinic. With his white face and partially shaved head, he looked like an aging punk rocker. At first he seemed animated and strong, but then he began to bump into bushes. M. J. looked concerned. We took him inside, and a few minutes later the call came from the lab, where Theo had run the sample: no white blood cells.

I held the fax that M. J. had handed to me. The columns of numbers bounced across the page.

M. J. said, "I'm really sorry." Then she began to talk about Merle's quality of life and that it might be time to euthanize him. Seeing that I didn't want to hear this, she immediately added, "I'm here if you need me."

"Thank you," I told her, "you did a great job," and I turned to leave. Merle, who was keeping an eye on me, got to his feet. Without any help, he walked out the door and continued across the parking lot to stand by our car.

"God," said M. J., genuinely surprised, "he is a strong old boy."

I bought food in the grocery store, seeing too many people I knew, some of whom had heard about Merle and asked how he was. I had to keep my jaw clenched, telling them about his condition, so as not to break down. Not that I'm averse to shedding tears in public—I've done my share at funerals—but who wants to be a wreck in the produce aisle?

On the drive home, I watched him in the rearview mirror, lying on his green bed, sleepy from the Valium M. J. had given him. Looking up, I saw dozens of peaks we had climbed and skied, and I could not believe that it was all over and time to say good-bye. It seemed like he had just stepped out of the night, dug a nest by my side on the banks of the San Juan River, and said, "You need a dog, and I'm it." Then, alone in the car with him, I began to cry.

I carried him into the house like a frankfurter, simply folding his bed around him. Feeling completely played out, I lay on the deck with my eyes closed. A few minutes later Paul Cuddon called. He had gotten the lab results and wanted to reiterate that the prednisone would keep the swelling down in Merle's brain, while the potassium bromide would prevent any further seizures. Merle would have to stay on both drugs for the rest of his life.

He sounded matter-of-fact, even positive, and his phrase "the rest of his life" had a hopeful ring to it. Confused, I said I was being told that it might be time to put Merle down.

"Euthanasia is forever," he answered, sounding quietly passionate rather than judgmental. "Merle is still recovering from his post-seizure phase. I'm a very patient man, and I'm a neurologist who sees lots of sick dogs." He paused and said it again, "Death is forever. Let's give the prednisone a try for fourteen days. Is his quality of life good now? No. But you look at dogs with neurological disorders, and they look horrible, but then they do better. I've had dogs in Merle's condition go on for a year or more. It won't hurt to give steroids a chance."

He strengthened by the day. Paul had said there would be bumps in the road, and there were. Initially, Merle couldn't make it through the dog door in time. Several times a day I was down on my knees, cleaning up the mess. When he regained his balance, he began to do loops around the house, his head and gait straightening as he walked slowly and purposefully along the edge of the lawn like someone at a sanatorium doing laps to restore his health.

He took his meds and supplements in ground raw elk—it was what he wanted more than anything else—and it made the potassium bromide, a vile, salty brew, palatable. Soon, he was well enough to sit on his haunches in the front seat of the truck as we went to the landfill, an idiotically happy smile on his face as he looked out the open window.

I kept the dog door closed at night, and ten days after his first seizure, at just about the same time—two in the morning—my eyes flew open as he panted in my face: "Could you please open the door?"

Groggily, I said, "How did you get up here?"

"Ha!" he exclaimed. "I climbed the stairs."

And to prove it, he walked back down them—slowly and carefully—and waited for me to open the door. Jumping off the deck, he relieved himself.

That morning it snowed an inch, and he went outside again, walking through the aspen and sage while watching the snowflakes fall around him. Lifting his head to meet their descent, he let a soft smile play on his mouth. He seemed touched by the sudden reappearance of winter, and when he came in, he wagged his tail at me, just its tip, for the rest seemed paralyzed: "Ah, snow."

I thought about it long and hard that day, and that evening left his dog door open. The night had always been his province, part of his identity and doghood, and having access to it would bolster him, I felt, as much as eating elk.

From upstairs I heard him go out. When he didn't return in ten minutes, I dressed, took a headlamp, and began to search for him, clapping and whistling. After a pass around the edge of our land, I found him near the clump of aspens that he had claimed as his own—I had been searching too far out. He was sound asleep, lying curled with his nose under his tail, and breathing softly. The snow, still falling, had covered him with a white blanket.

Gently, I touched his shoulder, but he was hard to wake. Finally, he stood, unsure, it seemed, of where he was.

"I don't think it's a good idea to sleep outside right now," I told him, "nice as it feels. The drugs you're taking make you sleep too deeply, and you don't know if some coyotes or a mountain lion might come walking by."

Back in the house, he shivered as I toweled him off in front of the fire. I gave him some of his favorite penny-size liver treats, and after chewing them he lay before the woodstove. I sealed the dog door.

When I went downstairs in the morning, I found a pile of poop directly in front of it. He was lying on his bed, and when I turned

to him, he didn't look despondent, as he had on the many occasions during the past days when he had soiled his bed or the floor.

"Ha!" he panted. "I tried."

When it stopped snowing, I reopened his door, and he came
and went on his own, staying close to the house. One evening, a
lively bluegrass tune began to play on the radio just as he came
through the door. I coasted away from the kitchen counter and two-
stepped across the great room toward him. With a wide grin on his
face, he gimped toward me and began to pick his paws up and
down rapidly.

"You dance, Sir!" I cried.

"Ha-ha-ha," he exulted back. "Yes, I still dance."

Three days later, as I was coming downstairs at six-thirty in
the morning, I heard him go out his door. I walked into the mudroom to see what he was doing and found him squatting on the
grass and peeing. Like many male dogs, he had been unable to lift
his leg in his old age because of his arthritis.

Done, he walked with some purpose toward the spruce trees,
but on his way a smell pulled his nose down. He snuffled the grass
and prodded it with his paw—the right one, as always. The sun
had just risen, its beams lancing through the conifers and striking
Merle's head and right shoulder with golden light, the rest of him
in greenish shadow. I stood, transfixed. He was two weeks from his
fourteenth birthday, eighty-nine years old in our terms, and his
coat was as finely burnished as when I had met him, his muscles
still ropy under his fur. Had I been able to, I would have halted
the sun in its rising, its beams gilding both of us where we stood:
he setting off, I watching him.

He continued to read the text of the grass—nostrils dilating,
eyes half closed in reflection; then, lifting his head, he ambled
through the trees and down the trail he had cut into the earth
through nearly a decade of use. Hobbling slightly, he made his way
across the road to Gladys's house, where his old friend Josie, the
chocolate Lab, was visiting.

About an hour later, as I wrote, he returned—slap, slap. He drank at his bowl, came to my desk, and put his chin on my thigh. I scratched it, and he rubbed it hard against my fingers—he was unable to lift his rear leg and do it himself.

"A good morning out there?" I asked.

His eyes shone and held mine: "You don't know what you're missing."

"Someone's got to work," I replied.

"Ha!" he snorted. "I am working," and he turned and left.

A few seconds later, I heard the dog doors slap. Following him out, I saw him hop off the porch, but instead of heading northwest to Josie's place, he went the other way, around the Subaru, and down the drive. At its end, he paused, as if deciding which way to go—left and back to Josie's, or right and off on his traditional mayoral rounds.

After a few moments' consideration, he turned right, walking slowly and carefully like an elderly person. But he soon picked up speed and began to step out with a purposeful stride, his eyes gazing eagerly toward the creek and the village beyond. He was back on the job.

I had always known that both Merle and I experienced similar emotions, but as I watched him disappear down the road, the tip of his tail wagging contentedly, the answer to one of my longstanding questions about him was finally answered. I had always wondered if he dreamt, not merely twitching his paws and running after subconscious cattle and bison, but also dreamt in the other meaning of the word: to aspire. There had been a couple of times that his actions had made me think he did. Scott Landale, for instance, had told me a story about hunting with Merle. As they had sat on a high bluff, a bull elk had walked beneath them. It was the end of the season and only cow elk were legal to shoot, and Scott raised his rifle and simply looked at the elk through the scope.

When he didn't shoot, Merle looked at him piercingly, his eyes lit with demand. When Scott still didn't shoot, Merle quickly looked at the elk and back to Scott, back and forth, back and forth, in an ever more demanding way. When Scott still didn't pull the trigger, Merle began to stomp his paws in frustration. "Shoot, shoot," he was saying. "What's wrong with you?"

Scott, of course, wouldn't shoot, and as they walked back to the truck, Merle gave him the cold shoulder. In a huff, he walked far ahead of Scott, not paying attention to his calls, and in the truck he looked out the window, his back turned to Scott in anger and disgust.

On another occasion, Merle and I skied to the peak at the south end of Teton Pass. Because Merle's rear end had become unstable by this time, I wasn't willing to ski downhill with him and began to head back the way we had come, on the shallow grade of the skin track. Seeing me depart, Merle lingered.

"Come on," I called. "We're not skiing into Black Canyon. No more downhill powder for you. It's too steep and bad for your back. You know that."

He eyed me soberly, turned, and jumped off the peak, skiing down into the steep bowl.

He was, as always, a dog who knew what he wanted.

Were these aspirations? The word has such a lofty sound. But I have numerous friends—fine members of our community— whose major aspirations have been to hunt elk each fall and ski powder as many days as possible in the winter. Some of them have gone to their daily work with far less enthusiasm than did Merle, setting off so faithfully on his rounds that he eventually cut well-worn paths from our house to the road.

The philosopher Raymond Gaita says that "we do not write biographies of animals" because they do not have "distinctive identities" and cannot make or fail "to make something of their lives." Consequently, they are unable to find in their lives a "reason for joy and gratitude."

Watching Merle set off on his rounds that morning with gratitude illuminating his face, and a lifetime of sound if not extraordinary accomplishments behind him, I knew for certain that being accorded a biography isn't dependent on one's species or one's fame. When he returned an hour later, I walked into the great room and greeted him as he came through the dog door.

"How was it?" I asked.

His eyes were alight as they hadn't been for three weeks. "Ha-ha-ha," he panted happily. "The best!"

The aspen leafed; the rivers rose. He continued to go on his rounds; I wrote.

He accompanied me to town, and when not on his rounds he lay behind my chair as my fingers moved over the keyboard. I would look around and catch his eyes, fixed on my back.

How are you?

Better now.

I am glad.

So am I.

Eyes locked: together.

When I told Paul Cuddon of Merle's improvement, he suggested putting him on a lower dose of prednisone and having his potassium levels monitored. I called Theo Schuff to give him a report, and to make an appointment for the blood draw and to pick up the new prescription. Sounding pleasantly surprised, he said, "I didn't think we'd see him live through the prednisone he had. Why don't you bring him in right now."

I drove into Jackson, but our appointment was delayed by an emergency euthanasia. As I took a seat, a husky man came into the clinic, carrying a fifteen-year-old black Lab, an enormous fellow with a handsome blocky head, giant paws, and weighing close to one hundred pounds. The dog was groaning and slavering, and the receptionist told me that he had been having seizures.

The man placed his dog on the same stainless steel table where Merle had gotten his IV three weeks before. There were double doors to the room and no one thought to close them, so I watched Theo and the two vet techs shave the dog's hock, the electric razor making its dreaded buzzing, which I had come to associate with Brower's euthanasia and Merle's spinal tap. It took a while for Theo to find a vein, the man standing by his dog's head. Finally, Theo injected the solution, and the Lab's groaning slowed; then his legs fell limply off the table.

The husky man came out of the room and stood with his face to the wall, his shoulders heaving. As he wiped at his eyes, Theo came into the waiting room, and the man turned to him quickly. I could see his jaw clenching, just as mine had clenched in the grocery store.

"Thank you, doc," he said, and shook Theo's hand.

They talked about picking up the dog's ashes, and, as the man left, the two vet techs slid the dog into a plastic body bag and carried him out to await cremation.

I fetched Merle from the car, and he came into the clinic pretty smartly, panting a greeting to the receptionist before I led him into a smaller examination room. There, Theo took a blood sample and recommended feeding him yogurt for his gut, which the potassium bromide was keeping unsettled.

On our way home, I thought about the euthanasia I had witnessed, wondering how the man had decided to put down his dog. I didn't know his circumstances, so I couldn't say. But I knew what my circumstances had been, and how I had come to the conclusion that, if at all possible, Merle deserved to die when he wanted to.

Later, I discovered that my intuitive decision-making tree was identical to the one suggested by the veterinarian Bernard S. Hershhorn in his book *Active Years for Your Aging Dog*. Hershhorn suggests that a dog owner consider six criteria before euthanizing a dog, adding that *"Chronological age, in itself, is never one of them!"* (The italics are his.) Here are his questions and my answers for Merle's and my situation:

1. Is the condition prolonged, recurring, or getting worse? (Yes.)

2. Is the condition no longer responding to therapy? (Don't know.)

3. Is your dog in pain or otherwise physically suffering? (After hearing from the neurologist, Paul Cuddon, my answer was no.)

4. Is it no longer possible to alleviate that pain or suffering? (No.)

5. If your dog should recover, is he likely to be chronically ill, an invalid, or unable to care for himself as a healthy dog? (Don't know yet.)

6. If your dog recovers, is he likely no longer to be able to enjoy life, or will he have severe personality changes? (Don't know yet.)

Hershhorn goes on to say that if one's answers to all six questions are "yes," the dog should be euthanized. If the answers to question three and four are "no," then perhaps the dog should be allowed to die naturally. However, one must answer three more questions:

1. Can you provide the necessary care? (I could.)

2. Will such care so interfere with your own life as to create serious problems with you or your family? (It wouldn't.)

3. Will the cost involved become unbearably expensive? (No.)

My choice had been the right one for Merle and me. He had resumed his life—a little crippled to be sure, but glowingly happy.

In the days ahead, as I walked around the house, he would fix his eyes upon me as if following a star. In turn, I would watch him and say, "It has been so wonderful being with you. The absolute best."

"Ha!" he'd answer. "The very best!"

It was as if our thirteen years together had been allowed to stay on the vine a little longer, accumulating the maximum sugar content possible. Now, they had turned into an intensely sweet dessert wine, which he and I were savoring sip by sip.

———

Two weeks went by during which he rallied. He resumed his rounds; we drove to parties; our life began again. Then he went downhill. He began to stumble, his back legs splaying out, and his incontinence returned. I stapled plastic sheets to the floor and laid old beach towels over them, stapling their corners so they wouldn't slip under him. When they were soiled, I'd pick them up, wash them, and tack new ones down. I did half a dozen washes a day, sponging off Merle almost as many times. Occasionally, just as I finished cleaning him, he'd walk toward his dog door and fall directly into the pile of poop he had left as he had tried to get outside.

If he was really messy, and the weather was cold, I'd lead him to the guest bathroom downstairs. Stripping, I'd get into the shower with him and give him a complete shampoo.

"Oh, he's a clean machine," I'd say as I'd lift him out and towel him off.

"Ha-ha-ha," he'd pant. "That feels so much better."

And he'd weave his way toward the woodstove, lie down on the towels in front of it, and rub his cheeks and head against them, finishing the drying.

If it was warm outside, I'd bring hot buckets of water onto the porch, wash him down, then hose him off, toweling him dry and letting the sun fluff his fur.

One morning, when I came back to see what he was up to, I found him at the end of the porch, gazing down the drive to the start of his mayoral rounds. Then he gazed to the trail going to Gladys's house. He hopped off the deck and went toward the trail, and a minute later I found him lying where the trail met the road. He was sitting like a sphinx, his eyes panning up and down the road as if he were making his rounds in his mind.

He sensed me behind him, turned, and grinned, tapping his tail: "I'm here. I got this far."

I went inside and as I washed the breakfast dishes he came through the dog door, crossed the great room, and insinuated himself between my legs. Shutting off the tap, I leaned over and pressed my nose to the top of his head, so we were looking directly into each other's eyes.

"Oh, you smell good," I said.

And he did: nutty and crisp, overlaid by mountain air, and with that sweet hint of lanolin.

He took a deep breath and chattered his teeth: "You do too."

We remained looking at each other, eye to eye, for a long time. He didn't flinch; he didn't look away. Keeping his pupils directly on mine, he made three little yips.

At last, it was he who broke the spell, walking through my legs and toward his bowls, where he had a drink. I followed him and knelt. He turned and walked his head directly into my chest, keeping it there as I clenched my fingers in the fur of his shoulders. Then he backed away and gave me a look of utter love and something more, the look I had seen so many times since the day I had opened the door of the truck on the San Juan River and had said, "You're a Wyoming dog now—if you want." And his eyes had replied, "Thank you for believing in me." As they did now.

"Thank you," I told him, "for choosing me."

He began to have difficulty getting in and out of his doors. He'd make it through the first one and get stuck in the second. I'd stand in the great room, rooting for him, willing him through the outer door in which he was hung up, and then I'd finally help him. Often, he'd go to the end of the porch, look toward the road, and simply turn around, returning to the house and his bed.

Sometimes, he'd make it through both doors and off the porch, and I'd find him at the end of his path, sitting with head erect, his paws touching the road as if he might be assimilating the rounds he had once made. Turning his head left and right, he'd study the occasional car going by. Some of the cars stopped, the drivers saying, "Mr. Mayor, it's good to see you out and about again." The tip of his tail would wag: "Good to see you, too."

How he got to the road, I sometimes wondered. But he did—falling down, picking himself up, resting, going on. When he'd return, he'd ask for something to tide him over until dinnertime: a dog biscuit; his liver treats; occasionally I gave him an elk bone, and he'd work on it, holding it between his paws and gnawing on its end with his eyes closed in delight. I had learned that he had no use for plain yogurt, but loved the kind flavored with vanilla. Obviously, he still had his sweet tooth, and, remembering how he had loved wild berries, I bought him some organic blackberry sorbet. He could have finished cartons of it.

One evening, after he had eaten his dinner, he began to scrabble to his feet. I helped him up, but his back end immediately collapsed. His front end looked strong, though, so I put a towel under his waist and supported him as he set off on a tour of the house.

First he went to my office, turned a circle around it, and sniffed the rug on which he had lain for years. Then he proceeded into the guest room, where he rarely went, and gave it an inspection. Upon coming out, he looked at the stairs to our bedroom and decided against them. Instead, he walked through the great room, outside onto the deck, jumped off it, and towed me around the entire perimeter of the lawn, before coming back onto the deck and leading me into the house, where he lay directly before the great window, under the ridge log that we had cut together, equidistant from every corner of the room, in the very center of the house.

"Ha-ha-ha," he panted up at me. "I needed one last look around."

And, indeed, it was his last. He did not rise again. But this didn't mean we stayed at home. I carried him to the car, the Subaru becoming a traveling hospice. If I met someone for dinner, I chose an outdoor café, where I could sit at a table directly by our car and Merle could watch me through the open windows. Passersby who knew us would stop and, after chatting with me, they'd sit with Merle awhile, saying good-bye to him. Some brought their dogs, and Merle and the dogs would also have a last visit, his friends pressing their noses to him and appraising his changed state.

Back at home, I'd carry him inside and put him to bed. If he couldn't eat, I'd chop his elk in small pieces and hold it in my hand for him to lick it up. Sometimes he couldn't hold his head up to lap water from his bowl, so I'd syringe it into his mouth. Then, as I put away kitchen things, his eyes would follow me, saying, "Oh, it is so good to be seeing you!" And I'd walk back to him, lie down before him, nose to nose, and say, "Oh, it is so good to be seeing you. Simply the best!"

On a morning when the weather turned fine, I came downstairs to find that Merle had soiled himself as usual. I carried him to the front porch, washed him down with warm water, then laid him on the grass between the house and the spruce trees. As I went inside to put the towels in the washing machine, I heard him whimpering plaintively. He hadn't made a sound in days, and I hurried back outside.

Lying on his side, he was moving his paws as if trying to paddle himself across the grass. When he saw me, he whimpered more loudly. I knelt over him, and he held my eyes. The look in them said, "I don't want to be here." Instantly, I understood.

I picked him up and carried him through the house and out the south glass doors. As I stepped onto the deck, he began to wag his tail, the entire length of it, which amazed me, since he hadn't wagged it fully since before his seizures. His eyes were fixed on his clump of aspen trees.

"Ha-ha-ha!" he panted happily, in relief. "Yes, there. There is where I want to be."

I laid him on the grass under their shade, and his whole body—from nose to tail to toes—relaxed as he let out a long breath.

And that is where we passed the next eight days—he lying on his side, I sitting beside him. I wrote on my laptop, or tried to, and answered the phone, keeping my eyes on him as he kept his eyes on me. Every so often, I would lie down before him and say, "Do you know you're the pup of my dreams?" And then I'd sing his song—"I know a dog"—and he'd chatter his teeth and exhale "Ha!" when I reached his name. Then we'd just gaze at each other, our eyes saying, "You know, I just want to keep looking at you."

Often, he would stare at the snowcapped Tetons, rising above the sagebrush. And I'd say, "They sure are purtacious, aren't they?" It was the word we shared for when something or someone was remarkably pretty. And he'd turn his eyes back to me, acknowledging what I'd said, before returning his eyes to the mountains.

He had always liked to gaze into big spaces, and now, with so many directions to look—up, down, to the prayer flags, the aspens, or to me—he'd so often hang his eyes upon the mountains rising above the great sage prairie. His tranquil gaze made me think that he was still finding peace there—in those wide open spaces that had been his shelter.

During this week people visited and said good-bye to him, sitting on the grass by his side, leaning close, and speaking in soft voices. The Landales came and Benj and Allison, and the many neighbors who had been his ports of call. Two of his favorite people did not come. Donald Kent had died four years earlier, and Gladys had died a month before Merle had become gravely ill. When Donald had been deep in his Alzheimer's, I had visited him in the nursing home, and he had not recognized me or anything I had said until I had told him, "Merle says, 'Hi.' He misses you." Donald had raised his head and replied, "He is a good dog."

Among the many people who called from far away was my mother, checking in as she had been doing. This time she said that she had just blessed Merle's photo on her refrigerator with the *themiato*—the censer with which devout Greek Orthodox direct incense toward the people they wish to protect. Her gesture touched me. Though what she had done wasn't heresy, it did go beyond the canons of the Church, which with respect to animals

are clear. Since animals don't have souls, one doesn't pray for
their afterlife. And that my mother had been doing this became
apparent a few moments later when she said, "Merle is such a
good dog. Who knows where his s—" She stopped herself short,
unable to use the "soul" word for him. "Who knows where Merle
might end up."

A little later my neighbor David Shlim rang. An M.D. and a
Buddhist scholar, he offered to give Merle some *ngundrup*—black
particles the size of tiny seeds. Made from the relics of lamas, they
contained centuries of sacred wisdom and would purify Merle's
karma, helping him to find a higher reincarnation.

After fetching the *ngundrup*, I placed most of them inside
Merle's mouth, and, for good measure, I ate several myself. The
thought did cross my mind, however, that Merle might desire nothing more than to come back as the dog he had been, and I, certainly, couldn't imagine a finer reincarnation than repeating the
life I had shared with him in Jackson Hole.

At last a morning came when he didn't want to eat or drink. His
cheeks had grown hollow; he seemed to be departing himself. I
called the Landales and they stopped by again. Scott, on his way
to the office, came first. He knelt beside Merle and ran his fingers
though his ruff. Then he looked into his eyes and said, "Hey, Merley, want to go find some elk? Do you want to go hunting?"

Merle didn't move. His brown eyes, their centers more pur-
plish than ever, stared at Scott.

I walked out toward the prayer flags and heard Scott say,
"Thank you for all those hunts, Merley." Leaning very close to
Merle, he said some things I couldn't hear.

When he stood up, his face seemed to be coming apart in all
directions, his eyes like two blue rain clouds. I followed him inside. At the door, he turned and clutched me hard. Then, without
a word, he was gone.

I resumed my vigil beside Merle. His eyes grew more sunken, his breath softer. He seemed to go ever farther away.

A while later, April and the girls came by, and April and Eliza sat around Merle, their hands on him, as most everyone's hands had been on him, as if he were some sort of reference point, a headland that needed to be rounded.

Stoic, Tessa stood nearby. April had told me that when Tessa had put down the phone after my call, she had burst into tears.

"His fur is so soft," said Eliza, stroking his golden flank. "Will you bury him? We buried our rat at school."

I told her that I had thought about leaving Merle high on the Sleeping Indian, because he had begun his life as a wild dog and that's how a wild dog would end his life. But that's not who Merle had become, and so I was going to bury him by the prayer flags, with some elk bones to send him on his way. Then we could always be close.

"That's a good idea," she said.

"He loved bones," Tessa interjected, stepping closer.

And they all began to recall Merle's love of food and how he would get into the kitchen trash when they left him alone in the house. When they'd return, he'd look off into the distance and instead of being guilty or afraid, he'd say, "Garbage? I don't know a thing about no garbage."

"Remember how he'd walk down to Kelly, looking for you when you were gone?" said Tessa.

"Yes," said April, "someone at the school would call me and say, 'Do you know this big red dog?'"

"He's not red," corrected Eliza.

"Oh, yes, he was red when he was a pup."

"I remember him when he was a puppy," said Eliza.

I laughed. "You weren't even born when he was a puppy."

She gave me her elfish smile.

Stepping still closer, Tessa chimed in, "He's lived a good life."

"He's ninety-eight," said April.

"Ninety-eight!" Tessa exclaimed.

"Or thereabouts," I added. "In fact, I think it was just his fourteenth birthday, or what I've made his birthday."

"He loved to sing 'Happy Birthday,'" said Tessa.

"We should sing him 'Happy Birthday,'" I said.

And so we put our hands on him and sang, at the top of our lungs, "Happy birthday, dear Merle. Happy birthday to you."

But the most he could muster was to blink his eyes.

I had to get up and blow my nose. Coming back, I said, "Historians will now calculate time as BM, DM, and AM—Before, During, and After Merle."

April laughed. "I don't know how good BM sounds."

"We've had plenty of those," I answered.

And we all laughed, as people do around the dying when they can no longer stay sad.

The girls had to get to school, and so they all leaned down to give Merle a last pet and kiss. April stood up with her eyes wet. "Hoo," she exclaimed, letting out a long breath. "You don't get this upset about some people."

I sat the rest of the morning with him, often lying nose to nose, my hand on the back of his head, as his eyes sank and rose, and he seemed to fall in and out of consciousness. "You fly on, Merle," I told him gently. "Chase those bison, find those elk. Thank you for being my dog."

At noon, he still lived, and light-headed from hunger—I hadn't eaten since the previous day—I went inside, fixed an antelope sandwich, and came back to the deck, sitting on its edge with my legs in the grass, my bare feet just touching his back.

As I brought the sandwich to my mouth, I saw his nose twitch. His right eye, the upper one, opened, and he stared directly at me. He looked suddenly perfectly lucid, and I knew that look as well as I knew his name.

Taking a piece of meat from the sandwich, I held it over his nose, and he reached up and snagged it. Swallowing, he looked very smug.

"You faker," I said. "People are weeping over you."

His eyes went from mine to the sandwich: "I could use another bite of that."

Going back inside, I cut the remaining antelope steak into slivers and fed it to him. He swallowed each piece voraciously, his filmy eyes brightening, his hollow cheeks seeming to fill out.

"Sir," I said. "You are a wonder."

One brow went up, the other down, and he turned his gaze to the mountains, watching them contentedly.

We continued to sit together through the afternoon, and there were no more river trips, no more powder days, no more cruising the high country for elk. There were no more mayoral rounds and staying in Kelly because what I was doing in town was too boring for a dog of his wide interests. There were no more assignments to take me away. There were no more conditions. There were only the two of us, touching and unable to take our eyes from each other.

At one point his eyes widened considerably. He reached out with his right paw and dug his nails into the grass as a worried and frightened look crossed his face. Something was going on inside of him, some physiological Rubicon, and he knew it. He looked at me. Lying next to him, I put one hand on his cheek and one on his flank, and said, "I'm right here. I'm right here."

And then whatever was happening stilled.

"How you doing with all this?" I asked gently. "Do you want to hang in there?"

He gazed directly at me, and his eyes were scared and also remarkably sad. I looked at him carefully, trying to see whether he was simply frightened and low from being so ill or if he knew that he was dying. I thought that he did know he had come to his end, and it didn't surprise me. From a pup, mortality had been his shadow. There had been that bullet behind his shoulder. There had been his having to kill his own food to survive. Then, hunting with me, he had seen the life go out of many big animals, animals who were just like us.

Once, we had even found a coyote on the Kelly road, struck dead by a car and perfectly intact except for her broken tail. At the sight of the coyote, Merle had shaken with excitement, but when I had let him out of the car, he had stopped in his rush toward her and raised a paw, expanding and contracting his nostrils like a bellows as he sucked in her scent. In an instant, his excited shivering—"let me at that coyote"—ceased and he became extraordinarily still. With great care, he leaned forward and put his nose a few inches from her belly. Then he eased his nostrils directly into her fur, breathing deeply. Pulling himself back, he looked at me with the sober expression I had seen him wear before.

"Dead," I agreed.

Gravely, he sat down, cocked his head, and stared at the coyote with the attention that people reserve for unprecedented occurrences. I wondered if this might be the first occasion that he had realized dogs could die.

Now he seemed to know that he was on the other side of that sober look he had given to so many of his fellow beings.

I kissed him on the nose, and held his head between my hands, and said, "I will go through this as long as you want." I tried to make my voice reassuring, but his eyes stayed sad and a little frightened and made mine fill with tears.

"I will miss you so much," I said, my voice breaking as I tried not to sob in front of him and make him sadder and more fearful for my grief. Swallowing my tears, I added softly, "Love you forever."

It wasn't my words; it was the tone behind them. His eyes calmed, and he sighed.

"Forever," I repeated.

And he sighed again, looking peaceful.

Some big cumulus clouds covered the sun, and I went upstairs to get a long-sleeve shirt. Glancing at his corner—now empty of his bed and soon, I knew, empty of him—I had a sudden vision of the house filled only with photographs and memories. Without warning, the thought broke me. My mouth shook violently; my body felt as if it were being ripped apart. I had known loss before, but never like this. Others had held the door ajar for me; Merle was the door through which I had passed, allowing my heart, so careful of giving completely, to fling wide open. I could no longer hold it together. Doubling over, I fell on my bed and bawled.

Paul Cuddon, Theo Schuff, and Marybeth Minter called later that day, within hours of each other, as if heeding some distant signal. They wanted to know how Merle was doing. I told them that I thought he was beyond medical help and thanked Paul in particular for giving us this extra month and a half together. Theo asked me what I wanted to do now and I said, "Just let Merle go on his own." There was a sigh of relief on the other end of the line, and Theo said, "That sounds like a good plan. I'd hate to be the one to put him down." Marybeth said the same thing, adding, "You're doing the right thing, letting the process happen. He's not in pain. It's what we see in dying that is uncomfortable to us."

He began to go in and out of sleep or consciousness—I couldn't translate which. His temperature went up; so did his heart rate and his breathing; he began to shiver; I covered him with a light blanket. That night I slept by him, downstairs, putting my arms around him when he shook. A few moments later, he grew still and calm. I pressed my lips to his head and looked into his eyes, and he looked into mine.

"Hey, my lightfoot lad," I said, but all he could do was mince his eyes.

When we awoke, he was unable to eat. I held a piece of elk in front of his nose, and he looked at me with a soulful expression that said, "I wish I could, but I can't."

After days of clear weather, the sky had turned dark and the rain pounded. Stepping outside, I tossed the elk to the wind. Then I called the Landales, who stopped on their way to school and said good-bye once again.

During the day, Merle's eyes became dry and tracked back and forth. His breaths came in soft shallow puffs that lifted his lips. His pulse, once so strong—like a kettledrum—was light and fast, 150 beats per minute. I sang his song. Even in his condition, he managed to raise an eyebrow when he heard me sing his name, "Merle!"

It was so cold I built a fire. Lying by his side, I syringed many doses of water into his mouth, the water running down his tongue and out the lower side of his jaw, while his back legs jerked a little. His breath had begun to smell acidic and full of ketones. He swallowed the water and smiled again, that grateful smile, his eyes lighting happily. Then I lay with him, nose to nose, and we looked directly at each other. "You and me," I said. His eyes glowed warmly at the touch of my hands. "Wherever I am, you'll be there too." I tapped my index finger to the side of my head several times. "And here, always." I tapped my heart.

We stared at each other and time, unmarked by us, moved along. His eyes half closed, and I kissed his head. He sighed.

In the late afternoon, I called my friend Bill Liske in Colorado. Twenty years before, in the Hunku Valley of Nepal, he and I had met the Khyi together, the friendly Tibetan Mastiff whom I had carried over the Amphu Labtsa in my pack, Bill jumaring on the rope ahead of me. Since then, Bill and I had traveled around the world together, consoling each other during the deaths of our fathers and at the breakup of love. On two adventures, he and I had nearly died together.

Now he said, "Give Merle a head butt for me," alluding to how Merle would greet Bill by planting his head into his chest and pushing hard, his tail wagging passionately. Merle had known, in an instant, the connection Bill and I had.

Merle was lying by the woodstove, in the center of the house, facing the great window, though there was nothing to be seen there now except clouds and rain. Walking to him, I noticed some foamy saliva on his lips and I wiped it off, as I had been doing during the past couple of hours.

"This is from Bill," I told him. Putting my head against his head, I scratched his ruff. His eyes remained vacant, and he breathed in small puffs.

He had messed his towels while I was on the phone, as well as himself, and I got the bucket and began to sponge him off. The towel directly beneath him had also become urine-soaked, and I decided to change that at the same time.

Taking him by his outstretched legs, I rolled him over, and as his head came around, his mouth opened in a snarl. I petted him and said, "I'm sorry, I'm just trying to get you clean." When I had rolled him onto his other side, I smoothed the snarl of his lips and flapped his ear onto his cheek. Removing the wet towel from beneath him, I began to swab off his urine-soaked flank. As I went to rinse the cloth, I saw his chest stop rising and falling. I dropped the towel and raced around to his face. His eyes were filmed over with the silver-white cloudiness that is the end.

"Merle! Merle!" I cried.

But his chest was still. There had been no warning or death rattle, no slowing of his breath that was supposed to warn me to lie before him, as I had been doing for days, and say a final good-bye.

"I know a dog—" I began. There was no response and I buried my face against his flank, which smelled of urine and soap. I had to put my nose into his ruff to smell his sweet nutty odor. His mouth opened and closed several times, remaining agape. I closed it gently and smoothed his lips over his teeth.

Rocking back on my heels, I wondered how this could be— his going off while I was cleaning his butt. Somehow, it seemed apt. A dog is always more interested in another dog's rear end than in its eyes. Half laughing, half crying at this thought, I suddenly

felt all my joints lose cohesion, as if what had been holding me together had suddenly dissolved.

"My dog," I said to the empty house. "My dog."

We buried him by the prayer flags, though it took a couple of days.
He died at five-thirty on a Thursday afternoon, and there was nothing to be done that night except clean him off and carry him to his
round green bed, which I placed under the great window, a vase
of yellow wildflowers on the sill, flanked by two red candles.

Looking at him from the balcony that evening, I thought he
might stand up and walk off, he looked so perfectly gold and calm,
so untarnished by death. "Fly on, Merle," I said. "And may flights
of elk sing thee to thy rest."

Allison and three other friends helped me dig his grave—a
round one the size of his bed and three feet down. It took three
hours, picking and shoveling through the rocky ground, and when
we were done we stood around the grave, gazing at its perfectly
vertical sides. One of my friends, who owns many Springer
Spaniels, said, "That is a damn good hole for a dog."

"Damn good," I said.

Though it was cool after the rain, Merle had begun to bloat.
Allison, who had kept Brower's body by her hearth for two days
before she took him to be cremated, said not to hurry. She went
into town and bought dry ice, and we packed him in it, covering
him with one of his favorite blankets, imprinted with great stags,
and leaving his head out so people who came by could look him
in the eye. The silver cloudiness had gone from them, and they
were brown and bright.

Midday on Saturday, many of Merle's and my friends gathered
around the prayer flags. I had built a low catafalque and covered
it with Merle's stag blanket, and we put him and his bed on it, taking the ice away. My four-year-old godson Reed, who had been
picking wildflowers, laid blue and yellow ones by Merle's back,

and Allison placed a gold *kata* around his neck—one of the silken scarves used by Tibetans as an auspicious symbol of greeting or a good-luck token upon one's departure.

Then people spoke, remembering him. I told some of my favorite stories about him—counting coup on the coyote, skiing deep powder, and how we had found each other on the San Juan River.

Allison read the poem I had translated for Brower, in which he told her not to cry for him, because I was definitely crying. As were many others. In fact, later that day Tessa told her mother that she had never seen her father cry before.

Allison gave Merle an eagle feather, one I had brought home from Alaska for her when she was in a transitional place, to lift him, as she said, on his journey. She also gave him an elk tooth from one of the first elk she had shot—the debutante who had become a hunter after hanging out with a half-wild dog and his man.

Scott gave Merle a great pile of elk steak, and I gave him two big bones. I also laid several photos next to him. They were of him, Brower, Allison, and me, hiking and skiing. There was a photo of Scott and Merle, hunting. And there was a photo of Merle and me on the summit of the Sleeping Indian, his face pressed to mine. I taped an elk tooth to the photo, one of a pair from an elk I had shot on the mountain as Merle had sat by my side. Between the tooth and the photo, I nestled a lock of his hair and a lock of my hair, lying across our hearts. The other tooth of the pair was in my pocket.

Looking over to a friend, I nodded. He tripped a switch, and from the speakers I had brought outside came the "Hallelujah Chorus." The prayer flags snapped in the wind, the clouds sailed over the Tetons, and we listened to Merle's favorite sing-along. And listening to music that had made kings rise to their feet, I wondered if some of my friends thought all this too much ceremony for a dog. Then I remembered those people, twelve thousand years ago, who placed their loved ones in the same graves with dogs—the forehead of the person and the forehead of the dog nodding toward each other. And I thought that this was no more than my nod to Merle.

Finally, we put a tanned elk hide over him, the same rich dark reddish gold as he was, and carried him to his grave on his bed, wrapped in, surrounded by, and sent off with elk.

Allison, Scott, and I lowered him down, and I took one more look at his face—those brows, those deep brown eyes—before touching my nose to his forehead and breathing in his scent: sweet, crisp, nutty, with a hint of lanolin. Then I gently pulled the elk hide over him and, climbing out of the hole, helped Allison and Scott shovel in the earth.

There were over thirty people at his party later that afternoon, and others drifted in and out, dogs running through the house and children playing everywhere. Allison had taken care of the food and arrangements, making people comfortable as she handed out drinks and appetizers—Merle's party allowing us to share a domesticity we had never enjoyed while he and Brower were alive.

As we were eating, one of Donald and Gladys's daughters walked into the great room, looking ill at ease, perhaps from the size of the group, perhaps from the old issue of her parents' having sold me land. I had learned from Donald and Gladys that some of their family had resented the diminishment of their legacy.

Walking up to me, she said, "We're really sorry about Merle. We really liked him." Declining any food or drink, she gave me a tiny nod of her head, the way old Wyoming people do when they're at a loss for words, as if they were still wearing cowboy hats and the slight dip of the brim toward the person they're addressing— like the tiny movement of Wilhelm von Osten's hat toward Clever Hans—conveys all that needs to be said. And, in this case, it did. Grateful for a visit that had made her uncomfortable, I walked her to the door and thanked her into the dusk.

Around 9:30, as the sky grew lavender, folks began to make their good-byes. I went out to the deck and stood with Allison, our arms around each other's waists as we looked at the summit of the Sleeping Indian, where we had sat with our dogs just a year before.

"Too soon over," I said.

She turned around and looked at the prayer flags, limp in the cool night air, and Merle's freshly filled grave beneath them.

"Too soon over," she replied.

When everyone was finally gone, I walked across the grass and sat by him, just feeling him, as if he might be a kind of osmotic pressure, pushing out to the edge of the universe.

My head nodded and I fell asleep. An hour later, the stars bright, I went inside and up to bed, feeling the same outward bulging of the house, Merle's spirit still full within it. Sometime in the night, I heard the dog door slap, and his claws come across the floor and climb the stairs—tok, tok, tok.

He blew a breath in my face, and when I opened my eyes he was right there, reddish-gold, one brow going up, the other down, saying, "You need a dog, and I'm it." I leapt out of bed, crying, "Merle! Merle!" and started roughhousing with him on the floor, only to wake and find myself tangled in the sheets.

Slowly, I looked to the corner of the room where he had slept. Of course, it was empty. I went downstairs and walked to his grave, where I stood, listening to the hum of the river and feeling the universe still pressed out to its farthest corners by him. And I couldn't tell if the bigness was him or how we had filled each other's hearts or if there was any difference between the two. Looking down, I imagined him lying on his green bed. Even though he would now always be close, it seemed like too confined an end for a dog who liked to roam.

I needn't have worried. When I looked up, he was bounding across the grass toward me, already as much starlight as dog.

Tail lashing, front paws dancing, he twirled before me.

"You dance, Sir!" I cried.

"Ha-ha-ha!" he panted. "I dance! *I DANCE!*"

WITH MANY THANKS

To Kim Fadiman, who read each word, some of them many times, who talked over issues of tone and meaning, who suggested important changes, who helped to find a subtitle, and who has been an enduring friend. To Allison von Maur for her careful read of the manuscript, her helpful comments, her humor through thick and thin, and her unstinting support. To Dr. Theo Schuff, D.V.M., for his review of the manuscript for veterinary accuracy and his reminding me not to be afraid to ask the deepest question about dogs. To Lorraine Bodger for insisting that this was the book I should write. To Marian Meyers for helping me discover some of Merle's origins. To Molly Breslin for listening to many of these chapters several times. To Douglas Smith of the Yellowstone Wolf Project for his enthusiastically answering my questions about wolves, year after year, and to Marc Bekoff for his read of my early manuscript. To Richard Appleman for our many discussions about the canine world. To Noelle Naiden for pointing out key readings in the dog literature. To Benj and Janet Sinclair for those many days at Hunter's Rest. To Lyn Benjamin and Tater and Tot for their love and friendship. To Len Carlman, Anne Ladd, and Mayo and Susan Lykes for their comfort when I needed it most. To Carol Connors and Steve Whisenand of the Teton County Library for processing hundreds of Interlibrary Loan Requests.

To Jane Backer, Jo Cleere, Jim Billipp, Sylvaine Montaudouin, and Anna Dank for help in translation. To Tim Bent and Tina Pohlman for their editorial counsel. To David Hough for his scrupulous and fun-filled production of the book. To Russell Galen for guiding me through the publishing world with the patience he would have shown a young inexperienced dog. And to Merle's vets—Jack Konitz, Tim Gwilliam, Theo Schuff, M. J. Forman, Erick Egger, Paul Cuddon, and Marybeth Minter—for their care of my friend.

NOTES

CHAPTER 1: From the Wild

PAGE

2 **"Smell is our oldest sense"**: Diane Ackerman, *A Natural History of the Senses* (New York: Vintage, 1995), 20.

3 **"whom they call 'Four-Eyes'"**: Marion Schwartz, *A History of Dogs in the Early Americas* (New Haven: Yale University Press, 1997), 20.

3 **"their expressions were easier to read"**: Stanley Coren, *How To Speak Dog* (New York: Free Press, 2000), 112.

7 **"acclaimed Newfoundland Seaman"**: Mark Derr, *A Dog's History of America* (New York: North Point Press, 2004), 104, 109–120.

7 **"most sagacious animal"**: John James Audubon, *The Birds of America*, vol. U, Plate CCCLXVIII, "The Great White Heron," Web version at http://www.audubon.org/bird/BoA/F38_G1f.html.

10 **"ability to transmit a rich array of information"**: Irene Pepperberg, "Cognitive and Communicative Abilities of Grey Parrots: Implications for the Enrichment of Many Species," *Animal Welfare* 13 (2004): S203–208.

Jane Goodall, "Behaviour of Free-Living Chimpanzees of the Gombe Stream Area," in *Animal Behaviour Monographs*, vol. 1, part 3 (London: Baillière, Tindall & Cassell, 1968), 165–311.

For a cautionary view of chimpanzees' ability to sign and use language as humans do, see Marian Stamp Dawkins, *Through Our Eyes Only?: The Search for Animal Consciousness* (Oxford, England: W. H. Freeman, 1993), 71–79; C. N. Slobodchikoff, "Cognition and Communication in Prairie Dogs," in *The Cognitive Animal: Empirical and Theoretical Perspectives on Animal Cognition*, ed. Marc Bekoff, Colin Allen, and Gordon M. Burghardt (Cambridge, Mass.: MIT Press, 2002), 257–264; V. M. Janik, L. S. Sayigh, and R. S. Wells, "Signature Whistle Shape Conveys Identity Information to Bottlenose Dolphins," Proceedings of the National Academy of Sciences (23 May 2006); Fred H. Harrington and Cheryl S. Asa, "Wolf Communication," in *Wolves: Behavior, Ecology, and Conservation*, ed. L. David Mech and Luigi Boitani (Chicago: University of Chicago Press, 2003), 66–103; Marc Bekoff, "Social Communication in Canids: Empirical Studies of the Evidence for the Evolution of a Stereotypical Function of Play Bows Mammalian Display," *Science* 197 (1977): 1097–1099; Sophia Yin and Brenda McCowan, "Barking in Domestic Dogs: Context Specificity and Individual Identification," *Animal Behaviour* 68 (2004): 343–355.

11 **"[T]he difference in mind"**: Charles Darwin, *The Origin of Species* and *The Descent of Man* (New York: The Modern Library, no date), 444–495, 912.

19 **"Stray dogs,"**: L. Boitani, F. Francisci, P. Ciucci, and G. Andreoli, "Population Biology and Ecology of Feral Dogs in Central Italy," in *The Domestic Dog*, ed. James Serpell (Cambridge, England: Cambridge University Press, 1995), 217–244.

CHAPTER 2: The First Dog

PAGE

27 **"a variety of wild ancestors"**: Charles Darwin, *On the Origin of Species* (New York: Heritage Press, 1963), 8–9, 10. See also Charles Darwin, *The Variation of Animals and Plants Under Domestication*, vol. 1 (Baltimore: Johns Hopkins University Press, 1998), 21.

28 **"little submission and less obedience"**: Konrad Lorenz, *Man Meets Dog* (New York: Kodansha International, 1994), 28.

29 **"is descended from wolves"**: Carles Vilà et al., "Multiple and Ancient Origins of the Domestic Dog," *Science* 13, vol. 276 (13 June 1997): 1687–1689.

29 **"Dogs are gray wolves,"**: Robert K. Wayne, "Molecular Evolution of the Dog Family," *Trends in Genetics* 5, vol. 9 (June 1993): 220.

29 **"as long as 135,000 years ago."**: Carles Vilà et al., "Multiple and Ancient Origins of the Domestic Dog."

30 **"There were no wolves in Africa"**: Ronald M. Nowak, "Wolf Evolution and Taxonomy," in *Wolves: Behavior, Ecology, and Conservation*, ed. L. David Mech and Luigi Boitani (Chicago: University of Chicago Press, 2003), 239–258.

32 **"Murie watched a wolf family"**: Adolph Murie, *The Wolves of Mount McKinley* (Washington, DC: United States Government Printing Office, 1944), 45–50.

36 **"outcompete their brawny cousins"**: Raymond and Lorna Coppinger, *Dogs: A New Understanding of Canine Origin, Behavior, and Evolution* (Chicago: University of Chicago Press, 2001), 60–61.

37 **"sniffing and licking the researchers"**: "Early Canid Domestication:

The Farm Fox Experiment," http://www.freerepublic.com/focus/news/807641/ posts.

38 **"found to be ninety-five hundred years old"**: Stanley J. Olsen, *Origins of the Domestic Dog: The Fossil Record* (Tucson: University of Arizona Press, 1985), 71.

38 **"lived fourteen thousand years ago"**: Juliet Clutton-Brock, "Origins of the dog: domestication and early history," in *The Domestic Dog: Its Evolution, Behaviour and Interactions with People*, ed. James Serpell (Cambridge, England: Cambridge University Press, 1995), 10.

38 **"six thousand years before agriculture"**: Jared Diamond, *Guns, Germs, and Steel* (New York: W. W. Norton & Company, 1997), 181.

38 **"seventeen thousand years old"**: Mikhail V. Sablin and Gennady A. Khlopachev, "The Earliest Ice Age Dogs: Evidence from Eliseevichi I," *Current Anthropology* 5, vol. 43 (December 2002): 795–799.

38 **"rather a common practice"**: Peter Savolainen et al., "Genetic Evidence for an East Asian Origin of Domestic Dogs," *Science* 22, vol. 298 (November 2002): 1610–1613.

39 **"founded some of today's breeds"**: Jennifer A. Leonard et al., "Ancient DNA Evidence for Old World Origin of New World Dogs," *Science* 22, vol. 298 (November 2002): 1613–1616.

43 **"pacifying an angry wasp"**: Francis Galton, *Inquiries into Human Faculty and Its Development* (New York: Everyman's Library reprint of the 1883 edition, 1907), 185–193.

44 **"ability to read us extremely well"**: Brian Hare et al., "The Domestication of Social Cognition in Dogs," *Science* 22, vol. 298 (November 2002): 1634–1636.

44 **"substitute objects like dogs"**: Konrad Lorenz, "Part and parcel in animal and human societies" (1950), in *Studies in Animal and Human Behaviour*, vol. 2 (Cambridge, Mass.: Harvard University Press, 1971), 154–156.

44 **"kisses it on the snout"**: Carl Lumholtz, *Among Cannibals* (New York: Charles Scribner's Sons, 1889), 178–179.

44 **"ridiculous affection"**: George Forster, *A Voyage Round the World*, vol. 1 (Honolulu: University of Hawaii Press, 2000), 206.

45 **"happy expression on its face"**: Marion Schwartz, *A History of Dogs in the Early Americas* (New Haven: Yale University Press, 1997), 54.

45 **"astute, human-reading dogs"**: Howard Hughes Medical Institute Bulletin (Fall 2004), http://www.hhmi.org/bulletin/fall2004/dogs/dogs2.html.

45 **"wolf and human remains"**: Juliet Clutton-Brock, "Origins of the dog: domestication and early history," in *The Domestic Dog: Its Evolution, Behaviour and Interactions with People*, ed. James Serpell (Cambridge, England: Cambridge University Press, 1995), 8.

45 **"morphologically distinct"**: Carles Vilà et al., "Multiple and Ancient Origins of the Domestic Dog," *Science* 5319, vol. 276 (13 June 1997): 1687–1689.

46 **"most remarkable of these memorials"**: Simon J. M. Davis and François R. Valla, "Evidence for domestication of the dog 12,000 years ago in the Natufian of Israel," *Nature*, vol. 276 (7 December 1978): 608–610.

46 **"a newly domesticated wolf"**: Tamar Dayan, "Early Domesticated Dogs of the Near East," *Journal of Archaeological Science* 21 (1994): 633–640.

46 **"The grave wasn't unique"**: Eitan Tchernov and François F. Valla, "Two New Dogs, and Other Natufian Dogs, from the Southern Levant," *Journal of Archaeological Science* 24 (1997): 65–95.

47 **"a deliberate display of friendliness"**: L. David Mech, "'Standing Over' and 'Hugging' in Wild Wolves, *Canis lupus*," *The Canadian Field Naturalist*, vol. 115 (2001): 179–181.

CHAPTER 3: The Synaptic Kiss

PAGE

51 **"a 'critical period' for object play"**: Patricia McConnell, *The Other End of the Leash* (New York: Ballantine Books, 2002), 95.

59 **"that never felt a wound"**: William Shakespeare, *Romeo and Juliet*, act II, scene ii, line 1.

60 **"those protoplasmic kisses"**: Santiago Ramón y Cajal, *Recollections of My Life*, vol. 8, part 2 (Philadelphia: American Philosophical Society, 1937), 373.

61 **"remarkable changes began"**: Edward L. Bennett et al., "Chemical and Anatomical Plasticity of the Brain," *Science* 30, vol. 146 (October 1964): 610–619.

61 **"20 percent bigger brains"**: Raymond Coppinger and Richard Schneider, "Evolution of Working Dogs," in *The Domestic Dog*, ed. James Serpell (Cambridge, England: Cambridge University Press, 1995), 33.

62 **"more adept at moving"**: Ashish Ranpura, "Weightlifting for the Mind: Enriched Environments and Cortical Plasticity," http://www.brainconnection.com/topics/printindex.php3?main=fa/cortical-plasticity.

62 **"increased branching created"**: Fred R. Volkmar and William T. Greenough, "Rearing Complexity Affects Branching of Dendrites in the Visual Cortex of the Rat," *Science* 30, vol. 176 (June 1972): 1447.

62 **"escaping from pens"**: Steven R. Lindsay, *Handbook of Applied Dog Behavior and Training, Volume One: Adaptation and Learning* (Ames, Iowa: Blackwell Publishing, 2000), 18.

62 **"learning engaging tasks"**: William T. Greenough, James E. Black, and Christopher S. Wallace, "Experience and Brain Development," *Child Development* 58 (1987): 539–559.

63   **"a large, object-filled space"**: Edward L. Bennett et al., "Chemical and Anatomical Plasticity of the Brain," *Science* 30, vol. 146 (October 1964): 610–619.

63   **"rarely permitted to solve problems"**: Jon Katz, *The New Work of Dogs* (New York: Random House, 2004), 18.

CHAPTER 4: In the Genes

PAGE

68   **"killed by other wolves"**: Douglas W. Smith, Leader Yellowstone Wolf Project, interview with author, Mammoth Hot Springs, Wyoming, 18 March 2005.

75   **"of other loud noises"**: David S. Tuber et al., "Treatment of Fears and Phobias in Dogs," *Veterinary Clinics of North America: Small Animal Practice* 4, vol. 12 (November 1982): 607.

76   **"potentially traumatic experiences"**: Michael W. Fox, *Behaviour of Wolves, Dogs and Related Canids* (New York: Harper & Row, 1971), 145.

83   **"called the subethmoidal shelf"**: Julio E. Correo, "The Dog's Sense of Smell" (July 2005), Alabama Cooperative Extension System, http://www.aces .edu/pubs/docs/U/UNP-0066/.

83   **"vomeronasal-like organ"**: "The Vomeronasal Organ," Dr. Michael Meredith, Florida State University, http://www.neuro.fsu.edu/research/ vomeronasal/human.htm.

83   **"Merle was a young dog"**: "How Well Do Dogs and Humans Hear?" http://www.lsu.edu/deafness/HearingRange.html.

84   **"sound's distance and position"**: Richard F. Thompson, *The Brain: A Neuroscience Primer* (New York: W. H. Freeman and Company, 1993), 259–260.

85   **"elk sneaking away"**: Rickye S. Heffner and Henry E. Heffner, "Evolution of Sound Localization in Mammals," in *The Evolutionary Biology of Hearing*, ed. Douglas R. Webster, Richard R. Fay, and Arthur N. Popper (New York: Springer-Verlag, 1992), 691–715.

88   **"print's olfactory strength"**: J. B. Steen and E. Wilsson, "How do dogs determine the direction of tracks?", *Acta Physiologica Scandinavica* 239, (1990): 531–534; E. Miller, R. Houghton, and W. J. Carr, "Chemosensory tracking in dogs: Enhancing the track's polarity," *Chemical Senses* 20 (1996): 743–744.

88   **"programmed to compute"**: Linda Aronson, "The Nose Knows," http:// www.beaconforhealth.org/The_Nose_Knows.htm.

88   **"a memorable *sillage*"**: Chandler Burr, "The Scent of the Nile," *The New Yorker*, 14 March 2005, 78–87.

90   **"tints of yellow or blue"**: J. Neitz, T. Geist, and G. H. Jacobs, "Color vision in the dog," *Visual Neuroscience* 3 (1989): 119–125; G. H. Jacobs

et al., "Photopigments of dogs and foxes and their implications for canid vision," *Visual Neuroscience* 10 (1993): 173–180.

91 **"my visual acuity"**: Paul E. Miller and Christopher J. Murphy, "Vision in Dogs," *Journal of the Veterinary Medical Association* 12, vol. 207 (15 December 1995): 1623–1634; "Ruff Work," http://www.avalanche.org/~doghouse/3%20canis%20familiaris/1%20a%20Dogs%20BRAIN.htm.

95 **"a woman Sykes named Helena"**: Bryan Sykes, *The Seven Daughters of Eve* (New York: W. W. Norton, 2001).

96 **"so well-balanced a relationship"**: M. R. Jarman, "European Deer Economies and the Advent of the Neolithic," in *Papers in Economic Prehistory*, ed. E. S. Higgs (Cambridge, England: Cambridge University Press, 1972), 125–149.

CHAPTER 5: Building the Door

PAGE

97 **"quickly stopped barking"**: Charles Darwin, *The Variation of Animals and Plants Under Domestication* (Baltimore: Johns Hopkins University Press, paperback reprint of the original 1868 edition, 1998), 27.

97 **"wolves are practically mute"**: L. David Mech, *The Wolf* (Garden City, NY: Natural History Press, 1970), 95–110.

98 **"less vocal than coyotes"**: Joel Berger, a senior scientist at the Wildlife Conservation Society who has studied large mammals in both North America and Africa, suggests that the question of whether coyotes bark more than jackals can be addressed by inference. "Coyotes," he says, "live in an environment where only two predators habitually prey upon them— wolves and mountain lions. The cost of a coyote announcing itself to another coyote by barking is thus rather low. Jackals, on the other hand, live among lions, hyenas, leopards, cheetahs, and wild dogs, all of whom would be more than happy to make a meal out of a jackal. Therefore, the cost to a jackal, for revealing its position by barking, can be quite high." (Joel Berger, telephone conversation with author, 22 July 2005.)

98 **"wild dogs are impressionable"**: Desmond Morris, *Illustrated Dog Watching* (New York: Crescent Books, 1996), 31.

99 **"great bayers"**: Benjamin Hart, "Analyzing breed and gender differences in behaviour," in *The Domestic Dog*, ed. James Serpell (Cambridge, England: Cambridge University Press, 1995), 65–77.

CHAPTER 6: Growing Into Himself

PAGE

114 **"Dogs learn by observing other dogs"**: J. M. Slabbert and O. Anne E. Rasa, "Observational learning of an acquired maternal behaviour pat-

tern by working dog pups: an alternative training method?", *Applied Animal Behaviour Science* 53 (1997): 309–316.

114 **"in nine seconds"**: Leonore Loeb Adler and Helmut E. Adler, "Ontogeny of observational learning in the dog (*Canis familiaris*)," *Developmental Psychobiology* 10 (1977): 267–271.

114 **"lying down at dinner"**: Elizabeth Marshall Thomas, *The Social Lives of Dogs* (New York: Pocket Books, 2000), 85.

122 **"an Arabian stallion"**: KBR Training Information Sheet, "The Story of Clever Hans," http://www.kbrhorse.net/tra/hans.html.

122 **"a Russian trotting horse"**: Oskar Pfungst, *Clever Hans (The Horse of Mr. Von Osten)* (Bristol, England: Thoemmes Press, 1998), 18.

123 **"the time of Darwin"**: Ibid., 2–3.

123 **"serious and incisive investigation"**: Ibid., 253–254.

123 **"experimental animal and human psychology"**: Ibid., title page.

123 **"future studies of animals"**: Robert H. Wozniak, *Classics in Psychology 1855–1914, Historical Essays*, http://www.thoemmes.com/psych/pfungst.htm.

124 **"who was talking to him"**: Oskar Pfungst, *Clever Hans*, 30–33.

124 **"counting with his hoof"**: Ibid., 63.

125 **"revolving on a drum"**: Ibid., 115–117.

125 **"It was enough"**: Ibid., 125.

125 **"truly microscopic movements."**: Ibid., 108.

125 **"experimenter's own expectations"**: Robert H. Wozniak, *Classics in Psychology 1855–1914, Historical Essays*, http://www.thoemmes.com/psych/pfungst.htm.

126 **"and targeted zebra"**: Hans Kruuk, *The Spotted Hyena* (Chicago: University of Chicago Press, 1972), 146–275.

127 **"spoken to the horse"**: Oskar Pfungst, *Clever Hans*, 91.

129 **"falls into their bowls"**: "Circadian Rhythm," *Wikipedia*, http://en.wikipedia.org/wiki/Circadian_rhythm.

129 **"a twenty-eight-day period"**: Sabah Quraishi, "Circadian Rhythms and Sleep," http://serendip.brynmawr.edu/bb/neuro/neuro01/web1/Quirashi.html.

130 **"listen to a dog"**: The Monks of New Skete, *How to Be Your Dog's Best Friend* (Boston: Little, Brown and Company, 1978), 17.

132 **"eat as much as"**: L. David Mech and Luigi Boitani, *Wolves: Behavior, Ecology, and Conservation* (Chicago: University of Chicago Press, 2003), xv.

137 **"meet those needs"**: Oskar Pfungst, *Clever Hans*, 242.

139 **"a pleasurable taste"**: James C. Boudreau, "Neurophysiology and Stimulus Chemistry of Mammalian Taste Systems," in *Flavor Chemistry: Trends and Developments*, ed. Roy Teranishi, Ron G. Buttery, and Fereidoon Shahidi (Washington, DC: American Chemical Society, 1989): 122–137.

139 **"The wolf's general alertness"**: Michael W. Fox, *The Soul of the Wolf* (New York: Lyons and Burford, 1992), 32, 81.

140 **"greater complexity than any wolf"**: Raymond and Lorna Coppinger, *Dogs: A New Understanding of Canine Origin, Behavior, and Evolution* (Chicago: University of Chicago Press, 2001), 23–25.

141 **"hope over experience"**: James Boswell, *The Life of Johnson* (Hammondsworth, England: Penguin Books, 1979 reprint of the 1791 edition), entry for 1770, 153.

143 **"letting them run free"**: Patricia McConnell, *The Other End of the Leash* (New York: Ballantine Books, 2002), 165.

144 **"never forgotten the trauma"**: Steven R. Lindsay, *Handbook of Applied Dog Behavior and Training, Volume One, Adaptation and Learning* (Ames, Iowa: Blackwell Publishing, 2000), 62.

CHAPTER 7: Top Dog

PAGE

147 **"heavy loads of intestinal parasites"**: Bruce Fogle, *The Dog's Mind* (New York: Howell Book House, 1990), 144.

149 **"hopes of reducing fleas"**: "Respiratory toxicity of cedar and pine wood: A review of the biomedical literature from 1986 through 1995," http://www.trifl.org/cedar.shtml.

152 **"groomed each other"**: Michael W. Fox, *Behaviour of Wolves, Dogs and Related Canids* (New York: Harper & Row, 1971), 100–101.

155 **"leads to acrimony,"**: Douglas W. Smith, Leader Yellowstone Wolf Project, interview with author, Mammoth Hot Springs, Wyoming, 18 March 2005.

156 **"three to five weeks old"**: Clarence J. Pfaffenberger, *The New Knowledge of Dog Behavior* (New York: Howell Book House, 1963), 124.

156 **"retaliate by attacking them"**: Steven R. Lindsay, *Handbook of Applied Dog Behavior and Training, Volume Three, Procedures and Protocols* (Ames, Iowa: Blackwell Publishing, 2005), 522.

158 **"a serotonin reuptake inhibitor"**: Ilana R. Reisner, "Assessment, Management, and Prognosis of Canine Dominance-related Aggression," *Veterinary Clinics of North America: Small Animal Practice* 3, vol. 27 (May 1997).

161 **"dogs express dominance"**: Stanley Coren, *How To Speak Dog* (New York: Free Press, 2000), 144–145.

164 **"his study is out of doors"**: Henry David Thoreau, "Walking," in *Walden and Other Writings of Henry David Thoreau* (New York: Modern Library, 1950), 599, 601.

166 **"blow of the shoulder"**: Rudolf Schenkel, "Submission: Its Features and Function in the Wolf and Dog," *American Zoologist* 7 (1967): 321, 322; Fred H. Harrington and Cheryl S. Asa, "Wolf Communication," in *Wolves:*

Behavior, Ecology, and Conservation, ed. L. David Mech and Luigi Boitani (Chicago: University of Chicago Press, 2003), 95.

CHAPTER 8: The Gray Cat

PAGE

171 **"humans persuade cats":** Juliet Clutton-Brock, *A Natural History of Domesticated Animals* (Cambridge, England: Cambridge University Press, 1987), 133.

CHAPTER 9: Estrogen Clouds

PAGE

181 **"secret, and self-contained":** Charles Dickens, *A Christmas Carol* (London: Chapman & Hall, 1843), 3.

183 **"thoroughly enjoying herself":** Bruce Fogle, *The Dog's Mind* (New York: Howell Book House, 1990), 53.

183 **"two to four million dogs are euthanized":** American Humane Society, "Animal Shelter Euthanasia," http://www.americanhumane.org/site/PageServer?pagename=nr_fact_sheets_animal_euthanasia; Stephanie Shain, Humane Society of the United States, e-mail communication with author, 30 January 2006.

183 **"a laparoscopic vasectomy":** L. D. M. Silva et al., "Laparoscopic vasectomy in the male dog," *Journal of Reproduction and Fertility, Supplement,* vol. 47 (1993): 399–401.

184 **"incidence of testicular cancer":** Race Foster and Marty Smith, "Neutering—Why It's a Good Idea," PetEducation.com, Drs. Foster and Smith's source for expert pet information, http://www.peteducation.com/article.cfm?cls=2&cat=1625&articleid=911.

184 **"loss of her reproductive organs":** Race Foster and Marty Smith, "Spaying—Why It's a Good Idea," PetEducation.com, Drs. Foster and Smith's source for expert pet information, http://www.peteducation.com/article.cfm?cls=2&cat=1625&articleid=926; "Feedback on Pet Overpopulation," http://www.pelagus.net/animal/v03.html.

184 **"castrating dogs predisposes":** "Prostate Problems," Vizsla V-Source, Vizsla Health Topics, http://users.lavalink.com.au/theos/Prostate%20problems.htm; Mary C. Wakeman, "Issues Regarding Castration in Dogs," http://www.showdogsupersite.com/kenlclub/breedvet/castrationindogs.html; E. Teske et al., *Molecular and Cellular Endocrinology* 197 (1–2) (2002): 251–255; Sorenmo K. U. et al., "Immunohistochemical characterization of canine prostatic carcinoma and correlation with castration status and castration time," *Veterinary and Comparative Oncology* 1 (1) (2003): 48–56.

185 **"desire to fight other males":** Benjamin Hart, D.V.M., Ph.D., Center for Companion Animal Health, University of California Davis, Fall 2003,

"Understanding the Effects of Neutering on Problem Behaviors in Male Dogs," http://www.vetmed.ucdavis.edu/CCAH/Update08-2/upd8-2_behav-neutering .html.

186 **"in fact what they do"**: Karen Pryor, *Lads Before the Wind* (New York: Harper and Row, 1975), 171.

187 **"faithfulness is the norm"**: L. David Mech and Luigi Boitani, "Wolf Social Ecology," in *Wolves: Behavior, Ecology, and Conservation,* ed. L. David Mech and Luigi Boitani (Chicago: University of Chicago Press, 2003), 3.

CHAPTER 10: At Home in the Arms of the Country

PAGE

197 **"spoke the same language"**: Marion Schwartz, *A History of Dogs in the Early Americas* (New Haven, Conn.: Yale University Press, 1997), vi.

199 **"labile study in conversation"**: R. Schenkel, "Expression Studies of Wolves," *Behavior,* vol. 1 (1947): 96.

202 **"They love being dogs"**: Jeffrey Moussaieff Masson, *Dogs Never Lie About Love* (New York: Crown Publishers, 1997), 36–37.

205 **"many a lightfoot lad"**: A. E. Housman, *A Shropshire Lad* (New York: Buccaneer Books, 1983), 99.

CHAPTER 11: The Problem of Me

PAGE

213 **"there was no difference"**: Marion Schwartz, *A History of Dogs in the Early Americas* (New Haven, Conn.: Yale University Press, 1997), vi.

213 **"humans had souls"**: Bernard Singer, "History of the Study of Animal Behaviour," in *The Oxford Companion to Animal Behaviour,* ed. David McFarland (Oxford, England: Oxford University Press, 1981), 262.

213 **"[I]n animals, there is neither intelligence"**: Nicolas de Malebranche, *The Search After Truth,* trans. Thomas M. Lennon and Paul J. Olscamp (Columbus: Ohio State University Press, 1980) (first edition, *De la Recherche de la Verité,* Paris: 1674–75), 494–495.

214 **"destructive and murderous idea"**: Henry More, "*Epistola Prima H. Mori ad Renatum Cartesium,*" in *Collection of Several Philosophical Works* (London: William Morden, 1662), 64.

214 **"beasts are endow'd with thought"**: David Hume, *A Treatise of Human Nature* (Baltimore: Penguin Books, 1969) (first published 1739), 226.

214 **"the lives of 'dumb animals,'"**: Harriet Ritvo, *The Animal Estate* (Cambridge, Mass.: Harvard University Press, 1987), 126–127.

215 **"Morgan called 'sense-experience'"**: C. Lloyd Morgan, *An Introduction to Comparative Psychology* (New York: Charles Scribner's Sons, 1902), 301–302.

215 **"lower in the psychological scale"**: Ibid., 53.

218 "'cognitive map'": Edward Chace Tolman, *Purposive Behavior in Animals and Men* (New York: Appleton-Century-Crofts, 1967), 48–50; Edward C. Tolman, "Cognitive Maps in Rats and Men," http://www.wadsworth.com/psychology_d/templates/student_resources/0155060678_rathus/ps/ps10.html.

218 "window into its subjective experience": Robert Boakes, *From Darwin to Behaviourism* (Cambridge, England: Cambridge University Press, 1984), 153.

218 "which are much like ours": Robert M. Yerkes, *Introduction to Psychology* (New York: Henry Holt and Company, 1911), 239.

219 "Russian physiologist Ivan Pavlov": Mark Ridley, "Pavlov," in *The Oxford Companion to Animal Behaviour*, ed. David McFarland (Oxford, England: Oxford University Press, 1981), 447–449.

219 "Give me a dozen healthy infants": John B. Watson, *Behaviorism* (New York: Norton, 1924), 104.

220 "reinforcement will follow": B. F. Skinner, "How to Teach Animals," *Scientific American* 185 (1951): 26–29.

220 "'purely mechanical' fashion": B. F. Skinner, *The Behavior of Organisms* (New York: Appleton-Century-Crofts, 1938), 55.

220 "The world of introspection": B. F. Skinner, *About Behaviorism* (New York: Alfred A. Knopf, 1974), xii.

220 "Let [the child] believe": Quoted in B. F. Skinner, *Beyond Freedom and Dignity* (New York: Alfred A. Knopf, 1971), 40.

221 "absolutely no unsupervised freedom": Kevin Behan, *Natural Dog Training* (Xlibris Corporation, 2001), 93–94.

221 "control of your dog's access to everything": Jean Donaldson, *The Culture Clash* (Berkeley, Calif.: James & Kenneth Publishers, 1996), 132–133, 111.

222 "the thinker should have": Marian Stamp Dawkins, *Through Our Eyes Only?* (Oxford, England: W. H. Freeman, 1993), 105.

223 "would likely select the career": Steven R. Lindsay, *Handbook of Applied Dog Behavior and Training, Volume Three, Procedures and Protocols* (Ames, Iowa: Blackwell Publishing, 2005), 710.

223 "What they needed was less control": E. G. Sarris, "Individual Differences in Dogs," *American Kennel Gazette*, four-part series: 1 November 1938; 1 December 1938; 1 January 1939; 1 February 1939.

226 "seeing the world in vivid detail": Temple Grandin and Catherine Johnson, *Animals in Translation* (Orlando, Fla.: Harcourt, 2005), 51–57.

227 "Dogs and people coevolved": Ibid., 306.

227 "our brains are the same": Paul D. MacLean, *The Triune Brain in Evolution* (New York: Plenum Press, 1990), 3–18.

227 "Machiavellian intelligence": Richard W. Byrne and Andrew Whitten,

Machiavellian Intelligence: Social Expertise and the Evolution of Intellect in Monkeys, Apes, and Humans (Oxford, England: Oxford University Press), 1989.

227 **"what to do in constantly changing social situations"**: Marian Stamp Dawkins, *Through Our Eyes Only?* (Oxford, England: W. H. Freeman, 1993), 173.

228 **"dog pretending to be sad"**: Jeffrey Moussaieff Masson, *Dogs Never Lie About Love* (New York: Crown Publishers, 1997), 31.

230 **"basic similarity between"**: Nicholas Dodman, *If Only They Could Speak* (New York: W. W. Norton & Company, 2002), 9–10.

231 **"Experiments with chimpanzees and dolphins"**: Susan D. Suarez and Gordon C. Gallup, Jr., "Social Responding to Mirrors in Rhesus Macaques (*Macaca mulatta*): Effects of Changing Mirror Location," *American Journal of Primatology* 11 (1986): 239–244; Irene M. Pepperberg et al., "Mirror Use by African Grey Parrots (*Psittacus erithacus*)," *Journal of Comparative Psychology* 2, vol. 109 (1995), 182–195; Gordon G. Gallup, Jr., "Chimpanzees: Self-Recognition," *Science,* vol. 2 (January 1970), 86–87; Diana Reissue and Lori Marino, "Mirror Self-recognition in the Bottlenose Dolphin: A Case of Cognitive Convergence," *Proceedings of the National Academy of Sciences of the United States of America* 10, vol. 98 (8 May 2001), 5937–5942.

233 **"Yep, that's me."**: For two different views on what "Yep, that's me" might mean see: Gordon Gallup, Jr., "Can Animals Empathize?: Yes.," *Scientific American* 9 (1998), 66–71; Daniel J. Povinelli, "Can Animals Empathize?: Maybe Not.," *Scientific American* 9 (1998), 67–75.

CHAPTER 12: The Mayor of Kelly

PAGE

238 **"The fundamental mistake"**: B. F. Skinner, *Beyond Freedom and Dignity* (New York: Alfred A. Knopf, 1971), 99.

243 **"punishment to be effective"**: N. H. Azrin and W. C. Holz, "Punishment," in *Operant Behavior,* ed. Werner K. Honig (New York: Appleton-Century-Crofts, 1966), 410.

243 **"pain that is inflicted beneficially"**: Steven R. Lindsay, *Handbook of Applied Dog Behavior and Training, Volume One, Adaptation and Learning* (Ames, Iowa: Blackwell Publishing, 2000), 303. See also some of the original work done on the effects of punishment from which Lindsay developed his ideas: Richard L. Solomon, "Punishment," *American Psychologist* 19 (April 1964): 239–253.

243 **"[A] puppy does not automatically love you"**: John Paul Scott and John L. Fuller, *Genetics and the Social Behavior of the Dog* (Chicago: University of Chicago Press, 1965), 177.

245 **"the two porpoises had learned"**: Karen Pryor, *Lads Before the Wind* (New York: Harper & Row, 1975), 251–253.

246 **"the 'structure of a situation'"**: Wolfgang Köhler, *The Mentality of Apes* (London: Routledge & Kegan Paul, 1925), 190.

246 **"nervous animals investigate their environments"**: Temple Grandin, *Animals in Translation* (Orlando, Fla.: Harcourt, 2005), 222.

CHAPTER 13: The Alpha Pair

PAGE

254 **"alpha wolf as a 'top dog'"**: L. David Mech, "Alpha Status, Dominance, and Division of Labor in Wolf Packs," *Canadian Journal of Zoology* 77 (1999): 1197.

254 **"wolves sharing *leadership*"**: Rolf O. Peterson et al., "Leadership Behavior in Relation to Dominance and Reproductive Status in Gray Wolves, *Canis Lupus*," *Canadian Journal of Zoology* 80 (2002), 1405–1412.

255 **"These older, non-alpha wolves"**: Douglas W. Smith, interview with author, Mammoth Hot Springs, Wyoming, 18 March 2005.

255 **"but also has free will"**: Douglas W. Smith, e-mail communication with author, 7 February 2005.

255 **"automatically become alphas"**: L. David Mech, "Alpha Status, Dominance, and Division of Labor in Wolf Packs," *Canadian Journal of Zoology* 77 (1999), 1197.

255 **"This enhances their nutritional condition"**: Jane M. Packard, "Wolf Behavior: Reproductive, Social, and Intelligent," in *Wolves: Behavior, Ecology, and Conservation,* ed. L. David Mech and Luigi Boitani (Chicago: University of Chicago Press, 2003), 57.

256 **"who, in the wild, are 'contemporaries'"**: Constance Perin, "Dogs as Symbols in Human Development," in *Interrelations Between People and Pets,* ed. Bruce Fogle (Springfield, Ill.: Charles C. Thomas, 1981), 80.

256 **"permitted by their owners"**: John Paul Scott and John L. Fuller, *Genetics and the Social Behavior of the Dog* (Chicago: University of Chicago Press, 1965), 415.

256 **"instituted a benevolent reign"**: Douglas W. Smith and Gary Ferguson, *Decade of the Wolf* (Guilford, Conn.: Lyons Press, 2005), 78–82.

257 **"the hallmarks of the syndrome"**: http://en.wikipedia.org/wiki/Stockholm_syndrome; http://www.mental-health-matters.com/articles/article.php?artID=469; http://web2.airmail.net/ktrig246/out_of_cave/sss.html.

257 **"$15 billion Americans spent"**: Animal Feed Manufacturers Association: http://www.afma.co.za/AFMA_Template/1,2491,6552_1645,00.html; Number of U.S. Dog Owners: http://answers.google.com/answers/threadview?id=177303.

257 **"reversal of millions of years of evolution"**: Kevin Behan, *Natural Dog Training* (Xlibris Corporation, 2001), 316.

258 **"left out in the wild"**: Jon Katz, *Katz on Dogs* (New York: Villard, 2005), 92.

258 **"only females and their pups used them":** L. Boitani et al., "Population Biology and Ecology of Feral Dogs in Central Italy," in *The Domestic Dog*, ed. James Serpell (Cambridge, England: Cambridge University Press, 1995), 222.

258 **"her mate will only occasionally":** Jane M. Packard, "Wolf Behavior: Reproductive, Social, and Intelligent," in *Wolves: Behavior, Ecology, and Conservation*, ed. L. David Mech and Luigi Boitani (Chicago: University of Chicago Press, 2003), 50.

258 **"They sleep in the open":** L. David Mech, *The Wolf* (Garden City, N.Y.: Natural History Press, 1970), 121, 190–191; Douglas W. Smith, head of Yellowstone Wolf Project, e-mail communication, 3 May 2006.

258 **"The calmest moments her dogs":** Elizabeth Marshall Thomas, *The Hidden Life of Dogs* (New York: Pocket Books, 1993), 108–121.

259 **"who may not reach full adulthood":** L. David Mech and Luigi Boitani, "Wolf Social Ecology," in *Wolves: Behavior, Ecology, and Conservation*, ed. L. David Mech and Luigi Boitani (Chicago: University of Chicago Press, 2003), 7.

260 **"Dogs who had a strong dependent relationship":** J. Topál, Á. Miklósi, and V. Csányi, "Dog–Human Relationship Affects Problem Solving Behavior in the Dog," *Anthrozoös* 10 (4) (1997), 214–224.

260 **"living creatures are not a bunch of machines":** Karen Pryor, *Don't Shoot the Dog* (New York: Bantam Books, 1999), 94.

CHAPTER 14: White Muzzle

PAGE

276 **"love what it loves":** Mary Oliver, "Wild Geese," in *Dream Work* (New York: The Atlantic Monthly Press, 1986), 14.

277 **"according to one dog–human age comparison":** A. LeBeau, "L'age du chien et celui de l'homme. Assai de statistique sur la mortalité canine," *Bulletin de l'Academie Veterinaire de France*, vol. 26 (1953), 229–232.

277 **"It factors in a dog's weight and breed":** Gary J. Patronek, David J. Waters, and Lawrence T. Glickman, "Comparative Longevity of Pet Dogs and Humans: Implications for Gerontology Research," *Journal of Gerontology: Biological Sciences* 3, vol. 52A (1997): B171–178.

282 **"Veterinary AP (acupuncture)":** American Veterinary Medical Association Guidelines for Alternative and Complementary Veterinary Medicine, *Journal of the American Veterinary Medical Association* 6, vol. 209 (15 September 1996).

282 **"the use of 'nutraceuticals'":** Kurt Schulz, *The Pet Lover's Guide to Canine Arthritis & Joint Problems* (St. Louis, Mo.: Elsevier Saunders, 2006), 140–141, 90–109.

283 **"use more energy when they're hot"**: Bernard S. Hershhorn, *Active Years for Your Aging Dog* (New York: Hawthorn Books, 1978), 12.

CHAPTER 15: What Do Dogs Want?

PAGE

289 **"They know the same"**: Barry Lopez, *Of Wolves and Men* (New York: Charles Scribner's Sons, 1978), 86.

296 **"they want each other"**: Elizabeth Marshall Thomas, *The Hidden Life of Dogs* (New York: Pocket Books, 1993), 134–135.

297 **"Johannsen was an early champion"**: Alice E. Johannsen, *The Legendary Jackrabbit Johannsen* (Montreal: McGill–Queen's University Press, 1993).

301 **"What happens among cells"**: Antonio Damasio, *Descartes' Error: Emotion, Reason, and the Human Brain* (New York: Penguin Books, 2005), 109.

CHAPTER 16: A Looser Leash

PAGE

304 **"Ten thousand people live in the valley"**: http://info.chamonix.com/infoGeoEn.php.

306 **"a national law mandating"**: *"Divagation des Chiens et des Chats et Mise en Fourrière,"* May 2006, http://www.carrefourlocal.org/vie_locale/cas_pratiques/police/divagation.html.

306 **"an animal-welfare organization that was founded in 1845"**: *Société Protectrice des Animaux* Web site, *"Un Peu d'Histoire,"* http://www.spa.asso.fr/association/histoire.asp.

309 **"[L]eash laws may be short-circuiting"**: Temple Grandin, *Animals in Translation* (Orlando, Fla.: Harcourt, 2005), 160.

309 **"Off-leash areas are essential"**: "Benefits of Off-Leash Recreation," San Francisco SPCA, 2002.

310 **"FIDO believes"**: "FIDO's Mission," http://www.fidobrooklyn.org/mission/mission.html.

310 **"4.7 million dog bites"**: "Nonfatal Dog Bite–Related Injuries Treated in Hospital Emergency Departments—United States, 2001," Centers for Disease Control and Prevention, http://www.cdc.gov/mmwr/preview/mmwrhtml/mm5226a1.htm.

311 **"most comprehensive review of dog bites"**: Linda S. Shore, "The Question of Dogs, Off-leash Recreation, and Safety: A Review of the Literature on Dog Bites," http://www.dogexpert.com/Literature/Offleashsafety.htm.

311 **"increase in dysfunctional canine behavior"**: Nicholas H. Dodman, *If Only They Could Speak* (New York: W. W. Norton & Company, 2002);

Patricia B. McConnell, *The Other End of the Leash* (New York: Ballantine Books, 2002).

312 **"incidence of depression and psychosis"**: Kristina Sundquist, Gölin Frank, and Jan Sundquist, "Urbanization and Incidence of Psychosis and Depression," *The British Journal of Psychiatry,* vol. 184 (2004): 293–298.

312 **"without environmental enrichment"**: Nicholas H. Dodman, *The Dog Who Loved Too Much* (New York: Bantam Books, 1996), 228–229.

CHAPTER 18: Through the Door

PAGE

341 **"do not write biographies of animals"**: Raymond Gaita, *The Philosopher's Dog* (New York: Random House, 2002), 79.

343 **"before euthanizing a dog"**: Bernard S. Hershhorn, *Active Years for Your Aging Dog* (New York: Hawthorn Books, 1978), 216.

INDEX